Wicked Takes the Witness Stand

Wicked Takes the Witness Stand

A TALE OF MURDER AND TWISTED DECEIT IN NORTHERN MICHIGAN

Mardi Link

University of Michigan Press
Ann Arbor

♾ Printed on acid-free paper

Hardcover ISBN-13: 978-0-472-07169-2
Paper ISBN-13: 978-0-472-05169-4
Ebook ISBN-13: 978-0-472-02943-3

2018   2017   4   3   2

Link, Mardi.
    Wicked takes the witness stand : a tale of murder and twisted deceit in Northern Michigan / Mardi Link.
        pages   cm
    Includes bibliographical references.
    ISBN 978-0-472-07169-2 (hardback) — ISBN 978-0-472-05169-4 (paperback) — ISBN 978-0-472-02943-3 (e-book)
    1. Murder—Michigan—Case studies. 2. Murder investigation—Michigan—Case studies. 3. False imprisonment—Michigan—Case studies. 4. Criminal justice, Administration of—Corrupt practices—Michigan—Case studies. I. Title.
HV6533.M5L56 2014
364.152'3092—dc23

                                        2014039496

To Bruce, Ray, and Stuart:
The Head, the Heart, and the Muscle

ACKNOWLEDGMENTS

Imagine if someone showed up to your work first thing in the morning with a laptop computer, a reporter's notebook, and a whole bunch of questions. Imagine if the person stayed there, just feet from where you were trying to get your work done, for hours and even until your office closed in the evening. And then imagine they returned, day after day, for weeks.

That's what I put the fine women who worked in the Otsego County Clerk's office through, and yet I was always greeted with a smile and a willingness to not only answer questions, but retrieve boxes and boxes of files from distant warehouses, provide a chair and table for me to use as a desk, and even lend an extension cord for my overworked computer. Thanks especially to County Clerk Susan DeFeyter and Chief Deputy Clerk Lynn Branch.

Maureen Derenzy, Director of the Otsego County Library, was helpful in my quest for so many seemingly unrelated details and taught me how to access certain library archives and indexes from my home computer. The people of Gaylord should be proud to support such a vibrant public library with so many free resources online.

Esther Moore supplied to me a big cardboard box containing years of newspaper clippings, prison newsletters, and other ephemera she'd collected, welcomed me into her home, and willingly agreed to remember a very difficult time for the Moore family. Jim Grisso, publisher of the *Gaylord Herald Times* for forty years, provided helpful information, as did Dean Robb and Terry Moore. I do not know Vicki Naegele or Norm Sinclair personally, but reporters have no trouble recognizing talent in fellow reporters. These two, working for the *Gaylord Herald Times* and the *Detroit News*, respectively, were, quite simply, excellent at their jobs. I thank them both for providing objective, accurate, and ongoing records of police investigations and complex court proceedings that no journalist could have prepared themselves for.

I would not have embarked on this project at all if not for Stuart Hubbell. He was an amazing man and a skilled lawyer and it will forever be a great regret of mine that the book was not completed before he died in September of 2010. Special gratitude also goes to Ray MacNeil and Stuart's son, Dan Hubbell. They provided every document I asked for, answered every question I could think of, and showed a great deal of patience with my writing efforts, which often moved forward at the pace of molasses in winter.

It has been my privilege to know Don and Lisa Heistand. They began as victims of this terrible injustice, became two of my sources in reporting this story, and, finally, friends. Thank you.

Finally, sincere appreciation to the staff of the University of Michigan Press, and especially Editor Scott Ham, for their peerless dedication to books (including this one), writers, and readers.

AUTHOR'S NOTE

Want to receive some strange email? Become a true crime author.

Soon after my first book, *When Evil Came to Good Hart*, was published in June of 2008, my in-box filled up with book suggestions, notes from prisoners claiming to be wrongly convicted, anonymous tips about unsolved cases, and lengthy rants penned by the obviously disturbed. Many of these missives began with the same five words: "I'm not a nutcase but . . . ." It is impossible to predict what will ignite my writing nerve, and so I learned to politely decline the story ideas and ignore the cranks and the crazies.

Then in December of 2008, a man named Dan Hubbell wrote me a short note. In it he said that his father, Stuart, had been involved with a case that "generated some notoriety" and might make a good book. I did not know Stuart Hubbell, but I knew of him. He'd once been the prosecuting attorney in my town for more than a dozen years. Certainly not a crank or a crazy.

"Some notoriety" turned out to be an understatement, and six years later, there is finally a book. I believe you will find the case to be as fascinating as I did. I must warn you, though, that the redemption finally achieved at the end is small, especially in comparison to the twists, turns, lies, ambition, and acute suffering participants both perpetuated and experienced along the way.

Although it was the defense attorneys who first brought the case to my attention, I was trained as a reporter first and an author second; when I undertook the project, I committed myself to tell the story objectively. Alas, most of it had to come from the extensive police reports, seemingly endless court documents, psychiatric and medical reports, and published newspaper accounts, as for reasons known only to them, many of the participants declined to be interviewed. That is their right, to let the documented record speak for them. All quotes that are not from personal interviews are taken directly from these official documents and have not been edited of their legalese or awkward grammar, so some may read a little strangely. Welcome to the Tobias case.

CONTENTS

PART 3 The Unraveling 299

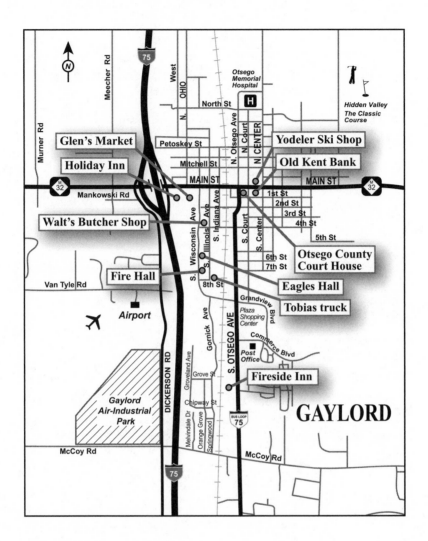

Map of Key Locations

PART 1

. . . . The Crime

Chapter 1   Found Frozen

. . . . Monday, December 8, 1986, 4 PM

If there is a more inhospitable place to die than the back of a long-bed pickup on a winter night in northern Michigan, it doesn't come quickly to mind. With no coat, no hat, and no gloves, any sane man would have to be liquored up, high, passed out, or dead to spend it like this: flannel shirt hiked up, bare skin to metal, a body exposed to the mitten state's legendary deep freeze.

And that's exactly what Jerry Tobias was. Dead. Frozen stiff as winter laundry forgotten on a backyard clothesline. Townspeople would speculate for decades whether he'd been only half dead when he was tossed in, but he was definitely all the way dead by the time a State Police trooper peered over the truck's tailgate and took in the sight: a young guy wearing only jeans, a flannel shirt and cowboy boots, lying on his side.

The Michigan State Police trooper was Ken Burr, and he took off one of his gloves, reached out a finger, and touched the man's bare stomach. Cold and hard.

Burr patrolled the back streets of Gaylord, an Alpine-themed resort town in the northern part of Michigan's lower peninsula. It was a series of computer entries that led Burr to Jerry Tobias' blue Ford pickup. Late Monday afternoon, Jerry's wife, Jackie Tobias, hadn't seen her husband since Friday morning, and she was starting to worry. Jerry was an oilfield worker, and although he was frequently in the field for days at a time, she'd expected him home by Sunday. When Monday arrived and no Jerry, Jackie called his boss, his boss called the State Police, and a dispatcher entered the missing man's license plate number—"HD 2850"—into Michigan's Law Enforcement Information Network (LEIN). LEIN was a statewide database of missing persons, criminal activity, personal protection orders, arrests, suspicious vehicles and the like; if the law knew where Jerry Tobias might be, chances were better than average that they'd find a clue to his whereabouts somewhere in the recesses of LEIN. It was often the first place police looked when someone went missing.

Finding a missing person wasn't always this easy, but when Burr checked the database he received an immediate hit. Not on Jerry Tobias himself, but on his truck. An officer on road patrol noticed it Sunday night, apparently abandoned, and ran "HD 2850" to see if the vehicle was stolen. The plate came back clean, and the officer, Karen McCann, went on about her rounds. Even though nothing came of that inquiry, LEIN still logged the activity into the system and dutifully fed it back to Trooper Burr on Monday afternoon, along with a location. The truck was last seen parked at the corner of South Illinois and Eighth Streets, on a quiet edge of downtown Gaylord, just behind the Fire Department.

And so at 4:25 PM on Monday, Dec. 8, 1986, Burr found the snow-covered vehicle exactly where LEIN said it would be. But the frozen body in the back came as a shock. Burr had to wonder if Jerry Tobias had been just lying there the night before, when Officer McCann shined her cruiser's brights directly at his tailgate.

The dead man's cowboy-booted foot stuck up out of the truck bed, clearly visible to Burr even from several yards away. It was hard to believe anyone could have missed that.

On the surface, Gaylord is one of a handful of small towns in northern Michigan that successfully transitioned from lumbering and trapping in the 1800s to golfing, snowmobiling, and skiing in the 1900s. In the glossy tourist brochures the town boasts it is "Northern Michigan's heart."

Tourists from Detroit and Chicago came north for the quaint downtown, sparkling ski hills, and pristine fairways. An easy exit off I-75, the freeway that connects the southern suburbs to the northern resort areas, "Gaylord" means "meeting place" in Ojibwa. By the 1970s, it was already a well-known gathering spot for families on vacation, executives on corporate golf outings, and men at their annual fall deer camp. A decade later, Gaylord gained a reputation as the waypoint for another type of traveler, and one who certainly wasn't going to be lauded in any of those tourist brochures.

In August of 1986, the *Detroit Free Press* uncovered a massive drug smuggling operation that began in Barranquilla, Colombia, and ended at the tiny Antrim County Airport, just thirty miles west of Gaylord. At the time, it was the largest drug smuggling operation ever uncovered in U.S. history, according to the report. In October of that same year, an area drug raid netted several pounds of pot and a grocery bag–sized stash of pills, the result of a yearlong undercover operation. Eight northern Michigan counties pooled their resources and instituted an undercover task force, the Straits Area Narcotics Enforcement (SANE), to address what they viewed as an out-of-control drug problem.

In November, Gaylord's Police Department, the State Police post, and the Otsego County Sheriff's Office formed yet another group, the Local Law Enforcement Partnership (LLEP), to fight the local spread of illegal drugs. All levels of the population were suspect, from teenagers to businesspeople. There were sweeps at Gaylord High School with drug-sniffing dogs, and the owner of the local Little Caesar's Pizza franchise was suspected in a cocaine deal that led to a kidnapping. A grand jury indicted drug users and dealers and sent dozens of them to prison.

By the winter of 1986, it began to seem to police and townspeople alike that hard drugs were everywhere in Gaylord. As Trooper Burr stared down at Jerry's body, it's likely he would have had three parts of the same question on his mind: *Drug dealer, drug user, or both?*

Trooper Burr didn't know Jerry Tobias personally, but he did know of him. The dead man was no stranger to Gaylord's seedier side, and in some ways his life mirrored the dual nature of the town. Jerry was a fun-loving outdoorsman, a husband, a loving father, and a hardworking oilfield roughneck, but he was also a drinker and a flirt who ran around on his wife with women he met in bars—a trait caused, or at least enhanced by, his regular alcohol and drug use. Pot and cocaine were his first choices, but friends said he'd do pills when they were offered. And Tobias dealt a little to support his habit, too. Nothing big; he wasn't listed in any of the front-page drug busts, and he barely had a police record, just a decade-old delivery of marijuana charge. Still, Jerry was a partier, and Burr remembered hearing his name in conversations about the Gaylord drug scene at least once or twice.

But the lifeless man the trooper stared down at was hardly the grinning blond and blue-eyed charmer his friends and family adored. Tobias' body was pressed against the rear of the truck, his bare back against the tailgate, knees bent, one foot resting awkwardly on a gasoline can, the other stuck up over the edge of the truck bed.

His plaid shirt and white undershirt were yanked up to his armpits, exposing bare flesh. His face was bruised and there were scratches on the side of his forehead. Patches of scalp showed through his thinning hair. Tobias' left arm was flung over his head, a set of jumper cables was coiled near his wrist, and accumulated road clutter—hand tools, an empty jug of windshield wiper fluid, a spare tire, litter—were scattered around the truck bed. A crust of snow-cloaked random surfaces. Inside the truck, there was more detritus, and behind the driver's seat was something that looked a little out of place: frozen packages of meat wrapped in white butcher paper.

Snowflakes dusted Tobias' bare skin, and if this image caused Burr to shiver involuntarily, no one could fault him for it. He'd been a trooper for 23 years, with all but a few of those years spent patrolling Gaylord and the surrounding area. Burr was used to writing traffic tickets, running down stolen snowmobiles, confiscating dime bags of pot, and busting drunks, not stumbling upon dead bodies.

The officer looked down at the snow drifting on the ground and back at his own footprints, visible in a direct line from the door of his cruiser to Jerry's truck. For the first time he noticed that someone else had already been to the truck. Older boot prints, blurred and half filled with snow, tracked from the ground in front of the passenger side door of Jerry's truck, around to the back of the bed, and then down the street.

Burr's eyes followed the mystery footprints north, away from the truck and up the snow-covered street, until they disappeared.

Chapter 2   Wild Game

. . . . Three Days Earlier, Friday, December 5, 1986, 9 PM

O nly the most experienced and wide-ranging carnivores recognized the smells wafting from the Northland Sportsman's Club the first Friday after gun season. Venison was on the menu, and so were partridge, duck, and rabbit. But there was also elk steak, buffalo, an antelope roast someone brought back from an excursion out west, greasy black bear stew from a beast shot in the Upper Peninsula, wild boar sausage, and a couple of wild turkeys, roasted like it was still Thanksgiving.

The social event of the season in Gaylord was not a charity ball, an art gallery opening, or a concert—it was the Northland Sportsman's Club's annual Wild Game Dinner. This was a stag affair—men only, and all were welcome. Doctors and lawyers filled their plates next to plumbers and electricians; politicians came to shake the hands of farmers and shopkeepers. Bartenders with the night off might be waited on by teachers; oilfield drillers could enjoy a roast prepared by an apron-wearing lawyer.

This once-a-year combination of camaraderie and cooking attracted local businessman, Laurie Moore. A hunter himself, and outgoing in a way some called fun-loving and others just called loud, Laurie had been looking forward for weeks to this evening of meat, men, and drinking.

Despite the coarse nature of some of the attendees, this was still no tacky buffet. Some members came in suits and ties, tickets went for $20 or more, a raffle generated thousands for the Club, and a cash bar served up draft beer, but also martinis and carafes of local wine. It was a gourmet-themed celebration of the hunting lifestyle so popular in the north.

Opening day of Michigan's deer season for rifle hunters is Nov. 15, and to many in the state it is more of a holiday than Presidents Day, Memorial Day, and Labor Day combined. Many schools are closed so that sons and daughters can go hunting with their fathers, many of whom take a vacation day from work for the privilege. Michigan businesses that cater to deer hunters—sporting goods stores, gas stations, bars, restaurants, hotels—enjoy sales that rival Christmas shopping on black Friday.

The Northland Sportsman's Club was founded in the 1930s to encourage hunting and target shooting and to be a local affiliate of the National Rifle Association. Laurie Moore was one of nearly 200 members and, like most, wouldn't think of missing the annual Wild Game Dinner. It was tradition to celebrate the end of the hunt, and from noon until dinnertime volunteers cooked and served a variety of meats and side dishes, buffet-style, to their willing diners.

Moore worked in his parents' store, a local combination butcher shop, deli, and small grocery store known as Walt's. Hunting season was particularly busy because Walt's specialized in processing deer for hunters who'd drop off their deer, pay a fee, and a few days later pick up steaks, ground venison, and venison sausage. So although Moore liked a good party, even the prospect of good company and strong drinks couldn't tempt him to leave work early during deer season. He locked the front door of Walt's at the regular time—6 PM—but stayed in the back processing deer with two of his part-timers, the Morey brothers, for another three hours. When the men were down to their last three deer, Laurie left, telling the Moreys to lock up when they were through.

By the time Laurie walked into the Sportsman's Club, it was after 9:30. Most of the others had finished eating, but a couple of his friends knew what he liked, made him up a plate, wrapped it in tin foil, and set it aside. So Laurie ate, got a drink, got another drink, and pretty soon he was, according to those in attendance, "feeling no pain."

"We stood together at the bar, he was loud, and he was drunk," attorney and Sportsman's Club member Mike Nelson would remember later. "But then, Laurie was always loud."

Drunk or not, Laurie was in control enough to make a phone call. From the telephone at the Sportsman's Club he rang up a friend, Debra Deitering, around 11 PM. Deitering's boyfriend, Tom Kearbey, lived downstate but had a cabin in Gaylord. He and Laurie were friends, had partied together, and, according to Kearbey, did the occasional drug deal. Just weekend partying, he called it—nothing big.

Laurie's phone call to Kearbey's girlfriend was brief. According to her, it went something like this:

"Hey, is Kearbey there yet?" Laurie asked.

"No," said Deitering. "But he just called to say he's on his way. Won't be here for a while though. Couple hours."

"All right, maybe I'll call back later."

If Laurie was feeling no pain by 11, he was downright hammered by 1 AM.

"Hey! Heyyyy!" Laurie hollered from the top of the stairs at the Sportsman's Club. "Everybody! Woo-hoo!"

The din in the room stopped for a moment as the group looked up at Laurie and raised their drinks in salute. The hunters in the room who were either lucky, accurate, or patient enough to get a deer that year would not have had venison steaks in their freezers if not for the skill and work of this man. He was obnoxious, but they could forgive him a drunken outburst, especially a happy one.

"Chug-a-lug!" someone called out and then the laughing, the conversations, and the card games started up again.

At 1:30 in the morning, Laurie made his way through the thinning crowd toward Nelson, who was standing at the end of the bar. The pair talked awhile, and then took their half-full drinks out to Laurie's van. When their glasses were empty, Nelson went back inside and Laurie drove off.

"Sure you can drive?" Nelson called out.

Laurie, grinning, raised his fist and gave an enthusiastic thumb's up.

"Is he there *yet*?"

"No."

"I'm coming over."

That was the gist of the second phone call between Laurie Moore and Debra Deitering. Minutes later, she heard a loud knock on her door, looked out her front window, and there was an intoxicated Laurie, swaying on her front step.

"Let's go out to the cabin," Laurie said, when she opened the door. "I'll drive."

"Are you *kidding*?" Deitering said. "You're way too drunk to drive."

"I'm fine!" Laurie insisted. "C'mon! Don't you want to see Tom?"

"Laurie, I'm not riding with you," Deitering told him. "You shouldn't be driving at all."

"Oh, c'mon!"

"Ok, ok, we can go," Deitering said, resigned. She knew Laurie well enough to know that it was impossible to argue with him when he was drunk and had his mind set on something. "But let me drive. We can take your van, but I'm driving."

The pair arrived at Tom Kearbey's cabin on Otsego Lake, a four-and-a-half-mile trip, sometime after 2 AM. They walked into the cabin just in time to help Kearbey build a fire in his woodstove. The three smoked a joint together, and then Deitering went into the other room while the men talked.

"You should have seen all the food at the Club!" Laurie said to Kearbey. He went on to list each entrée, how it had been prepared, who had done the cooking, and how much of it he had eaten. Kearbey let him ramble on, even though he was thinking about how much he wanted Laurie to leave so he could be alone with Deitering. The couple hadn't seen each other in a week, and yet here was Laurie, oblivious to anyone but himself, going on and on about the best way to prepare an antelope roast.

Eventually, Laurie got around to the reason he'd come, and the two discussed cocaine. Kearbey and Laurie were both casual users, but on that night, neither man had any. As soon as Laurie learned that, he blurted out that he was ready to leave. He hadn't sobered up much at all, and Deitering and Kearbey both offered to drive him home, but Laurie politely refused. He left the cabin as quickly as he'd come, got into his van, smiled and waved, then drove off, telling them nothing about where he was headed next.

By 3 AM his destination was no mystery, at least not to his wife. Back at their home, Janet Allen was doing what most people did in Gaylord at 3 AM—sleeping—until she heard a revving engine and then the grinding sound of tires burying themselves in the snow over and over again. She got out of bed, walked to the front of the house, and pulled the front curtains back. There was her husband. Miraculously, he'd made it through his tipsy travels without incident, but then got his van stuck in his own driveway.

Janet marched to the front door and yanked it open. She stuck her head out into the cold and prepared to yell something, but then an unexpected sound stopped her. Laurie had his window rolled down and she could hear him singing. Whatever song was blasting from the radio was apparently just too good to turn off. When he saw his wife standing in the doorway in her nightgown, Laurie threw back his head and grinned, but also kept right on singing.

"Get in the house!" Janet called into the night.

Her voice was angry, but it wouldn't stay that way for long. It was easy enough to get mad at Laurie, but a lot harder to stay that way.

The next morning, a Saturday, it was the more routine sounds that got the day going at the Moore and Allen household. A telephone, ringing. A spoon against the inside of an empty cereal bowl. And dogs, somewhere outside, barking at nothing. Not a one was a welcome sound because Laurie had a headache. His stomach didn't feel all that good, either.

Saturday was usually a work day for Laurie, especially on the weekends between deer season and the holidays, but he flopped back down. Across town the deer were stacking up at Walt's, hunters would be calling the butcher shop wanting their venison, and people would be making special orders for Christmas, but Laurie still spent most of the morning in bed.

Janet went to the shop instead, took special orders, did the week's accounting, and answered the phone.

"I wouldn't do that if I were you," she told a customer who said he was going to call Laurie at home. "He's awful grouchy."

Laurie slept until 11, and then dragged himself to work, bringing his headache along with him.

"Laurie's got a hangover," the teenaged girls who worked the cash register giggled to each other. They had brothers and fathers. They knew what men looked like after a night of drinking. They looked puffy and haggard and bloodshot. They looked exactly like Laurie.

Laurie lasted at Walt's until the middle of the afternoon before he surrendered and went back home. At least the butcher shop was closed on Sundays, and he could come in at his leisure after church and get caught up. By the end of the day Monday, most of the venison would be picked up and paid for and his walk-in cooler would be emptied out. Everything could get back to normal.

Chapter 3   A Pretty Good Beating

. . . . Monday, December 8, 1986, 8 PM

The end of Illinois Street, a nondescript gravel turnaround with little to distinguish it on any other day, was a crime scene. By the time State Police Detective Fred LaBarge arrived, the place was teeming with uniformed officers, detectives in dark overcoats, firemen working their regular shifts at the fire barn, and curiosity-seekers milling around in the snow.

When Burr called dispatch and reported that he'd found a frozen Jerry Tobias in the back of his pickup, the dispatcher called Gaylord Police Chief Frank Dufon, and Dufon called the State

Police and their crime lab. The State Police assigned a detective to the case and the lab sent a crime tech. Soon the scene was populated with Latent Print Specialist James Besonen, Otsego County Undersheriff Richard Cook, and Chief Dufon's second in command, Sergeant Paul Dunkelberg, along with Otsego County Prosecutor Norm Hayes, and the medical examiner, Dr. Charles Iknayan. Trooper Burr and Officer McCann had set up road barricades and remained with Jerry's truck. Someone had to keep people away—even after the sun went down and the temperature dropped into the teens it didn't look like the crowd of onlookers would be going away anytime soon.

Into this solemn gathering of stamping feet, fingers flexing inside gloves, and exhaled breath rising in the chill drifted the figure of Detective Fred LaBarge. A man of averages in size, looks, smarts, and temperament, LaBarge was in his late 50s and had been ambling toward the end of a long, if unassuming, police career. For 35 years he'd toed the line, followed the rules, kept his head down.

LaBarge parked his cruiser, stepped out into the snow, and greeted the group. A man of little ceremony, he introduced himself to those he didn't know, and then set about examining the body and taking a good long peek inside the cab of the pickup. He took a small notebook out of his pocket and laboriously printed his observations.

With the creation of the Field Investigation Section in 1981, the Michigan State Police was at the end of its transition from a good ol' boy network to a highly educated, obsessively trained, and sophisticated group of law-enforcing professionals. By December of 1986, officers wore an updated uniform, had a new union, and worked in facilities across the state that were being upgraded. Mandatory training programs had been instituted as part of this change, and career advancement was increasingly tied to high scores on written tests.

LaBarge, a poor reader, writer, and speller, had not always been a willing participant in this transition. His notes written at the crime scene bear this out. Printed in block letters, all caps, they read:

"JERRY ROBERT TOBIAS. W/M. 1.7.55, 5'-10"—155 BRN-BLUE.

FACE BEAT UP. WALLET MISSING.

MEAT IN BACK WITH GROCERYS. LEFT HANED.

SMOKE'S MARBORO'S. DRINKS BUDWISTER."

In Northern Michigan in the 1980s, the brand of beer you drank and the cigarettes you smoked were part of your character description, almost as important as your D.O.B., your eye color, your height, and your profession. Tobias' choices weren't particularly revealing—Budweiser and Marlboro were standard issue, the "acme" of beer and smokes.

LaBarge classified Tobias' death as suspicious. Not a homicide, at least not yet, but his truck was still regarded as a possible crime scene and couldn't be driven. With the body still in the bed, a tow truck operator inflated a flat tire, winched up the rear axle, and towed the truck to the city garage. Following behind were LaBarge in his State Police cruiser, several city police officers in their patrol cars, and other officers in their personal vehicles, the whole procession making for a macabre winter parade.

Waiting for them at the city garage was a somber man wearing a black suit, black leather gloves, and a black wool overcoat, and a younger woman, short and plump, in jeans and a puffy ski jacket. The undertaker and the pathologist.

Once inside, everyone watched in respectful silence as Jerry's frozen body was lifted out of his truck and onto a table to thaw.

Dr. Patricia Newhouse examined the body, but it didn't take a pathologist to see that Jerry took a pretty good beating before he died. Anyone could tell that, just by looking at him. Her initial overview revealed he wasn't shot or stabbed, no bones looked broken, and there were no significant wounds anywhere, but somebody did beat the tar out of the guy.

A small amount of dried blood was smeared on the right side of his face, he had a black eye, and there were small bruises on his shoulders, chest, back, and right side. A scabby scrape wrapped around the right side of his waist like a rope burn, and there was an uneven welt on his shoulder.

Gaylord's medical examiner, Dr. Charles Iknayan, had been called away to the Upper Peninsula on another case, so this one would belong to Dr. Newhouse. In any suspicious death, be it from accident, suicide, or by more nefarious means, standard procedure is for a pathologist to conduct an autopsy and determine cause of death. In Jerry's case, that wasn't going to be easy.

Police couldn't tell the doctor when the man died, or where. They didn't know how long he'd been in the bed of his truck, whether he'd crawled in by himself or was dumped in by someone else. Had he been unconscious at the time but still alive? Police didn't know that either. They didn't know who he'd been fighting with, or why. When it came right down to it, police didn't know much of anything at all.

To complicate matters, the body was frozen solid. Dr. Newhouse hadn't been practicing long, but she did know that freezing a body complicated an autopsy. That much she remembered from medical school. Once she became a licensed pathologist, she had done one such autopsy—a frozen snowmobiler killed in an accident. Newhouse decided to wait a day for the body to thaw before she began her work. Because Jerry's body could contain evidence of a crime, officers took shifts guarding it in the police garage overnight.

The next day, Tobias was moved to the Nelson Funeral Home and late Tuesday afternoon, Dr. Newhouse began the autopsy. With the help of an assistant, and while a handful of police looked on, it took her four hours to complete. She found that Jerry had suffered "pulmonary edema," or blood inside his nose, throat, and lungs. Newhouse also found two tiny circular scratches on his right temple—perhaps the source of the dried blood she initially observed—and he had eight fresh needle marks on his arms. But he had no broken bones, no damage to any of his internal organs, and nothing had obstructed his breathing in the minutes before he died. And, Jerry's last meal was a hearty one—meat, some kind of green vegetable, and potatoes.

Before she finished, Newhouse collected the standard blood and urine samples and sent them to the lab, requesting a routine screen for alcohol and illegal drugs. As per her wishes, these were treated as just a formality. Whether Jerry had been drunk or high when he died was irrelevant, as far as Dr. Newhouse was concerned. She'd found bleeding in his brain and so before the autopsy was even over, she determined that's what had killed him.

Jerry, Dr. Newhouse decided, had been murdered.

"The pathologic findings associated with the immediate cause of death were in the central nervous system," she wrote in her autopsy report. "In summary, the immediate cause of death was . . . blunt trauma to the head. Death appeared to be . . . homicide."

Chapter 4   The Task Force

. . . . Tuesday, December 9, 1986, 10 PM

While Dr. Newhouse finished up her autopsy, across town the cops were having a sit-down. Tobias' death was about to be officially declared a homicide, and that was a good enough reason for State Police Lieutenant John Hardy to make an appearance in Gaylord. Hardy commanded the State Police's 7th District, a large area encompassing nine posts in nine northern cities, covering nineteen counties and fifteen hundred square miles of forests, inland lakes, highways, and tourist towns, stretching from the middle of the mitten all the way to the Mackinaw Bridge.

Lieutenant Hardy brought along Detective Don Chappell, and asked another detective, Scott Croton, to drive down to the meeting from his post in Petoskey Post. The three met with LaBarge, Burr, and Dufon.

Five "Blue Geese," as Michigan State Police officers fondly called their cruisers, were parked outside Gaylord's tiny Police Department. Undersheriff Cook and Officer McCann were still in the loop, too, and a new face was added to the group: Jerry Borema, the investigator who worked for the prosecutor's office, would be on the team, too.

The group's first order of business was to list what they knew so far:

- Unidentified boot and palm prints were found on the top right edge of Jerry's truck, exactly where someone would place their hand and foot if they were climbing into the bed of the vehicle.

- Jerry had been wearing Levis, a gray long-sleeved t-shirt, a plaid flannel shirt, white underwear, white socks, and Dingo-brand cowboy boots. Two of his belt loops were torn and his belt was missing. There were scuffmarks on the heels and sides of his cowboy boots, as if he'd been dragged. His jeans were unbuttoned and the zipper was unzipped. He had $114 and a nickel in his left front pocket and $3.42 in his right front pocket.

- Deer hair was found on Jerry's shirt and in the back of his truck.

- There were rumors of infidelity. Jackie had recently discovered Jerry at a local bar with a supposed girlfriend. A confrontation ensued, and Jackie pulled the woman's hair in front of dozens of witnesses.

- Behind the front seat of Jerry's truck police found several bundles of frozen meat and seafood, wrapped in white butcher paper, and labeled "Walt's Meat Market." These included a package of oysters, a package of salmon, a package of Kowalski® Stadium kielbasa, two packages of red snapper, a Brookfield Farms® corned beef, a package of ground lamb, one whole boneless lamb shoulder, and a package of New York strip steaks.

This last detail was the one that piqued the interest of police. All told, they found more than $200 of specialty meat and seafood from Laurie Moore's butcher shop. What, the officers wondered, was an oilfield roughneck doing with pricey cuts of meat better suited to a gourmet restaurant?

Whatever the reason, the meat hadn't traveled very far. Walt's Butcher Shop was on Wisconsin St., only two blocks from where Jerry and his truck had been found.

As the meeting wrapped up, the newest member of the team, prosecutor's investigator Jerry Borema, was given the task of finding out how all that meat got into Jerry's truck. And so as soon as the meeting was over, he made the short drive to Walt's, walked in, and saw Laurie there working behind the counter.

"I need to ask you a few questions about Jerry Tobias," Borema said, in a low voice.

"Ok," Laurie answered, wiping his hands on his apron and coming out from behind the counter.

There were several customers in the store, and Borema had been hoping for a private place to talk, but the store was busy and Laurie said he couldn't leave, so the investigator decided to make do with a corner inside the store.

"You heard about him?" Borema asked, pulling out his notebook.

"Yeah," Laurie answered.

"When was the last time you saw him?"

Laurie thought a minute. "Well, he was in here Thursday, I think it was. He had his kids with him and he was asking about his deer. I had to tell him it wasn't ready, but that he could pick it up on the weekend. I wanted him to pick it up as soon as it was ready because my walk-in is jammed full."

"So, you know we found him in the back of his truck?"

"Yeah," Laurie said, shaking his head, "that's what I heard."

"There was a bunch of meat from your store behind the seat," Borema told Laurie. "New York strips. Polish sausage. Some fish, some corned beef. Do you know how it got there? Or when he would have bought it?"

Laurie looked puzzled. "I don't remember him buying any of that," he said.

Maybe Borema should talk to a couple of the other employees, Laurie suggested. Walt's was staffed by a lot of part-timers and the women who worked in the front part of the store might remember Jerry's purchases. A clerk named Sue Davis, and Laurie's teenaged niece, Kim Moore, might know something. Davis was in the store, and Borema talked to her, but she turned out to have no more information than Laurie did.

Borema thanked Laurie for his help, left Walt's, and drove to the high school. He flashed his investigator's I.D. badge at the principal, and said he wanted to talk with Kim Moore. The principal made a few phone calls, trying to get permission from Kim's parents, but couldn't reach anyone. He finally got a hold of Laurie, back at Walt's, and Laurie said it was ok with him if Kim talked to Borema. The pair met in the principal's office.

"Do you know a Jerry Tobias?" Borema asked.

Kim nodded.

"Did you work at Walt's on Friday?"

"Yeah, I went there after school and worked 'til 6."

Borema took a piece of paper out of his pocket, unfolded it and showed it to Kim. It was the list of meat police had found in Jerry's truck.

"Do you remember him buying any of this?"

Kim read through the list, looked up at the investigator and shook her head no.

Jerry's body had been found late Monday afternoon; by Thursday morning, the assorted group of officers, troopers, detectives, and investigators looking into his death was now considered a task force. They had one singular goal: find his murderer. Dr. Newhouse officially declared Jerry's death a homicide, and the crime dominated area radio stations. Gaylord's local newspaper, the *Gaylord Herald Times*, was a weekly, and the Thursday, Dec. 11, 1986 edition ran news of the crime on the front page and above the paper's own masthead:

INVESTIGATION CITES UNNATURAL CAUSES

Probe death of man, 31

———————

The article included a photograph of Jerry and one of his truck. It declined to state the cause of death and didn't reveal that Tobias had been found in the bed of the truck and not the cab. The story did ask for help from readers.

> "Officials are requesting information on the where-abouts of Tobias from Friday afternoon, Dec. 5 through mid-morning of Saturday, Dec. 6. They did not acknowledge any suspects in the incident and no arrests had been made."

At their Wednesday and Thursday morning meetings, the task force worked on developing a rough idea of where Jerry had been and what he had been doing the first week of December. They interviewed Jerry's wife, Jackie, and her friend and boss, Becky Nelson. They interviewed Jerry's bosses at the oil company and his co-workers. They interviewed an old girlfriend, Marie Ross, and a couple of Jerry's other friends, too, Sue Forcier and Sherry Payton. They even checked Sherry Payton's time card at the ski lodge where she worked, learning she'd been punched in from 6:42 PM on Friday, Dec. 5, to 1:36 AM on Saturday Dec. 6, and then again on Saturday evening from 6:51 PM until 11:43 PM. It was a 45-minute drive from the Boyne Mountain ski lodge to Walt's, so police ruled Payton out as a suspect. They interviewed bartenders, deer hunters, oilfield workers, and all of the employees at Walt's.

From these interviews, police put together a rough schedule of Jerry's last days:

Wednesday, December 3, 1986
Early evening—Jerry drops a deer off at Walt's Butcher Shop to be processed.

Thursday, December 4, 1986

Early evening—Jerry stops by Walt's with his two young sons to ask about his deer. Laurie Moore tells him it wasn't ready, but that it would be sometime over the weekend.

Friday, December 5, 1986

8:00 AM—When Jerry's wife, Jackie, wakes up after Jerry has already gotten their two sons off to school, she goes to McDonalds and brings home breakfast for the two of them.

9:30 AM—Jerry gets a phone call from his boss, Tom Valeika of Acme Tool Co. Valeika tells Jerry to come to the office to get his regular work truck. The two-tone Ford he usually drove back and forth to the oilfields had been in the body shop but was now repaired. Jerry leaves his home in Gaylord at 11:30 AM and heads for the Acme Tool Co. office in Kalkaska, an hour away.

12:30 PM—Jerry arrives at Acme Tool, exchanges trucks, and leaves for home about a half hour later. On his way, Valeika contacts Jerry on his pager and asks him to check on a job in Gaylord. Jerry checks in there between 3:30 and 4 PM.

4:00 PM—Jerry pages his boss from the job site, says the job is fine, but that he's not feeling well and is going home.

5:30 PM—Acme foreman Bob McCullick calls Jerry at home and tells him to take the weekend off, but to report to a job in Reed City 100 miles south of Gaylord, first thing Monday morning. Jerry agrees.

7:30 PM—Jerry stops in at the Yodeler Ski Shop where Jackie is working. He tells Jackie and Jackie's boss, Becky Nelson, that he's headed to Reed City on a job and won't be back until noontime Saturday at the earliest. He asks his wife for some pocket money, and she gives him $40.

9:00 PM—Jerry is in the Swamp Bar in Frederic, a small town ten miles south of Gaylord, drinking. He brags to a group of friends that he has $5,000 in cash on him. His pockets are bulging with $20 and $100 bills, and he buys several rounds. Over the next three hours he drinks eight or nine White Russian cocktails and two beers, and leaves the bar a little after midnight. He tells his friends he's headed to Gaylord to buy some cocaine, but that he'll be back by 1:30 AM for last call. He's driving his blue Ford work truck, and this is the last time anyone reports seeing him alive.

Saturday, December 6, 1986

12:30 AM—On his way home from a late night at the bowling alley, a Gaylord fireman and local busybody, Mel Green, sees Jerry's truck parked in front of the fire hall, where it would be found a day and a half later by police.

9:00 AM—Several hours later, Green is on his way back to the bowling alley to take his young son bowling, and again sees Jerry's truck parked in the same place. When the Greens leave the bowling alley at noon, the truck is still there. Green notices footprints by the driver's side door leading north. He writes down the truck's license plate number—HD 2850—and stuffs it in his pocket.

6:00 PM—Jerry's bosses from Acme Tool Co., Tom Valeika and Bob McCullick, call Jerry's house to ask where he is. They need to give him details about his next work assignment. Jackie says he's in Reed City. They tell her he didn't have to report there until Monday morning.

Sunday, December 7, 1986

11:00 AM—Jackie Tobias and Becky Nelson take their kids to Traverse City to do some Christmas shopping and to see a movie; they're gone most of the day. Jerry's bosses try several times to contact Jerry by phone and via his work pager with no success.

6:00 PM—Jackie and the Tobias children return home from shopping. Jerry still isn't home, and she's worried he might be with a girlfriend.

10:00 PM—Officer Karen McCann patrols Illinois St., sees Jerry's truck from the window of her patrol car, and enters the license plate number into LEIN.

Monday, December 8, 1986

11:00 AM—Tom Valeika calls the Kalkaska post of the Michigan State Police to file a missing person's report. The Kalkaska post calls the Gaylord Post and speaks with Trooper Burr. Burr contacts Jackie Tobias and a missing person's report is filed. Burr types the plate number into LEIN, gets a location, and finds the frozen body of Jerry Tobias in the back.

Looking over the itinerary, the task force could now account for Jerry's whereabouts until midnight Friday, Dec. 5. He was found dead Monday, Dec. 8 at 4:25 PM. That meant 64 hours of his life remained unaccounted for. Sometime within those missing hours, he'd been murdered, according to Dr. Newhouse, though she couldn't say with any accuracy, exactly when or how. Because his bosses at Acme Tool could pinpoint when they couldn't get in touch with him, and because Jerry Tobias was known as a responsible employee, police suspected it was sometime Friday night or in the wee hours of Saturday.

Where had Tobias been in the meantime? And with whom?

Other questions also confronted detectives. For example, the suspected cocaine deal and the money. Jerry had asked his wife for $40 at 7:30 PM on Friday night, but then supposedly had as much as $5,000 on him only an hour and a half later. Where did he get it?

And why did he lie to his wife and tell her he was headed out of town on a job, when he didn't really have to report to Reed City for three days? Was it because he didn't want her to know about a drug deal? Or was it because he was planning on meeting a girlfriend? And finally, who beat him up?

When Trooper Burr found Jerry, his body appeared plenty bruised, but his knuckles were also scraped up, so he may have given as good as he got, or at least tried to.

Complicating matters, the test results from the autopsy came back from the lab and Dr. Newhouse added them to her report. Jerry's blood alcohol was .02 when he died; such a minute amount that it wasn't even considered tipsy. Yet witnesses in the Swamp Bar said that Jerry had drunk at least eight White Russians and two beers in three or four hours. Witnesses said he was so drunk that he had a hard time playing a game of pool, dropping his cue stick several times and staggering around the pool table.

White Russians—a mixture of vodka, Kahlua, and cream or milk—pack a wallop, and eight of them, plus the beer, would have put a stumble into the step of even a seasoned drinker. If Jerry was killed later that night or early Saturday morning, his blood alcohol should have measured as much as ten times higher than .02.

All of these questions would have to be answered if police were going to find out who killed Jerry and build a case against his murderer. With little physical evidence to go on, they expanded their interviews. Jerry and Jackie's friends, family, co-workers, and neighbors were interviewed and re-interviewed. One person called in for a second interview was Jackie's boss at the ski shop, Becky Nelson. While the blood alcohol level was a scientific inconsistency, Becky's answers provided the case's first human one.

When an investigator interviewed him in the butcher shop, Laurie Moore said he hadn't seen Jerry since Thursday night, but when they called Becky Nelson into the station and sat her down in an interview room, she told Detective LaBarge there was more to both her and Laurie's stories.

"I haven't been one hundred percent honest," she said. "The last time I saw Jerry wasn't at the ski shop."

Becky told police that she did see Jerry at the ski shop when he came to visit his wife on Friday afternoon and ask for some money, but then later that night he also came to her house. She and her husband, Don Nelson, gave Jerry $200 to buy them a bag of pot. He left at 8 PM with the money, and that was the last time she saw him. The interview ended, but then a few hours later, Becky returned to the police station again, this time with her husband and their attorney.

Again, she said she hadn't told them the full story. What she said about the pot deal was true, but incomplete. It was the Nelsons' understanding that Jerry was going to buy the pot from Laurie Moore, and then return to their house with it that same night. When they didn't hear from him she went to the butcher shop the next day, Saturday, and spoke to Laurie. According to Becky, Laurie said, "the stuff did not go."

With this new information, Detective LaBarge decided to take a closer look at Laurie Moore and Walt's. Could the store be a front for drugs? If so, the place sure operated way under the radar.

The butcher shop was a longtime Gaylord fixture. Laurie's father, Walter Moore, started the business in the 1960s when he moved his family to Gaylord from Ann Arbor. When the Moore patriarch died in a car accident in 1983, Laurie and his mother, Esther Moore, worked together to keep the place running. The shop had a well-stocked deli, sold specialty meat and seafood, provided butchering services, and often contributed to community events by collecting money for local charities. The Moores employed more than a dozen people, and Walt's was especially busy during deer season when hunters brought in their kills to be processed into steaks and sausage and during the holidays when special orders were at their highest.

Regardless of the business' good reputation, it was obvious to police that Laurie Moore would have to be interviewed again, and interviewed properly this time; not some quiet chat in the corner of his store, but a traditional interrogation in a police interview room.

Although he'd put Detective LaBarge in charge of the Tobias investigation himself, Lieutenant John Hardy wasn't sure whether he was the best person to handle such an important interview. LaBarge was a solid enough cop, but not the sharpest tool in the shed. A better choice would be Detective Chappell, and although he was bright and ambitious, Hardy wasn't sure he wanted him to do the interview, either. When it came right down to it, Hardy wasn't sure he wanted to farm the job out at all. In the end, he decided to make the two-hour drive from Traverse City to Gaylord, and conduct the interview with Laurie Moore himself.

Hardy invited Chappell and LaBarge to sit in and observe, and the three detectives met at the Gaylord Police Post and strategized their approach while they waited for Laurie Moore to show. The main purpose of the interview would be to learn as much as they could about Laurie's relationship with Jerry, and determine why the expensive meat was in the dead man's truck.

After suggesting several time options with Laurie, the interview was finally scheduled for 3 PM and Laurie arrived a few minutes early. He came alone, straight from work, and reiterated that he hadn't seen Jerry Tobias since he'd dropped his deer off at Walt's sometime during the week before he died, probably Thursday. Laurie said he didn't know Tobias all that well, but had heard he had a reputation for picking up women in bars.

"Where were you Friday night?" Hardy asked.

Laurie said he worked at the butcher shop until 9 PM, and left the Morey brothers, Todd and Bill, to process and package three deer and then clean and lock the store. The brothers had their own key, Laurie explained, and they often closed up after Laurie had gone home. On Friday, Dec. 5, Laurie went to the Sportsman's Club dinner, he told Hardy, and then went home.

"What about that meat we found in his truck?" Hardy said. "It came from your shop and yet no one remembers selling it to him."

Laurie said he couldn't explain it. He was as mystified by it as the police were. Hardy left the interview for a few minutes, and when he returned he was carrying a cardboard box and set down in front of Laurie. Inside were the meat and seafood found in Tobias' truck.

"It blows my mind," Laurie said, when he looked inside. He said he hadn't sold any of it to Tobias, and was particularly perplexed by the bundle of New York strip steaks. The meat wasn't cut into individual steaks, but just wrapped up in one large hunk of meat. Laurie told Lieutenant Hardy that Walt's never sold steaks that way. The New York strip meat arrived at the store like that from the wholesaler, but was always cut into individual steaks before it was sold to retail customers.

"I am the only guy who cuts meat in the store," he told Hardy, "and I would remember cutting that for him or for anyone else. And I can't remember ever selling it like that."

But Laurie agreed that the meat had definitely come from Walt's. He couldn't have denied it even if he wanted to. His own handwriting in black grease pencil was on some of the packages.

"Are any of your employees friends with Jerry?" Hardy asked. "Maybe they've been selling him meat out the back door after closing?"

Laurie explained that he had more than a dozen employees, and many of those were part-timers he hardly knew and had only recently hired for deer season. Sometimes, he said, to make the work go faster, he provided employees with beer after hours, but he lied and said he wasn't a drug user or dealer. Laurie wasn't sure if any of his new employees were good friends with Jerry, but even if some of them were, he still couldn't imagine how they could steal that much meat. Plus, he trusted his employees. They were all loyal to the store, and to him and his mother, and he refused to believe any of them were thieves or drug dealers.

"Can anyone verify your attendance at the wild game dinner?" Hardy asked. Dozens of people could place him there over several hours, but Laurie was rattled by the interview, and by Jerry's death, and said he couldn't think of anyone in particular.

Chapter 5   A Suspect

. . . . Friday, December 12, 1986, 3 PM

After confronting Laurie with the box of meat and getting little reaction, Lieutenant Hardy told LaBarge to find out if Laurie's alibi held up. They made the drive from the butcher shop to the Sportsman's Club, to Debbie Deitering's place, and then out to Tom Kearbey's cabin on Otsego Lake. From there, they drove back to Walt's Butcher Shop and to Laurie's own house. They computed the miles, the likely traffic, and the time it took them to make the trip.

If they drove fast, didn't encounter any traffic, stoplights, or obstacles, and if all the times witnesses gave them were tweaked here and there, police decided Laurie could have been at the butcher shop when Dr. Newhouse said Jerry died.

It was time to bring him back in for questioning, which they did the afternoon of Friday, Dec. 12.

"We're going to advise you of your rights," Detective Chappell told Laurie.

"Why?" Laurie asked. "Am I under arrest?"

"No," the detective said, "you're not."

"Well, then I don't understand why you're going to advise me of my rights. Maybe I should have someone here. You know, like a lawyer."

The day before, Detectives LaBarge and Chappell had paid a surprise visit to Walt's and found Laurie getting ready to go to a Christmas party. He offered to come by the State Police post the next morning, and the detectives agreed that would be fine, but then at the appointed time, Laurie had called and said that Walt's was busy with customers and that he couldn't leave. Besides hunters picking up their venison, it was only three weeks until Christmas and people were ordering their turkeys and hams. Laurie offered to come by at 3:00 that afternoon. The officers again agreed, and Laurie showed up again a few minutes early, at 2:55.

Detective Chappell conducted the interview this time while Detective LaBarge sat in and observed. Chappell didn't get very far. After a few questions, Laurie decided he wanted to call his wife, Janet. Besides giving him moral support, she was an attorney, and could offer him legal advice, too. The police waited, Janet arrived, the two talked privately, and Janet told Detective Chappell that, for the moment, her husband was not going to answer any more questions.

"I want to talk to Norm first," Janet told the detectives, referring to the Otsego County Prosecutor, Norm Hayes.

After the couple left, LaBarge and Chappell compared notes and agreed that Laurie's denials struck them both as suspicious. Neither man was a local cop, and neither was acquainted with Laurie or Janet. Detective LaBarge lived more than an hour east of Gaylord in Alpena, near the Lake Huron shore. Chappell lived an hour west of Gaylord in Petoskey, a swanky tourist town within sight of Lake Michigan. So neither officer knew that behind Janet's seemingly straightforward statement about speaking with the Otsego County prosecutor was a complicated history.

Prosecutor Norm Hayes and Janet Moore, who still went by her maiden name, Janet Allen, knew each other quite well. In 1986 Otsego County was small, rural, and except for Gaylord's town center, sparsely populated. With Hayes on one side of the law as the prosecutor, and Janet on the other side as a defense attorney, the two knew each other professionally. Even the out-of-town detectives couldn't have missed that Janet always referred to the prosecutor by his first name.

But what LaBarge and Chappell didn't know was that Prosecutor Norm Hayes had once been sweet on Janet. In the summer of 1983, the two were both single and lived in the same apartment complex. People would remember Norm pursuing Janet romantically, but that Janet only considered Norm a colleague. She would later characterize their friendship this way: "It was a small town. We were both attorneys, both single. We were friendly. We would have dinner together occasionally, drinks together occasionally. It was not an exclusive type relationship."

While the prosecutor never considered Janet his girlfriend, it became apparent to people who saw them together that he may have wished she were. Then Janet Allen met Laurie Moore, fell in love with the rowdy, life-of-the-party shop owner, and no longer had the time or the desire for casual get-togethers with Norm Hayes. Since Norm and Janet lived in the same apartment complex, the prosecutor would often see Laurie coming and going from Janet's apartment.

"You don't know how it tore my stomach up to see him go over and see Janet," a fellow attorney said Hayes once confided to him. Laurie and Norm were close in age and had not only attended Gaylord High School together, but Norm had sometimes been the target of Laurie's cruel teasing. That was the shared past of Laurie Moore, Janet Allen, and Norm Hayes.

As soon as Janet and Laurie left the police station, LaBarge called the prosecutor, and minutes later Hayes arrived and discussed the case with Chappell and LaBarge. The detectives didn't know, couldn't know, what had transpired between Hayes, Laurie, and Janet. Even if they had known, it's impossible to say what they would have done about it, if anything. Perhaps this early in the investigation, youthful misdeeds and past romantic longings were irrelevant. Perhaps not. Only the prosecutor himself knew the intensity of those "tore up" feelings, and whether or not they remained with him three years later, when Laurie was being questioned about Jerry Tobias' death.

Either way, no one mentioned any of it to the detectives. What Hayes did tell them was something much more pragmatic: There was enough probable cause for a search warrant of the butcher shop. A judge agreed and just after midnight on Saturday, Dec. 13, 1986, LaBarge, along with Chappell, Chief Dufon, and two officers from the State Police crime lab, gathered at the front door of Walt's, warrant in hand.

Laurie was called and a contingent of the Moore family—Laurie, Janet, Laurie's mother, Esther Moore, and his brother, Howard—all showed up at Walt's at midnight with a key to the shop. Bundled in their winter jackets, the family sat in Laurie's van for more than three hours while the police went through the butcher shop, the garbage dumpster behind the shop, and an adjacent garage. The store and the garage were built from cement block, and there were no windows in the back of the buildings, so while they waited and watched, the Moores still had no idea what police were collecting inside, if anything.

The warrant stated that Walt's was believed to be the scene of a homicide, but if police were expecting to find the place trashed and bloody inside, they must have been disappointed.

"The (butcher shop) appeared to be clean and in order. Nothing appeared to be disturbed," read the police report. "The (dumpster) was searched with nothing remarkable being found. A single car garage . . . used by Walt's Butcher Shop to hang deer prior to processing (had) deer hairs and dried blood stains observed on the floor. Nothing else remarkable was noted."

Knives, meat hooks, bone saws, and grinders. It didn't take a crackshot detective to find potential murder weapons inside a butcher shop. Yet compared to the dozens of glinting and bladed implements available inside Walt's, the items police actually confiscated appeared surprisingly harmless: a white butcher's apron, a white butcher's smock, sweepings from the cement floor, hair entangled in a mop, barbecue seasoning, a butcher's steel, and a chicken skewer.

This last item was thin, flimsy, and looked innocent, but actually turned out to be powerful enough to raise the dead. Because after police showed their finds to pathologist Patricia Newhouse, it was the chicken skewer she was interested in. She examined the two prongs and speculated that the sharp points, designed to skewer a whole raw chicken for roasting, could have caused the tiny scratches on Jerry's right temple. And there was only one way to find out: exhume Jerry's body.

With Jackie Tobias' approval, a sixteen-item "Motion for Disinterment" was filed with the Otsego County District Court by the prosecutor and granted by a judge. Ten days before Christmas, cemetery workers attacked the frozen ground with heavy equipment and hand tools, and Jerry's frozen body was taken to the Nelson Funeral Home once more. Dr. Newhouse held the spindle points up to the scratches on his temple and declared a match. Not only were the marks on the side of Jerry's head made by the confiscated chicken skewer, she said, a blow from the cooking implement was also probably what killed him.

"What you have here," Newhouse told police, "is the murder weapon."

Although the primary purpose of the exhumation was to compare the scratches on the side of Jerry's head to the skewer, buried within the prosecutor's Motion for Disinterment was item number fourteen: "[H]air samples and fingernail samples of the deceased were not obtained at the time of the postmortem examination."

Despite the fact that Dr. Newhouse had ruled Tobias' death a homicide, and despite the fact that Tobias had skinned knuckles and defense wounds on his forearm, and even despite the fact that at the time of the autopsy police had no suspects, no murder scene, and no murder weapon, the pathologist hadn't taken any hair samples or fingernail scrapings from the victim before she released his body for burial.

Newhouse had either forgotten, overlooked, or didn't think it was necessary to collect these at the autopsy. Exhumation gave her the chance to remedy her error, she collected the samples, and police entered them into evidence along with whatever effect time, snow, embalmment, burial, exhumation, and disinterment might have brought to bear upon them. This was only the first of what would turn out to be many more amateur blunders.

Primary among them was something that had yet to come to light: Tobias' blood and urine hadn't been properly analyzed for drugs or stored correctly at the police lab. A high level of security and a particular handling protocol is supposed to attend fluids from a homicide victim. Such samples are well marked, kept refrigerated if necessary, and are never destroyed without official permission. That would have been the way that Jerry Tobias' blood and urine were handled too, if lab personnel had known that they were taken from a murder victim. But they didn't know that because, for reasons known only to her, Newhouse never told them.

The police task force soldiered on, and officers continued to escort people to the post to be interviewed. With all information from Jerry's friends and family exhausted, detectives combed the fringes of the dead man's life.

One man on those fringes was a sometime drinking buddy named Vincent Andrews. Andrews told police he'd been at several bars with Jerry just two nights before he died. He and Jerry chatted for several hours, and the dominant topic was Tobias' "business on the side," by which, Andrews said, Jerry meant both infidelity and drugs. Andrews told police that Tobias was trying to manage romantic affairs with several different women, some of them married, all while holding down his oilfield job, being a family man, and occasionally dealing drugs. Andrews said he didn't know any of the women himself, but as far as Tobias' drug dealing was concerned, he did remember one name: Dennis O'Rourke.

Police were aware of O'Rourke. According to their files, his name was already on their radar as a suspected drug dealer. So, although detectives must have heard the ring of truth in Andrews' story—LaBarge had even found a slip of paper in Jerry Tobias' wallet with Dennis O'Rourke's phone number on it—the lead apparently went nowhere. It was either never followed up on or was a dead end, but no record of any interview with O'Rourke or investigation of him in relation to Jerry Tobias' death was included in the police report.

Police also interviewed two other men they suspected of being involved with illegal drugs, Gary Mayer and Tony Schultz. According to Jackie Tobias, Jerry and Tony Schultz had dealt drugs together on at least one occasion. And Mayer was friends with Jerry Tobias and had gone out drinking with him on December 1, just four days before they believed Jerry died. The two men even stopped into Walt's Butcher Shop together, but that was the last time Mayer said he ever saw Jerry Tobias. According Detective Chappell's report of the interview, Mayer was an ex-felon with "violent tendencies." The bartender at the Fireside Lounge told police that Mayer had been in on Friday, Dec. 5 at about 8:30 PM asking for Tobias. But that lead, too, apparently went nowhere.

Perhaps Andrews, O'Rourke, Schultz, and Mayer were deemed unimportant because police already had a suspect, and his name was Laurie Moore. Because in the days following their interview with Laurie, any leads that might have pointed to someone else killing Tobias appeared to be discounted. On Dec. 15, Prosecutor Hayes spoke to Janet and gave her some startling news.

"Number one, we know, *we know*, that he was involved in a dope deal," Hayes told her. "We know that, the evidence supports that. Number two, I am not interested in prosecuting people involved in a drug deal out of what happened. Ok? If that is what concerns Laurie, he should not be concerned with that. We want Laurie to come in, waive his rights, and tell us everything he knows."

Janet took a long moment and tried to process this news.

"Just for clarification," she finally asked, "when you say he was involved in a dope deal, do you mean in connection with this Tobias case?"

"Yes," Hayes said. "Yes, I do."

Chapter 6 A Witness?

. . . . February, 1987

Winter set in and despite the conversation between Janet Allen and the prosecutor, weeks passed without an arrest. There were no additional interview requests made of Laurie, and no more searches of Walt's. But behind the scenes the police and the prosecutor's office were both working hard to build a case against him. LaBarge's office was not at the Gaylord Police Post; it was inside the prosecutor's office and as part of their work together, some new evidence came to light.

A Gaylord city patrolman, Officer Dan Dallas, was on his scheduled overnight patrol on Friday, Dec. 5, the night police still believed Jerry died, despite there being blood alcohol evidence to the contrary. Officer Dallas approached Detective LaBarge and told him all the talk at the police station about the crime, as well as the articles in the newspaper and the radio reports, jogged his memory. After the State Police interviewed Laurie, Dallas suddenly remembered driving past Walt's on Saturday, Dec. 6, at 2:30 in the morning. He told LaBarge that there were lights on in the back of the shop that night and a pickup truck parked by the back door. As he was driving away, Dallas said he watched a light-colored van approach the shop and park in the alley near the truck. An unidentified man got out of the van, went in the back door of Walt's, and Dallas continued on his way.

"Why didn't you tell us any of this earlier?" LaBarge asked.

Dallas said he'd already documented the reason in his written report, and provided LaBarge a copy. The report stated that Dallas "did not feel the situation to be suspicious as u/o (undersigned officer) has observed employees on several different occasions in the past enter the building through the rear door in the early AM hours."

It was only after Jerry Tobias' body was found, and Laurie Moore was considered a suspect in his murder, that Dallas said he remembered his drive past Walt's. When he learned that Laurie Moore drove a tan-colored Chevy Astro van, he knew he had to come forward.

The investigation was now funneling everything learned about Jerry Tobias' death down onto one man: Laurie Moore. The evidence against him included illegal drugs and stolen meat, and with officer Dallas' account, there was even a possible match on their suspect's vehicle. All this combined to give Prosecutor Hayes and Detective LaBarge a specific theory on how and why Tobias was murdered, and by who. They believed Laurie Moore killed Jerry Tobias inside Walt's Butcher Shop in a drug deal gone wrong. Then he dumped Jerry's body in the back of his pickup truck, drove it a couple blocks away from the shop, and left it there.

While Tobias' death and the search for his killer dominated the front page of the *Gaylord Herald Times* and was a constant topic of conversation around town, it was not the only crime attended to by the Otsego County prosecutor's office.

Gaylord and the surrounding area saw its fair share of breaking and entering, domestic violence, drunk driving, and felony firearm possessions. Not to mention an almost constant stream of illegal drug possession with intent-to-deliver cases. With much of Prosecutor Hayes' time and energy focused on the Tobias case, these lesser crimes were relegated to the chief assistant prosecutor, Dawn Pyrek. She sent the county's serial shoplifters, drunk drivers, home invaders, and druggies to jail and handled many of Gaylord's seemingly unending domestic disputes. So while Hayes was busy tabulating any evidence that surfaced against Laurie Moore, it was Pyrek who handled one particularly bizarre domestic violence case.

The Parmentiers, a young married couple living on the out-skirts of town with their young children, were in the process of getting a divorce. Each parent had retained an attorney, but even with experienced and objective professionals to handle the back and forth, custody negotiations were not going well.

Debbie Parmentier had left her husband, Leonard, and moved in with friends. She'd taken their two sons with her, but on Christ-mas Day, the three of them went back home for a visit so the fam-ily could try to celebrate the holiday together. That was the plan anyway, Debbie told Pyrek. It was working out just fine she said, until her husband Leonard attacked her with a pair of scissors. Not only did he try to stab her, he also tried to rape her with them. Debbie called the police, and then an officer interviewed her and forwarded Debbie's allegations to the prosecutor's office.

The attack sure sounded cruel and violent, but Pyrek had enough experience to know that divorcing couples often embel-lished the details of disputes with their soon-to-be exes. Plus, according to the police file, Leonard Parmentier and the couple's two sons had been interviewed, and all three denied the attack ever happened. Leonard told police that his wife had a history of mental problems and often made up bizarre stories to try to get him into trouble.

Pyrek called Debbie into her office and shared this information with her, but Debbie remained undaunted—she was afraid for her life, she said, and she wanted Leonard in jail.

"Do you have any proof?" Pyrek asked. "Anything else that isn't in this report?"

"I had to go to the doctor," Debbie told her. "I was hurt bad and needed treatment."

Pyrek asked if Debbie would be willing to sign a form that would allow the prosecutors' office access to her medical records. At first Debbie refused, but when Pyrek told her there would be no case against Leonard without those records, she changed her mind.

On Feb. 18, 1987, Pyrek followed up and sent a letter to Debbie's primary care physician, Dr. Williams, asking for her complete medical history.

"Kindly remit to our office a complete case history including copies of all perscriptions (sic), medical reports, records and medications relating to your patient, Debra Dawn Parmentier. Should you have any question or concern in this regard, please do not hesitate to contact me."

Dr. Williams, a D.O. in Gaylord, mailed Pyrek a nineteen-page report. Between 1981 and 1987, Debbie was in and out of hospitals and doctor's offices in Ann Arbor, Petoskey, Traverse City, and Gaylord complaining of headaches, stomach aches, bad vision, cramps, shortness of breath, and muscle pain. She'd reported being attacked, operated on, said she had brain tumors, migraine headaches, miscarriages, and seizures. Included in the report was a personal note to Dr. Williams from another physician, Dr. Jack R. Postle, who was on staff at Petoskey's Burns Medical Clinic's Department of Obstetrics and Gynecology.

"As you know," the note read, "she gives a very long history of multiple crisises (sic) occurring with her pregnancies and between, over the last several years. It is difficult to separate what is real from what is her interpretation of the actual events. Her general examination is normal. She professes to be exquisitely tender but her reactions are somewhat rehearsed and inappropriate. I am sure she has had some difficult problems in the past, however, I think there is a . . . moderately severe hypochondria. Ultimately, we may need to . . . confront her with the realistic facts of her illness including possible psychiatric care."

Pyrek read through the medial file but found nothing to substantiate Debbie's allegations about the scissor attack. Some spouses did indeed embellish, changing the details of every little argument or dispute to make themselves appear to be the victim, and the other spouse the villain. The scissor story seemed unbelievable from the start, and after reading through Debbie's medical records an inference could easily be drawn: The scissor attack seemed unbelievable because it never happened. It was a fiction, made up by Debbie to get her estranged husband in trouble. Pyrek recommended to Hayes that Leonard not be charged with anything, and she put the file aside.

On the surface, Debbie's accusation about Leonard seemed to have nothing to do with the Tobias case. But somewhere in the prosecutor's office, deep in a file cabinet or buried under a pile on a desk, there may have been another file with Debbie's name on it. It would have been a thin file, or perhaps even a single piece of paper with a few notes written on it. Maybe there was no file at all. Maybe all that existed was a notation on the office phone log, and maybe not even that. But whether or not it was officially documented, Debbie had already intersected at least once with the Otsego County Prosecutor, and that contact related directly to Jerry Tobias' death.

On Dec. 1, 1986, Leonard Parmentier filed for divorce from Debbie. His attorney was a man named Bernard Caspar, and Leonard told Caspar something about Debbie that sounded crazy, but on the off chance it was true, Caspar had gone to the prosecutor with it. Caspar informed Hayes that Debbie had told Leonard she witnessed Jerry Tobias' murder. Debbie said she saw two men stab Tobias to death in a parking lot behind Glen's Market, a grocery store in Gaylord. Debbie explained that Tobias was involved in selling illegal drugs and she was holding onto $30,000 of his drug money when he was killed. She couldn't lay her hands on the money because she'd hid it; so well in fact that even she couldn't remember where it was.

Leonard told Caspar he believed none of it, but Caspar relayed all of it to Prosecutor Norm Hayes, just in case. The prosecutor listened to what the divorce attorney had to say, thanked him for the heads up, but dismissed the tale as completely fabricated. Hayes knew from the autopsy report that Tobias hadn't been stabbed, and the idea that someone could "lose" $30,000 was ludicrous. The tip was so bizarre it didn't even necessitate a police report.

Debbie Parmentier was persona non grata as far as the Otsego County Prosecutor's Office was concerned. She'd lied about witnessing a murder, and then she'd lied about being attacked by her husband. It seemed like she was just another crazy low-life, out to use the justice system for her own means.

Chapter 7 In Their Panic

. . . . Monday, March 2, 1987, 8:30 AM

On a Monday morning in late winter, a tanned and bewildered Laurie Moore was arrested in the parking lot of his wife's law office. It was only a few weeks past the Moores' first wedding anniversary and they returned to northern Michigan just the night before from a belated honeymoon in the Cayman Islands. With the memory of sand under his fingernails and still smarting from Caribbean sunburn, Laurie was welcomed home with an arrest warrant.

The police and the prosecutor's theory was that Jerry owed Laurie either money or drugs or both and was killed when he didn't either pay up or deliver the drugs. They believed Laurie went to Walt's in the early morning hours of Saturday, Dec. 6, after he left the Sportsman's Club dinner and before he went to Debra Deitering's house. He and Jerry met at Walt's to conduct a drug deal, an argument escalated, and Laurie beat Jerry to death, or at least unconscious, with a weapon of opportunity, the chicken skewer. Laurie then dumped Jerry in the back of the pickup truck, drove it two blocks away and parked it in front of the fire hall where it was found two days later by Trooper Burr.

The Moore family knew full well that Laurie was under investigation, but the actual arrest came as a shock. In the three months since Jerry's body had been discovered, the message to the public from the police and the prosecutor's office was of a wide-ranging manhunt throughout the region for the rough character responsible for Jerry's death. The shadowy side of the tourist town would be scoured, and police assured the public that they were using every tool of detection available. A long list of outliers, troublemakers, junkies, dopers, and petty criminals had been hauled into police headquarters and interviewed, and sometimes their names were even fed to inquiring reporters.

The Moores' shock was not unfounded. In a front-page story in the *Gaylord Herald Times*, Police Chief Dufon blamed "drug transients" and "less than desirable" drifters for a marked increase in crime throughout the waning months of 1986. Though he didn't mention the Tobias case by name, the image in the minds of the public was that their small Alpine-themed town was being overrun with drugs from dealers hailing from the big cities to the south— Grand Rapids, Detroit, and Chicago.

Laurie's arrest came as a shock to many locals, too. He was not a drifter, not a criminal, not a transient, and though he was, by his own admission, a casual drug user, he didn't have a drug record. He was just a local businessman with a large extended family who liked to party and had a big personality. Regular customers at the butcher shop were particularly surprised by the news. Laurie was the man who put the paper frills on their crown roast of lamb and carefully trussed their special occasion veal shoulder. This affable and outgoing green-eyed charmer, this man who was a dead ringer for Jimmy Buffet, this friend of deer hunters was a *murderer*? He could be loud, often to the point of obnoxiousness, and he did like to drink. A lot. But a *killer*?

But the police assured the public that they had their man. After an exhaustive and meticulous investigation, leadership from Prosecutor Hayes, and unprecedented cooperation among the State, County, and City Police Department, meticulous detective work had excluded all other suspects and ultimately led to Laurie. Gaylord was safe again because Jerry's killer had been arrested.

While a long and exhaustive investigation was the scenario police and the prosecutor must have wanted to inspire in the public's mind, the actual police report told another story. Laurie had been their only real suspect from the get-go, and any information that led elsewhere—Gary Mayer, Dennis O'Rourke, the Morey brothers, Tony Schultz—was discarded, ignored, or explained away.

Sitting in a jail cell certainly gives a person time to think. Even people who find themselves in a cell for a few days—an overnight or even just a couple hours—often report having a good old-fashioned heart-to-heart with themselves. Being confined has a way of making someone take stock of their life.

"To bear witness, to stay sane, to keep their heart pumping, to not be eaten up by rage or despair, to figure out how they got there, or to discover what truly matters," is what prisoners think about, according to Sister Helen Prejean, author of *Dead Man Walking*.

After the initial shock of the arrest, Laurie surely went through some of these same thought processes inside his cell at the Otsego County Jail. Eventually, he probably spent at least some of that time thinking back to his Gaylord High School days. Thinking back to when he and Norm Hayes were both students at Otsego High School, but never friends despite living near each other and riding the same school bus. It would be difficult, if not impossible, to imagine that while sitting alone in his cell even for a few hours, Laurie didn't zero in on one particular memory.

Moore would later say, under oath, that on that memorable day it was late afternoon and the school bus Laurie rode home every day was nearing the end of its route. Most of the other kids had already been dropped off; there were only a few students left in their seats, including himself and Norm Hayes.

Laurie was a new kid in town and had just learned something terrible about Norm's family that most of the other kids already knew: Norm's father had committed suicide two years before. Someone must have whispered this news to Laurie because none of the kids on the bus or in the halls at school talked about it publicly, where Norm might overhear. But Laurie, at 15, was not that polite. Brashness had long been his dominant character trait, even when he was only a teenager.

"I know why your old man killed himself," Laurie said to Norm, out loud, on the school bus. "If I had a wimpy son like you, I'd kill myself, too."

The few other kids still on the bus stopped talking and looked away. Later, Laurie remembered saying it but couldn't articulate why. There had been several times over the years that he thought about apologizing to Norm, but for one reason or another, he never did. More than a decade later, Laurie was in a jail cell for something he said he didn't do and Norm Hayes had put him there. It was far too late to apologize, that was for sure.

Did that cruel insult, and the animosity between the two teenagers that followed, have anything to do with Laurie's arrest? Michigan State Police records indicate that despite public statements to the contrary, both Hayes and the police had Laurie, and only Laurie, in their sights as Jerry Tobias' sole killer as early as Dec. 18, 1986, ten days after the body was found. A property report following the search of the butcher shop listed one confiscated item, "Stainless Steel Rotisserie Spindle," with an estimated value of "none." The report was signed by Detective LaBarge, and on the line for "Suspect's Name," was typed, "Laurie Moore."

The charge on Laurie's arrest warrant was "Open Murder," a catchall giving the prosecutor the option of later charging Laurie with anything from manslaughter to First-Degree Murder depending upon what, if any, evidence came to light before trial. Seven officers, including LaBarge, Burr, Dufon, and an investigator from the prosecutor's office, all showed up for the arrest. The show of force was unnecessary. Laurie cooperated, insisting that they had the wrong guy.

His family agreed. The entire Moore clan remained steadfast in their belief that Laurie was innocent, and after his arrest their first task was to hire a defense attorney. Although Janet was a well-respected attorney, she was no expert on criminal law and even if she were, she wouldn't have been expected to defend her own husband against murder charges. It would be emotionally impossible, and she had her own clients who were particularly important now; with her husband in jail, Janet was their only source of income.

The best litigator Janet knew was a Traverse City attorney by the name of Dean Robb. Known for his civil rights work, Robb had fought McCarthyism in the 1950s, marched with Dr. Martin Luther King, Jr., in the 1960s, and then represented people wronged by insurance companies, big business, and the government. Robb was such a mesmerizing force in the courtroom that when he was practicing in Detroit law students would flee their classes and crowd into the courthouse when word got out that he was trying a case. Dean Robb and Janet Allen only knew each other peripherally, from their membership in various law organizations, but after meeting with Janet and Laurie, he agreed to take Laurie's case.

"I was a civil trial lawyer almost always representing the plaintiff, and when you're a civil trial lawyer you function a lot like a prosecutor, trying to prove wrongdoing," Robb said. "In the Laurie Moore case I didn't think it was my duty to prove his innocence. I thought it was my duty to help him tell his story. And besides, all they had was a thin, thin, circumstantial case."

To a defense attorney, the charge of "open murder," meant police and the prosecutor already knew they didn't have all the facts or evidence in the case yet, only enough for an arrest. To Dean Robb, such a general charge, and the time that had elapsed between Laurie's interview with police and his arrest, meant that the prosecutor had some doubts. His first act as Laurie's attorney was to go straight to the media with this idea.

"The delay in issuing a warrant is probably indicative of the strength of the case," Robb told a news reporter. "Pretty sketchy."

After Laurie was arraigned, Janet spoke to the local television news reporters and continued to deliver that message.

"My family and I have full faith in my husband's innocence," she said. "We are deeply disappointed in the trial by rumor that has originated from police sources since this unfortunate homicide took place. In their panic to find a solution, they have unjustly charged my husband. At present, we know very little about the facts concerning the case. However, we are confident once all the facts are known Laurie will be vindicated, and he will be found innocent. Our only hope is that the police will continue their investigation."

Chapter 8   "Makes no sense at all."

. . . . April, 1987

In the weeks following Laurie's arrest, Dean Robb dug in to his new case with gusto. According to Robb, the sheer wealth of material, coupled with the confusing nature of the investigation and the willy-nilly way the prosecutor provided updates, meant that preparing a defense was going to take significant time. Robb believed himself to be equal to the task and was soon getting to his Traverse City office early, leaving late, and spending regular parts of his days talking to himself in frustration.

"This doesn't add up!" he'd yell, pacing back and forth in front of his desk. "Makes no sense at all!"

These exclamations became Robb's muttering refrain as he worked through police documents, lab reports, conflicting witness statements, and crime scene photographs. Robb couldn't understand why the police had not focused more on the Morey brothers, Bill and Todd. They'd been the last people at Walt's on Dec. 5, the night police said Jerry died, yet Robb could find only one brief mention of the brothers in the police report. He was certain there had to have been a reason they weren't interviewed more diligently, but he couldn't think of one.

He began to ask around, and ultimately it was his own client who provided a possible answer. Laurie told Robb that he and Janet both asked the police not to drag the Morey brothers into the investigation if it wasn't necessary. They were still employed by Walt's and were helping Laurie's mother, Esther, run the store while Laurie was in jail. Esther couldn't do it alone and without Bill and Todd, Walt's would have to close. Laurie had Janet to depend on, but Esther only had the butcher shop, and Laurie told Robb he couldn't bear to see his mother lose her business simply because he was in a mix-up with police. If the store could just stay open until police found out who really killed Jerry, Laurie was convinced everything would get back to normal.

Robb tried to explain to him that by protecting Esther, Laurie wasn't doing his case any favors, but once Laurie's mind was made up about something there was no talking to him. So Robb continued to prepare for trial, with or without the Moreys.

Although Robb practiced mainly in the few northern Michigan counties west of Otsego, he and Prosecutor Hayes had opposed each other in the courtroom once before. Robb knew that when

Laurie's case went to trial, Hayes would be well-prepared, opinionated, and probably even condescending. That was his style, according to Robb, who'd clashed with him years earlier when a labor dispute at U.S. Plywood, one of Gaylord's biggest employers, turned violent. In 1978, members of the Woodworkers Union went on strike, and picketed near the plant entrance, and a man was arrested for throwing rocks at cars. Dean was hired to defend him, and Hayes, then an assistant prosecutor, tried the case for Otsego County. Robb prevailed, the jury found the man not guilty, and Robb remembered Hayes being furious over the verdict.

"I really didn't know the nasty side of Norm until that trial," Robb said.

The memory of Hayes' fury had lost none of its shock in the intervening years, and Robb was glad he remembered it so well. It would help him prepare for trial, and because of that experience Robb believed he knew what he and Laurie were up against.

He was wrong.

Back in Gaylord, Janet was trying her best to maintain some kind of regular schedule. The Moores needed her income now more than ever, and while she was committed to doing whatever she could to help Laurie's case, she also went to work every day. But the stress was taking a toll. Her work didn't suffer but her outlook on life certainly did. Janet's co-workers picked up on her understandably dark mood, and it was especially apparent to her law partner, Gene Petruska.

Ever since Laurie's arrest, Janet had not been herself and Petruska knew that was to be expected. But as the days passed, he noticed her demeanor getting progressively more serious and distant. On a morning she seemed particularly distraught, Petruska prodded her with questions throughout the day in an effort to find out what was wrong. He knew Janet was a private person, not a complainer or a gossip, so getting her to talk about personal matters was not always easy. But he also believed Janet trusted him, and they'd shared personal issues with each other before. Whatever was bothering her was certainly related to Laurie's case, and whether it was warranted or not, Petruska felt some responsibility for it. He was the one who had introduced Janet and Laurie.

In the early 1980s, when Janet was new in town, she went to Walt's on her lunch hour to pick up some groceries. Laurie was behind the meat counter, and although Janet was far too reserved to let him know it, he'd caught her eye. Back at the office, Janet asked Petruska who the handsome guy at the butcher shop was. Petruska knew Laurie from the Sportsman's Club and introduced them to each other a few days later. Laurie and Janet began dating, and married in December 1985. Laurie was arrested fifteen months later. Petruska couldn't help wondering if all that would have happened without his introduction.

The next step in Laurie's case was the preliminary exam, when the prosecutor would have to prove in front of a judge that there was enough evidence against Laurie for the case to go to trial. Most preliminary exams were a formality, and unless Laurie's case was an obvious candidate for dismissal, it would probably go forward, so Petruska thought that might have been what was worrying his partner.

"Janet, please," Petruska said one morning at their office. "Tell me what's bothering you. Maybe it's something I can help with."

Janet brushed him off, blaming her mood on her full schedule, but suggested the two of them might be able to talk later. They each had a heavy appointment schedule and it wasn't until early evening, when everyone else had left for the day, that Janet walked into Petruska's office, closed the door, and sat down.

"We got a death threat," she said, without preamble.

"*What?*" Petruska asked.

"Someone called the house and said they were going to kill Laurie," Janet explained. "They said they were going to drive by and shoot him and we'd never see it coming."

Well that certainly explained it, Petruska thought. Janet had spent months worrying about her husband's legal troubles, and now she was afraid for his life. To make matters worse, Janet said there hadn't been just one threat, but several.

"What should we do?" she asked him, almost pleading.

"I'll call Norm," Petruska told her. "Laurie obviously needs police protection."

That evening, Petruska called Prosecutor Hayes at home and told him about the threats. His reaction was not at all what Petruska expected.

"I'm not going to have any cop protect an asshole," Petruska remembered Hayes screaming into the receiver. "Besides, I know he's guilty. Dean never had him take a lie detector test, and Dean *always* has his clients take one. Always."

Petruska didn't know whether that was true or not, but he did wonder where Hayes got the information. Wasn't a lie detector test an issue of trial strategy and something for Laurie and Dean to discuss privately? Any defense attorney in his right mind is not going to alert the prosecutor that his client doesn't plan on taking a lie detector test, especially one privately scheduled and paid for. So how did Hayes know about it? The idea unsettled Petruska, but he tried to salvage the discussion.

"Why don't you just approach Laurie," Petruska asked, "in a way that he could talk to you and tell you what he knows about all this?"

"Well," Hayes challenged, "why do you think he didn't take the lie detector test? Huh?"

"I have no idea," Petruska said. "But why haven't you checked out any of the other leads? It seems to me there's a lot of leads you never looked at."

Petruska had read the police report. Like Dean Robb and the Moore family, he believed there were still tangents in the investigation left unresolved by police. After Laurie was identified as a suspect, as far as Petruska knew, no one followed up on the Morey brothers, Dennis O'Rourke, Gary Mayer, or Tony Schultz. And, why didn't the alcohol content in Tobias' blood jibe with his supposed time of death?

The telephone conversation between Petruska and Hayes lasted more than an hour, and Petruska tried to raise those issues. But according to his testimony, the sixty-plus minutes the two men were on the phone, Petruska remembered Hayes calling Laurie "an asshole" twenty times or more. When he was certain nothing productive could come from prolonging it, Petruska hung up. Police protection for Laurie was out of the question. But more troubling for Laurie was the prosecutor's attitude and Petruska dreaded to think what it meant for Janet, and for Laurie's upcoming trial.

Petruska's worry aside, the preliminary exam was not a forgone conclusion for Robb, and he felt confident he could sway a judge away from an indictment. There simply wasn't much credible evidence against his client, especially where the butcher shop was concerned. The meat found in Jerry's truck hadn't been fingerprinted and although it enabled a search warrant, the police went over Walt's from the front door to the garbage cans and found nothing. On May 5, 1987, the preliminary exam got underway and Robb immediately stressed the complete lack of physical evidence against Laurie and repeated it in his summation.

"From a fight with Jerry Tobias . . . then in the stealth of night clean up that act, clean up that butcher shop, somehow toss that big man into the back of that truck, drive him a third of a mile or however far it is from Walt's Butcher Shop to South Illinois Street, not leave any evidence *in* the truck or *on* the truck, not leave *any evidence* in a four hour search, a minute-type search, a microscopic-type search, not leave any evidence—*any evidence*—this, I say, defies imagination."

Robb's summation was a powerful one, but apparently not powerful enough. Laurie's preliminary hearing lasted six days, included more than 150 pieces of evidence, dozens of witnesses, and generated a transcript that ran close to 1,000 pages, and at its close the court bound him over for trial. The charge was Second-Degree Murder; meaning no planning was involved but that a death had still resulted from an assault.

As far as Gene Petruska knew, the Moores had not received any more death threats, but with the result of the prelim, the phone calls seemed irrelevant. If Laurie were convicted of Second-Degree Murder, he could face a life sentence. Plus, Hayes asked the judge to revoke his bail.

"There's a good place downstairs where we can assure his appearance in court," Hayes said, referring to the Otsego County Jail located in the basement of the courthouse.

"We need him," Robb argued to the judge. "We need his help. We need his advice. He needs to be free. Let Mr. Moore continue to work, continue to help us with his defense."

Laurie remained free on $75,000 bail, a small but important victory for the defense. But come fall, he would stand trial for the murder of Jerry Robert Tobias.

"I am satisfied that the People have established, as a matter of fact, that the decedent and the Defendant did meet in the early hours of Dec. 6 at the store known as Walt's Butcher Shop," the judge wrote in his decision. "The People have further established to my satisfaction that the rotisserie spit caused the blunt trauma to the decedent's head that ultimately caused death.

"What transpired incidental to the assault upon the decedent remains a mystery. But I am satisfied that the total record shows that the Defendant did reasonably and probably commit murder upon one Jerry Tobias."

The official charge of Open Murder had been refined by the prosecutor to Second-Degree Murder. That meant that Hayes believed there hadn't been any premeditation on Laurie's part, or if there had been, he couldn't prove it. With the trial still several months away, Hayes and the police continued to search for evidence against Laurie in the event they could amend the charge to first degree before trial. Perhaps that was why the prosecutor reconsidered the strange tip he'd received months ago from Bernard Caspar.

Caspar was the attorney representing Leonard Parmentier in his divorce from his wife, Debbie. The tip was that Debbie had told Leonard she'd seen Jerry Tobias stabbed to death behind a local grocery store. Since Tobias wasn't stabbed, Hayes originally dismissed it but after Laurie's trial date was set, he reconsidered. No matter how outlandish Debbie's account sounded, there was no harm in checking it out, and Hayes assigned his investigator, Jerry Borema, to look into it.

Borema located Debbie Parmentier at the Beaver Creek Resort, a campy collection of tourist cottages just outside Gaylord on Otsego Lake. Debbie worked part-time as a housekeeper, where her job was to clean the cabins after the guests checked out. She agreed to talk to Borema about the murder, but when the two sat down, it soon became obvious she was more interested in discussing Leonard and his supposed attack on her with a pair of scissors.

Why, she wanted to know, hadn't the police arrested her husband? Borema said he didn't know anything about that, and only wanted to talk to her about Jerry Tobias. Did she know anything about his death? Did she really witness his murder?

Yes, Debbie told him, she knew all about his death because she was with him when he was killed. Debbie told Borema about the stabbing, but it wasn't the same story that had made its way to Prosecutor Hayes. In this version there were three men attacking Jerry. Debbie said she didn't know whether or not one of the men was Laurie Moore, but she emphasized how brutal the men had been. Not only did they stab Jerry, they took turns beating him with a baseball bat. With no prompting from Borema, Debbie volunteered to testify about what she saw in court.

After the interview Borema hardly knew what to think but he reported back to Hayes, and soon Debbie's name and her account of the crime were shared with the task force. The consensus was that while Debbie's story did not fit the evidence, she still might be helpful to the prosecution. Debbie wasn't in any trouble herself, and hadn't asked for any money or other support from Borema. She must know something. Why would anyone make up an eyewitness account to a murder, when there was nothing to gain from it?

Finding out exactly what Debbie witnessed went to the top of the task force's to-do list and over the next several months various members took a crack at unraveling her story. Between April and June of 1987, Debbie talked to Investigator Borema, Detective LaBarge, Prosecutor Hayes, and Chief Dufon. She changed her story a few more times during those interviews, most notably to positively identify Jerry Tobias' three killers. In December 1986, she told her husband Leonard she had no idea who the killer was, but by June 1987 there were three killers, and she said she knew them all. Laurie Moore was one, and the others were two men she worked with, Doug Brinkman and Mark Canter. Debbie had briefly dated Brinkman, and Canter was Brinkman's best friend. The men worked on the maintenance crew at Beaver Creek Resort, but according to Debbie that was just a front. During the day they painted cabins and mowed the grass, but at night and on the weekends, they sold drugs and guns, stole sensitive court documents, and even smuggled stolen U.S. military weapons into Canada.

"They're dangerous criminals, all three of them," Debbie told police, "and you need to get them off the street."

At any other time, her claims might have been laughed at. But this was the late 1980s in a town increasingly ravaged by illegal drugs and crime. New arrests for robberies, drug dealing, and possession of increasingly larger and larger quantities of cocaine were announced in the newspaper almost every week. And so instead of being dismissed, her story fed a bigger fear creeping up on law enforcement. If drug dealers gained access to military grade weapons, it could be nothing short of a disaster.

Debbie's story of smuggling stolen military hardware had a sickening plausibility to it. Just twenty-five miles south of Gaylord on I-75 loomed Camp Grayling, the largest National Guard training facility in the nation. Some 20,000 soldiers from Indiana, Illinois, Michigan, Ohio, and even Canada trained there. The facility and grounds took up 147,000 acres—230 square miles—specifically for visiting soldiers to train and test large artillery, tanks, helicopters, and other military aircraft and weapons. The facility was sometimes opened up to local law enforcement for their training, so officers knew the camp had something else, too: an armory.

For those officers who might have been skeptical of her gun stealing and gun smuggling stories, what Debbie lacked in specifics she made up for with dramatic details. In one of her interviews with Borema, Debbie said she was with Mark Canter when he tested a stolen rocket launcher. She and Mark stood on the woodsy shore of an area lake, Mark aimed the weapon at a small island, and fired. It was a direct hit, she said, and he and Debbie watched while the entire island exploded into debris.

Borema didn't know quite what to make of Debbie and her stories—Who would?—but he did know that stealing military weapons was a federal crime, and beyond the scope of a murder investigation or the local police's expertise. He passed his interview notes immediately on to Prosecutor Hayes, Lieutenant Hardy, and Detective LaBarge. They discussed it with Gaylord Police Chief, Frank Dufon, but didn't know what to make of Debbie, either.

"I tried specifically to get her to give me something that could be substantiated, but she didn't do it," Dufon would later say. "I didn't know whether to believe her or not."

Which was why Dufon passed the information to the Bureau of Alcohol, Tobacco and Firearms (ATF). When the Feds heard Debbie's stories, they were interested enough to send an agent to Gaylord to find out more. Yet another interview was set up with Debbie, this time with ATF agent Valarie Goddard, while Borema and LaBarge observed. Debbie didn't back away from her stories, but rather added to them. Helicopters were using secret landing strips outside Gaylord to dump bundles of cocaine, she said, and the military weapons Mark Canter stole from Camp Grayling were being smuggled into Canada hidden in car tires. Before the interview was over, Debbie reasserted to Agent Goddard that Laurie Moore, Mark Canter, and Doug Brinkman were the ones who killed Jerry Tobias, and they did it with a knife and a baseball bat.

Agent Goddard finished the interview, went over the transcript, then contacted her superior, a man named George Stoll, with this assessment: "Information appears good." The ATF would be actively investigating Debbie's information about military weapons theft, illegal gun sales, and international smuggling. The task force could go back to gathering evidence against Laurie Moore.

By July Debbie had been interviewed by city, county, state, and national law enforcement. She assured whoever would listen that she'd seen an island blown up with a stolen rocket launcher, a U.S. Army weapons cache robbed, an international border breached, and Jerry Tobias murdered.

The start of Laurie's trial was only two months away, but whether by design or oversight, no one informed Dean Robb of Debbie's claims. Not that she'd witnessed illegal gun and drug deals and not that she'd witnessed Jerry' murder. Neither Robb nor Laurie had ever heard the name Debbie Parmentier, and didn't even know she existed.

Chapter 9 *People v. Laurie Moore*

. . . . Tuesday, October 20, 1987, 9:00 AM

In a small courtroom an hour north of Gaylord, Judge Livo looked out through his oversized glasses at sixty prospective jurors assembled and gave them his standard greeting: "It is an ancient tradition and a part of our heritage that a person accused of a crime be afforded the opportunity to be judged not by one person, but by a group of twelve of his fellow citizens selected to be impartial and fair."

A murder trial was big news in northern Michigan, and the courtroom was full but the judge said nothing to indicate what a hot potato Laurie's trial had become. Prospective jurors didn't know that the only reason Livo was hearing the case at all was because three of his judicial colleagues had been disqualified.

Judge Patrick Murray, who had presided over Laurie's preliminary exam, couldn't hear the case because the defense had been granted a change of venue, from Gaylord to Cheboygan. Judges Alton Davis of Grayling and William Porter of Gaylord each recused themselves, citing their professional relationship with Laurie's wife, Janet. Those men both knew and respected her, and that might compromise their objectivity toward her husband. So Laurie was being tried in Cheboygan, a ramshackle coastal town fifty miles north of Gaylord, and Judge Livo would preside over the case.

For a change of venue, the town was an obvious choice. Cheboygan County was mostly rural, just like Otsego County, and had experienced many of the same problems—drugs, transients, unemployment—as Gaylord had, just without the Alpine veneer. Cheboygan's one bright spot was that it served as the homeport of a U.S. Coast Guard cutter *Mackinaw*. The area was otherwise known for good hunting, good fishing, its cement plant, its toilet paper plant, and its nearly thirty percent poverty rate. Laurie's jury would be drawn from the county's 20,000 residents, scattered over 900 square miles of pine scrub, oil wells, hunting camps, and Lake Huron coastline.

After he welcomed the prospective jurors, Judge Livo reminded everyone it was an honor to serve on a jury and that the country's justice system depended upon people just like them.

"Each side in a trial is entitled to jurors who approach the case with open minds and agree to keep their minds open until a verdict is reached." The judge gave this admonition, or something similar, to every jury he presided over. It was just part of his regular jury instructions, though the words would soon come to mean more in Laurie's trial than one country judge's rote instruction.

While the prospective jurors got their bearings, Judge Livo, Prosecutor Hayes, and Robb began digging in. With a witness list numbering 42 and growing, and with more than 100 pieces of evidence already logged with the court, Laurie's trial was expected to last as long as a month. Even before the jury was selected it was ramping up to be as adversarial as any in the north in recent memory.

Those assembled could already feel the animosity between the defense attorney and the prosecutor, but the antagonistic nature of the case wasn't limited to the inside of the courtroom. Two of the newspapers that covered the case, the *Gaylord Herald Times* and the *Detroit News*, squared off, too.

"It's the sort of trial that weekly newspaper reporters rarely get to cover," wrote reporter Thomas BeVier in an article for the *Detroit News*. "It threatens to lay bare the whispered side of Gaylord society, the side behind a downtown façade of Alpine storefronts and Chamber of Commerce promises of fairy tale vacations. Talk of drugs and sex, and the granting of immunity from prosecution to key witnesses, supposedly are the stuff of big city trials."

BeVier's Detroit editors felt the Laurie Moore trial was newsworthy enough to send a reporter north, and BeVier had been poking around Gaylord and Cheboygan for a couple of days. His story ran on the *Detroit News'* front page on the Sunday following the start of jury selection, and its tone did not sit well with its local competition. The *Gaylord Herald Times* ran an angry editorial in response.

"We are disturbed to see sensationalism like the *Detroit News* distributed in its . . . front page article. Written by a reporter who is not sitting in on the entire trial, the story seems to promise seamy goings-on in the 'fairy tale' vacationland of Gaylord. Where is the attribution? The facts? Reporting actual testimony is the fundamental approach to covering a murder trial, and that is what the *Herald Times* intends to do."

Dean Robb didn't care much about newspaper rivalries, but he was willing to talk to any reporter any time about Laurie's case, whether they worked for an urban daily, a small town weekly, or any size publication in between. The prosecution's case, he told the *Traverse City Record-Eagle*, was built on thin circumstantial evidence and "loaded with doubt." By naming Laurie as their only suspect and ignoring other leads, Robb accused those heading up the investigation as suffering from what he viewed as a common law-enforcement malady: tunnel vision.

"This homicide remains unsolved and I've asked the prosecutor and the police to re-open the case," Robb said. "There were many suspects and leads and pieces of evidence that were never followed up on. These things should have been investigated and weren't."

The newspaper article didn't list any of those suspects, leads, or evidence, but one look at Robb's trial notes would have revealed them: "Investigate Schultz. Police did not comb area. What about Needle Marks? This was a drug dump, not a murder."

The name that most aroused Robb's suspicion came from Jackie Tobias herself, and Robb found it hiding in plain sight in the police report. "Schultz" referred to Anthony "Tony" Kevin Schultz, an oil driller who once worked with Jerry. Robb checked him out and learned that Schultz had a conspiracy and an illegal drug charge on his record. According to what Jackie told the police, in the early 1980s Schultz and Tobias botched a drug deal. Several years before he died, Jerry and Tony Schultz put together a $3,400 cocaine deal, and Jerry ended up owing Schultz the money and had to get a loan from his grandmother to pay off the debt. This was similar to what the prosecution said the arrangement between Laurie and Tobias was, and yet to Robb it seemed like the police hardly investigated Schultz at all.

Which was curious, considering that another source, James Sherriff, was interviewed by police three times and told them he knew Jerry Tobias, knew he was into coke and pot, knew he got his drugs from Tony Schultz and Schultz's unnamed Lansing supplier. Sherriff, Tobias, and Shultz all worked together in the oilfields. After Tobias died, Sherriff said Schultz "dropped out of circulation" and "did not want to be found." The police knew of Schultz, but for some unknown reason declined to pursue him.

Another fact Robb found troubling was something the police missed completely. Officers couldn't have combed the area surrounding Walt's and the fire barn very well, because the day before Jerry's body was found someone reported finding fresh blood on the ground near where his truck was parked. A pool of blood was spotted not at Walt's but a block away behind the Eagles Hall and next to its dumpster. Before police could investigate, a snowplow passed by and the evidence, if it was evidence, was destroyed. The Eagles Hall, known for hosting raucous parties, was only a block from where Jerry was found.

Finally, Robb wanted to know more about the eight needle marks the pathologist said were on Jerry's forearms when he died. According to Dr. Newhouse's autopsy report, they were fresh, and yet she found no cocaine in his system. That, along with his Friday night drinking binge but low blood alcohol test results, just didn't make sense.

Telling a *Traverse City Record-Eagle* reporter on the record that the police hadn't conducted a very good investigation probably felt pretty good to Robb at the time. But it earned him the ire of Lieutenant John Hardy, the powerful commander of the 7th district detectives. While LaBarge was officially heading up the investigation, Hardy was LaBarge's boss, and the man calling all the shots.

In northern Michigan legal circles, Hardy was nicknamed "Supercop" for his demeanor, his intelligence, and his work ethic. He didn't appreciate having one of his investigations lambasted in the press as incompetent and, even worse, lazy. He clipped the article out of the newspaper and mailed it to Prosecutor Hayes, along with a typed letter on State Police letterhead:

> "I feel we should call his bluff somehow," Hardy wrote to Hayes, "perhaps publicly, perhaps through the court system. . . . I guess we all know or feel Mr. Moore is guilty. If he isn't, then he certainly knows who is and probably was present or involved somehow. Can you think of a way we can force Robb's use of these wild accusations to come back and haunt him? Would any response on our part be utilized by him later, to show somehow that we were uncertain about our case? Is this just a typical defense tactic which I should not even worry about? Call me after you think about this and let's talk about this case some more."

Dean Robb knew nothing of this letter, or of the plan to organize the police and the prosecutor's office against him, but it would not have worried him much even if he had known. Robb was a master at proving wrongdoing, usually by large corporations and insurance companies, but sometimes by the government. He was used to being plotted against by those in power. His clients tended to be hippies, rabble-rousers, activists, the disenfranchised, and the downtrodden, so to be on the outs with Michigan State Police's Supercop was nothing new.

Robb's habitual alignment with the underdog hadn't hurt his career any. If anything, it earned him respect and accolades. By the time Robb took Laurie's case, he had served as president of the Michigan Trial Lawyers Association, as national chairman of the American Trial Lawyers Association, and had helped start Trial Lawyers for Public Justice, a civil rights initiative that harnessed the skill of dozens of trial lawyers to work on socially significant cases.

When Janet contacted him in March about representing Laurie, Robb took the case on as a job. But after getting to know Laurie, and working on his defense for months, Robb became convinced that his client was innocent and being prosecuted as a vendetta. The more he researched the case, the more obvious that became to him. So obvious, in fact, that Robb didn't plan on spending a lot of his work with the jury arguing in support of it. In his trial strategy notes he jotted, "I don't have to prove it, but I know it happened Saturday night or Sunday morning, not Friday night. There's just no connection with Laurie Moore. No reason why Moore would risk everything for this."

Robb believed that his main job at trial was to simply explain the random circumstances that landed his client in the defendant's chair. If he did that, Robb believed there was a good chance that Judge Livo would dismiss the case before it went to the jury. The worst-case scenario was that Laurie and his family would have to endure an entire trial, but that he would be acquitted. Since that was his sincere belief, he had no qualms about stating it publicly.

"I feel rather confident that Mr. Moore will be cleared," Robb told the *Gaylord Herald Times*. "I don't think the police have found the people who put that poor man in the pickup truck."

Chapter 10   A Thirsty Man

. . . . Monday, October 26, 1987

"**P**lease stand, sir," Prosecutor Hayes said to Laurie. "Ladies and gentlemen, I want you to . . . I want you to look at the Defendant. The Defendant is the gentleman . . . right here in the white sweater."

"Wait a minute!" Robb said, standing. "What's this all about?"

"I want to see if they have any sympathy for the Defendant, Your Honor," Hayes answered.

"Your Honor," Robb argued, "that would be wrong." He was already feeling exasperated and the trial hadn't started yet. This was only jury selection.

"Well your Honor, for the record . . . just so Mr. Robb doesn't think I'm . . . trying to pull something, I'm not, ladies and gentlemen. Now, if Mr. Moore will so indulge me, I would like to have him stand so you can see him. And I want to ask you, ladies and gentlemen, if the People overcome the presumption of innocence, and we prove to you beyond . . . I want to ask if any of you would hesitate to return a verdict of guilty."

All sixty heads turned toward Laurie, who was sitting at the defense table along with Robb and Janet. Prompting from the prosecutor for him to stand like some carnival freak didn't just irritate Robb, it irked Laurie, too. He was already upset about being there at all, and when Hayes put him on display it must have made him furious. Because with every prospective juror looking right at him, Laurie did something just plain peculiar.

He stood up, just as the prosecutor had asked him to, but instead of standing calmly for a moment, and then sitting back down again, he walked out from behind the defense table, past the judge, and headed directly toward the jury box. Once there, he stopped at a small table that held a pitcher of water and several empty glasses. Laurie paused, then picked up the pitcher, poured a glassful, lifted it to his mouth, looked directly at the prospective jurors, and took a long swallow.

Though unexpected, this might have been simply the action of a thirsty man, if not for a few other details. First, ever since his arrest he'd been wearing a permanent sneer on his once-handsome face. Second, the week before he'd climbed onto his roof to replace some shingles and fallen off and injured his leg, and third, a damaged eye from childhood rounded out the picture. Instead of a man they were supposed to assume was innocent until the evidence told them otherwise, what the jury saw at the water table was a limping, sneering, one-eyed menace.

The sight was so startling one woman seated in the jury box let out an involuntary yelp. Judge Livo excused her from duty, but the damage was done. The introduction of Laurie to his prospective jury couldn't have gone any better for the prosecution if Hayes had scripted it himself.

"Would any of you hesitate?" Hayes asked them, and Robb was sure he saw the corners of his mouth turn up into the faintest hint of a smile. "Would you?"

The prosecution's case was entirely circumstantial—no eyewitnesses, no direct physical evidence, no confession. Hayes admitted as much, and even told the prospective jurors that during the trial he wasn't going to put anyone on the stand who saw Laurie kill Jerry, or who even saw Laurie with Jerry the night he died.

The prosecution would enter more than a hundred pieces of evidence, but not one would tie Laurie to Jerry's murder. No blood, no hair, no fingerprints, nothing. There wasn't one single witness, or any physical evidence, connecting Laurie with Tobias's truck, or with the butcher shop on the night the prosecution said the murder took place.

All the prosecution had was circumstantial evidence, which meant, Hayes explained, evidence that didn't bear directly on Laurie's guilt, but would require the jury to *infer* that the prosecution was correct in their theory of the crime. This had not deterred the police from arresting Laurie though, and it wouldn't deter Hayes from prosecuting him.

"Circumstantial evidence is good evidence, ladies and gentlemen," Hayes told the jury pool. "Good evidence. Use your common sense."

What Hayes offered the prospective jury was conjecture, and a lot of it. Logical conjecture is the basis of circumstantial cases, and people are found guilty with only this kind of evidence every day in courts all over the country. What the prosecution did have was a grieving widow, Jerry's pickup truck with a package of meat from Walt's Butcher Shop behind the front seat, and four participants in two unsuccessful drug deals who would testify, thanks to an immunity deal with the prosecutor.

Hayes decided not to call Debbie Parmentier as a witness. She was too unreliable and so as far as the jury knew, there were no eyewitnesses to the crime. Another weakness of the prosecution's case was the victim himself. There was simply no way Hayes was going to be able to keep Jerry's infidelity, drinking, and drug use out of the court record. Jerry's wild nature was too much a part of his life to be conveniently hidden away in death.

Hayes' solution to mitigate that was to begin his case with Jackie. For all his faults, Jackie obviously loved her husband, and

Hayes believed that love would come through when she testified. Jackie wasn't a drug user or a heavy drinker. She was a wife and mother, and if anyone could convey Jerry's good side, it was Jackie. As soon as a jury was seated, and it was time to call prosecution witnesses, Hayes put her on the stand.

"The week before he died we were on very good terms," Jackie told the jury, between sobs. "He had been home every night and we talked about Christmas shopping. We had our problems, like any other marriage. We were working them out."

Jackie was no naïve wife—she said she was well aware of her husband's infidelity and drug use, but said she believed it was all in the past. She knew of only one instance when Jerry mainlined—injected—cocaine, and it was several months before he died. As far as she knew, Jerry had quit the drugs, quit the girls, and had been faithful to her.

Robb took the opportunity to cross-examine Jackie, but asked only general questions about their relationship. He saved his questions about Jerry's hard living for a State Police laboratory scientist. Jackie very well might have believed her husband had turned his life around, but Robb knew there was plenty of evidence to the contrary. For starters, the four pubic hairs found on Jerry's clothing and inside the body bag used at the crime scene.

"You compared the hairs with hairs of his wife?" Robb asked Connie Swander, the scientist.

"Yes," Swander said.

"You checked the hairs of several other individuals?"

"Comparison studies were made," she said.

"The source of the four hairs—was it ever found?" Robb asked.

It was not, Swander said. Despite putting Jerry's widow and several local women through the indignity of having their pubic hair collected and compared to the hairs found at the crime scene, the lab did not find a match. The news that her supposedly reformed and faithful husband died with eight fresh needle marks in his arms, his belt gone, his pants unzipped, and four unidentified pubic hairs on his body must have come as quite a shock to Jackie.

Despite that, she was a good witness and Hayes was wise to lead off with her. Jackie had loved her husband, despite his faults, and that came through in her testimony. Until the weekend of December 5, 1986, she had even been hopeful about their future together.

Chapter 11   The Pathologist and the Pumpkin

. . . . Tuesday, October 27, 1987

If the circumstances hadn't been so dire, the courtroom actions that came next could almost have been considered comical. After the opening arguments, after the 150 items were introduced into evidence, and after a few other witnesses testified, Hayes called Dr. Patricia Newhouse to the stand. The prosecutor wanted Newhouse to demonstrate exactly how a flimsy two-pronged chicken skewer could have killed a healthy full-grown man. In order to accomplish this, Newhouse would need someone to play the part of Jerry. Trooper Burr, who first found Jerry's frozen body and who was in the courtroom observing the trial, volunteered.

As the jury watched, Newhouse stood in front of the witness stand and straightened up to her full height of barely five feet. Trooper Burr, measuring a fit and muscular six-foot plus, sat down in a chair directly in front of her. Newhouse griped the chrome skewer in her pudgy fist, cocked her arm back, and pretended to strike Burr in the side of the head with it. While she flailed at him from behind, she narrated her actions for the jury.

"You will note that I am standing somewhat behind the victim but off to the right," Newhouse explained, nearly out of breath but still with all the dignity she could muster. "As we look at the wounds that were present, you will note that we had a wound high, and a wound approximately 7.5 centimeters below that. And what I would like to show is how that might have occurred."

While the pathologist swung the chicken skewer toward Burr's temple, Hayes handed the jury a close-up of Jerry's frozen face. They passed the photograph around, each juror silently taking in the image. It was in color and there were red scrapes on his skin, purple bruises, white scaly frostbite, and two tiny dark red dots. The prosecution contended that those two dots, each smaller than a freckle, were harbingers of the cause of death.

"You're going to come around," Newhouse continued, as the photograph made its rounds, "and because this (skewer prong) is hitting, first you are going to create a relatively round wound without going straight in. The injury to the underlying brain is a coup injury. Which is consistent with a blow to the movable—freely movable—head."

The pathologist couldn't discuss the presence of trace evidence—blood, skin, hair, or fingerprints—on the chicken skewer seized from Walt's because there wasn't any. In their search police confiscated five similar chicken skewers from the butcher shop, all stored neatly in their regular spot underneath a deli scale but not one contained a cell of evidence suggesting they had been used as any kind of weapon.

Robb pointed this out in his cross-examination, as well as the fact that Dr. Newhouse did not possess top qualifications. She was an M.D., but she wasn't board certified in forensics. Newhouse simply had a "special interest' in medical forensics, but hadn't passed the exam that would have certified her in the discipline. Newhouse's autopsy identified sixteen to twenty injury marks on Jerry Tobias' body, but only two that might have been caused by the skewer. One of those wasn't on his head, but on his shoulder. The dots on his head near his temple did not cause a skull fracture, Robb pointed out, or any external bleeding. They didn't even break the skin. How could the doctor be so sure they caused his death?

Still on the stand, Newhouse backpedaled a bit under Robb's cross.

"I can't assume that that was the lethal injury," she admitted. "I have got multiple blows to the head. That one certainly *could* have been a lethal injury. It *could* have caused the head to turn rapidly. But I have other sub-galeal hematomas that were significant. I have them on both sides of the head. And either of those could have caused the motion of the head required for death to occur."

In plain English, she was arguing that Jerry Tobias died from whiplash by chicken skewer. Robb believed that explanation was ridiculous, and had plans for a courtroom demonstration of his own to prove it.

"I tried to think of several ways that you could possibly help us understand that," Robb said to Newhouse as he reached below the defense table and lifted out something round, orange, and heavy. The defense attorney carried the orb toward Newhouse and held it up like an offering. "Would you—I have a pumpkin. It's not related to the fact that Halloween is here. But would you be so kind as to . . . hit that?"

The question landed in the courtroom like a comedic mortar and caught everyone off guard, especially Hayes. What prosecutor expects to have to argue against a ten-pound squash? A pumpkin was being introduced into court, or at least that's what the defense was trying to do, and only four days before Halloween, too. Miraculously, Hayes maintained his composure.

"This should be taken outside the presence of the jury," he argued to Judge Livo. "He has not laid a proper foundation that a pumpkin is the same as a human head."

"Well," Robb countered, "I'm not going to offer any *real* human head."

That quip released the tension in the room, and the jury, the spectators, and even some of the police officers erupted in laughter. Hayes failed to see the humor and grumbled back, "I don't expect him to."

Judge Livo sent the jury out of the courtroom so that he could discuss the legalities of entering a ripe pumpkin approximately the size and shape of a human head into evidence. Ultimately, he ruled against it, but said he would allow Robb's second choice of display into evidence: a mannequin head covered in modeling clay and topped with a wig.

Livo brought the jury back in and addressed them briefly.

"This demonstration with the clay model does differ from the same demonstration if made with a human head, which can't be done for obvious reasons. So, with that limiting observation, you may conduct your demonstration, Mr. Robb."

Robb picked up his mannequin head, walked to the witness stand and held it out in front of Dr. Newhouse. The pathologist seemed surprisingly game for the unorthodox activity and gripped the chicken skewer in her right hand, reached back, aimed, and then took a good swing. But missed.

"I missed!" she said to Robb, embarrassed. "I'm trying too hard not to hit you."

"Don't worry about that," Robb said. "I will heal."

"I would feel bad," she said, then swung again, and this time connected.

The marks the skewer made in the clay-covered manikin were immediately examined by Newhouse, Robb, and Hayes. It was obvious that they did not come close to matching the scratches on Jerry Tobias' temple. These new marks were crescent shaped, not round, and there were impressions from the skewer's crossbar that connected the two spindles also evident in the clay. No crossbar impressions were visible in the photographs of Tobias' face.

Robb asked Dr. Newhouse if she wanted to change any of her findings following his demonstration, but Newhouse said she remained steadfast in her original conclusion. Jerry had been beaten with a chicken skewer, and not just any chicken skewer but one of the five confiscated from Walt's. Robb remained unconvinced, and while he still had Newhouse on the stand, he introduced the defense's theory on cause of death.

"Doctor," Robb asked, "could this man have died from a drug overdose?"

"I would think that would be very highly unlikely," Newhouse said.

Robb seemed to dismiss her answer, because he asked the question again.

"Doctor, could this man have died from a fatal drug reaction or drug overdose? Cocaine?

"I have no evidence to support that," she said.

"Could he have died from a cocaine overdose?" Robb repeated.

"In my medical opinion, no."

At the preliminary hearing, Newhouse had testified that a cocaine overdose was a possibility; at trial she seemed to be changing her testimony, and Robb asked her to clarify.

"If you're asking for my medical opinion on what he did die of, no," she said. "If you're saying could that be a possibility, it's a possibility."

While the autopsy revealed an unknown amount of cocaine in the dead man's urine, Newhouse testified at the preliminary hearing that she'd found none of the drug in his blood. More than a dozen times Robb had asked her about it during the preliminary examination, and more than a dozen times her answer was the same: There was no cocaine in Jerry's blood when he died. None.

"Certainly we looked at the blood samples," Newhouse told Robb again. "No cocaine was present in the blood."

"And why?" Robb asked.

"There wasn't any there," Dr. Newhouse said.

"And why?" Robb asked again.

"Cocaine is rapidly metabolized," she explained. "It did not surprise me that there was no cocaine in the blood because it is rapidly metabolized."

Newhouse told the jury that if Jerry had injected enough cocaine to stop his heart or cause unconsciousness, there would have been chemical evidence of that in his blood, and there wasn't any. But Robb discounted that explanation, and still believed that Tobias wasn't murdered, and certainly wasn't murdered by Laurie, but rather died of a cocaine overdose. He hammered Newhouse on the blood test results so many times that Hayes finally objected, complaining that Robb was badgering the witness.

Judge Livo agreed and ordered Robb to either move on or let Dr. Newhouse step down from the witness stand. Robb excused Newhouse, then called his defense expert who disputed her findings.

Dr. Laurence Simpson, a forensic pathologist for Sparrow Hospital in Lansing, took the stand and said not only was the chicken skewer not the murder weapon, but Jerry Tobias didn't die "as a result of any head injury whatsoever." In order for the chicken skewer to be the murder weapon, Tobias would have to have been stabbed by it. If that were the case, the marks on his body would not have been tiny round dots, they would have been deep puncture wounds, traumatic and violent enough to cause a skull fracture.

"Like this," Simpson said, pulling a handful of orange Play-doh out of his jacket pocket and stabbing it with the skewer, in yet a third reenactment. Or rather, a third reenactment of a murder the defense was contending never actually happened.

Jerry Tobias had died from exposure, Simpson said, brought on by unconsciousness caused from abusing drugs and alcohol. Newhouse had it all wrong. Many of the discolorations she identified as bruises from blunt force trauma were actually caused by Jerry's skin freezing and thawing.

As the prosecution and the defense debated the science, physics, and chemistry of the case, the jury looked like they were beginning to understand their two choices. Was Jerry beaten unconscious with a chicken skewer inside Walt's, dragged to his truck, heaved into the back, and left to die by Laurie Moore? Or was he drunk and high, sleeping with a woman who was not his wife, beaten up and left to die in his truck by someone yet to be identified?

As the first two weeks of trial wound down, Robb felt pleased with the way things were going. His notes, handwritten on a yellow legal pad, were resolute and optimistic:

> "Police & Prosecutor have not found the right man. Case crys (sic) out for solution: Should be in book of Unsolved Murders. These blows would not kill people. Dr. Newhouse said <u>no words</u> about Needle Marks. Motive: None. No jury would convict this man."

Chapter 12　The Case for the Prosecution

. . . . November, 1987

Prosecutor Hayes held an opposite opinion of what a jury, specifically this jury, would or wouldn't do. Over the next several weeks, bit by methodical bit, he unspooled the rest of his well-wound case.

He established that Jerry's blue Ford was found only a quarter mile from Walt's, with that package of expensive meat, wrapped in white butcher paper, behind the front seat. During the police investigation the defendant himself had identified the meat as coming from his store, though he had no explanation for how it got inside Jerry's truck. Hayes showed the jury that police found deer hair in the bed of the truck under Jerry's body. Two days before he died, Jerry had taken a deer to Walt's to be processed.

Next, Hayes put Gaylord City Police Officer Dan Dallas on the stand. Dallas was the city patrolman who remembered driving past Walt's the night the prosecution believed Jerry died and seeing late-night activity at the butcher shop.

Dallas told the jury that he regularly worked the 11 PM to 8 AM shift and was on routine patrol in the early morning hours of Saturday, Dec. 6, 1986. He testified that he had cruised past Walt's, had seen the lights in the back of the store on, had seen a pickup truck parked nearby, and had seen a light-colored van arrive, driven by a white male. He also said that driver got out and appeared to go inside the butcher shop. Dallas couldn't say what specific color, make, or model the van was because it was too dark outside to identify it. The fact that Dallas admitted he was patrolling with his headlights off didn't help.

Not a word about this was included in Dallas' daily log, and on his cross-examination Robb waved a copy of it in the air as he questioned the patrolman. According to the log, not only was there no mention of a drive past Walt's, the patrolman actually reported being in an entirely different part of town at 2:30 AM. Robb made sure the jury knew that Dallas didn't file the report on Walt's, the pickup truck, the light-colored van, and the white male until several days after Jerry's body had been found and when Laurie was already a suspect.

Officer Dallas said the attention surrounding the crime had jogged his memory and that the activity around Walt's had not looked suspicious to him at the time, which was why he didn't record it in his log.

"We never charged that he was lying," Robb said later, "but his memory was too convenient. And Dallas' description of the pickup truck was somewhat unbelievable. His report was after the fact, all too convenient for the prosecution, and in my mind, highly questionable."

Of the more than forty people on Prosecutor Hayes' witness list, none were more important than Don and Becky Nelson. If Jerry really had been murdered in a drug deal gone wrong, the jury was going to expect Hayes to produce evidence of a drug deal. The Nelsons were that evidence.

Becky Nelson was a friend of Jackie Tobias' as well as her boss at the Yodeler Ski Shoppe. Unbeknownst to Jackie, Becky had an entirely different kind of relationship with Jerry: She was his customer. Hayes put Becky on the stand, and she testified that Jerry arrived at her house about 8 PM on Friday, Dec. 5, and that she and her husband, Don Nelson, gave him $200 to buy drugs. Although Becky initially told police the money was for pot, on the stand she admitted it was actually for cocaine.

Hayes asked Becky to explain the drug deal to the jury.

"He (Jerry) was going to meet Laurie Moore at Walt's Butcher Shop around midnight," Becky said. In her first interview with police, Becky said that Jerry might have been going to Walt's, but said she didn't know if he was meeting Laurie. On the stand, she changed that part of her story too. Not pot but cocaine; not maybe Walt's but definitely Walt's, and definitely Laurie.

After he bought the coke, Jerry was supposed to go back to the Nelsons the same night to deliver it, but he never returned. The following afternoon, Becky said she went to the butcher shop to ask Laurie what happened.

"I asked him if he'd seen Jerry. He told me yes—he told me he'd met him there at midnight, said nothing had come through."

Becky's testimony was the only thing tying Laurie to Jerry and to a drug deal, and was damning evidence if she was telling the truth. Under Robb's cross-examination, details about the Nelsons emerged that uncovered more questions than they answered. On Sunday, Dec. 7, Becky and her children spent all day in Traverse City with Jackie and the Tobias children, shopping for Christmas presents and seeing a movie. They left Gaylord at 11 AM and didn't return home until dinnertime, yet Becky didn't say anything to her friend about the supposed drug deal with Jerry.

Robb said he found that hard to believe. The two women had been friends since high school, Jackie had worked for Becky for three years, and on very the day after Becky was looking for Jerry, the two women drove an hour and a half to Traverse City from Gaylord, spent the whole day together, then drove the hour and a half back home, and *nothing* was said about the supposed drug deal? Becky said Jackie was against drug use and so she never talked about it with her.

Robb also asked Becky to explain why she had changed her story so many times:

- On December 9, she told police she and her husband did not socialize with Jerry and Jackie, that everyone in town knew Jerry had a girlfriend, and that she had no idea whether or not Jerry was "into" drugs.

- On the morning of December 11, a detective visited Becky at her store and asked her why she went to Walt's to ask Laurie if he'd seen Jerry. Becky said Jackie was worried that Jerry was having an affair, and Becky thought Laurie might have some information. But Laurie told her that he didn't see Jerry on Friday night, because he'd spent the evening at the Sportsman's Club dinner.

- Later that same day, Becky went to the State Police post, and detectives interviewed her a third time. She admitted to being involved in a drug deal with Jerry, but said the money her husband gave Jerry was for pot.

▪ And, finally, Becky returned to the State Police post a fourth time and brought along her husband, Don, and an attorney. She changed her story yet again, adding in the details about Walt's. But even that wasn't her final version because it wasn't until yet another interview with police, one that took place March 7, 1987, and that Becky told the story she was now testifying to under oath. That interview was tape-recorded.

"I had not told the complete story," Becky admitted to Robb. "It was not true, what I told the police. I made that up. I am telling the truth today."

Robb said he found it convenient that each time she changed her story, it was more favorable to the prosecution. Buying cocaine, withholding evidence, and lying to police are all serious crimes, felonies punishable by up to ten years in prison. But the Nelsons were not worried about serving any jail time, because in exchange for their testimony, Hayes had given them immunity from prosecution.

How much help they were to Hayes' case against Laurie was difficult to measure. Becky Nelson did testify about a drug deal, and according to her latest story, it did involve Jerry Tobias and Laurie Moore. But Robb believed the Nelsons, and Becky in particular, came off pretty sketchy to the jury. She was cooperating with the prosecution, but not so long ago both she and her husband had been on the other side of the case. They'd been interviewed by detectives, and even asked for alibis. Plus, Becky was one of the women police collected a pubic hair sample from. And Don drove a tan-colored van.

Hayes' final witness was Lieutenant John Hardy and he was questioned about only two things: Laurie Moore's alibi and the package of meat found in Jerry's truck.

"Mr. Moore really could give no explanation," Hardy said. "He identified it, said it came from his store. He's the only person who packages that kind of meat. He didn't recall selling it to Jerry Tobias, but said, 'It was possible Mr. Tobias stole it from the market'."

The jury could look at that evidence in two ways. Perhaps the meat was suspicious, and a key to Jerry's death. But perhaps Laurie didn't have an explanation for it because he really didn't know anything. Either way, the cryptic image of the expensive meat and seafood from Walt's, stashed behind the seat of the dead man's truck, inches away from his frozen body, was the last thing Hayes wanted to leave in the minds of the jury.

On Tuesday, Nov. 3, 1987, the prosecution rested.

Chapter 13   The Case for the Defense

. . . . Wednesday, November 4, 1987, 9 AM

Robb arrived at the Cheboygan Courthouse Wednesday morning "loaded for bear," as they say in northern Michigan when someone is angry, focused, and prepared.

All through the trial he and Hayes had taken repeated, petty, and personal swipes at each other. Robb called the prosecution's case against Laurie "sloppy," "biased," and "vengeful" and said that Hayes's circumstantial theory was nothing more than "inference piled on inference." Robb also accused Hayes of withholding police and autopsy reports that could be exculpatory (favorable) to the defense—a very serious charge if true.

For his part, Hayes portrayed Robb as a slick, conniving, out-of-town lawyer expecting to take advantage of the less-than-sophisticated locals, good people who were just trying to do their civic duty by serving on a jury.

A typical exchange between the two went like this: "Criticizing my conduct in front of the jury is improper," Robb complained to Judge Livo. "He is sort of trying to try *me* in a funny way. He's not the poor little innocent lawyer."

"I'm not going to stand by and let Mr. Robb take control of this case," Hayes countered. "I'm not going to allow him to put impermissible comments before the jury. He's not going to bulldoze me."

Perhaps that was a reference to the last time the two met in court, back in 1978, when Hayes was an assistant prosecutor and Robb beat him at trial in that labor dispute. What initially looked like a slam-dunk for the prosecution was decided in favor of the defense. If Robb really had "bulldozed" his way to victory then, Hayes wasn't about to let it happen again.

Either way, the little digs and sarcastic comments became ubiquitous in the courtroom, and by the time Robb began to present his defense, Judge Livo was fed up with both of them.

"I'm concerned about running commentary between counsel distracting the jury," he said, disgusted. "You gentlemen are charged with the responsibility for representing your clients. You ought both be aware of the consequence of letting yourselves be distracted by this constant harangue."

The judge made a valid point. Because of their constant bickering, the jury was repeatedly directed in and out of the jury box, sometimes for only five minutes at a time, so that the attorneys could argue minute points of law without the jury hearing. It was excessive and causing an already long and complicated trial to drag out even further.

"I'm sure if I let you two argue we won't get out of here this year," Livo said, after one go-round he must have considered particularly pointless. "But I'm not going to preclude either side from having their day in court."

With that, Robb opened the defense's case by re-calling Dr. Simpson, the forensic pathologist from Lansing's Sparrow Hospital. Again Simpson testified that blows from a chicken skewer didn't kill Jerry Tobias. According to Simpson, no head injury caused Jerry's death; the bleeding in the brain tissue that Dr. Newhouse found during the autopsy wasn't caused by blows to the head, it was caused by the freezing and thawing of the dead man's body. Jerry had been beaten up, the doctor said, but not badly enough to kill him. He froze to death, probably because he was unconscious after a drug and alcohol binge.

"The skin would tear and bone would break with a blow of the velocity necessary to cause brain stem damage," Dr. Simpson said. And even though Jerry's skin was scratched, it wasn't torn and he had no broken bones. "One could reasonably say this is a drug-related death. The actual mechanism of death may have been exposure."

For emphasis, Dr. Simpson, with an expression of disdain and disbelief on his face, held up the chicken skewer for the jury. "I do not believe he was beaten to death and I *certainly* don't believe he was beaten with a weapon like this."

Simpson was a good witness for the defense. He was believable, not too technical and, for a pathologist—a profession that juries often found repulsive and strange—he was even likable. Still, Robb's optimism about the trial's outcome had faded a bit. He had enough experience with juries to know that drugs had permeated the entire trial and so far, all in favor of the prosecution. One good witness wouldn't be enough to get Laurie acquitted.

If the defense was going to prove that Jerry wasn't murdered but had died of exposure after overdosing on cocaine, there was a crucial piece of evidence missing. The science. If there had been enough cocaine in Tobias' system to kill him, or at least make him pass out and freeze to death, the drug would have been found in his blood. Why didn't the autopsy reveal any? If Robb couldn't answer that, Laurie was in real trouble.

Gone was the defense attorney's earlier hopes of a dismissal or a mistrial, and Robb began focusing on an acquittal. Time was waning, and with no idea how to get around the blood test, Robb did what any good defense attorney would do: He sat down that night in his hotel room, miles from home, and painstakingly re-examined the evidence. He went over witness testimony, the police report, the autopsy, and all the lab test results.

The hours ticked by, but before morning Robb found something interesting. Or rather, he didn't find something that he thought he should have. That blood test Dr. Newhouse said over and over again was negative for cocaine? There was no paperwork on it.

Robb looked through the autopsy report again. He found paperwork for the actual autopsy, paperwork for the urine test, paperwork for the pubic hair comparisons, and paperwork for the unidentified fingerprints and palm prints the police found on Jerry's truck, but there was no paperwork for the blood test. None.

Was that simply an innocent oversight, and the results just accidently omitted from the discovery evidence provided by the prosecutor's office? Or, did the case file include no cocaine test results because they didn't exist? In his gut, Robb suspected the latter.

Chapter 14 The Missing Blood Test

. . . . Wednesday, November 4, 1987

" Anything for the record, gentlemen, before we call the jury in?" It was early Wednesday morning and Judge Livo was ready to get the trial back on track. If Robb or Hayes planned any of their usual shenanigans, he wanted to get them out of the way first thing.

"I had something, but I need more time to study it," Robb said. "Dr. Newhouse testified that there were blood samples, blood tests done for cocaine, and I found no report of that, no lab report. And Mr. Hayes says it's contained in her autopsy report, and I need to look at that further. But I was wanting to have that cleared up."

Judge Livo perked up. This was a substantive request, and not simply more sniping between the two attorneys. He looked at Hayes.

"I believe the witness indicated that there was a screening done, a test done of the blood, and no cocaine was detected," Hayes said. "Obviously, if there was cocaine present in the blood, that would be contained in her autopsy report, of which Mr. Robb has a copy. There's no mention of any cocaine in the blood because none was present."

Hayes' answer didn't satisfy Robb, but that wasn't unusual. Of note was the fact that for once it didn't satisfy Judge Livo, either.

"Well, I don't really care what the results of any tests are," the judge said. "If you have any documentation, and test results in that regard, you're to furnish them to Mr. Robb. And if you don't have them, you can't furnish them. To me, it's that simple."

But nothing was simple about this case anymore, certainly not whether the victim's blood had been tested for drugs. On the contrary, that usually routine test was turning out to be strangely complex and mysterious.

The autopsy report showed Dr. Newhouse had drawn both urine and blood from Jerry's body for "toxicologic studies." The accompanying report from the testing lab, Advance Medical & Research Center, stated Jerry's urine was negative for amphetamine, barbiturate, methadone, and opiates (pot, hash, opium) but positive for cocaine. It was impossible to determine the amount of cocaine present, however, because Dr. Newhouse had only ordered a drug screen, not a drug analysis. A screen was essentially yes or no, while an analysis provided amounts.

A second screen on the urine to confirm the results of the first test was also done, and again the sample tested positive for cocaine. The second drug screen report stated the amount was ">than 1000 NG/ ML, " meaning that the screen found an amount of cocaine in Jerry's urine greater than 1,000 nanograms per milliliter. That determination was still not exact, although it was generally accepted by the medical community that a dose above 1,400 nanograms per milliliter could be fatal. Still, a drug screen only tested for the presence of a particular drug. A drug analysis was required to determine how much of the drug was present.

Whether or not cocaine was a factor in Jerry's death was now, at least as far as Robb was concerned, very much up for debate. More than a dozen times Dr. Newhouse had said, under oath, that Tobias' blood had been tested for cocaine but none was found. According to her own lab report, she was either lying or woefully misinformed. A second report from the same lab that tested Jerry's urine also tested his blood. That report stated that Tobias' blood registered .02 for ethanol (alcohol) and was negative for methanol (carburetor cleaner sniffing), acetone (glue sniffing), and five prescription barbiturates. Cocaine wasn't even mentioned. It wasn't mentioned, Robb believed, because the lab never tested for it. And the only reason they wouldn't have tested for it was if Dr. Newhouse didn't ask them to.

Robb found something else in the lab reports that bothered him. Jerry probably died late on Saturday, December 6, or very early on Sunday, Dec. 7. Dr. Newhouse conducted the autopsy on Tuesday, Dec. 9, and signed the death certificate the next day listing "homicide," "blunt trauma to the head," and "hit with blunt instrument" as the cause of death. On Thursday, December 11, a press release from the prosecutor's office announced her findings. A search warrant was issued for Walt's Butcher Shop on Friday, Dec. 12, naming Laurie Moore as a suspect. And yet the toxicology reports that Newhouse ordered, the ones that showed alcohol and cocaine in Jerry's system, weren't completed until Monday, Dec. 15.

The police, the pathologist, and the prosecutor all decided Jerry had been murdered and that Laurie Moore had done the deed days before they knew the results of the drug tests. It was no wonder, Robb thought, the prosecution seemed to have no interest in what those results actually were.

Dr. Newhouse returned to the witness stand on Thursday afternoon to face Robb's new questions. Gone was the woman from the week prior who confirmed the prosecution's every supposition. Gone was the doctor completely confident in her methods and in her understanding of medical science. Present instead was a nervous woman visibly irritated at having to return just to second-guess her own abilities.

When she took the stand, her disdain for Dean Robb was impossible to ignore. Newhouse acted so openly antagonistic to the defense that there's a legal name for it.

"Are you calling her as an adverse witness, Mr. Robb?" Judge Livo asked.

Robb said he was.

Pathologists are supposed to be neutral in court cases, just like witnesses and the judge. Their role is to present their conclusions objectively and then let the jury decide how much weight to give to them. But Dr. Newhouse wasn't objective at all. Her alliance with the prosecutor was obvious. So obvious that the judge allowed the defense to treat her as a hostile witness, which gave Robb latitude in how he phrased his questions.

"Dr. Newhouse," Robb began, "why did you testify that the blood was tested?"

"I felt it *had* been tested," she said. "I asked for it to be tested, and I, I, as I said, falsely assumed that it had been."

"Doctor," Robb pressed, "I don't understand how that could be. That you could say that a blood test was done and it had no— let me read (from the court transcript) what you said: 'Certainly we looked at the blood samples. No cocaine was present in the blood.' You told us that you had tested the blood for cocaine."

"I told you I had sent it," she said, appearing to make an effort to stay calm. "I—I do not do the tests myself."

"On the blood test, you didn't get back anything on cocaine?" Robb asked again.

"That's—on the urine, we did get back that cocaine was present."

"So you got back a screening test a few days later finding cocaine to be positive?"

"That's correct."

"Before you signed the death certificate?"

"Yes."

"So you just didn't follow up on it?"

"I received the results back on the urine that said it had been confirmed (for cocaine) and that the quantity was insufficient (for an analysis)," Newhouse explained. "And again, my initial under-standing of the blood was that there had been *no* cocaine—my assumption was there was no cocaine in the blood. That was a false assumption on my part."

"Well, one of the reasons you gave, rather vehemently, that you wouldn't assume that this could be a death caused by cocaine . . . was that you didn't have cocaine in the blood."

"That's true," Newhouse, admitted.

"But you gave this jury the result of the quantification without having *done* it?"

Throughout this line of questioning, Robb's face, voice, and posture traveled a gamut of emotions—curiosity, disbelief, shock, anger. But with this last question, his whole being conveyed some-thing new: utter astonishment.

"Again," Newhouse said, obviously irritated. "I requested quantification of the specimens, and I was under the false impression it had been done."

"But did you tell this jury what I just suggested?"

"I gave them what I thought was the truth."

Under repeated questioning, Dr. Newhouse was finally forced to admit that she didn't have the report from the lab stating the volume of the blood sample was not enough for a drug analysis. Nor could she remember the name of the person at the lab who had told her that. But Robb was not finished.

"The cocaine . . . could it be a lethal dose?" he asked.

"I have no idea what the dose is," Dr. Newhouse answered.

"Could it have been a lethal dose?" Robb asked again.

"I could not exclude that."

Robb exhaled. He had what he wanted. Newhouse finally admitted that Jerry Tobias could have died from a drug overdose. Robb couldn't prove that Dr. Newhouse's actions constituted outright fraud, but he felt he'd shown the jury that she was, at the very least, incompetent. For the first time in the trial, Robb felt like he'd given the jury all they needed to accept a defense attorney's two most precious words: reasonable doubt.

This was victory that turned out to be only temporary.

Hayes was well-prepared and quite competent in front of a jury, but if he had one particular courtroom skill, it was an ability to cut through cloudy details and drop the well-timed bombshell.

"Let me ask you this," Hayes said, as soon as he had the opportunity to re-examine Dr. Newhouse. "Does cocaine cause sixteen to twenty blows to the body?"

"Of course not," she said.

One of the last remaining defense witnesses Robb had scheduled was Laurie's wife. Hayes rested the prosecution's testimony with the unexplained package of meat, and Robb wanted to leave the jury with something equally powerful. And that, he believed, was Janet.

She testified that her husband arrived home the supposed night of the murder at about 3 AM, drunk, happy, and singing. Not exactly the demeanor someone would expect from a man who'd just committed a murder. Physical evidence bore this out. Laurie wasn't cut, he wasn't bleeding, and he wasn't bruised.

"He didn't look like he'd been in a fight or anything," Janet said.

In fact, Janet told the jury, her husband had actually been the opposite of angry or violent. Even though she'd been perturbed at Laurie for coming home late, obviously drunk, and for waking her up, when she got out of bed to tell him to come inside, what she saw in her driveway immediately softened her mood. When she opened their front door to tongue-lash her new husband, there was Laurie, sitting in his van with the windows rolled down, and she could hear him singing.

After learning that, how could anyone on the jury believe he'd just beaten a man to death? With Janet's obvious love for her fun-loving, hard-partying, hard-working husband on full display, the defense rested.

Chapter 15   Closing Arguments

. . . . Friday, November 6, 1987

All that remained before Laurie's case went to the jury were each side's closing arguments and the judge's instructions. Closing arguments were the last opportunity for the prosecution and the defense to summarize their cases, to stress what each believed were the most important points of evidence and testimony, and to offer a theory on what really happened to Jerry Tobias. If a trial were a newspaper, closing arguments were the editorials. Not just facts, evidence, and testimony, but the addition of each attorney's opinion.

Opinions, Judge Livo reminded the jury, weren't evidence, but in their closing arguments, each side was allowed to speculate on the evidence and what it, along with witness testimony, really meant. According to custom, the prosecution went first.

"It is the theory of the people that this was a dope deal gone bad. It was an opportunity for Mr. Moore to get rid of someone. The defense has tried to try Jerry Tobias. There's no question Jerry Tobias used cocaine—that does not excuse what happened to him."

Hayes detailed Laurie's first interview with police, when he failed to mention his late-night trip to that Otsego Lake cabin after leaving the Sportsman's Club dinner. Hayes went over the testimony of Don and Becky Nelson, who had said that Jerry was going to buy them some cocaine and that they believed he was meeting Laurie at Walt's to do it, but then they never saw Jerry again. Hayes also detailed the search of the butcher shop, took hold of the chicken skewer while he talked, and held it up for the jury.

"Some instruments in and of themselves are dangerous. Some instruments are designed for peaceful purposes. What determines if it is a dangerous weapon is how it is used."

For emphasis, Hayes slapped his open palm sixteen times with the chicken skewer. The sound of the thin metal rods connecting with his skin reverberated through the courtroom as Hayes turned a withering gaze on Laurie. Dean Robb's defense table was overflowing with reports, exhibits, evidence, transcripts, and police files, leaving no room for the defendant. Laurie was seated in the row directly behind the table, an arrangement Hayes decided to bring to the attention of the jury.

"It's really interesting, ladies and gentlemen," he said, pacing in front of the jury box and pointing over at Laurie. "He hasn't sat at that table yet, has he? But he *is* the individual there in the blue sweater. He may be trying to hide from you. I don't know. But he hasn't sat at that table yet."

Hayes also reminded the jury that Laurie didn't testify in his own defense. "He's clothed in a shroud of—of innocence throughout this trial. But each piece of evidence rips away at that shroud of innocence. And he's standing right there to where you can see him. Oh, he's tried to hide. But you can see him."

A cornerstone of the American justice system is that defendants are not required to testify on their own behalf. And there are many legitimate reasons why they might not—trial strategy, their attorney's advice, nervousness, an off-putting manner or unsympathetic personality, etc. By law, juries cannot presume guilt if a defendant decides not to testify, and Robb repeatedly objected during Hayes' closing argument, but never more vehemently than when Hayes accused Laurie of "hiding."

Robb complained to Judge Livo that Hayes was attacking Laurie's right to remain silent and his presumption of innocence. Judge Livo agreed and admonished the prosecutor. Hayes offered no apology, and instead seemed to take offense that he'd been reprimanded.

"The People of the State of Michigan are going to get a fair trial in this case," Hayes snapped. "And let's try the prosecutor. I forgot that, too. They're gonna try *me*."

Court rules didn't allow the defense to actually "try" the prosecutor, but in his own closing argument, Robb bent that rule as far as he could without breaking it.

"The Republic isn't safe when Congress is in session," Robb told the jury, paraphrasing Mark Twain. The quote fit well. Robb actually looked a little like the famous author as he marched his tall thin frame in front of the jury box and shook his head of bushy white hair. What he really meant was, the people of northern Michigan weren't safe when Norm Hayes was prosecuting. "None of us is safe if a case like this can come to trial."

Robb was convinced his client was innocent, and that he had given the jury more than enough evidence for them to infer reasonable doubt. His notes and the official trial strategy he filed with the court bear this out. Twelve items, from questions about the cause of death, to an incomplete police investigation, detailed what Robb saw as the biggest holes in the prosecution's case. The package of meat was never fingerprinted, for example, and the palm print found on the tailgate of Jerry's truck didn't match Laurie and was never identified. When the truck was last parked, perhaps by Jerry Tobias himself, the radio was left on and tuned in to a hard rock station with the volume turned up as loud as it would go. Would someone trying to hide a body really do *that*?

There was no physical evidence, not so much as a single hair or partial fingerprint, connecting Laurie to Jerry, or Jerry to the butcher shop. The neighborhood where the truck was found was never canvassed. Worst of all, said Robb, Laurie Moore was identified as the police's only suspect even before the toxicology tests from the autopsy were complete. That was shoddy police work, he added, considering there was physical evidence proving Jerry was with an unidentified woman just before his death. Finally, Officer Dan Dallas' testimony—that he saw a light-colored van at Walt's in the wee hours of Saturday morning—was just too convenient to be believed.

The prosecution's case against Laurie wasn't built on evidence, Robb reminded the jury, but rather on a series of unlucky circumstances involving his client: A reputation for partying; a vocation (butcher) that the prosecutor tried to make seem sinister; and a pathologist more interested in aligning herself with the prosecutor than finding out what really happened to Jerry.

"She lost her objectivity," Robb said, about Dr. Newhouse. "She was so sold on the police's idea that this was a homicide, she just didn't look at this case."

Like most criminal defense attorneys, Robb had an abiding faith in juries. Throughout his career, time and time again, inside of many different courtrooms, and in hundreds of cases, jury after jury had proven to him this faith was warranted. Give a group of twelve citizens the facts, give them the law, give them good logic, and Dean believed that they would come to a just conclusion.

At a few minutes past noon on Friday, Nov. 6, 1987, eleven months to the day after Jerry Tobias died, the case of *People of The State of Michigan v. Laurie Monroe Moore* went to the jury. Robb's faith—in juries, in justice, in the whole American system—was about to be tested.

Chapter 16   Jury Deliberations

. . . . Friday, November 6, 1987, 12:15 PM

It was nearing midnight and the jury had been deliberating for almost twelve hours, but there was no verdict. The trial had been long and arduous. The jury members were tired, and they just wanted to go home. Jury Foreman John Pearson sent a note to the judge.

"We cannot conclude this matter tonight," it read.

Judge Livo knew that twelve hours of deliberation and still no verdict meant the jury was either split, still deliberating, or both. There were either a couple of holdouts refusing to vote with the majority, or there was evidence yet to be discussed. He called them back into the courtroom and gave them some surprising news.

They'd be spending the night at a local motel and sequestered for the duration of their deliberations.

There were some sighs and expressions of shock and irritation at this news, but Livo ignored them. He instructed the group not to talk about the case, not to make any telephone calls, and not to watch the television news or read a newspaper. The jury was to get a good night's sleep and return to the courthouse by 9 AM Saturday morning, fully awake and ready to resume deliberations.

Livo's instructions followed the letter of the law, but ignored an unwritten code of courtroom etiquette: Keep juries comfortable. When they were selected to serve, no one told them they might be sequestered, so not one of the twelve had so much as a toothbrush, let alone pajamas or a change of clothes. One juror had a sick daughter at home. The smokers in the group were running low on cigarettes, and Livo wouldn't allow them to phone home and explain to their families what was going on. Court staffers tried to contact each juror's family, but it was past midnight and some couldn't be reached.

The next morning, nine of the jurors returned to court in the same clothes they'd worn the day before, and had slept in at the motel. The men were unshaven, the women unkempt, and all were irritated. But they filed into the jury room just the same, and began their second day of deliberations.

At 10:40 AM, another note to the judge: "When did Dan Dallas tell detectives he had seen a light-colored van at Walt's? Was it right away, or had some time passed?"

Since this seemed to be an important question, and one that could affect the verdict, Judge Livo called Hayes and Robb into his chambers to discuss it. How would each side like this information communicated to the jury? Robb said that Dallas' few lines of relevant testimony should be read back to the jury. Hayes disagreed, and said that the officer's entire testimony, all two and a half hours worth, should be read to them. The judge didn't agree with either.

"This question is non-specific and I don't intend to have any portion of Officer Dallas' testimony read," he said. As usual, an argument between Hayes and Robb ensued, and as usual, Judge Livo was visibly disgusted by it. To clear up the issue, he called in the court reporter and asked her to begin reading Dallas' testimony out loud. He agreed to listen to her for a bit, and then make a ruling.

This arrangement temporarily appeased both attorneys, but soon irritated the judge. As the testimony was read, Livo grew increasingly agitated by what he heard. The court record included not only Dallas' testimony but everything said by Robb and Hayes, too. It must have seemed like torture to the judge to have to re-live all that bickering between the two men, because even ten minutes of it was too much.

"Stop!" Livo said, holding up his hand.

The court reporter stopped, but Hayes objected and asked her to continue. She did, without Judge Livo's approval, and the petty arguing from the trial was audible once again. But Judge Livo refused to listen to it, stood, and left his own chambers without saying a word. He hadn't made a ruling, or answered the jury's question, and neither of the attorneys or the court reporter knew what to make of the strange behavior.

In the meantime, the jurors were waiting patiently in the jury room and had no idea that their note had sparked such a quarrel. All they wanted to know was when Officer Dallas told detectives he had seen a van at Walt's. By not answering, Judge Livo had left the jury in a kind of deliberation purgatory, but sequestered in the jury room they had no way of knowing it.

"There was only so much I could absorb and respond to in a rational, fair and logical manner," Livo would say later. "And when I went past an imaginary point where I felt that I didn't want to listen to any more, I got up and left."

Eventually Livo did respond and sent them back a note of his own: "Do you still want an answer to your last question RE: Officer Dallas, before coming into the courtroom? Please write your answer on this paper. R.C. Livo."

An hour and a half had passed. The jury had waited and waited. The only people who would ever know what went on in the jury room during that time were the members themselves. But whatever happened, they no longer needed an answer to their question, and the Foreman wrote the judge back.

"NO," the note read, "we are Ready."

While the attorneys squabbled, the judge disappeared, and no answer to their question was ever provided, the jury had reached a verdict.

Chapter 17   A Verdict

. . . . Saturday, November 7, 1987, noon

The news spread and Judge Livo, the attorneys, Laurie, Janet, the rest of the Moore family, the police, and miscellaneous court watchers filed into the courtroom. They whispered and murmured until the jury foreman stood. Silence enveloped the room and his shaky voice echoed: "Guilty of Voluntary Manslaughter."

Laurie's mouth opened in an "O" of disbelief. Robb put his hand on his client's shoulder, while Janet could do nothing but drop her face into her palms.

"Do you want the jury polled, Mr. Robb?" Judge Livo asked.

"Yes, your honor."

Polling the jury was almost always simply a formality, a way for the defense to force each juror to take personal responsibility for the verdict. In a jury poll, each juror was asked by the judge whether or not "guilty" was indeed their verdict. Robb already knew that each juror always answered, "Yay." He'd never participated in a trial where that wasn't so. That's how the poll of Laurie's jury unfolded, too, for the first eleven jurors anyway.

Then Judge Livo came to juror twelve, a woman named Michelle Cronan.

"Is that your verdict?" Judge Livo asked, almost rhetorically.

But juror twelve didn't immediately answer, not the way the other eleven had. She refused to look at the judge and instead just hung her head. After a pause she finally did open her mouth to answer, but the sound that came out was unintelligible.

"Could you repeat that please?" the judge asked.

"Yay," Cronan finally squeaked out, crying softly.

Judge Livo exhaled. "Thank you, ladies and gentlemen," he said. "You have had a very arduous case. I won't make it any worse by stretching it out. You're free to go."

Laurie's bond was revoked, he said his shocked goodbyes to Janet and his family, and he was escorted into a police car, which would transport him back to Gaylord and the Otsego County Jail to await sentencing. Robb stood at the curb in front of the Cheboygan courthouse and watched the car drive away while Hayes held an impromptu press conference.

"I feel that with the jury's verdict today, a lot of people in Gaylord are vindicated," Hayes said. "Defense counsel has been saying throughout the case that it should never have been brought to trial. However, the court repeatedly denied motions for dismissal. And now the jury has spoken, and they believed in our case as well."

A reporter broke from the group and approached Robb. Did he plan to file an appeal?

"This case has got so many issues to appeal, I wouldn't know where to start," Robb said.

Privately Robb had already given it some thought and believed the case practically begged out for an appeal, despite what he told the reporter. But Robb had just watched his client, a man he believed was innocent, be carted off to jail, so he couldn't concentrate on the specifics of the law. He was just plain weary. Weary of arguing, weary of Norm Hayes, weary of the whole thing. He needed a break. Maybe he'd think about the appeal tomorrow. Or, the next day. Or maybe not until the day after that.

Back in his chambers, Judge Livo was tired, too. He was relieved the trial was finally over, but he had one last task to complete before he could close the file and try his best to forget about it and move on. Still in his robe, the judge sat down at his desk, pulled out a notebook, and began writing. He made it a practice to write post-trial notes for all the cases he presided over, but in this case there were specific issues he felt compelled to document, and he wanted to make sure he did it while they were still fresh in his mind.

Judge Livo thought, and wrote, and thought and wrote some more, eventually filling four pages. He read them over to make sure he hadn't left anything out, tore the pages out of the notebook, added them to the case file, and closed it.

Just over a week after the verdict, a greeting card arrived in Esther Moore's mailbox. It was a sympathy card, the kind usually sent to the family of someone who has just died. But there hadn't been a death in the Moore family since the patriarch and namesake of the butcher shop, Walter Moore, died several years ago.

The verdict was still fresh, Laurie was headed for prison, and so Esther thought she knew why someone would send her a sympathy card. She opened it and read the handwritten note inside.

"I'm sorry," it read. "I know I did wrong and I'm so sorry, but I just didn't know."

The card was signed, "Michelle Cronan, Juror #12."

Chapter 18   "I believed him."

· · · · · · · · · · Monday, November 16, 1987

By the time Laurie's mother opened up that greeting card, Laurie was spending his tenth night in the Otsego County Jail. That was enough time for Robb to rest up, try to put his disgust over the trial aside, and start the appeal. The first step was to file a motion asking Judge Livo to declare a mistrial. If that didn't work, then Robb would file a formal appeal. Somehow, some way, Robb vowed he would get Laurie out of jail and exonerated.

"Everything they teach you in law school, and every instinct I've got as a lawyer, says don't automatically believe it when your client tells you they're innocent," Robb said. "But Laurie never said or did *one thing* to make me think otherwise. I believed him. I believed him from the start. And I remain convinced that the whole case against him smells. Stinks to high heaven."

A mistrial can be declared by trial judges if they believe there has been a procedural error, attorney misconduct, or juror misconduct significant enough to prevent defendants from receiving a fair trial. Robb was certain that errors and misconduct occurred in Laurie's trial; he just had to decide which infraction offered the best chance of reversing the verdict.

Was it the personal attacks on Robb by Hayes? Was it the lack of response to the jury from Judge Livo during deliberations? Was it that Laurie was charged with Second-Degree Murder, but found guilty of Voluntary Manslaughter? Or was it the prosecutor's closing argument and his accusation that Laurie was "hiding" under a "shroud of innocence"? There was plenty of ammunition and Robb needed to choose a single bullet.

When a judge rules in favor of a mistrial, the ruling is almost always made before the verdict. In rare cases, it can also be made after the verdict but before sentencing. Laurie's sentence hearing had yet to be scheduled, and Judge Livo agreed to hear mistrial arguments from Robb, and rebuttal from Hayes, on November 20.

Once the date was set Robb decided to focus his mistrial efforts on the prosecutor's closing argument. Because he planned to allege prosecutor misconduct, Robb sought advice from the other side of the aisle. Who better than another prosecutor to assist him in arguing that the prosecution of Laurie had been unjust? Robb asked the prosecutor of nearby Antrim County, Charles Koop, for help in drafting the mistrial motion. Koop accepted the assignment and together the two men drafted an eighteen-page motion on prosecutor misconduct and other issues, including jury irregularities, and delivered it to Judge Livo.

"The prosecutor's bald assertion that Mr. Moore was hiding something was an inexcusable infringement on Mr. Moore's rights to be physically present and to be presumed innocent until proven guilty by legally admissible evidence," the motion read. "The prosecutor's suggestion that Mr. Moore was cloaked in a shroud of innocence was highly inflammatory. A 'shroud' is commonly defined as, 'A cloth to wrap a body for burial.' This obviously highly charged word was extremely prejudicial in this murder trial. No defendant 'hides' behind the presumption of innocence. Rather, this principle is the 'bedrock' of criminal law. The Court cannot allow this or any prosecutor to turn this principle on its head by arguing that Mr. Moore used the presumption of innocence to hide his guilt."

Robb felt confident that he and Koop had made an excellent argument in support of Laurie. He was even optimistic that Judge Livo would agree with their contention, declare a mistrial, and possibly dismiss the charge, or at least grant Laurie a new trial. But he'd been optimistic before, and it hadn't gotten him very far. So when he visited Laurie in jail, he kept his opinion to himself.

"Sit tight," he told his client instead. "There's nothing more we can do but wait, as difficult as that is."

Still, in his own mind, Robb believed Judge Livo would rule in Laurie's favor. And he might have if he were the judge who ended up ruling on the mistrial motion. But he wasn't. An hour before he was to hear oral arguments from Robb and Prosecutor Hayes, Judge Livo recused himself from the case.

Robb was stunned. Hayes said the recusal was nothing out of the ordinary. Often, he told the *Gaylord Herald Times*, judges recuse themselves because of illness, a schedule conflict, or some other benign matter.

But Judge Livo didn't have a scheduling conflict, and he wasn't sick. At least, not in the usual sense of the word. The real story was that he was mentally and emotionally sick of the Laurie Moore case, and of the two attorneys arguing it.

"The two of you—the thing hasn't changed, you see—is the reason that I withdrew from the case," Judge Livo told the men. "The contention between counsel was so constant that I'm tempted to lose my objectivity. It wasn't an inability to listen . . . but when I had to hear the same argument for the umpteenth time, I found that I just could not stomach it anymore. And I—that's the reason I withdrew from deciding the motion for a new trial."

Circuit Court Judge William R. Brown of Traverse City was appointed to rule on the defense motion, and by early December, denied all of the issues but one. Judge Brown would not grant a mistrial, would not acknowledge any prosecutor misconduct, and would not agree that a conviction of Voluntary Manslaughter had been improper. He also would not consider the affidavits of four Moore jurors who now said, under oath, that they had made a mistake. Diane MacInnis, Annette Myers, Sandra Crawford, and juror number twelve, Michelle Cronan, each contacted Robb and asked him how they could change their verdict.

"I offer these people to you for your inquiry!" Robb said, incredulous at the judge's decision. "I didn't know these people before. They came forward after this case was over. They were so upset they had gone along with this verdict that they couldn't sleep. Now I ask, in fairness Judge, at least you hear these people out!"

But Judge Brown would not be budged.

"I have indicated my conclusion, based upon my research of the matter, and that is my ruling," he said.

Only one issue remained—the motion for a new trial. It was the defense's final chance and Robb asked the judge for more time to file and he agreed. While Robb wrangled with the law and the judge, Laurie waited in jail.

Chapter 19   "That was Debbie."

. . . . Tuesday, December 8, 1987

With Laurie in jail and his fate undecided, it was not going to be a happy Christmas for the Moore family. Esther's youngest son, Howard Moore, came home from college for holiday break. In between trying to comfort his mother, visit his brother in jail, and sort out what had been happening with Laurie's case, he stopped in at the Cedar County Ambulance Corps. During high school, he'd volunteered there and considered the other drivers and the EMTs his friends. Howard was just planning to say hello and wish everyone a Merry Christmas. Although he'd been away at college, he still knew most of the staff and volunteers, including his supervisor, Mary Evans.

"There's someone here who wants to talk to you," Evans told Howard, after the two shared their hellos.

"Really? Who?" Howard didn't understand how anyone could want to talk with him. He'd come by the Ambulance Corps on a whim. No one knew he was coming, so how could anyone be expecting to talk with him?

Before he could ask, a woman he'd never met approached him and asked if they could talk privately. She was petite, dark-haired, and pretty in a "hard-looking" kind of way. Howard had no idea what she wanted to talk to him about, but he was always willing to help out a fellow Corps person, so he followed her into one of the bunkrooms reserved for volunteers on overnight shifts. The woman pulled the door closed and told him something startling: She knew secrets about Jerry Tobias' death.

"Laurie had absolutely nothing to do with it," she whispered to Howard. "I know who the real murderers are, though. They're people to be afraid of. But if you tell anyone I told you all this, I'll deny it."

Howard was blindsided. Who was this woman? And how did she know his brother was innocent? Whoever she was, she assured Howard she knew exactly what happened and where Jerry's missing boots and belt were hidden. The police had looked all over for them, she told Howard, but they'd never been found.

"Who *are* you?" Howard blurted. "And how do you know all this?"

"I shouldn't have told you," the mystery woman said, reaching for the door. "And if you repeat this to anyone, I'll deny we ever met."

"Wait!" Howard said, still confused. "If you have information that could help my brother, you need to come forward. You need to tell the police!"

His words had no effect on her and she scurried out of the bunkroom, down the hall, and left the building. Howard followed her out of the room and went straight to the front desk. Mary Evans was still at her post, and Howard asked her who the woman was.

"That was Debbie," Evans said. "Debbie Parmentier."

It was a name Howard had never heard before. But soon he and everyone else with any connection to the Jerry Tobias case would know the name well. Whether they wanted to or not.

Winter raged. The more Robb thought about it, the more the conviction of Laurie bothered him. Robb was not one to shy away from controversy or unpopular clients. Yet never before had it seemed like every rule of law he held dear was just flung out the window by the very people sworn to uphold it. For his own satisfaction, Robb tallied up what he believed were the most grievous offenses:

- A death classified as a murder that was more likely a drug dump.
- Evidence—the package of meat—the police never fingerprinted.
- Blood that wasn't tested for cocaine, even as the prosecution insisted their case revolved around drugs.
- Prosecution witnesses who changed their testimony multiple times.
- Jurors who wanted to recant.
- A prosecutor who seemed bent on destroying both Robb and his client.
- And, finally, at the bottom of his list, Robb added a name: Debbie Parmentier.

After his strange encounter, Howard went to Robb with the story of a supposed mystery witness who could exonerate Laurie.

With his motion for a new trial still to be filed, Robb's defense of Laurie was not over, but he'd need a full-time investigator to help him follow up on all the case's misdeeds and tangents. Investigating the crime wasn't supposed to be a defense attorney's job, but Robb was not satisfied with the police work in the case and didn't trust them to find Howard's mystery witness. Robb didn't know that Debbie had already been dismissed by the police and the prosecutor as a crank. He just knew she told Howard Laurie was innocent. Robb didn't have the time to run down the mystery woman. He was busy working on Laurie's motion for a new trial, his strategy for appeal if the motion were denied, plus trying to keep the rest of his law practice going.

Law firms frequently employed private investigators for just this kind of task. In Robb's case, his son, Blair Robb, often filled that role. Blair could check out Howard's story, find out who Debbie Parmentier was, and what she knew about Jerry Tobias' death.

On Feb. 1, 1988, Robb filed the motion asking Judge Brown to grant Laurie a new trial based on prosecutorial misconduct. It was going to be an especially tough motion for the judge to rule on, Robb warned. The trial was rife with an undercurrent of conflict and complexity, Brown had not been the trial judge, so he was not privy to all the subterfuge.

"Much of the prosecutorial misconduct involved nuances, insinuations, innuendo, and vindictiveness which occurred throughout the trial and created an atmosphere that only the trial judge would be aware of," Robb explained in his motion. He wanted the judge to understand the mood of the trial, but that was going to be impossible. Mood is not something communicated very well in a trial transcript.

Robb had other issues tugging at him, too. After an expensive legal defense his client, once a successful businessman, was broke. On the day Robb filed the motion for a new trial, Laurie's bank balance was $86.57, and he owed Robb's law firm more than

$90,000. But finances aside, since the verdict Robb had grown even more committed to his client's innocence, and he still believed the law would rule in their favor if he could just get a judge to take his prosecutorial misconduct motion seriously.

"He may prosecute with earnest[ness] and vigor—indeed, he should do so," read a decision in an often cited case, *Berger v. United States*, regarding the duties of the prosecutor. "But while he may strike hard blows, he is not at liberty to strike foul ones. It is as much his duty to refrain from improper methods calculated to produce a wrongful conviction, as it is to use every legitimate means to bring about a just one. It is fairer to say that the average jury, in a greater or less degree, has confidence that these obligations, which so plainly rest upon the prosecuting attorney, will be faithfully observed. Consequently, improper suggestions, insinuations, and, especially, assertions of personal knowledge are apt to carry much weight against the accused when they should properly carry none."

Robb knew *Berger v. United States* well, and passionately agreed with every word of it. He hoped, for Laurie's sake, that Judge Brown did, too.

"Is Debbie there?"

"This is Deb."

"My name is Blair Robb. I work for Dean Robb, an attorney, and I understand you have certain information on the Laurie Moore case."

"Yes."

"Would you be willing to meet with me, and tell me what you know?"

Blair Robb didn't have to do any detective work to find Debbie Parmentier. He just looked her up in the phone book and gave her a call. But like all good investigators, he knew the best way to find out what she knew was to interview her in person. The location she chose—a backroads bar—was not his first choice. He didn't know the place, and he didn't know her. But this was a murder case, not the Junior League. He'd meet with her there, find out what she knew, and report back to his dad.

The bar she chose was the Swamp, a dusty little dive in Frederick, a tiny town twenty miles south of Gaylord. It must have seemed an odd choice to Blair Robb. He'd read the case file, and he knew it was the same bar Jerry Tobias had been in, buying drinks and stumbling around the pool table, the night before he died. Did Debbie choose it on purpose? Or was it just a convenient spot? Blair didn't know, but as it turned out, it didn't really matter either way, because they wouldn't be going inside.

Debbie told Blair not to go in because she didn't want anyone to see them together. Blair was to meet her in the parking lot. She'd be the woman alone, driving a small black Chevy.

"Are you taping me?"

This, thought Blair, was an odd first question from a potential defense witness. If she wanted to set the record straight about Laurie's conviction, why would she worry that her story might be taped? Not that it mattered, because Blair didn't have a tape recorder along, and he told her as much.

"I don't want you taping me," Debbie said, "and I don't want you taking no notes, neither."

Blair agreed.

"I wish I never said nothing to nobody," Debbie continued. "But they're barking up the wrong tree. Laurie didn't have nothing to do with it. He's innocent."

Jerry Tobias was killed by a man named Mark Canter, she said, and an accomplice she could only identify as someone named John. This "John" person was her ex-boyfriend, but Debbie refused to tell Blair his last name, explaining that she didn't know it. She did say that Canter and John were dangerous men, criminals, who not only killed Jerry Tobias, but were also involved in drug dealing and gun running.

If Blair thought it odd that Debbie didn't know the last name of her own boyfriend, he didn't get a chance to ask her about it. His meeting with her wasn't a conversation, it was an exhale. Debbie's story came out in a strange and dreamy stream of consciousness. She showed little emotion while she talked and barely stopped to breathe.

"They're drug traffickers," she said, "taking drugs into Canada. I got it all down in my diary. Fifty machine guns from a helicopter, AK-47s, gun running outta the National Guard at Grayling headed up by this crooked sergeant. A plane landed near Gaylord to pick stuff up and drop stuff off. I took all this to the FBI and the ATF and they wanted to talk with me too, but I just froze up."

Debbie explained she tried to tell authorities what happened to Tobias, but a strange feeling came over her. She "froze up" and couldn't speak about it. Verbal paralysis did not seem to be a problem for her with Blair, however. She told him all of this through her window, when they were parked in the Swamp's parking lot and before he even got in her car.

But she eventually invited him to get in her passenger seat. He did, and for the next hour and a half she drove him around the snowy back roads of Frederick, Michigan, chattering away.

"Here's what happened. During the day, Mark and John and I rode around, and we called Terry and Doug. We planned to meet up at the butcher shop, to straighten everything out with Jerry. They went to the Fireside Lounge, Mark and John went in to meet with Jerry, and I waited in the car."

The two new people she named, "Terry and Doug," were Terry Moore, Laurie's brother, and another local man named Doug Brinkman. While she waited in the car, Mark Canter, John (no last name), and Jerry Tobias came out of the Fireside Lounge and she said they were arguing. They apparently left Jerry behind, because Debbie said that she, Mark Canter, and John drove around downtown Gaylord for several hours, getting high and selling drugs. They were either in Debbie's car or Mark's, she couldn't remember, drinking liquor straight from the bottle, snorting cocaine, and smoking pot. They went to Walt's Butcher Shop because Jerry owed the men money from a past drug deal and a private place was needed to discuss repayment.

After a half hour of non-stop talking, Blair finally interrupted her.

"How do you *know* all this?" he asked.

"Cause I was dealing coke with Jerry," Debbie said. "I dealt with him all the time, and so that's how I knew he was shafting people."

"Have you gone to the police with this?" Blair asked her. "You really need to go to the police."

"I'm scared," Debbie said, in a monotone Blair found strange.

He didn't buy her story. First, downtown Gaylord was only about two square miles. It would take ten minutes, at the most, to cruise it, not several hours. Second, Debbie didn't look afraid or "froze up." Blair took in her small size, her square jaw, her wild eyes, her flat tone. She didn't look scared to him at all, she'd looked manic. Crazy even.

Then as quickly as she began, Debbie said she was finished talking and drove Blair back to his car. Before he got out, he again urged her to go to the police but her answer remained the same— she was too scared to do that. Scared of what or of whom, Blair would never know because Debbie refused to elaborate and, as soon as he got out of her car, she drove off.

As an investigator, Blair believed he was a pretty good judge of human nature. He'd interviewed all kinds of people, watched them when they didn't know they were being watched, asked the hard questions, confronted criminals. And yet, he couldn't get a read on Debbie. He had no idea whether any part of her story was true, whether she could help Laurie's defense, or even if he'd ever see her again. Blair headed home to type up a report of the encounter for his dad. Maybe the older Robb could make some sense of Debbie.

As it turned out, Blair didn't have long to wait until he'd see Debbie again. He didn't even have to call to arrange another interview or drive to Gaylord. The very next afternoon, while he was staying at the Robb family farm north of Traverse City, the doorbell rang. He opened the front door, and there was Debbie on the doorstep.

"I just want to ask you one question," she said, without preamble. "How can I get in protective custody? You know, police, FBI. That kinda thing."

Blair wasn't sure how she'd found the farm, but it was February and bitter cold outside, so Blair invited her in, took her coat, invited her to sit down, and asked if she'd like anything to drink or something to eat. She declined, and reminded him of their conversation the day before. Her information was valuable stuff, she said. No one else knew what she knew about the drugs, the drinking, the driving round, the killing.

By then Blair had had some time to think about their conversation, and to speak with his father about it. Neither Dean nor Blair were convinced Debbie knew much of anything. The information she said was so valuable wasn't specific enough to be verified, and a lot of what she'd said had been reported by the media and was public knowledge.

"You know a lot of this was in the papers, right?" Blair reminded her.

"Yeah," Debbie snapped, "I know that."

"Well, can you give me anything more?" he asked.

Debbie said she couldn't, but asked him again if he could help her get into protective custody.

"Here's the best advice I can give you," Blair said. "Go to the police. Tell them what you know."

Debbie had no response, and just put her coat back on and left.

Blair Robb had only been alone with Debbie two times and was not sure which parts of her story were true, if any. But he did get a sense of her as a person.

"I would say she was determined. It was very important to her that she make people believe her. Extremely determined. Motivated, that would be a good word to describe her, too. Motivated and determined."

Chapter 20   The Death Threat Letter

. . . . March, 1988

Supplemental Report Date MAR 08, 1988. "Undersigned officer this date, approximately 3:00 PM received a telephone call . . . from a NORM HAYES (Prosecutor from Otsego Co.). Mr. Hayes advised undersigned officer that he had additional information in regards to the murder of Jerry Tobias. He requested undersigned officer contact one Debra Dawn Parmentier." Signed, D/SGT LaBarge.

Three days after Blair Robb urged Debbie to contact police, her name appeared for the first time in the ever-expanding police report on Jerry Tobias' death. She had come to the attention of Detective LaBarge not of her own volition, but from the prosecutor. Hayes called LaBarge to discuss the possibility that Debbie may have witnessed Jerry's murder. Whether the meeting between Debbie and Blair, and then the phone call between Hayes and LaBarge, were related, or just a coincidence, was unknown.

Within days of Debbie's name appearing in the police report, Dean Robb received a letter. In his office mail was a plain white envelope hand addressed to, "Dean Robb, attorney at law, Traverse City, Mich."

Inside was a single sheet of paper torn from a yellow legal pad. It read:

```
If you continue with your investigation into

the Laurie Moore afair we will kill you! We

will be taking care of the one who knows.
```

Startled, Robb read the letter again, then turned the paper over, found no more writing and no signature, and then read it a third time through. His confusion turned to shock and then worry. He put the letter on his desk and immediately made two phone calls. The first was to Judge Brown to tell him about the letter and to ask what he should do with it. Brown's advice was to call the authorities and that's what Robb did. But instead of the police or the prosecutor's office, Robb called the FBI.

Robb suspected the State Police and Hayes of hiding documents, coaching witnesses, and manipulating the medical examiner. He did not feel like he could go to them for help and, although it was an instinctual feeling, he was self aware enough to recognize the irony—here he was, a well-respected and experienced attorney, threatened by an unknown correspondent, and yet not comfortable reporting it to the State Police.

The FBI had an office in Traverse City, staffed by agent Larry Hoffmeister. Agent Hoffmeister came immediately to Robb's office, collected the letter as evidence, and took Robb's statement. Hoffmeister said he wasn't going to be able to avoid the State Police. The letter would have to be checked for fingerprints and the handwriting analyzed in a crime lab, and the closest one to Traverse City was in Grayling, and it belonged to the State Police.

Robb had no idea who wrote the letter, or who was "the one who knows," but he was certain of two things. One, since the letter mentioned Laurie Moore, this was obviously about the Tobias case. Of all the cases he'd tried in his long and rather colorful career, it was the only one crazy enough to inspire a death threat letter. And two, he wanted out. Now.

Robb believed Laurie deserved a new trial and he hoped that he was going to get one. But if he did, Robb wouldn't be the attorney defending him. His next phone call was to deliver that news to the Moores.

On Robb's recommendation, Laurie hired another Gaylord attorney, Karen Jackson, to take over his defense. The change was made official in Judge Brown's chambers with Laurie, Detective LaBarge, Prosecutor Hayes, and Robb all present. The meeting was a formality, but before he officially withdrew, Robb wanted assurance from the prosecutor and the police that the death threat letter would be investigated, and that if any evidence uncovered was favorable to Laurie, it would be immediately made available to Laurie's new attorney. In any other case, this kind of thing was understood, but after his experience with Hayes, Robb said he wanted it written down and included in the court record. Judge Brown listened to the request, then asked Hayes to respond.

"It is my statement, for this record, that the investigation at this point, has not revealed anything exculpatory as to Mr. Moore, in this present case, and furthermore, it is my statement that if, in fact, the investigation reveals—I don't know exactly how far or what the FBI is doing. However, I assume that any information that I receive, that would appear to be exculpatory, as to Mr. Moore in this case, would obviously be revealed to defense counsel."

Robb had mixed feelings about leaving the case, but with only one motion pending—the motion for a new trial—he believed Karen Jackson qualified to handle it. As it turned out, there was little Jackson could do for Laurie. Within days of Robb's withdrawal, the motion was denied. Although it was no longer his case, Robb still felt the blow.

"It's a terrible, terrible case of the justice system gone crazy," he said. "Three judges disqualifying themselves, four jurors saying he was innocent, a prosecutor with a vindictive vendetta-type attitude. I'm just not used to this in America."

Chapter 21   An Eyewitness Account

. . . . March 9, 1988, 1:41 PM

At Prosecutor Hayes' direction, LaBarge contacted Debbie and set up an interview with her. She refused to come to the police station so at her suggestion, LaBarge met her in a conference room at the Gaylord Holiday Inn. The interview was taped, and the tape later transcribed.

Detective LaBarge: Could you basically tell me in your own words what you saw, what you observed, when it was, where it was, and then, from then on, I will ask you some questions on it, and who you were with, to the best of your ability.

Debbie: It all started on the fifth.

LaBarge: Ok. Can you tell me how it—ah—how it started that day, or what your day's events were?

Debbie: Well, Mark picked me up. Mark Canter. We kind of rode around, and stopped at a few places for drugs and to make drug deals. We had coke and, um, there was, well they call them 'shrooms; they're mushrooms. Mark had some of those anyway, and he had some pot and stuff. Anyway, the biggest thing in there was the coke.

LaBarge: Ok. What happened then?

Debbie: Well, we just kind of drove around, made a couple of connections. Killed some time. Mark got a hold of some people and wanted to know where he could find, um, Jerry.

LaBarge: Jerry?

Debbie: Tobias. This was later on in the afternoon. I'm not real, I don't have all the times exact, but this is later. We made some phone calls, I don't know, he got a hold of, tried to get a hold of Laurie. Laurie was out at, he was out at the shooting range. The Sportsmen's Club.

LaBarge: Ok. Laurie is who?

Debbie: Laurie Moore. Anyway, they talked for a few minutes, and we killed some more time. We sold some more coke. Mark got high, he shot up; he was also drinking at the same time.

LaBarge: Then what happened?

Debbie: Anyways so it's getting later now. Um. We, ah, I don't know this is later, it's quite a bit later. You know, we did some things, and Mark got high and stuff like that, and was drinking. We went to the butcher shop.

LaBarge: What butcher shop was that?

Debbie: Walt's Butcher Shop. Anyways, so we went there, there wasn't anybody there. So we kind of drove around a little bit, and we picked up Terry.

LaBarge: Terry who? Picked up Terry, what's his last name?

Debbie: Moore. He went with us the first time we went there. There wasn't anybody there. The second time when we returned, Jerry's truck was there in the back. Laurie let us in the back door. I seen, at the time when we first entered in there, there was Laurie, Terry, Mark, myself, and then John came out from behind.

LaBarge: Do you know John's last name?

Debbie: No.

LaBarge: Then what happened?

Debbie: Laurie started getting really upset. He'd asked Jerry where the stuff was, and Jerry said he didn't have it. And then Laurie had made a statement, "You're into me for $4,000." And then Terry hit Jerry alongside the back of the head.

LaBarge: So Terry hit him?

Debbie: Yeah.

LaBarge: Then what happened?

Debbie: Laurie hit him a couple of times, and he picked up something, and I turned to Mark at that point and said I wanted to leave, I wanted to get out of there. Mark just held on to me and said, 'Shut up, don't say a word and don't move.' And when I turned back around, he had thrown this thing across the room. Jerry was laying on the floor. He tried to fight back, but they just kept hitting him.

Debbie said another man, Doug Brinkman, arrived at some point in the melee. Shortly after he got there, she noticed a car driving slowly by the back of the butcher shop, its headlights shining in through the shop window. When she looked closer, she said she could tell it was a police car, but instead of stopping, it just drove past.

It took all five men to lift Jerry into the back of his pickup truck and then Terry Moore drove it away from Walt's and parked it behind the fire station where police eventually found it. Doug and John left separately, and Debbie, Mark, and Terry left together in Mark's car. The three of them went to Mark's house, and then Terry went home.

LaBarge: Did you ever have any conversation after that with anybody regarding this?

Debbie: No, I was just warned. "Don't ever, ever say anything about this because if you do, you're dead."

LaBarge: Why have you not come forward with this information to the police before this?

Debbie: Because they threatened me. I would never have come forward at all if they would've left me alone. But I got a phone call and my name got dropped, and I had no choice but either to go to the police, or run for the rest of my life.

After the interview, LaBarge arranged for Debbie to take a polygraph test. She passed. There were some irregularities, but none significant enough to convince the examiner she was lying.

LaBarge tried to wrap his mind around all the information this woman, who seemed to come out of nowhere, had just given him. Could there really be four murderers walking around in their midst? Right here in Gaylord, and on the loose? LaBarge considered the possibility, and eventually came up with an idea that might help him find out. Debbie Parmentier's eyewitness account, and her polygraph test results, might be enough probable cause to ask a judge for a wiretap.

LaBarge called Hayes and they decided Debbie would have to be questioned again. This time, the prosecutor wanted to sit in on the interview, and ask her some questions himself. He needed to get a sense of who she was, what she had really seen, and whether or not she'd make a good witness. A second interview was scheduled and Hayes, Detective LaBarge, and another State Police detective, Carl Goeman, met with Debbie.

Hayes: Let me ask you initially, how long have you known Terry Moore?

Debbie: Maybe a year. Year and a half. Acquaintance. I met him and it was about that, and then . . . It really wasn't like a friend or anything like that.

Hayes: If this happened in December of '86, did you know Terry Moore prior to that? December of '86?

Debbie: What the deal is that we had . . . it was only for really a relatively short time, that we . . . that I'd really met him and knew who he was and what we were doing. It was just . . . we really got involved in a lot of . . . things.

Hayes: Now when you say dealings, do you mean, ah, drug dealings?

Debbie: Drugs. Guns. Yeah.

Hayes: He was involved in guns, too?

Debbie: Yeah.

Hayes: Who was he with, how did you meet him?

Debbie: There was a Jeff. A Dave. Shawn. Umm. I don't remember.

At this point in the interview, Debbie launched into a long ramble, similar to her first communication with Blair Robb. Debbie said she'd met Terry Moore and Mark Canter at a local ski resort. It was in October of 1986 and she spent the day skiing at Sylvan Resort. During the afternoon or early evening, she went into the lodge to take off her gear and relax. A rock band was playing in the bar, so she went in to listen and Terry Moore and Mark Canter were there. She struck up a conversation with them, and that's how the three met.

Hayes and LaBarge had lived in Michigan for much of their lives. They had to have known there was never enough snow to open the area ski resorts until late November at the earliest. Usually, there wasn't enough snow until mid-December, and some years not until Christmas. Still, the men must have believed that Debbie's story was at least partially true because after interviewing her himself, Hayes said he was in favor of LaBarge's wiretap idea. Together, Hayes and LaBarge petitioned a judge for a tap on Terry Moore's home telephone. It was granted.

Chapter 22   Terry Moore, Meet Debbie Parmentier

. . . . March 17, 1988, 1:43 PM

This is from the transcript of the second taped conversation between Debbie Parmentier and Terry Moore. In the first conversation, Debbie said she wanted to meet with Terry. He said she didn't know who she was but would meet with her and asked her to call back later.

Terry Moore: Hello?

Debbie Parmentier: Terry? This is Deb.

Terry: Hi.

Debbie: Um. I'm not really sure if I want to meet, um, I'm really scared.

Terry: Why?

Debbie: I don't know if I can trust ya.

Terry: Trust me for what, Deb? I mean, you know, I was kind of illusioned [sic]. I mean, what do you want from me?

Debbie: Well, I just kind of wanted to talk to you about what's been happening and stuff. I've been getting, um, threats and I've—.

Terry: You have?

Debbie: Yeah . . . Do you know why I've been getting these threats?

Terry: Um, no. . . . why do you want to talk to me?

Debbie: I just, I don't, I don't want to really talk with somebody else there because I don't want anybody to know. I'm in a lot of trouble, and I could go to jail. I don't want to go to jail. You know what happened. . .

Terry: No, I don't really know what happened.

Debbie: But see, I just want to talk to you. I want to be left alone. What I know I'll keep with me forever. I just wanted to talk to you, and I guess I want assurance from you.

Terry: Assurance of what?

Debbie: I just don't like the threats I'm getting.

Terry: You surely don't think they're coming from me, do you?

Debbie: Yeah.

Terry: You do?

Debbie: Yeah.

Terry: Oh, come on!

Debbie: I'm serious.

Terry: I don't even know you! I, I honestly can't, unless you can relate to me why I should know you. I don't have any idea who you are. In all honesty.

Debbie: I can't do that over the phone.

Terry: Huh. Can you give me one—have I seen you before?

Debbie: Ah—yes.

Terry: Could you tell me where?

Debbie: At the Butcher Shop . . . I was there the night that Jerry Tobias was murdered.

Terry: Well I sure as hell wasn't there!

Debbie: Ok.

Terry: I mean, you may know a name, could it have been some-one else using my name?

Debbie: No.

Terry: Have you met me before that?

Debbie: Yeah.

Terry: Do you know what I look like?

Debbie: Yeah.

Terry: This is awful crazy.

Before ending their conversation, Debbie and Terry made a plan to meet later that day in the parking lot of the Big Boy restaurant in Grayling. The police staked out the restaurant and Debbie wore a wire. Everyone took their places as planned, and Debbie arrived at 4:30, along with six state troopers. They waited for more than an hour, but Terry never showed. LaBarge added a report of the event in the case file:

> "It is believed that the suspect was the second individual involved in a homicide that occurred in the City of Gaylord in December 1986. Object of this surveillance was to protect the witness Debra Parmentier from any danger by meeting with the suspect. During this meeting the witness supposedly is going to attempt to get the suspect to at least partially admit, if not more, having participated in some way in the murder of Jerry Tobias. Several TX's (telephone calls) were made to the suspect by Parmentier . . . however, with no results."

Debbie called Terry Moore the following morning to find out why he hadn't shown up.

This is from the transcript of the third taped conversation between Debra Parmentier and Terry Moore.

Terry: Hello.

Debbie: This is Deb. What happened to you yesterday?

Terry: I gave it a lot of thought, Deb, and I, ah, made a decision that, ah, it was probably best that we didn't meet.

Debbie: Ok. Why?

Terry: Because what you're saying is absurd.

Debbie: No, it ain't.

Terry: Yes, it is. I have nothing, no knowledge of, and had nothing to do with, and you're trying to indicate I did. That's absurd.

Debbie: I don't like being threatened. I hate that. I don't like somebody telling me that they're going to kill me.

Terry: I'm not threatening you . . . and your insinuation that I had threatened you, or have been threatening you, is absurd. And I had nothing to do with that. I don't have any idea—Deb, I wouldn't know you if you walked up to my door right now . . . there's something awful weird about all this . . . it's totally off-the-wall crazy in my book.

Debbie: Well, I'll tell you what. Seeing that you won't really talk to me about it, and you're not going to help me out . . .I don't have any choice but to get help other places.

Terry: Such as?

Debbie: Such as going to the police department and telling them what I know.

Terry: That's fine, you know, as far as I'm concerned, you may as well do that. Because what you know, and what you *think* you know, are two different things.

Debbie: It's a fact. It's a plain simple fact. I don't really think we're getting anywhere on this conversation any longer. I'm not going to try anymore.

Terry: You know, when you initially contacted me, I was thinking that you had something that could help my brother's case out, because I *know* that my brother is innocent.

At that point in their conversation a loud buzzing sound, likely caused by the wiretap, cut their conversation short. If the police were expecting Terry to confess to Debbie, they had to have been sorely disappointed. Not only didn't Terry confess to anything, he said he wasn't there, knew nothing about Jerry's death, and didn't even know who Debbie was.

Chapter 23   The Others

. . . . March 31, 1988

The wiretap of Terry Moore's telephone was a bust, but police remained interested in Debbie's account of the crime in large part because she gave them names of others she said were involved. Besides Terry Moore, there was also Mark Canter, Doug Brinkman, someone named John, plus a Jeff, a Shawn, and a Dave. LaBarge decided to begin with Canter and Brinkman. They'd probably be the easiest to find since he had their last names. As it turned out, bringing them in for an interview couldn't have been any easier. They were in the Otsego County Jail on unrelated charges (drunk driving, resisting arrest, parole violation) and all LaBarge had to do was ask an officer to get them from their cells and bring them to the post.

LaBarge and Detective Carl Goeman flipped through the police files on the two men. The first to be interviewed was Douglas James Brinkman, a white male, D.O.B. 4-5-61, 5-10, 170 lbs., brown eyes, brown hair, in jail on a resisting arrest and obstructing justice charge. He had a long criminal history of mostly minor infractions, such as drug use, shoplifting, larceny, and drinking and driving.

"What is your relationship to Debra Parmentier?" LaBarge asked him.

Doug said he wouldn't really call Debbie his girlfriend, but that he had gone out with her for a few months. They'd started dating in November of 1986, but broke up in the spring of 1987. They met while working together at Beaver Creek Resort. Debbie was unpredictable and vindictive, Brinkman said, and had caused him trouble at his job. He was fired because of her accusations, and his friend and co-worker, Mark Canter, quit in protest.

"Do you know the Moores?" LaBarge asked. "What was your involvement in Jerry Tobias' death?"

Brinkman said he did know the Moore brothers and Jerry Tobias, but he said he had nothing to do with his death. All he knew about it was what he'd heard on television. If police wanted him to Doug Brinkman said he'd be willing to take a polygraph test.

LaBarge took him up on the offer and made the arrangements. An hour later, Brinkman took the test. And failed.

Next, LaBarge and Goeman interviewed Mark Canter. Canter also said he knew the Moore brothers but had never met Jerry Tobias and had nothing to do with his death. Canter had heard the same rumors everyone else in town had, that Jerry's death was part of some big drug deal, but he didn't have any specific information about whether or not that was true.

"What is your relationship with the Moores?" LaBarge asked.

Canter said that Terry Moore had worked for Mark's stepfather years ago in the oilfields, and that he knew Laurie because he was an occasional customer at Walt's Butcher Shop. He'd been to the store a few times to pick up a sandwich. Canter said he knew Doug Brinkman. He was one of his best friends. Debbie Parmentier was Doug's sometime girlfriend, and Canter said he thought she was strange. There was something not quite right about her, he explained, but you just didn't criticize your best friend's taste in women. Even if it was bad.

By the time LaBarge interviewed Brinkman and Canter, Jerry Tobias had been dead for sixteen months. When they asked the men for their alibis the nights of December 5 and 6 in 1986, neither man could be sure of what they'd been doing or with whom. Brinkman wouldn't even wager a guess and Canter said he was probably home with his girlfriend. Like Brinkman, Canter also offered to take a polygraph test to prove he was telling the truth.

LaBarge took Canter up on his offer and made the arrangements. An hour later, Canter took his test. And just like Brinkman, he failed.

Back in his cell, Canter's head was spinning. Canter knew he wasn't going to win any good citizen awards; he used drugs, often drank to excess, cussed in public. But he wasn't a murderer. The questions the police asked were strange, and their rough attitude toward him was uncalled for. He had a sense that something about the whole interview wasn't right and he wanted a record of what just happened. He asked a corrections officer for a pen and some paper, sat down on his bunk, and wrote down his thoughts. He scribbled the date, Wednesday, March 30, 1988, at the top of the paper and then wrote the words, "What Happened" as a title underneath the date.

Then, he started to write:

> "Sgt. Davis came back to cell 5 and said someone wanted to talk to me up front. Sgt. Dunkelberg and State trooper Dick Boynton were there and said they were taking me to the State Police post for some questions. I was cuffed and taken there to the State Police post. There was two detectives there waiting, Det. Goeman and LaBarge. they took me upstairs. Det. Goeman read me my rights and started asking me questions.
>
> I answered to the best of my knowledge and answered honestly. Goeman asked me if I was familiar with the Tobias case. I told him just from what I had heard on TV and read in the papers. They read me my rights again and asked me about some guns. Then Goeman said he didn't care about anything else except what I knew about the Tobias case and started asking me questions again.
>
> He asked me where I was Dec. 6, 1986. I told him I wasn't sure but I thought that I was home with my girlfriend Wendy Brock. He asked me if I knew Tobias. I

told him I have never met him. He asked me if I knew Laurie Moore. I said yes. I know him but not very well. That I had seen him in the oil field a few times and in Walt's Butcher shop a few times. He asked me if I knew Terry Moore. I said yes, that I knew Terry for about 15 years. They asked me how. I told them that he used to work for my step Dad in the oilfield on a drilling rig, Cedco, and that he was a friend of the family also that I worked for Terry for about 4 or 5 days doing insulation. They asked why I told them that. I was low on money and that he was busy enough to hire me on for a little while so I could earn some extra money for bills and basic shit.

They asked me how many times I had ever been to Walt's Butcher Shop. I told them approximately 3 or 4 times. They asked on what occasions. I told them as a customer. They said they didn't believe me. They then started accusing me of things. They said they had an eyewitness that I was there the night Tobias was killed. they said that I helped do it, that I was in the back of the Butcher shop on many occasions, that I conspired with terry and Laurie to kill him, that I was making cocaine deals at Walt's.

They asked me if I had ever been to Walt's late at night or early in the morning. I told them no. They said they didn't believe me, that I was lying and they knew it because they had an eyewitness. I told them they were wrong or someone had lied to them because it was not possible for them to see me because I wasn't there and that they had false info. I then said, 'Hey I'll clear this all up for you right now,' that I would take a lie detector test and prove myself. Goeman said what if I made a call right now and you could take it right now? I said, 'Go for it, the sooner this is cleared up the better.'

They cuffed me and took me south of the post to the old skating rink on 27 South about 3 or 4 blocks south of the post. They put me in a very small room and locked me in until they were ready for the test. They took me out of the room and into another room with the polygraph machine in it. Some Mike guy started going over questions that he was going to ask me on the test. He asked me if there was any crimes I wanted to confess to, to get them off my chest or if there were any lies that I told that I wanted to talk about first. I said no. He asked me these questions without being hooked up to the machine.

This Mike guy then hooked me up to the machine and told me to answer all the questions in my mind but not to give him a verbal response so I did. He told me to close my eyes and answer the questions he asked. Then he told me to say 'no' to everything and then to say 'yes' to everything. Then the test was over and he said I was a liar and that I flunked the test.

Goeman and LaBarge come in there and started accusing me again. They asked me the same questions over and over, the ones about killing Tobias and seeing his body put in the pickup truck and said I was making cocaine deals at Walt's. They said they knew I wanted Tobias to die. That I helped plan it, that I was a liar, and this was my last chance. I told them over and over again I was not there, that I never did anything, that I never even knew Tobias. That I never met him ever before. That I didn't know what he looked like or anything.

They finally pissed me off and I told them I didn't think I should say any more without an attorney. Goeman said, 'Well that's it then. We think you're guilty; we know you are.' LaBarge agreed. I told them that I swear to God I don't know anything. LaBarge said he knows I'm guilty and that I'm a liar. They said this isn't going to go away and they have enough evidence to convict me on this.

I told them I couldn't believe this shit. That I'm innocent. God knows I'm innocent and <u>I will prove it !!</u>"

When he was finished, Mark lay down on his bunk and thought about his friendship with Terry Moore. When Mark was just a little kid, six or seven years old, Terry worked on the oil crew that his stepfather ran. In the summer, and on weekends, Mark would sometimes tag along. His stepfather would drive out to check on the rigs, and to make sure the guys were on the job and doing their work, and Mark would ride along with him. Terry was the only man on the whole crew who paid any attention to him. Mark hadn't seen Terry for years, until random bad luck brought the two together.

A few months ago, Mark had been in a car accident and was looking for part-time work to supplement his medical benefits. Terry Moore had a busy insulation business and hired him. But Mark screwed it up. He came to work hung over, or just didn't show up at all. Instead of firing him for it, Terry gave Mark some advice: Stop all the drinking and the partying, take work seriously, and if he could do that, he could build himself a good life. An adult life, a life of responsibility and accomplishment.

Those words of wisdom obviously didn't take, because Mark was sitting in jail for drunk driving and parole violation and the police thought he'd participated in a murder. If only he would have listened to Terry. Mark felt like he had no one to turn to, but Terry had always taken an interest in him, ever since he was a little boy. Maybe he'd help him again. He couldn't turn his life around until he got out of jail, and to do that he needed was bail money.

Mark got the pen and pad of paper back out, and started writing again. This time it was a letter to Terry Moore.

April 1, 1987

Terry,

Can you please post bond on me. As far as this girl calling you I have some ideas on how to find out who it really was and we need to talk about some things anyhow. I don't like talking about any thing in that booth or on the phone here. We need to talk in person. Don't worry about the money I have a few ideas to get it back to you pretty quick but I can't do any thing while I'm in here. I'm afraid to say or talk about <u>anything</u> in here because of the bugs and phone taps.

We can talk about the financial part of this when I get out. I'm sure with a couple phone calls I can find out what's going on. You can get on the other phone and listen in that way maybe we can identify some voices and get some info on these people. I have a good idea who's fucking with you. Well, hope you can get me out of here. I'm straight now and plan on staying that way and I don't know if you trust me or not, but I don't lie to you. I don't figure I have to.

Leave a message with the guard if you are going to get me out of here tonight. Will talk to you later in person I hope.

Appreciate it a lot.

Mark

The next day Terry received the letter and posted Mark Canter's bond.

Jerry Tobias, found frozen in the back of his pickup truck, December, 1986. (Defense exhibit #20A)

Jerry Tobias' Ford pickup truck after it was towed to the Gaylord city garage, December, 1986. (Courtesy Ray MacNeil)

Rear of Walt's Butcher Shop, Gaylord, the night it was searched by the Michigan State Police. (Courtesy Ray MacNeil)

Interior of Walt's Butcher Shop, Gaylord. (Courtesy Ray MacNeil)

Norman Hayes in 1988 when he was Otsego County Prosecutor. (Used by permission of the *Detroit News*)

Debra Dawn Parmentier. (Used by permission of the *Detroit News*)

Courtroom drawings of Laurie Moore's trial, held in Cheboygan County, by artist Julie Lovelace. Above: Judge Robert C. Livo listens to testimony. Below: Prosecutor Norman Hayes questions a witness; in front of the witness stand, a table contains exhibit items.

Chapter 24   Attorney Ray MacNeil

. . . . April 1, 1988

It might have been April Fool's Day, but for Gaylord attorney Ray MacNeil, the morning started out just like any other work day. He was sitting in his office, going over his appointments for the day when his secretary transferred in a phone call.

"Ray, I need a favor."

MacNeil recognized the voice: It was Patrick Murray, a judge with the district court.

"Sure, Judge," MacNeil replied, "What can I do for you?"

"I want you to take a murder case," Judge Murray said, forgoing the usual small talk. "We've got a number of people charged here, and I need a competent attorney. I don't want to assign it to just anybody."

The client was a local man named Mark Canter, Murray explained. He was one of four men just arrested for conspiracy and murder. The victim was Jerry Tobias.

MacNeil knew the case. Everyone in Gaylord knew the case. But MacNeil didn't understand the request at all. Wasn't Laurie Moore already in prison for killing Tobias? What made the judge's request even stranger was that MacNeil was a general practice lawyer. Divorce, custody, your everyday misdemeanors, those were his specialties. He hadn't tried a felony case in a dozen years or more, let alone a murder case, making him a highly unlikely candidate for a referral from a judge to represent someone charged with murder. That was when MacNeil remembered it was April Fool's Day; if it hadn't have been for the serious tone in Judge Murray's voice, MacNeil might have thought the judge was pulling his leg.

Still, when a judge asked an attorney for a favor, it was ill-advised to say no, unless you had a pretty good reason. MacNeil didn't. Plus, chances were good there'd be a plea bargain and his newest client wouldn't even have to go to court. That's how felony cases were often settled. With that in mind, Ray agreed. He'd take the court appointment and represent Mark Canter.

Over in Grayling at the State Police crime lab, there was some news about the threatening letter sent to Dean Robb. The lab tech found fingerprints on the letter, compared them to the fingerprints on file for Laurie Moore and the four new men just arrested for Jerry Tobias' murder: Terry Moore, Mark Canter, Doug Brinkman, and Don Heistand, who police believed was the man Debbie knew as "John."

No match.

An out-of-state lab hired by the State Police to conduct advanced chemical analysis on a piece of Jerry Tobias' clothing also had news. A senior research microscopist for McCrone Associates, Inc., in Illinois tested the soles of Jerry Tobias' socks, the ones he'd been wearing the night he died.

"The socks were examined using a stereoscopic microscope. Suspected microtraces were recovered during this examination. Sticky tape was also applied to the soles of the socks in order to recover any additional microtraces. No fish scales, deer hair, fat, or brown rubber sweeping compound fibers were recovered. None of the microtraces recovered from the socks could be associated with the material contained in the debris identified as the sweepings from the concrete floor of the butcher shop."

That was a complicated way of saying that nothing from the soles of Jerry Tobias' socks matched anything collected by police from the floor of Walt's Butcher Shop. McCrone Associates also performed tests on the other items of physical evidence—the chicken skewer, the apron, the floor sweepings, the barbeque seasoning, etc.—but not even a stereoscopic microscope could tie a single atom to the five men police had in custody.

And yet, by the end of the first week in April, all four of the men Debbie named—Terry Moore, Mark Canter, Doug Brinkman, and Don Heistand—were arrested for Conspiracy and First-Degree Murder, arraigned, plead innocent, and were being held in the Otsego County Jail.

At the group arraignment, Mark Canter blurted to Judge Murray, "I don't know what's going on here! This is ridiculous!"

Canter was admonished by the judge for his outburst, but his emphatic words spoke for all of them. The men felt blindsided, and each one scrambled to remember what they'd been doing on December 5 and 6, 1986. The dates were a year and a half old. Who could remember what they were doing, or whom they'd been doing it with, that long ago?

The new arrests were the result of solid investigative work, according to the police. Even though tests run by their own crime lab revealed that none of the men's hair matched what was found on the floor at Walt's, and none of their fingerprints or palm prints matched those found on Tobias' truck, that did not sway LaBarge, Hayes, or the rest of the task force. They had Debbie's eyewitness account plus other information.

A police informant characterized Mark Canter as "hot-headed, crazy, always drunk or high, a real weirdo." The woman who had been Canter's girlfriend in 1986, Wendy Brock, was now his ex-girlfriend. She told police she couldn't remember if she'd been with Mark that night or not. What she could remember was that Mark's lip was swollen and Doug's knuckles were scraped sometime during the week of the murder. When she asked them what happened, Mark told her they'd been in a fight. Wendy Brock told police that the last time she'd heard from Mark, he'd been in jail and trying to remember where he'd been the night Jerry Tobias died. She recalled their telephone conversation with disdain.

"He kept on sayin', 'Don't you care? This is my life!'" Wendy told police. "And I says, 'You messed up my life too much. I can't help you no more.'"

Wendy Brock's status as a jilted woman who might have a motive to try to get her former boyfriend in trouble didn't worry police much, since they had Debbie Parmentier. A friend of Debbie's even corroborated her story. Cindy Gleason told police that Debbie's reports of being threatened by Tobias' killers were true. When Debbie's marriage fell apart, Debbie moved in with Cindy. And while Cindy admitted she didn't know whether or not Debbie had actually witnessed the murder, Mark Canter and Doug Brinkman were definitely after her. She'd seen them try to run Debbie off the road.

To police, Doug Brinkman and Mark Canter had bad tempers, were involved in a fistfight around the time of the murder, used drugs, had no an alibis, and had threatened an eyewitness. Debbie Parmentier might have been strange, but police believed she was also an innocent woman whose only crime was being brave enough to come forward. Hayes and LaBarge decided that was enough evidence to charge the men with murder.

So what if there wasn't any physical evidence, or that none of the men had confessed and continued to claim they were innocent. Everyone who's in jail says they're innocent, and perhaps the physical evidence was out there. If police kept looking, they were confident they'd find it.

Chapter 25   Sketchy, Vague, and Iffy

. . . . April 18, 1988

With four new men in jail, the police worked to nail down the details of Debbie's story. She'd been sketchy on times and places. Vague about what happened in the hours before Tobias died. And iffy on what actually happened inside Walt's. The State Police's plan was to interview people who knew her, especially those who might have useful information about Mark, Doug, Terry, and Don.

An obvious first step would have been to interview Debbie's husband. Although Doug Brinkman admitted Debbie had been his sometime girlfriend, the Parmentiers' divorce wasn't final and so Debbie still had a husband, Leonard. As her spouse, he couldn't testify against her, but he could be interviewed. This idea was floated, but ultimately discarded. Since Debbie and Leonard were estranged, and had been since a month before the murder, police decided to check for other boyfriends besides or in addition to Brinkman. The plan that seemed straightforward enough but turned out to be a little more complicated than expected.

Some digging by police revealed that from November of 1986 until April of 1988, Debbie had lived with her husband Leonard and then left him and moved in with Cindy Gleason and her husband, Mike. Debbie spent the Thanksgiving holiday with a man she'd just met at a bar, Steve Wise. This was during the time she was also dating Doug Brinkman. In early 1987, probably February or March, Debbie moved out of the Gleasons' house and went to live with Doug, sometimes sleeping with him in his car.

By spring, Debbie, Doug Brinkman, and Mark Canter were working together at the Beaver Creek Resort. Her relationship with Doug ended abruptly when he discovered her in bed with their boss, the resort's manager, Roger Becker. Becker was married, but Debbie immediately moved in with him, an event that ended his marriage, and the pair lived together in a cabin at the resort he received rent-free as part of his compensation package. But something happened between Debbie and Becker because police learned that in mid-1987, Debbie moved again. This time she'd taken up residence in a motel room at the Gaylord Best Western with another man, Jim Sage. Sage worked at the hotel, and like

Becker he too received room and board as part of his pay. Debbie lived with Sage for approximately six weeks, and then moved back in with Becker at the Beaver Creek Resort.

When State Police detectives finally made it to the end of the soap opera that was Debbie's love life, Detective Carl Goeman interviewed Roger Becker. Becker explained that he met Debbie when she came to work for him at the resort as a part-time housekeeper. She was dating another employee, Doug Brinkman, and when Debbie and Doug broke up, Debbie told Becker that he'd been stealing. Becker fired Doug Brinkman, Mark Canter quit soon after, and Debbie moved in with Becker, all over the space of a couple days.

Goeman listened to the romantic twists and turns of Debbie's life, and then asked whether or not Debbie ever told him anything about the Jerry Tobias case. Becker said Debbie not only told him she'd witnessed a murder, she talked about it non-stop.

But was her story true? Goeman asked.

Becker said he didn't know what to believe, but Debbie kept a diary and often wrote in it about the murder.

Where was that diary now? Goeman asked.

Becker hemmed and hawed, tried to stall or change the subject, but Goeman persisted and Becker finally gave him an answer. Debbie's diary was in a bank safe deposit box somewhere in Florida.

As if they didn't already have enough tangents to follow, the last week in April police were faced with another complication. While working to arrange interviews with all of Debbie's boyfriends, trying to make sense of the inconsistencies in her story, looking for any physical evidence, and tracking down her diary, something new captured the police's attention.

Debbie's friend, Cindy Gleason, called the State Police dispatch in a panic. She'd just received a letter threatening her life. It was unsigned but whoever sent it obviously knew where to find her because the letter was addressed to Cindy, care of the Best Western Hotel, where she worked as a hostess. Typed in all lowercase letters (spelling mistakes included), it read:

> keep your mouth shut or your dead

The next day, a similar letter arrived at Cindy Gleason's house, but was addressed to Debbie. Also typed in lowercase letters it read:

> you have been seen we will find you your dead

Laurie Moore received telephone threats on his life right before he went on trial. Dean Robb received a death threat letter when he was working on Laurie's appeal. Now Cindy and Debbie had received death threat letters, too. The common denominator in all four was Jerry Tobias' death, but police had no idea how the threats were related, or who was behind them.

Four of the five men police believed were responsible for Tobias' death were locked up; Laurie was in prison; three of the others were in the Otsego County Jail. There was no way the letters could have been sent from behind bars without being detected. Only Terry Moore had made bail—was he behind the death threats? And if so, why would he threaten the life of his own brother?

For the police, the prosecutor and the defense attorneys, the case was growing more confusing by the day.

May 1, 1988

The relationship between Becker and Debbie was soon off again. At least, police thought the couple must be on the outs since it looked like Becker had left town. Alone. A missing person's report had just been filed by Becker's estranged wife. The Beckers were going through a divorce and hadn't lived together for more than a year, since Roger Becker had taken up with Debbie. When he didn't show up for work, someone at the Beaver Creek Resort called his wife. She went to his cabin to look for him, but all she found was a short handwritten note:

> I'm sorry I have to leave. I hope you can understand and
> will see that my boys get my deer head. Deb will come and
> get her furniture. This is the hardest thing I've ever did and
> I'm sorry. I know that saying sorry doesn't help.
> Roger

On the table next to the note was Becker's unopened mail. In the small stack was a letter that explained what he meant about Debbie coming to get her furniture. The letter was from a local discount retailer, Tri-State Furniture. Inside the envelope was an overdue notice. Becker was three months behind on payments for a house full of furniture he bought for Debbie. In December Becker spent $2,400 on a sofa, a bedroom set, a loveseat, and a dining room table and chairs. He'd only made the January payment.

The new furniture was still right there in Becker's old cabin, but there was no sign of Debbie.

Chapter 26   Irony Piled on Irony

. . . . Tuesday, May 3, 1988

While police continued to investigate what they now believed was a five-man conspiracy to kill Jerry Tobias over a botched cocaine deal, Laurie was in court and about to be sentenced for Voluntary Manslaughter as the sole killer of the same man. No one in the prosecutor's office, the police post, or the court seemed to find this physically, morally, or even legally impossible.

After quieting the packed courtroom, Judge Brown leveled his gaze on Laurie. There was no mandatory sentencing rule in Michigan for Voluntary Manslaughter, so the judge had some latitude. He could sentence Laurie to as little as two years, making him eligible for parole in half that time, or he could sentence him to a term as long as seven to fifteen years.

"This was a most heinous crime," Judge Brown said, his voice the only sound in the room. "Although conviction was for manslaughter, death resulted from a particularly brutal beating. Punishment and community protection require a greater period of incarceration."

As the judge spoke, Laurie grasped Janet's hand but said nothing.

Then Judge Brown gave him the maximum sentence the state allowed for Voluntary Manslaughter—seven to fifteen years in prison. Laurie would be transferred immediately from the jail in the basement of the courthouse to Southern Michigan Prison in Jackson. There he'd be evaluated and then assigned a permanent location to serve out his sentence.

Convicted defendants have the option of addressing the court if they want to. Face stricken, skin pale against the gray of his sport jacket, Laurie let go of Janet's hand, took a moment to compose himself, and spoke.

"I didn't kill Jerry Tobias and I don't know who did," he said, his voice shaky but clear. "I did not beat a person to death, especially a friend I've known for years, for no reason. I hope my appeal will be heard and I will be vindicated. I've only been in one fight my whole life. I'm not a violent person."

PART 2

. . . . The Trials

Chapter 27 Positive

. . . . May 5, 1988

During Laurie's trial, Dean Robb had continually labeled the case one of "inference piled on inference." Court-watchers knew it had become one of irony piled on irony: A butcher being tried for murder with a package of meat as a key piece of evidence yet never fingerprinted; a tiny, flimsy chicken skewer identified as the alleged murder weapon of a healthy 31-year-old man; a prosecutor who characterized the crime as a cocaine deal gone bad, but a pathologist who didn't test the dead man's blood for cocaine; a trial that included more than 150 pieces of physical evidence, not one of which tied the defendant to the murder scene or the victim.

Those details paled in comparison to this one: On the exact same day, at the exact same time, in the exact same courthouse, Laurie Moore was sentenced in one courtroom by one judge as the sole killer of Jerry Tobias, while downstairs in the same courthouse, in another courtroom, in front of another judge, a preliminary examination was underway to charge Terry Moore, Mark Canter, Doug Brinkman, and Don Heistand with conspiracy and murder for the same crime.

After Laurie was led away, a reporter asked Hayes if it was legal. Weren't the new murder charges a conflict of interest, a miscarriage of justice, double jeopardy, something?

Prosecutor Hayes waved away the reporter's suggestion.

"These charges *in no way* affect the prior prosecution of Laurie Moore," he said and hurried away. His time was precious—he needed to be two places at once.

The four new arrests actually did impact Laurie Moore in one important way—they kept the police investigation open and active. Two days after Laurie was sentenced, his new attorney received some vindicating news from the Michigan State Police's crime lab. A second sample of Jerry's blood taken during the autopsy had been located by the Michigan State Police. And it tested positive for cocaine.

But with Laurie out of the local jail and lodged in Jackson prison, it was too little, too late. The test hadn't been run for Laurie's benefit, anyway. On the State Police's laboratory worksheet, there was a space to record "Suspect(s) Name." That line read, "Mark Canter, Edwin (Terry) Moore III, Douglas Brinkman, and Donald Leroy Heistand."

Detective LaBarge ordered the test and delivered the blood sample. A handwritten notation on the lab worksheet read:

> Received S/u 91 from D/Sgt Fred LaBarge (hand carried) on 4/13/88 at 11:00 AM CI #1 T—Approx. 6 ml blood.

U-91 was shorthand for "Unit-91," the name for the medical kit used to collect and store a blood sample. The kit included an insulator, a cardboard holder, and a glass tube. The resulting lab report stated Jerry's blood tested positive for "a moderate amount of cocaine" as well as "metabolites of cocaine."

During Laurie's trial, Dr. Newhouse testified that cocaine leached out of the blood quickly. That was why, she said, even if Jerry Tobias' blood was tested for cocaine, it was likely none would have been found. It was Newhouse's belief that the drug would have been out of his system by the time of the autopsy. The sample LaBarge gave to the lab was seventeen months old, but still tested positive—not for a trace amount, but for a much higher concentration.

It was a bittersweet time for Dean Robb's trial strategy to gain traction. Laurie was convicted, sentenced, and in prison, and Robb was off the case. There was still the appeal, and the first question for Laurie's new attorney was where the blood sample had come from. In her testimony at Laurie's trial, Dr. Newhouse said that the blood and urine samples taken from Jerry's body during the autopsy had been destroyed. She admitted she neglected to request the special "chain of custody" handling used in a homicide investigation, so by law the commercial lab she hired was free to destroy the samples a week after testing.

Newhouse's autopsy report was in the case file Robb passed on to Karen Jackson, and she read it over several times looking for clarification. What she found was a notation reporting that "two containers of heart blood" had been collected by Dr. Newhouse during the autopsy. Only one of those containers was sent to the commercial lab. Because Detective LaBarge delivered the second sample himself, Jackson surmised the other sample had gone to the Michigan State Police's crime lab. But why had the police waited so long to test it? And when they finally did, why hadn't the test results been more exact?

A "moderate" amount of cocaine was not a scientific analysis, but more of a guesstimate. If Newhouse was right and cocaine leached out of the blood quickly, and if there was still enough in the sample to register as "moderate," how much cocaine had been in Jerry Tobias' blood when he died? Enough to kill him?

Jackson began to wonder whether Dean Robb was right. Maybe Jerry Tobias wasn't murdered, but had died from a drug overdose. Unless she could get access to the remaining blood sample to conduct another test, she might never know. If that were the case, neither would Laurie.

It had been exactly a year and a half since Jerry Tobias died. In that time, Laurie Moore had faced three different charges (Open Murder, Second-Degree Murder, Voluntary Manslaughter), five different judges (three of which had recused themselves for personal reasons), one change of venue, a pathologist deemed incompetent, witnesses who admitted to drug use and drug dealing, four jurors who wanted to recant their verdict, an attorney who withdrew after receiving a death threat, a secret eyewitness, and four new suspects about to be prosecuted for the very same crime.

Four jurors who wanted to recant their verdict were enough to make the case extraordinary. Tack on all the other shenanigans, mistakes, and mysteries, and that should have been more than enough extenuating circumstances for one small town murder investigation. It should have been, but she was soon to find out it wasn't.

Chapter 28   Welcome to Kinross

. . . . Thursday, May 26, 1988

From the Otsego County Jail, Laurie was taken to the Michigan State Department of Correction Reception and Guidance Center in Jackson to be evaluated. He'd never been in prison before, and according to the inmate social worker who reviewed his file, he showed no signs of predatory behavior that qualified him for a high security facility.

The intake center that conducted the evaluation was located inside the Southern Michigan Correctional Facility in Jackson. The prison was built in 1839, and by the 1840s, it was the largest walled prison in the world. The place most people just referred to as "Jackson" was a maximum security facility, and so once Laurie was evaluated, he was transferred to the prison that would be his home for the next several years. On an uncharacteristically chilly spring afternoon, Laurie joined 1,300 other male inmates at the Kinross Correctional Facility in Michigan's Upper Peninsula, 179 of whom were serving life sentences. Barring any behavior problems, Laurie would be eligible for parole after five years, or sometime in 1993.

Prisoners not involved in active court cases are allowed weekly phone calls with their attorneys, so shortly after his arrival, Laurie learned about the second blood test. Even in his new and stark surroundings, he tried to feel some optimism. The appeal of his conviction would be filed soon, Jackson told him, and it had teeth.

Chapter 29   Don Heistand

. . . . May 26, 1988

The four new men arrested all said they felt confused and blindsided, but none more than Don Heistand. Heistand was new to Gaylord, having moved to town in June 1986 with his girl-friend, Lisa. They both soon found jobs—he as a truck driver and she as an assistant in a law firm. They were planning a late October wedding when Lisa got pregnant with twins. The pregnancy was a difficult one and the nausea was so severe she had to quit working. Without her income the couple was worried about money, and an attorney at the firm suggested Don get a second job. That attorney was Janet Allen and on her suggestion, Laurie Moore interviewed Don for a seasonal part-time job at Walt's.

"Laurie liked Don and hired him on the spot to start work one week after our wedding, two to three nights a week," Lisa said. "(He) was a nice-looking man . . . with a great sense of humor. Don enjoyed working with Laurie."

Although robust looking at 6'4" with a blonde crew cut and a weightlifter's physique, Don was also diabetic and had allergies. One of those allergies turned out to be to deer hair and his symptoms were so severe he lasted only two weeks at Walt's. He quit several days before Jerry Tobias died. When the Heistands couldn't make ends meet in Gaylord, they moved in with Lisa's parents in southern Michigan. When Don was arrested on April 6, 1988, his only intersection with the Tobias investigation was as a brief part-time meat-cutter at Walt's. The Heistands were the parents of twin boys and had recovered enough financially to rent a house in New Hudson, Michigan, but had no extra money for an attorney. The court appointed them one, Jack Felton, who shared an office with Ray MacNeil, Mark Canter's court-appointed attorney.

Like MacNeil, Felton was also a general practice lawyer and viewed court appointments as his civic duty. His fees were reimbursed by the county at an agreed upon hourly rate usually significantly less than what attorneys charged their paying clients. Still, being part of the rotation provided steady work of clients arrested for drunk driving, drug possession, fraud, or occasionally, assault. When he was assigned Heistand, Felton had been practicing for eight years but had never represented anyone accused of murder. Heistand was his first and, from the very beginning, Felton believed his client was innocent.

"I had no doubt that Mr. Heistand was innocent of the charges against him," Felton would say later. "He was pretty adamant in his denial. I never got any information, whatsoever, during the course of representation, that would suggest to me that the denial was anything but sincere."

Besides gut instinct, there was also evidence of Heistand's innocence. In the police report supplied to Felton by the prosecutor's office, Debbie was listed as the new eyewitness who identified Don Heistand as "John," no last name. She said he was between 5'9" and 6', with an average build, long brown hair, and brown eyes. Felton had met his newest client at the Otsego County Jail and that did not describe him at all. Heistand was a giant of a man, 6'4" and muscular, with striking blue eyes and blonde hair worn military-short. Plus, Heistand told Felton he had an alibi. At the time of the supposed murder, he'd been at home working on his car, getting it ready for his and Lisa's move back downstate, and then in bed sleeping.

Felton's caseload meant he didn't have time to knock on doors and find witnesses who could corroborate that, and Heistand couldn't do it himself because he was in jail. Felton asked for, and received, permission to hire a private investigator the court would pay for. A fellow attorney recommended Charles Rettstadt, of Research North, and Felton called him to discuss the assignment.

Rettstadt said he'd heard of the new arrests and even knew the man in charge, Detective John Hardy. Felton asked Rettstadt if that would prejudice him against Heistand, but Rettstadt assured him it would not. If anything, Felton thought Rettstadt's association with Hardy might be an asset to his client. Hardy was in charge of the whole region's detectives; Rettstadt's assignment was to locate witnesses who could corroborate Heistand's alibi and learn what really happened to Jerry Tobias. That had to be what the police wanted too, Felton believed, so he saw no conflict and hired him.

As the phone conversation was wrapping up, Rettstadt asked Felton if he'd heard the rumor about an eyewitness named Debbie Parmentier who could put Heistand at the murder scene. Felton said he had and discounted it.

"My theory on that?" said Felton. "Either she's telling the truth and she's got the wrong guy, or she's a complete liar."

In early June, Charles Rettstadt went house to house in the Gaylord neighborhood where Don and Lisa Heistand lived in November and December of 1986. At the time of Jerry Tobias' death, the Heistands rented a small cabin on Krys Road, a few miles south of downtown Gaylord. Another married couple, Johnnie and Linda Graham, were the Heistands' neighbors, and they still lived across the road when Rettstadt knocked on their door. Linda Graham invited him in and said she did remember seeing Don come home on Friday afternoon,

December 5, sometime between 2 and 3 PM. After dinner he spent several hours outside in the cold, working on his car. Don drove an old white Mustang plagued by a loud muffler and it took him a long time to fix it. Linda Graham said she saw the porch light at the Heistand's cabin go on at about 11 PM and off at about 2 AM.

The next day, Saturday, Dec. 6, Lisa said her husband and Don Heistand cut firewood together and then Heistand helped them install a television antennae on their house. When Rettstadt asked why she remembered a random weekend a year and a half ago, she told him her husband suffered a heart attack on Sunday, Dec. 7. He survived, but because it was such a traumatic event everything leading up to it and immediately following remained a clear memory for her.

Chapter 30 That Handwriting Looks Familiar

. . . . June 16, 1988

While Charles Rettstadt tried to run down Don Heistand's alibi, the police continued to search for evidence against the four new suspects. The key remained what Debbie did or didn't see the night Jerry died. In their effort to figure that out, they interviewed some people a second and even a third time. Some of those who had been easy to find for their first interviews had disappeared by time police wanted to talk to them again. One of those was Roger Becker, Debbie's on-again, off-again boyfriend. He'd disappeared at the end of April or the beginning of May, and after more than a month of looking for him, police had a lead on his whereabouts.

The local car dealership that sold Becker a pickup truck and financed it was receiving regular payments by mail. Becker had been making the payments with money orders and the envelopes he used were all postmarked in Rifle, Colorado. The money orders themselves contained a street address and Detective LaBarge believed that with a little effort, the police in Colorado could probably track Becker down. In the meantime, he added copies of the money orders, as well as the envelopes they were mailed in, to the investigation's case file.

By law, defense attorneys are entitled to copies of any evidence police uncovered related to the charges against their clients. So Ray MacNeil (Mark Canter), Jack Felton (Don Heistand), Michael Hackett (Terry Moore) and James Deamud (Doug Brinkman) all received batches of new police reports in their office mail every few days. The volume was difficult to keep up with but one of them, Ray MacNeil, developed a system to deal with it all.

At the end of every workday he'd go through his mail and if there was anything new on the Tobias investigation, that took priority over everything else. Like Hackett and Felton, MacNeil had many other clients, but the inconsistencies in the Jerry Tobias case hooked him, and he spent an inordinate amount of time on it. All his reading and thinking was leading him to feel the same way about Mark Canter that Robb felt about Laurie Moore and, that Felton did about Don Heistand. His client was actually innocent.

It was the end of June before copies of Roger Becker's money orders were in his mail. But MacNeil returned to his office from the courthouse at the end of another long day and followed his well-worn routine. He went through his mail, saw an envelope of new police reports from Detective LaBarge, and immediately read through them. Amidst another round of dead-end interviews and bureaucratic busywork were copies of Roger Becker's money orders, the envelopes they came in, as well as the goodbye letter Becker left behind at Beaver Creek Resort.

One quick look and MacNeil felt prickles of recognition creep up his spine. He examined each documents more carefully, but his reaction was the same. He recognized the handwriting. MacNeil opened his file cabinet and pawed through the rest of the police report until he found the other document he was looking for and yanked it out of the file folder. Back at his desk, he put the two documents side by side. His hunch was dead on. They matched.

The handwriting on the letter Roger Becker left behind in his cabin and the handwriting on the death threat letter sent to Dean Robb were exactly the same. MacNeil reached for his phone and dialed the prosecutor's office. It was well after 5 PM so the switchboard at the prosecutor's office was closed, but MacNeil knew the building's night number, and knew that Prosecutor Hayes usually worked late.

"Norm," he blurted, "I think I found something! Becker wrote the death threat letter!"

The defense attorney calmed himself, took a breath, and explained the handwriting match in detail. It could be the big break in the case they'd been looking for, MacNeil said, and suggested both letters be sent back to the State Police's crime lab and analyzed.

"Well," Hayes said, "you can't really tell anything from similarities in handwriting."

MacNeil couldn't believe it. The entire Tobias investigation had been devoid of physical evidence, and here was some that might help solve the case or at least reveal who threatened to kill Dean Robb. MacNeil could not understand why the prosecutor seemed uninterested in it.

"Look, I *know* I'm right about this," MacNeil insisted. "I'm absolutely certain. I'm telling you, it's the exact same writing!"

Detective LaBarge had his own desk in the prosecutor's office and was there when MacNeil called. Hayes put him on the phone and MacNeil repeated his story. He told LaBarge about the two letters, the handwriting, his hunch, and the match. To his surprise,

LaBarge's reaction was the same as the prosecutor's. It was probably nothing, LaBarge told him, and murder cases weren't usually solved by a defense attorney's hunch.

MacNeil heard the bored tone in LaBarge's voice. Handwriting analysis was a science and an art, and perhaps LaBarge and Hayes didn't think MacNeil had the ability to make an accurate comparison. What they did not know was that Ray MacNeil had been interested in handwriting analysis since college. So much so that it was a kind of hobby for him.

As a law student, the idea that you could tell something about a person from their handwriting interested him. He checked out books on the subject from the law library and enjoyed analyzing his own handwriting and that of his friends. When he opened his law office, he often bought books about the connection between a person's handwriting and their personality, and by the time he read Roger Becker's note, he'd amassed a small collection of them. What he learned was often helpful in dealing with clients. So helpful in fact, that MacNeil kept a favorite title, *Handwriting Analysis* by Karen Kristen Amend, in his desk drawer.

Hayes and LaBarge might not have confidence in his ability, but he did. Roger Becker's goodbye letter and the money orders were going to be tested by a professional, MacNeil insisted on it.

"You have to get an expert to look at these," he told LaBarge. "If you don't, I will."

A full week passed until MacNeil received another packet of police reports in the mail. Inside this batch was a report from the State Police crime lab's document unit. As MacNeil requested, a specialist compared the death threat letter sent to Dean Robb and the envelope it came in, with the letter Roger Becker left at Beaver Creek Resort.

"It is my opinion that the questioned letter and envelope, and the known writing by Roger Becker, were written by one and the same person."

The lab also found Becker's fingerprints on both documents. MacNeil felt vindicated, called Dean Robb with the news, and then took the rest of the day to map out his defense strategy for Mark Canter. With the blood test positive for cocaine and now the identity of the death threat correspondent known, he was gaining some traction for Mark. Police hadn't found Mark Canter's fingerprints on anything related to the case including the death threat letter, and they'd uncovered no evidence Mark even knew Jerry Tobias.

The only evidence against Mark was Debbie Parmentier's word. But she was linked to Roger Becker, who was now missing and suspected himself. Perhaps that would convince the police she was lying and as far as MacNeil was concerned, the break couldn't have come at a better time. The murder trials of Mark Canter, Terry Moore, Doug Brinkman, and Don Heistand were on the court docket. The first one, *People v. Terry Moore*, was scheduled to begin in just a few days.

Chapter 31   "You just can't imagine that girl."

. . . . June, 1988

But confirmation of MacNeil's hunch did nothing to slow Prosecutor Hayes' plan to use Debbie as a witness in the upcoming trials. Being Roger Becker's girlfriend wasn't a crime, and it didn't mean she had anything to do with the letter. Debbie said she witnessed a murder, she agreed to testify to it in court, and Hayes planned to put her on the stand to do just that.

MacNeil hadn't tried a murder case in more than a decade and was anxious over his lack of experience at it. He vowed to learn as much as he could about his opponents and for Mark Canter's trial, that was not only the prosecutor but Debbie Parmentier, too. She was the only link between Mark and Jerry Tobias, and as far as MacNeil was concerned, the police had not investigated her or her story very well. MacNeil would make up for that by investigating Debbie himself.

He shared his plan with Jack Felton and the two men agreed to work together in talking with people who knew her. It seemed odd that there was no record of Debbie's estranged husband being interviewed by police, so they decided to start with him. MacNeil and Felton went to Leonard Parmentier's house unannounced and knocked on his front door.

They had no idea what kind of reception they were going to get—a slammed door, insults, or even someone willing to talk. The worst that could happen was Leonard would refuse to speak with them, and they'd be no worse off than they were already. When Leonard answered his door, they introduced themselves and explained their visit. The door swung open. Leonard would be happy to talk to them about Debbie, and on tape too if they wanted. Leonard had been expecting the police to interview him and couldn't figure out why they hadn't.

MacNeil put a tape recorder on Leonard's kitchen table, turned it on, then he and Felton sat back and listened. Leonard explained he and Debbie had been married for fourteen years and their union had been volatile. They'd lived in four different states and come close to divorce at least a dozen times before he finally filed the papers. Debbie had severe psychological problems that Leonard could no longer deal with.

"I couldn't tell you the medical term," Leonard said. "Homicidal vengeance? I have no idea. You just can't imagine that girl. Have you ever seen a wild animal cornered? You get her cornered, and she attacks. I can't describe it, she's just like, totally insane."

Leonard said Debbie had received extensive psychological treatment. His experience as her husband might carry weight with a jury, but only if he were allowed to testify. For that to happen Debbie would have to waive her right to spousal privilege. Even if she did, Leonard wasn't a doctor so his medical opinion wouldn't be allowed into the court record. If the case went to trial and the defense had to impeach Debbie on the stand, they'd need a psychiatrist or a psychologist to testify she was insane. MacNeil asked Leonard if he knew what her doctors had diagnosed her with.

"They made the statement that she's totally un-helpable," Leonard said. "That she didn't want to be helped. That she uses people for her own benefit, that she has absolutely no compassionate feeling, and that she could kill you just as soon as look at you, and never have a bit of regret about it."

Leonard assured MacNeil that if he looked hard enough, he'd find reams of psychological records for Debbie at various hospitals in every place they had lived during their marriage: Alaska, New Mexico, Montana, and Michigan. There would be police reports to go along with those medical records, he explained, because Debbie had a pattern. First, she would accuse him of beating her and then she'd call the police. The police would investigate, determine she lied, confront her, and then she'd recant and end up committed to a hospital for mental problems. Sometimes she'd stay for a few days, sometimes several weeks.

MacNeil played devil's advocate and told Leonard that, just because Debbie had mental problems, it didn't necessarily mean she couldn't have witnessed Jerry Tobias' death. Leonard was the first person she told. Did he believe her?

"She wasn't in there," Leonard said. "There's no way you'll convince me she was in the back of that butcher shop that night. She may have been in there at another time, either after or before, but with all that goin' on, she would of noted every damn detail for future use for herself. She'd a drew you a diagram on that blackboard with the tiniest damn detail there were. If there would've been a cigarette butt in an ashtray, it would have been on there. She wouldn't a missed *anything*."

"But why would she lie?" MacNeil asked.

There wasn't any money in it for her, he reminded Leonard, and she wasn't in any trouble herself, so she wasn't doing it to save her own skin. It wasn't to get back at Leonard because he wasn't ever mentioned. What could possibly be her motive?

Leonard said he wasn't surprised that Debbie had wormed her way into the most sensational crime Gaylord had seen in decades. She loved attention, and this was just another one of her persecution fantasies. Plus, she had a hard time taking care of life's details, like food and rent, and was always looking for someone to do it for her. Maybe she thought if she said she was a witness, the police would take care of her.

From reading all the police reports, MacNeil knew about Debbie's frequent moves from one place to another—in with the Gleasons, then with Doug Brinkman, on to Roger Becker's cabin, and then Jim Sage's hotel room. Debbie had even asked Blair Robb how a person qualified for the witness protection program. If Leonard was right and that was her motive, her plan worked beautifully. The State Police put Debbie in protective custody in early March, and she'd been there ever since. MacNeil didn't know exactly where she was, but he knew she was living in a house or apartment, probably with a phone, cable TV, and full refrigerator, all arranged and paid for by the Michigan State Police. Leonard knew it, too.

"Right now she's got it made," Leonard said. "They're payin' her bills, they're supporting her, and everything's fine. Until she gets to the point where, 'I ain't got no freedom, I'm not happy.' And then they won't have her no more. She'll disappear from them just as quick as can be, anytime she wants to. Unless they got her under lock and key, there ain't no way in this world they're gonna have her if she doesn't want to be there, I can guarantee 'em that."

MacNeil shook his head in disbelief. How could anyone, in good conscience, send four innocent men to prison just to get temporary shelter from life? Despite Leonard's assurances, it was still hard for him to believe.

"You've got to appreciate somebody like me sitting here," Mac-Neil explained to Leonard. "I just . . . this is . . . it's the most incredible story I've ever heard."

"All I can tell you is, it's the truth," Leonard said. "And if you talk to her doctors, you'll find out it *is* the truth. I don't think any of you's know what you got there. I know Norm don't."

MacNeil thought back to Mark Canter's preliminary hearing, when Debbie testified she'd seen Jerry get beaten to death inside Walt's Butcher Shop. MacNeil was convinced she was lying and thought once he cross-examined her, he'd be able to shake her off her story. It hadn't turned out that way.

"See, we went in cold," MacNeil explained to Leonard, the "we" meaning all the defense attorneys—Felton, Hackett, Deamaud, and MacNeil himself. "We had never seen her, and we had no idea what to expect. I figured, well, like with any witness, if you're good at cross-examination, you should be able to trip up a witness. She did not trip up. She was a cool customer."

His characterization was no surprise to Leonard. His wife might only have a sixth grade education, he said, but she qualified for a Ph.D in lying.

"You won't trip her up," Leonard said, with a hint of admiration in his voice. "And this is another thing. She's an expert on drugs. She knows *exactly* what drugs to take to control her mind to do whatever she wants to do with it. And if she doesn't want to break under pressure, she'll take something before she goes on there and you won't break her. No way in hell will you break her."

The interview with Leonard lasted three hours. When the attorneys were finished, MacNeil felt exhausted, even though all he'd done was sit in a chair and ask questions. Back at his office, he found the energy to pick up the phone and share what he'd learned with Terry Moore's attorney, Mike Hackett.

MacNeil had both altruistic and selfish motives for making the phone call. If Terry was innocent like Mark, MacNeil didn't want him convicted and sent to prison. But of the four new men arrested, Terry Moore's trial was the first one scheduled. If Debbie testified and Hackett tripped her up on the stand and showed she was lying, and then the jury found Terry Moore innocent, the prosecutor might not be quite so gung ho about going after Mark Canter.

Chapter 32   Debbie's Courtroom Debut

. . . . Tuesday, June 28, 1988

Handwriting matches, positive cocaine tests, and mentally unbalanced witnesses aside, *People v. Terry Moore* got underway as scheduled. Terry did not ask for a court-appointed attorney and after seeing what happened to his brother, Laurie, Terry wanted to hire someone who knew how the prosecution's side of a trial worked. He chose Michael Hackett, a former prosecutor of Cheboygan County in private practice. MacNeil shared his research on Debbie with Hackett, and Hackett knew enough about her to call her eyewitness account into question on the stand. There were things about Debbie the jury needed to know, Hackett explained to Terry, things that would weaken the prosecution's case, and he began putting his strategy in motion even before the official start of the trial.

"Judge," Hackett said, "we're dealing with a fleck right out of the sky."

Hackett made a pre-trial motion that the jury be privy to Debbie's idiosyncrasies, tall tales, hospital commitments, and false police reports. He needed the judge's permission to have her examined by a psychiatrist.

"This case turns on the testimony of a female, emotionally distraught, drug dealer," Hackett told the court. "We're convinced we're going to win this case; there isn't a question in our mind. I'm going to suggest that this case is not strong at all, but hangs by the thread of Debra Parmentier alone, and that thread is weakening all the time."

Hackett knew all about MacNeil and Felton's kitchen table interview with Leonard. That was why he knew to ask the presiding judge, William A. Porter, for access to Debbie's medical records. It was not the first time he'd asked for them, and it wouldn't be the last. At Terry's preliminary examination, he'd asked, re-asked, and practically begged the judge for them.

Hackett argued that Terry was morally entitled to know everything about the woman accusing him of murder. Legally, Judge Porter said, the issue was not so clear cut.

For a woman with very little education, Debbie was either surprisingly astute about the law or was getting good legal advice. She refused to waive her doctor-patient privilege or her spousal privilege and she wouldn't voluntarily consent to be examined by a defense psychiatrist. Judge Porter wasn't sure her circumstance merited a court order, and the prosecutor certainly had no incentive to have her examined. At the start of Terry's trial, the most important issue for the defense was in limbo.

At the preliminary examination, Michael Hackett had been granted an "in camera" inspection of Debbie's medical records. They were subpoenaed, but only the presiding judge was allowed to read them, and he ruled that they contained nothing relevant.

But after listening to MacNeil's taped interview with Leonard, Hackett disputed that opinion. The preliminary exam was over, ancient history, and Terry had been bound over for trial. Hackett was convinced that if Terry was going to be found innocent, it would be because the jury didn't believe Debbie. The seeds of that disbelief were in her medical records, if he could just secure permission to dig them out.

"I am going to suggest that it is absolutely necessary and crucial that we be allowed to review and utilize and offer testimony about the medical, psychological, and psychiatric history of Debra Parmentier," Hackett said. "Judge, the issue ends up coming down to the question of credibility. When the history of psychiatric and psychological treatment demonstrates manipulative behavior, when they demonstrate drug abuse, we would suggest that we be allowed to impeach her and use these materials.

"They are significant to the case of Terry Moore, because Terry Moore cannot, of his own knowledge and background, say anything about Debra Parmentier because the man doesn't know her. It becomes absolutely *crucial* that we be allowed to look into this history. It is pretty apparent that we don't have the normal Suzy-Q walking down the street here."

The defense was essentially asking Judge Porter to waive Debbie's doctor-patient privilege and force her to undergo a psychiatric examination. Judge Porter eventually agreed, but the victory for the defense had a down side. Because of the court's busy calendar, such an analysis would take a month or more to arrange. Terry had been denied bail, and so he would have to remain in jail.

That was a decision too important for Hackett to make without consulting his client, and so while the court waited, Hackett walked to the defense table and conferred with Terry. The two men went back and forth for several minutes before Terry stood and addressed Judge Porter.

"Your Honor, I have missed my daughter's graduation," he said. "My daughter's running for Alpenfest Queen. I was really looking forward to being a free man to see that, and it's really upsetting that this is going to take that away from me now. I've raised my children myself, since 1978. And it's not easy, sitting down there in that jail, and watching my whole life, and my business, just continue on a downhill slide for something that I didn't have a damn thing to do with. I'm just asking the Court that please, can we get this under way as soon as possible?"

Terry didn't believe he was taking much of a risk by deciding not to wait the extra month to have Debbie examined. He didn't know Debbie and wouldn't recognize her if she was standing right in front of him, so how could she testify against him? She couldn't know anything, Terry told his attorney, because there wasn't anything *to* know. It was just an awful mistake, and the sooner the trial got underway the sooner he would be cleared.

It was already the end of June, but if the trial started immediately, Terry believed he'd be out of jail in a couple weeks. He'd still be able to take his boat out a few times and get back some of the insulation jobs going to other companies since he'd been in jail. He'd get caught up with his daughter and spend more time with his mother.

Hackett explained to Terry that if he was impatient, there was another option. Instead of sitting in jail and waiting weeks for Debbie to undergo an actual exam, Terry could opt to have Hackett hire an independent psychiatrist to review her records. It wouldn't be a full mental examination, but they could ask Judge Porter to allow the independent psychiatrist to testify about her mental instability. If that worked, Hackett could still question her story, share her instability with the jury, and it would cut out a month of jail time. Terry agreed.

"You desire then to have the matter set for trial, rather than having the Court hear a motion for an independent psychiatric evaluation?" Judge Porter asked.

"Yes, your Honor," Terry said.

And so, he rolled the dice. Terry chose to go forward with the trial immediately, instead of waiting. He was not the first man to underestimate the twisted mind of Debbie Parmentier, and though there wouldn't be much comfort in knowing it, he wouldn't be the last, either.

Chapter 33   Doug Brinkman

. . . . July 4, 1988

Doug Brinkman was the fifth man to get swept up in the Tobias investigation. Arrested in early April about the same time as Mark Canter, Terry Moore, and Don Heistand, Brinkman was no stranger to the Otsego County Jail. He had a police record stretching back to high school, mostly misdemeanor arrests and convictions resulting from his drug and alcohol abuse. Frequency of incarceration did not make jail any more palatable for Brinkman, however. The place was an especially unpleasant place to be on a national holiday.

In frustration of missing Independence Day fireworks and parties, Brinkman tossed his meager belongings around his jail cell. A can of shaving cream exploded when he threw it at the wall and the sound quickly brought a corrections officer, Debbie Davis, to his cell door. Scattered around cell #4 were a package of dominos, a Bible, and an apple. The outburst was over as quickly as it started and when Davis arrived, she saw Brinkman lying facedown on his bed, sobbing.

"I don't know what to do!" he wailed. "If I don't tell them what they want to hear, I go to prison for the rest of my life."

"Well," said Officer Davis, "if you just talk to LaBarge, everything will be all better."

"But I don't know anything about this murder!" Brinkman said. "I'm sitting here in jail for something I didn't do."

The corrections officer was unemotional, as she'd been trained to be. But his protests still would have reached some sympathetic ears. Next to him in cell #3 was Don Heistand, in cell #2 was Terry Moore, and in cell #5 was Mark Canter. They also had continually insisted they didn't know anything about Jerry's death, either.

The officer explained to Brinkman that the only person who could sign his release was Detective LaBarge. He was in charge of the investigation and the only person with the power to get him out of jail. Brinkman felt his desperation increasing. It was the Fourth of July weekend and his friends were out having fun while he was stuck in a cell for something he didn't do.

He weighed the pros and cons of talking to LaBarge. On the plus side, maybe he could get out of jail in a day or two, but on the minus side, he'd have to lie to make that happen. He didn't mind lying to police, but he didn't want to get other people in trouble. Maybe there was another way. Brinkman didn't know who killed Jerry Tobias, but he did have information about the Gaylord drug scene. Maybe he could trade what he knew for his freedom.

This train of thought went through his mind in a few short moments, while officer Davis stared at him and waited. Brinkman's holiday was probably already ruined, and the more he thought about that, the madder he got. It was satisfying to think about inter-rupting Detective LaBarge's plans and making him come to the jail instead of having fun with his family. If his holiday was going to be spent in jail, Brinkman decided, then so was Detective LaBarge's.

"I'll talk to him," Brinkman told the corrections officer, "but it has to be today."

Holiday or not, Detective LaBarge was all too happy to get Davis' phone call, and was sitting across from Doug Brinkman in an interview room at the jail within a couple hours. LaBarge listened to Brinkman's information about the Gaylord drug scene but said all he wanted from him was help with the Tobias case.

"Well, I'm sick of sitting in jail," Brinkman said. "What kind of deal can you give me?"

LaBarge kept his face blank, but inside he had to have felt excited. Finally, a confession in the complex case seemed like a distinct possibility. Maybe police would find out exactly what hap-pened to Jerry Tobias, maybe they would discover another eye-witness, maybe the men would all go to jail, and maybe he'd get credit for breaking one of the biggest murder cases in the history of Gaylord.

Across the table, Brinkman felt hopeful, too. If he told LaBarge what he wanted to hear, maybe he could get his entire criminal record expunged, and start life fresh. The detective might even sign him out of jail that very day.

"We'd have to work that out with your attorney and with the prosecutor," LaBarge said. "You might be able to get a really good deal, but I can't promise you anything."

"Well, I ain't sayin' nothing 'till I got a deal," Brinkman said, but then he did the exact opposite. He talked to Detective LaBarge for forty minutes about the investigation and about the drug problem in Gaylord. LaBarge listened but complained that the information Doug had was too general. He needed specifics, such as a make and model of one particular car. For Debbie's story to hold up in court, LaBarge needed to find out what car she and Mark Canter were driving around in during the hours before the murder. All LaBarge knew was that the car was red.

Doug Brinkman didn't know what had happened to Jerry Tobias, but he stopped saying that to LaBarge. He did know something about a red car, though. It couldn't be the car the detective was looking for because Brinkman knew Mark hadn't driven the car until *after* Jerry died. But he didn't tell LaBarge that, either. If all it took was a red car to get him out of jail, Brinkman would provide one. Since it was the wrong one, there'd be no harm done to his friend Mark.

"It was a red Chevy Nova," he told LaBarge. "It wasn't Mark's, it was a friend's, but he was borrowing it. That's the car you're looking for."

The interview wasn't taped, but Detective LaBarge took notes and filed a report:

"He stated that Mark Canter had Bill Przeradzki's red vehicle the night of the murder. He advised that Canter had borrowed the vehicle which is believed to be a red Nova from Bill."

LaBarge declined to offer Brinkman a deal, and Brinkman kept talking anyway. He told LaBarge he wasn't with Mark Canter the night Jerry Tobias died, but had happened to be driving past Walt's Butcher Shop, saw the red Nova parked there, knew Mark had borrowed it, and so he stopped in.

Inside, he saw Debbie Parmentier, Mark Canter, Laurie Moore, Terry Moore, and Don Heistand. According to Brinkman, Jerry was already on the floor, unconscious. The other men asked him to help load Jerry into the back of his truck, but he refused. They did it without him, and then someone, he wasn't sure who, drove the truck away.

"I thought they were taking him to the hospital," Brinkman said. "Now get me a deal and I'll testify."

LaBarge said Brinkman's account sounded good, but that he'd have to talk to Prosecutor Hayes before he could offer him a plea deal. Brinkman was returned to his cell and LaBarge called the prosecutor with the news. The two discussed a plea deal but didn't make a decision. They agreed they'd both sleep on it and talk again the next morning.

Back in his cell, Brinkman suffered from an immediate case of informant's remorse. He felt guilty about sacrificing one of his best friends just to get himself out of jail. It was the thought of Mark Canter in trouble that made Brinkman feel bad. He didn't care quite so much about Terry Moore or Don Heistand. How could he? He'd never even met them until they were all arrested and lodged in cells #2 through #5 in the Otsego County Jail.

Brinkman called out for Officer Davis. When she came to his cell, he told her he wanted to speak to his attorney. He wanted to tell Jim Deamud that the story he told LaBarge was a lie. Sure, he wanted to get out of jail, but he'd had some time to think about it and changed his mind. Brinkman wasn't really at Walt's Butcher Shop and had no idea what happened to Jerry Tobias.

Chapter 34   Driving with Debbie

. . . . July 4, 1988, 10 PM

Independence Day fell on a Monday, which meant a nice long weekend for all the people free enough to appreciate it, including Debbie Parmentier. She was celebrating the holiday her way—with a new boyfriend. The romance was fresh, so she was still on her best behavior, and the guy, Curt Beerens, couldn't believe his good luck. He'd never been particularly popular with women, and yet here was a petite, pretty, rough-and-tumble gal who seemed to really like him.

Beerens worked as an emergency medical technician (EMT) with Northern Emergency Services and had a part-time business as a licensed gun dealer. His EMT partner, Mark Kerry, knew Debbie, and had introduced her to Curt and, within days, he was completely smitten.

It didn't matter to Beerens that Debbie was a protected witness and that the police were always hanging around. It didn't even matter that one of the State Police detectives, Doug Wilt, had asked Beerens to keep an eye on Debbie and let him know if anything out of the ordinary happened. It was irritating when Wilt followed them to Beerens' cabin in the woods, but Beerens put up with it. He'd been lonely for a long time and was falling in love with Debbie. If an occasional police tail and spying on the object of his affection was the price for romantic happiness, he was willing to pay it.

So nothing mattered more to him over the holiday weekend than making Debbie happy. When she asked for a favor, he said yes before he even knew what it was. Debbie said her request wasn't anything out of the ordinary. She just wanted him to drive her to a few places in Gaylord, and it would take no more than an hour or so. Beerens liked spending time with Debbie, especially in a private place like the inside of his car—the police couldn't follow them there—so he was happy to oblige. Late in the evening on Independence Day, the couple got in his car and headed away from his cabin in Houghton Lake, north on I-75 toward Gaylord.

It was dark outside, hot and humid, and Beerens drove while Debbie navigated. First, they cruised to the outskirts of town, down the remote Thrumm Road, and Debbie asked him to pull over near Cindy and Mike Gleason's house. The Gleasons were Debbie's friends; she'd moved in with them when she left Leonard, and Beerens thought they might be stopping by for a visit. All the lights were off in the house though, and it looked like no one was home. Debbie sat quietly and just studied the house for a few minutes but when she spoke, what she said didn't quite compute in Beerens' brain.

"Let's shoot into their house," Debbie said. "Everyone's at the fireworks so it's the perfect time. Nobody's around so . . . no witnesses."

"*What*?" Beerens said. "What are you *talking* about? Are you serious? We can't shoot into someone's *house*!"

But Debbie was adamant. She came up with the idea herself, she told Beerens proudly, and it was a pretty good one. She knew that the Gleasons weren't home. If Beerens just fired into their living room a couple times, the police would think someone was after Cindy, and she could get into protective custody, too. If the police believed she *and* Cindy were in danger, they'd pay a lot more attention to her. Nobody would doubt her eyewitness account or make fun of her stories in court.

Beerens was shocked by Debbie's reasoning and even hoped she might be joking, but one look at her determined face, and he could tell she was serious.

"I don't care," he told her. "There is absolutely no way I'm doing that."

Debbie stared back at him and then went quiet. Beerens knew she was pouting, because she'd showed him this side of herself before, whenever she didn't get what she wanted. Beerens wanted to make her happy, but he had his limits. They could get in a lot of trouble doing something so crazy; plus, even though the place looked empty, someone could be inside and get hurt. As a gun dealer, if Beerens got caught shooting into a house, unoccupied or not, he'd lose his federal firearms license, his gun collection, and probably go to jail.

Debbie could stare at him all she wanted, but Beerens wasn't going to change his mind. It took her several minutes, but eventually Debbie seemed to let the idea go and she asked him if he'd mind driving her one more place instead. She wanted to go back toward town and take a slow cruise past Walt's Butcher Shop. It was after 9 PM and the shop was closed.

"Why there?" Beerens asked, happy to put the car in gear if it meant leaving the Gleason house behind.

Beerens knew that Debbie was a prosecution witness in the Tobias trials, but he wasn't aware of the specifics of her story or the case. All she'd told him was that she'd witnessed the murder and that it happened at the butcher shop. On the drive to downtown Gaylord, Debbie explained she'd testified in court about seeing the headlights of a police car shine through Walt's back window the night Jerry Tobias was killed. At the preliminary examination, one of the defense attorneys accused her of lying. He said Walt's didn't even have a back window and Debbie wanted drive past the butcher shop to see for herself.

In ten minutes, Beerens turned onto Illinois street and slowed the car to a crawl. He drove past the backside of the butcher shop, and Debbie looked at Walt's. No window.

Beerens said nothing, but remembered his assignment from Detective Wilt: Report anything out of the ordinary. A request to shoot at her best friend's house and checking for a window that didn't exist seemed *way* out of the ordinary to Beerens. When he and Debbie returned to his cabin, he waited until she was engrossed in a television program and then snuck into another room and called Detective Wilt. Beerens started to tell him what Debbie had been up to, but the detective cut him off.

"Don't tell me any more," Wilt said. "I've got someone else I want you to talk to."

That "someone" was his boss, John Hardy. The next day, Beerens talked to Hardy and detailed his and Debbie's strange Independence Day activities. Hardy asked him a few questions, and as they talked, it became clear that each man wanted something from the other.

Beerens knew Debbie was impulsive and strange, but he was in love with her anyway, and might even want to marry her someday. If that was ever going to happen, he had to remain a part of her chaotic life. As for Lieutenant Hardy, he was a busy man and didn't have the time or the manpower to watch Debbie every minute of the day. But he needed to know what she was up to and whether or not she was telling the truth about Jerry Tobias' murder. Hardy said he'd be willing to do what he could to keep Debbie and Beerens together if Beerens would report Debbie's activities to him.

Beerens agreed, and Hardy came up with a way for Beerens to report whatever information he collected. As an EMT, it was natural for Beerens to visit the Gaylord fire station. Hardy told him he needed to go there every couple days and call Lieutenant Hardy's office and the two would talk. No detail about Debbie was too small for Beerens to pass on; Hardy wanted to know everything.

While Hardy kept tabs on Debbie through her new boyfriend, Prosecutor Hayes focused on trial strategy. Right after the holiday weekend, Doug Brinkman's attorney informed him that Brinkman's story was fake, the product of a man desperate to get out of jail. With Brinkman out, Hayes zeroed in on Don Heistand. Heistand was not a Gaylord native; didn't hang out with the Moore brothers, Doug Brinkman, or Mark Canter; and was completely unfamiliar to the local police. He'd been arrested because Debbie identified him as the man she knew as "John," but besides a two-week stint at Walt's, Hayes could find no other connection between Heistand and the others. Perhaps that meant he'd testify against them in exchange for a reduced sentence.

Hayes called Heistand's attorney, Jack Felton, and told him if Heistand would plead guilty to Accessory After the Fact, testify against the other men charged, Hayes would dismiss the murder charge. He'd also limit Heistand's sentence to one year in the county jail and give him credit for time served.

The deal was a gift, Hayes said. If Heistand went on trial and was convicted of First-Degree Murder, he could face life in prison. But there was a catch: Hayes wanted an answer immediately. Jury selection in the Terry Moore trial was underway and when it came time for Hayes to call his prosecution witnesses, he wanted Heistand to be one of them.

Felton told Hayes he'd pass the offer onto his client, but Heistand was in jail and Felton wanted to talk to his client privately, out of the earshot of the inmates, guards, and the other defendants, all housed in cells right next to each other. Hayes agreed and arranged for Felton to meet with his client in a room at the local Holiday Inn. Felton could bring along his investigator, Charles Rettstadt, and Hayes would have two police officers escort Heistand from the jail to the hotel. When the interview was over, the officers would return Heistand to his cell and no one else would know what was discussed. Felton sent a note to Heistand that afternoon

"I have asked the prosecutor and sheriff for a conference between you, Charlie, and myself tonight at 6:00 PM. It will be outside the jail. Don't say anything to anyone. Two police will bring you to meet us."

LaBarge and two State Police troopers arrived at the hotel at the appointed time with Heistand in tow. When he arrived, Felton and Rettstadt were already in the room waiting for him.

"Initially, I laid out the offer to him, the pros and cons, and what he was charged with," Felton would recall. Felton was still convinced Heistand had nothing to do with Jerry's death, but as his attorney he was duty bound to present any plea offer made by the prosecutor. "I indicated to him that this was an extremely attractive offer, given the risk, and one that should be considered very seriously and not dismissed lightly if, in fact, he was there."

Heistand told Felton and Rettstadt that he couldn't testify to something he hadn't seen, and said he wasn't interested in a plea deal. He was innocent, and if his case went to trial, that was how he intended to plead.

"You have to know that there is a significant amount of evidence against you," Felton reminded him. He'd worked at Walt's and knew Laurie Moore. Debbie had picked him out of a photo line up as the man she knew as John. And there was the story, joke or not, about him "roughing up" someone for Laurie. Taken together, along with his large size and muscular build, the evidence would not look good to a jury especially if the other men were convicted by the time Heistand went on trial. Heistand listened to his lawyer, and then put his head in his hands and started to cry softly. He insisted again and again that he was innocent.

"I didn't even *know* anyone named Jerry Tobias!" he said.

Felton was at a loss for words and Rettstadt took over the interview. A former cop himself, Rettstadt increased the intensity of the questions and employed a police interrogation technique. He asked Heistand to visualize a circumstance in which he could have been at the murder. Heistand said there wasn't one.

"Is it possible that you were there and don't remember it?" Rettstadt asked, suggesting Heistand might have been drunk or on drugs and blacked out. But Heistand was a health nut—lifted weights and worked out—and never used drugs; as a diabetic, consuming alcohol to excess would have been dangerous for him so he never did it.

"I wasn't there!" Heistand insisted again, and Rettstadt's aggressive questions aroused his suspicion. "Who exactly are you guys working for anyway, me or the prosecution?"

Heistand refused the deal and said that he would rather go to trial and face the murder charge, knowing full well that if he were convicted he might get life in prison, than plead guilty to something he didn't do. He told Felton that bringing him to the Holiday Inn was a waste of time and that there was nothing more to discuss. Felton called Detective LaBarge and his officers back into the room and they led Heistand away, into a police car, and back to the jail.

"I think he's involved," Rettstadt told Felton, after Heistand left.

"Well, I don't," Felton said. "I think he just told the truth and I believe him."

"Crime doesn't take a holiday," police are fond of saying when they have to work while the rest of the world relaxes and celebrates. That was certainly true of the Tobias case over the days surrounding the Independence Day holiday in 1988. First Doug Brinkman confessed and recanted and then Hayes offered Heistand a plea deal which he refused. But that wasn't the end of the Tobias case fireworks.

Right after the Independence Day weekend, Cindy Gleason called 911 and told the dispatcher that someone just tried to kill her. She'd seen prowlers around her house, and so she and her children were staying next door. The dispatcher told her to stay where she was and sent two police officers to investigate.

When the officers arrived and checked out the Gleason home, they found a bullet hole in the front widow and a matching hole in an interior wall. A single slug on the kitchen floor was collected in an evidence bag and marked for delivery to the State Police's crime lab. One of the officers who responded was Ken Burr, the man who'd found Jerry Tobias' body. Cindy Gleason told him since the Fourth of July there'd been prowlers creeping around outside her house. This was especially frightening to her because she and her children lived out in the country and her husband worked nights, and so they'd been sleeping at a neighbor's house. She was sound asleep on her neighbor's couch when she heard a gunshot. It sounded like it came from her house, so she got up, ran to the window, and saw a small car speeding away.

Burr asked if there was anyone who might want to harm her, and Cindy said the attack had to be connected to the Tobias trial. As soon as she'd been listed as a prosecution witness, strange things began happening. She'd received a death threat letter at the Holiday Inn where she worked, began noticing prowlers around her house at night, and sometimes she was even followed in her car.

Burr took notes, told Cindy to contact him if she noticed any other suspicious activity, and then he and the other officer left. As soon as they were gone, Cindy called Debbie and told her what happened. The police had Debbie temporarily living at Curt Beerens' cabin, so he overheard Debbie's side of the conversation and felt sick to his stomach. Two nights prior she'd asked him to shoot into the Gleason house, but he refused. Obviously she'd found someone else to do it and as soon as she hung up the phone, he confronted her.

"I didn't have anything to do with it," Debbie told him. "That was not me."

Beerens was in love, but he wasn't stupid. It was obvious to him Debbie had everything to do with the shooting. The idea that she could put her friend and her friend's children in danger bothered him, but something else bothered him even more. Debbie must have a secret boyfriend that she convinced to do the shooting after Beerens refused. The thought of her with another man just about crushed him.

As soon as he could, Beerens went to the Gaylord fire station and tried to get a call through to Lieutenant Hardy, without success. He tried several times over several days but Hardy was always busy or away from his desk, and a week passed before the two men talked. When Beerens got him on the phone, he told him what Debbie had been up to. Hardy was astonished. Beerens confided he was more in love with Debbie than ever and felt torn.

"I'm a law-abiding citizen, and I want to do the right thing. I just don't want to get her in trouble."

Hardy listened to Beerens pour out his heart, and asked him to continue to spy on Debbie. The police needed him close by, to be their eyes and ears. If he really loved Debbie, he'd help them protect her from herself. Perhaps things were about to get better, Hardy said. The hotel they'd moved Debbie into from Beeren's cabin was getting expensive and Hardy was looking for a new place to put her. A change of scenery might put a stop to her crazy behavior.

While Beerens spoke with Hardy, Burr took the slug he found on Cindy Gleason's kitchen floor to the State Police's crime lab. They tested it and learned it was fired from a 30-30 caliber rifle, possibly a Marlin. They ran the information through LEIN but slug wasn't connected to any other crimes.

Chapter 35   Sand Hill Manor

. . . . Mid-July, 1988

Lieutenant Hardy made good on his plan to move Debbie to a new and less expensive location. Another State Police detective knew just the place: an apartment in Houghton Lake, less than an hour from Gaylord and close to Curt Beeren's cabin. The apartment was in the Sand Hill Manor complex and already rented by the State Police. It was for undercover officers to use for illegal drug investigations but was currently vacant.

Within days of Beerens' conversation with Hardy, Debbie moved into the apartment and for the first few weeks, life for Beerens and Debbie settled into a normal routine. Beerens went to work at his EMT job every day, and Debbie seemed content to spend her days in the apartment alone. The police paid her telephone bill, paid for her prescriptions, gave her spending money for groceries, and had cable TV installed.

The tranquility didn't last. Soon, when Beerens came home from work, he noticed Debbie wasn't spending her days watching TV and talking to Cindy Gleason on the phone anymore. Instead, she was obsessed with the news coverage on the Tobias case. By the third week in July, Debbie spent all her time collecting, clipping, reading, and studying newspaper articles and trial transcripts. She was methodical about it and used different colored paperclips for different parts of court testimony.

The activity itself didn't bother Beerens as much as the question of where she got the transcripts and the newspaper articles did. They didn't subscribe to any newspapers, and she didn't have a car so she couldn't just drive to the store. The transcripts had to have come from the court, but Beerens couldn't figure out how Debbie got those, either. When he asked her about it, she gave only vague answers. He didn't press her because he knew that would only make her mad.

As time passed Debbie's Tobias-related document collection grew. Soon she had so many clippings, notebooks, and stacks of stapled court documents, she needed big cardboard boxes to keep them all in. Beerens didn't know where the boxes were coming from but didn't want to ask about them, either. Debbie was increasingly defensive, and even the most innocent comment from Beerens led first to an argument and then the silent treatment, something he dreaded.

Eventually, Beerens' curiosity got the best of him. He waited until she was in a good mood then asked her where she was getting all of the documents and newspapers. Debbie only gave Beerens a partial answer, but it surprised him. The newspaper clippings were coming from Mark Kerry. Mark Kerry was Beeren's EMT partner and the man who introduced him to Debbie. But how could that be? Beerens worked right next to Kerry, day in and day out, and he hadn't said a word. Before Beerens could work the answer out, Debbie gave him one of her coy smiles.

"Everything didn't come from Mark though," she said, teasing. "Some of this came from someone else. Someone in the State Police."

Beerens' interior jealousy meter went to max and he begged her for a name, but Debbie refused. Beerens knew that the only State Police officers who had regular contact with Debbie were Detective Wilt and Lieutenant Hardy. If Hardy was giving her the documents, he would have told Beerens about it so he believed it had to be Wilt. When he asked Debbie, she told him it was none of his business.

"Well, what do you need all this stuff for, anyway?" Beerens said.

"It's my homework," Debbie said.

"Homework?" Beerens asked.

"Yeah," she explained. "I want to make sure I don't make any mistakes."

What Beerens didn't know was that over the next several days, he and Mark Kerry were scheduled to work different shifts. That wasn't a scheduling anomaly, it was set up by Kerry. He was attracted to Debbie, too, and the fact that she was his partner's girlfriend didn't seem to matter and so, while Beerens was at work, Kerry spent the day with Debbie. His job was to quiz her on the contents of the newspaper clippings and the trial testimony. Some days, Cindy Gleason came over and Kerry quizzed both of them. On the days Kerry and Beerens worked the same shift, Debbie and

Cindy studied alone. Cindy kept a diary, too, and the two compared their entries and made sure they matched.

"We've got to get our stories straight," Debbie told Cindy. Especially the entries for the weekend Jerry Tobias died.

As the strange days at Sand Hill Manor droned on, Beerens' love for Debbie began to wane. All she did was insult him and pick fights, and Beerens told Hardy he felt used. He didn't want to be her boyfriend anymore, or Hardy's spy. During one of his last reports, the two men discussed Debbie's diary. Hardy wanted to know if Beerens had read it, but Beerens said not only hadn't he read it, he'd never even seen it. He didn't think it existed, and if it did, it was probably a fake.

Chapter 36   *People v. Terry Moore*

· · · · · · · · · · · Friday, July 15, 1988, 9:23 AM

"Good morning, Ladies and Gentlemen of the jury. Thank you very much for attending this morning. We appreciate your attendance as jurors, as you are fulfilling your responsibility. It is a pleasure and privilege to welcome you to the 46th Judicial Circuit Court jury service."

People in northern Michigan could be forgiven for feeling a sense of déjà vu. Yet again someone from Gaylord was on trial for the murder of Jerry Tobias. Yet again the trial was moved to a neighboring county on a change of venue and, again, Norm Hayes would be the prosecutor. And, yet again the defendant was a man named Moore.

Laurie's younger brother's full name was Walter Edwin Moore III. The charges against him were First-Degree Murder and Conspiracy to Commit Murder, and his trial would be presided over by Judge William A. Porter. Porter was one of the judges who disqualified himself from hearing Laurie's trial because he knew Laurie's wife. He felt no such kinship with Terry Moore, and although he usually presided in Gaylord at the Otsego County Courthouse, a change of venue moved Terry's trial to nearby Kalkaska.

The defendant was new but Prosecutor Hayes had not changed his belief that Jerry Tobias' death was the result of a drug deal gone wrong. The theory of the crime he'd shared with Laurie's jurors, he repeated for Terry's. According to the prosecutor, the crime still happened in Walt's Butcher Shop, Jerry Tobias was still beaten to death and left to die in the back of his pick-up truck, after trying to buy or sell cocaine. But there was an important difference this time around. Hayes had Debbie.

"The evidence will show, ladies and gentlemen, that Terry Moore and Mark Canter were in the company of a woman by the name of Debra Parmentier. She was there that night. She observed what happened.

"I am not going to stand here and tell you that Debra Parmentier is the greatest person in the world. I am not going to do that. I am sure the evidence will show she is not the greatest person in the world. But ladies and gentlemen, you don't generally deal with the greatest people in the world in this kind of case. You just don't."

There were obvious similarities between the prosecution of Terry and the prosecution of Laurie, but there were similarities in the defense's case, too. Terry's defense attorney, Michael Hackett, was just as incensed by the case against his client as Dean Robb had been about the case against Laurie. Where was the physical evidence—the fingerprints, the hair or fibers, the blood, the footprints? There wasn't any. The autopsy was bungled, the toxicology was incomplete, and the logic was ludicrous. Terry could be loud-mouthed like his brother, but he was a church-going, business-owning, workaholic, not a drug-dealing murderer.

"Terry Moore is innocent. This whole case is horrendous," Hackett said, in his opening statement to the jury. "You are going to listen to the things that the Prosecutor puts in, and then you are going to listen to the rest of the story. The rest of the story will satisfy you that this case should not have even been brought. Terry Moore is not guilty, and he must be released. This charge is amazing. It is incredible."

Laurie Moore and Dean Robb never had to deal with Debbie. At least, not in the courtroom they didn't. Terry and Hackett did.

"It is going to be a long trial," Hackett warned the jury, "but the crux of this case is whether you believe the story of Debra Parmentier. This fantasy. There's not a fingerprint. There's not a footprint. There's not a bloodstain. There is no fabric. There is no evidence against Terry Moore. There is *nothing*. So we get back to Debra Parmentier. The story you are going to hear about Debra Parmentier is one that I am going to paraphrase for you. She is a dope dealer. She is a dope user. She is a liar. She is crazy. "

As the trial unfolded, the mental stability of Debbie was the elephant in the courtroom that, early on at least, only Hackett acknowledged. Hayes squeezed around it for as long as he could, and until Debbie took the stand, Terry's trial proceeded much like a carbon copy of the trial against his brother.

Trooper Burr found the body and testified to seeing a faint set of footprints in the snow, headed away from the driver's side door of Jerry's truck. These were never identified.

Jackie Tobias said she and Jerry argued the week before he died, that he'd been drinking more than usual, and that he spent Monday night at the bar instead of at home with her and their sons. This was particularly troubling to her in light of Jerry's past infidelities.

The Nelsons testified they'd given Jerry $200 to buy cocaine and then never saw him again.

None of this was particularly damaging to the defense, but rather simply set up the circumstances of Jerry's death. When Hayes put Dr. Newhouse on the stand, Hackett gathered himself to spring. Hackett knew all about the bungled blood test and was prepared to grill Newhouse about it as soon as he got the chance.

But Hayes used his time with the pathologist wisely. He encouraged Newhouse to go into great detail about the bruises on Jerry's body. To illustrate Newhouse's descriptions, Judge Porter allowed the prosecution to show the jury not just one but dozens of gruesome autopsy photos.

"I just want to prepare you, so it is not a surprise, and that you are not caught off balance, because these are difficult pictures to look at," Judge Porter warned the jury.

Hayes spent six hours, over two days, questioning Dr. Newhouse. He went over her qualifications, the autopsy process she used, the bruises found on Jerry Tobias' body, and the life-ending capability of a chicken skewer. He did not address Jerry's drug use or the toxicology reports, but Hackett focused directly on both during his cross-examination. He directed Newhouse to describe the needle marks in Jerry's arms and the cocaine in his system. He stressed there weren't just one or two needle marks, but eight, and they were fresh. Dr. Newhouse's failure to assign any importance to them in her autopsy report seemed odd, he said to the jury.

"Did you check or follow the testing of the blood?" Hackett asked her.

"Again, I was under the impression at that time the blood had been quantified," Dr. Newhouse said. "It was an erroneous assumption."

"That means you were wrong, correct?" pressed Hackett.

"It was an erroneous assumption, and so I did not pursue quantitative testing of the blood at that time. When I became aware that the blood had not been tested quantitatively, I did pursue that, and asked that it be sent for testing, and it subsequently was."

The blood test she was referring to was not the one she ordered immediately following the autopsy, but rather the test conducted by the State Police after Laurie's trial, and a year and a half after Jerry died. It was positive for cocaine but still hadn't been measured for an exact amount. Hackett's theory of crime was the same as Robb's: that Jerry wasn't murdered at all, but had overdosed on cocaine, passed out, was dumped in his truck by people unknown, and froze to death. The fact that his zipper was left undone could also have meant he was with a woman, perhaps the wrong one.

"Let's put it in layman's terms," Hackett said. "If you shoot it in your arm, you need less cocaine to kill yourself?"

"If you are talking about the actual quantity that you are putting in, yes," Newhouse said.

Hackett hammered on, but despite bungling the blood test, despite not knowing how much cocaine had been in Jerry's system when he died, and despite signing the death certificate days before the toxicology tests were completed, Dr. Newhouse held firm. She said she still believed Tobias was beaten to death.

Her assertion seemed almost silly, and the defense had made important progress in showing there could easily be doubt in what killed Jerry. Hayes had to have known this, but he was also quick with a rebuttal question and the prosecutor gave Dr. Newhouse a succinct opportunity to redeem herself.

"Do you see bleeding in the brain with a cocaine overdose?" Hayes asked in his re-direct.

"No," said Dr. Newhouse.

Chapter 37   The Competency Question

. . . . Thursday, July 21, 1988

Mike Hackett wasn't the only attorney interested in Debbie Parmentier's mental health. Mark Canter's preliminary hearing was underway, so Ray MacNeil was mighty curious about it, too. While Hackett and Hayes battled over the admissibility of Debbie's psychological records in front of Judge Porter in a Kalkaska courtroom, MacNeil and Assistant Prosecutor Dawn Pyrek battled over them in front of another judge, Alton Davis, in a Gaylord courtroom.

Of the four attorneys, MacNeil was the one who investigated Debbie most thoroughly. He was the one who'd met with Leonard Parmentier, and his motion to Judge Davis for the release of Debbie's records went beyond even what Hackett had asked for. Like Hackett, he wanted all her psychological, medical, and counseling records admitted into evidence, but MacNeil wanted her police record admitted, too. Once Mark Canter's trial began, he also wanted the jury to know exactly how much the Michigan State Police had spent on her upkeep.

When he had a free moment, MacNeil often sat in on Terry Moore's trial, and so he had some idea of what was in store for his client. The most helpful thing he'd learned from his hours of observing was not to be in a hurry. Terry was in a hurry and decided to go ahead with his trial and not wait for Debbie to be examined by a psychiatrist. To MacNeil, that miscalculation looked like it was going to be his downfall.

MacNeil would advise Mark they *had* to have a competency hearing for Debbie, even if that meant a long delay. Mark's trial was already two days overdue because Terry's was taking longer than expected, so he probably wouldn't get his day in court until the fall. Mark couldn't make bail, and he'd be spending the delay in jail. But after conferring with MacNeil, and learning it looked like the jury was buying Debbie's story, Mark agreed to be something Terry hadn't been—patient.

Debbie took the stand in Terry's trial on Tuesday, Aug. 2, 1988.

It was a stiflingly muggy day, the courtroom was hot and still. Under those conditions, any other day the jury would likely have felt irritated and restless. But that day was different. The jury had been waiting to hear what the prosecution's only eyewitness had to say, and they were finally going to get their wish.

"Would you state your name for the record, please?" Hayes asked.

In contrast to the big stir her entrance created, the woman who held up her right hand, said her name, and swore to tell the truth was surprisingly small. Her hair was shoulder length, middling brown, and kinky. She wore a blue flowered blouse, a white skirt, and low-heeled shoes. Her jaw was square, almost like a man's, and her face was hard and narrow, but pretty, even though she wore little, if any, make-up. She spoke softly; her voice was even and without emotion.

"Debra Parmentier."

There were many, many people who had already heard Debbie's story, or rather, various versions of it. In the past year and a half she'd told her tale to her estranged husband Leonard, to several boyfriends, to Assistant Prosecutor Dawn Pyrek, to Prosecutor Hayes and his investigator, Jerry Borema, several sheriff's deputies, Fred LaBarge and the State Police detectives, Gaylord Police Chief Frank Dufon, two ATF agents, two judges, and her best friend, Cindy. But Debbie was finally going to tell her story to a group of people who really mattered: a jury.

Prosecutor Hayes wasted no time in asking her about the night of Jerry's death.

"Did you have any contact with Jerry Tobias on December the sixth, 1986?"

"Yes, I did."

"Where did you see Jerry Tobias?"

"At Walt's Butcher Shop in Gaylord."

"Who were you with?"

"Laurie Moore, Terry Moore, Mark Canter, John, myself, Doug Brinkman."

The jury was familiar with Terry Moore—he was the defendant. They likely knew that Laurie Moore was Terry's younger brother and had been convicted of Voluntary Manslaughter for the same crime. The other men's names may not have been as familiar. Mark Canter was a handsome and friendly 24-year-old Gaylord native, known around town for working in the oil fields, drinking in bars, and occasionally selling drugs. Doug Brinkman, 27, was one of Mark's running buddies. "John" was thus far unidentified in court, but according to Debbie's statement to police, was Don Heistand, 30, a well-built, straight-laced, husband and new father who no longer lived in Gaylord.

"Would you please tell the jury what happened?" Hayes asked.

"They were talking. Laurie had asked Jerry where the stuff was, and Jerry says, 'I don't have it.' They started arguing more and more, and it got to the point where yelling began, and Terry hit Jerry Tobias in the back of the head and he fell down on the floor, kind of in a face-down position. Then Laurie hit him with his fist a couple times. Then, he picked up something and hit him with that. When Jerry Tobias came back toward us, Mark Canter had hit him and he fell back down and they kept hitting him, and hitting him, and hitting him, and wouldn't let up, and he didn't move no more."

Next, Debbie said Terry Moore hit Jerry in the back of the head with a butcher steel—a metal rod used to sharpen knives—and Laurie Moore hit him with a chicken skewer. Jerry lay on the floor unconscious and the men dragged him into the butcher shop's walk-in cooler. They discussed an alibi, and then lifted Jerry out of the cooler, carried him outside, and put him in the back of his truck. Someone, Debbie wasn't sure who, drove the truck away from Walt's and parked it by the fire station.

Hayes asked Debbie what the motive was. Debbie explained Jerry owed the Moore brothers $7,000 for cocaine and couldn't pay it. She said she knew the amount because Mark Canter and Terry Moore talked about it earlier that evening and she had overheard them. According to her, the three of them drove around Gaylord together Friday night, Dec. 5, before stopping at Walt's. Mark was driving a small red car, Terry was in the passenger seat, and Debbie sat in the back.

"Let me ask you this," Hayes said. "Why did you come to the Michigan State Police?"

"I had no choice anymore," Debbie said. "I had no alternative."

Debbie looked at the jury and said she went to the police because she was afraid for her life. The men who killed Jerry, the men she just named, threatened to kill her.

Chapter 38   Debbie's Past

. . . . Thursday, August 4, 1988

If you give a liar enough rope, the saying goes, they'll eventually hang themselves. That was the cross-examination strategy Michael Hackett planned to use with Debbie. Let her talk, he thought, let her trip herself up, and make sure the jury heard and understood it. So while Hayes kept Debbie on the stand for nearly two hours, Hackett just sat back and listened, offering few objections. His turn would come, he knew, and when it did, he was ready.

"Mrs. Parmentier," Hackett began, when Hayes finally finished with Debbie, "let's provide some history about you to the jury. Where did you last go to school?"

"In Michigan."

"What grade was that?"

"Sixth grade."

"And did you run away from home, as a youngster?"

"Yes, I did."

"How old were you when you ran away from home?"

"About eleven and a half."

"Where did you live when you ran away from home?"

"On the streets."

"How did you make money?"

"I sold drugs."

"Did you use drugs during that time?"

"Yes, I did."

"What drugs did you use?"

"THC, PCP, Acid, Purple Haze, Yellow Mesc and Orange Sunshine. There was a lot of them. Chocolate Mesc."

"Mrs. Parmentier, have you told this jury the truth as to what you observed, and what you did, on December 5, 1986, and December 6, 1986?"

"Yes, I have."

"And to *every* matter put to you? *Every* question?"

"Yes."

Hackett considered Debbie a liar and a crazy woman. He didn't believe her story, not the small details of it, and not the larger ones, either. Hackett believed that Debbie would lie for just about any reason, and more disturbing, sometimes for no reason at all.

"You told a different story to Mary Evans, right?

"Yes, I did."

"You told a different story to Cindy Gleason?"

"Right. Yes, I didn't tell them the truth."

"You told a different story to Howard Moore?"

"I didn't say much at all to Howard."

"You lied to the doctors, in the course of your treatment, isn't that true?"

"Yes."

"Are you telling us that you feel it is okay to lie if you have a reason to lie?"

"If the reason is good enough, yes."

It hadn't taken Hackett long to score an important point for the defense. The prosecution's witness admitted that she lied, not once but several times and to several different people, and would lie again, if the conditions were right. Hackett was convinced the conditions were right for her to lie, right there in the courtroom. He'd read all the psych reports, he'd seen the false police reports Leonard Parmentier tipped off Ray MacNeil to, and he knew at least some of what she was capable of.

The jury did not. They were probably under the common assumption that people needed a reason to lie. Hackett had to maneuver his cross-examination of Debbie to show she had a reason. A difficult task because what could be a good reason to lie about a murder? So far nothing was presented in court to explain why Debbie made up a story about a murder and then randomly selected five men to participate in it, like doomed characters in a stage play.

"Have you been arrested as an accessory to murder, or for delivery of cocaine, or delivery of controlled substances?" Hackett asked her.

"No, I have not."

"Mrs. Parmentier, do you know *why* you haven't been charged with the crime that you just testified to?"

"I don't know."

"Are you being paid for your living expenses at this point?"

"Yes."

"So all your expenses are covered, right?"

"Yes, they are."

"Are you working?"

"No, I am not."

"At the present time, your food is being paid for?"

"Yes."

"And your rent?"

"I don't pay nothing."

"How about your medications?"

"Yes."

"And you are receiving spending money?"

"It depends on what I need, and who I'm around. I tell them I need food and they give me fifty dollars, and sometimes twenty, sometimes forty, and sometimes that lasts me a week, or week and a half."

"And you get cash?"

"Yes."

"Do you know how long you are expected to be on this program, where all of your expenses and spending money is paid for by the Michigan State Police?"

"I don't know."

Hackett hoped the implication to the jury was that Debbie would be able to live off the largess of the Michigan State Police as long as she stuck to her story. And her story, that day anyway, was that she was a witness to a murder and that the murderers were threatening her life. Hackett wanted the jury to understand that the truth of Debbie's story didn't matter to her. She had a roof over her head, food in her refrigerator, cable TV to watch, prescriptions in her medicine cabinet, and spending money in her purse all because of it.

When Hackett ended his cross-examination for the day, perhaps it was Leonard Parmentier's words, and not Debbie's, echoing in his mind as he left the courtroom. If so, they were fitting.

"Right now she's got it made," Leonard had said. "They're payin' her bills, they're supporting her, and everything's fine."

Ray MacNeil shared the Leonard Parmentier interview tape with Hackett, and it made a pretty strong impression on him. Hackett believed that Debbie's estranged husband would make the same impression on the jury and his next move was to put Leonard on the stand. Spousal privilege didn't apply, Hackett believed, because Debbie and Leonard had been in the process of divorce for almost two years. Hackett planned to have Leonard describe what being married to Debbie was like and detail the elaborate lies she was capable of. Leonard said he was more than happy to testify.

But the next day when Leonard was called to the stand, Hayes objected citing spousal privilege. Judge Porter agreed and ruled most of what Leonard could have testified to would be inadmissible. Even though they were in the process of a divorce, Debbie refused to waive her spousal privilege and Judge Porter declined to break what the law almost always treated as a sacred trust.

Leonard could testify, the judge ruled, but he would not be allowed to mention Debbie's psychiatric history, her hospitalizations, or her false police reports. He also could not testify that Debbie told him she watched Jerry Tobias get beaten with a baseball bat and stabbed to death in a grocery store parking lot. All these specifics were out. Hackett was free to call Leonard as a witness, but he could only ask him general questions about his marriage.

"It was a very sporadic, nerve-trying marriage, a hard marriage," Leonard said, in his brief time on the stand.

"What do you mean, sporadic?" Hackett asked.

"Well, we would go along normal, real good for a while, and she would get bored with it, and start off on some type of a fantasy trip. She would go to doctors with this ailment or that ailment—female problems, headaches—and she would end up going to the hospital, and have all kinds of stories. She would go into spouse abuse, and various fantasy stories, ever since I have known her."

Judge Porter interrupted Leonard and fine-tuned his ruling. Debbie's husband was also not allowed to say anything about her "stories" or "fantasy trips," he said. Still, Hackett was a deft litigator, and managed to work at least one of Leonard's jaw-droppers into the court record. During their marriage, Debbie became interested in what Leonard called, "black magic."

"All of a sudden, there seemed to be several books on it around the house," Leonard said. "She borrowed them from somebody, and she started making the children believe that she could make objects move with her mind, and it was a real hassle."

It was up to him, Leonard told the jury, to assure their two young sons that people could not move objects with their minds.

While the jury might have been shocked by Leonard's characterization of Debbie, when they looked at Hayes for his reaction, they saw a calm exterior. The prosecutor acted almost bored by the revelation. Having a bad marriage was lamentable, he said, but it wasn't a crime. And it didn't have anything to do with the trial.

"Soap operas are great for the afternoon," Hayes told the jury, "but that's not why we're here."

Chapter 39   Terry's Defense

. . . . Wednesday, August 10, 1988

Hackett took two weeks to complete Terry Moore's defense. His main theme was rampant inconsistencies in the police's investigation and in Debbie's testimony.

For example, Becky Nelson told the same story in Terry's trial that she'd told in Laurie's. That Jerry came to her house the night before he died and her husband gave him $200 to buy cocaine. The deal was supposed to happen at Walt's Butcher Shop, and when neither she nor her husband heard from Jerry, Becky went to Walt's the next day to ask Laurie what happened.

But in Terry's trial she added a new detail. Becky said she went in the butcher shop via the back door and noted the barrels, boxes, and dumpsters filled with deer carcasses. Legs, heads, antlers, hides—a memorable and gruesome image. Yet when

Debbie described the butcher shop she'd made no mention of it, even though she was supposedly there just hours before, entering and exiting through the same door. Hackett asked the jury how Debbie could have missed such a sight, if she had really been there.

Next, Jim Giacalone, a part-time employee at Walt's, testified he had a key and opened the shop early Saturday morning. If the prosecution's theory was correct, that would have been the morning after the murder. When Giacalone arrived, everything was in order. The meat saw had been taken apart and washed, each section left on the table to dry, along with several knives and tools. In the center aisle of the walk-in cooler were two fifty-gallon barrels. These were to dispose of bones and other unsalable material, and had to be tightly squeezed into the cooler among trays of venison and special cuts of meat customers ordered for the holidays.

"At that time, there is a lot of meat that's in the cooler," Giacalone testified. "There is venison that has been processed, plus your domestic meat. It could be a little bit jammed at that time."

Then how, Hackett asked, did five men drag Jerry's body inside of it, as Debbie testified? The jurors had the opportunity to wonder this themselves on a field trip of sorts. On August 18, 1988, they were ushered out of the courtroom, onto a bus, and escorted to Walt's. But it was summer, not late fall, and the barrels weren't in the walk-in cooler during the tour. Still, Hackett hoped that when the door to the walk-in was opened and the jurors looked inside, they imagined it packed tight with holiday meat orders and two barrels of deer bones.

Next, Gaylord patrolman Dan Dallas testified the same as in Laurie's trial. He said he drove past the butcher shop in his patrol car with his headlights switched off sometime between 2 and 3 AM on Saturday, Dec. 6, 1986. Yet his daily activity log, entered as an exhibit by the defense, showed him patrolling several other areas of the city. His report said he was at the Air Industrial Park from 1:40 AM to 1:55 AM, at Glen's Alpine Plaza from 2:10 AM to 2:20 AM, passing through downtown until 3:00 AM, and went to the Michigan State Police post for a coffee break until 3:15 AM. There was no mention of driving past Walt's.

Hackett questioned Dallas about it.

"Sir, you have to realize we check these areas several times every evening. I am not going to jot it down every time I go through there, unless something significant happened."

Whether that was a believable answer was for the jury to decide. Next, Hackett called Blair Robb. Blair was Dean Robb's son and worked as his father's investigator in the Laurie Moore trail. One of Blair's tasks was to meet with Debbie, interview her, and try to determine if she knew anything about Jerry's death. Blair testified about their meeting, describing how they drove in her car from Frederick to Grayling while she talked non-stop about gunrunning and drug trafficking. Somewhere in this bizarre conversation, he said, she told him Laurie was innocent and she could prove it. She said she wrote it all down in her diary, and she knew where Jerry Tobias' missing belt and boots were, but refused to give him any details.

"It was a blocking conversation," Blair Robb said, meaning she was being evasive.

"Mr. Robb," Hackett asked, "did Debra Parmentier give you anything that you could verify?"

"No she did not."

"Did you ever obtain verification of the existence of the diary, the boots, belt, or anything that she had described to you?"

"No, I did not."

Next, *Gaylord Herald Times* Associate Editor Victoria Naegele testified that many of the things Debbie told police—details detectives insisted that only someone who witnessed the crime could know—had actually been published in the newspaper. These details included Jerry's body found frozen in the back of his truck, that drugs were involved, that he'd been beaten and dragged, that Walt's might have been the murder scene, and that Officer Dallas drove past the shop in the middle of the night. Naegele said she'd reported each of those in her coverage of the Tobias investigation. The newspaper also reported what Jerry had been wearing, right down to the colors in his plaid flannel shirt, that his belt and a pair of his boots were missing, that he'd been seen drinking heavily in the Fireside Lounge and flashed wads of money. The *Gaylord Herald Times* and other newspapers ran several detailed descriptions of the chicken skewer that was confiscated by police and later named as the murder weapon.

Next in Hackett's strategy was to offer real questions about when Jerry Tobias died. Like Dean Robb, Hackett believed Jerry died much later in the weekend than the prosecution was arguing. Hackett used the testimony of a local bartender and the results of Newhouse's autopsy to show Jerry could not have died in the early morning of Saturday, Dec. 6, 1986, but more than a day later.

The exact time of death was listed as "undetermined" on the death certificate, but the prosecutor contended Jerry died at approximately 3 AM Saturday morning, Dec. 6, 1986. Although she botched the cocaine test, Dr. Newhouse did have Tobias' blood tested for alcohol, and it registered .02. For a man his size, that was the equivalent of one beer or one mixed drink. And yet the prosecutor's own witnesses testified that Jerry was very drunk just three hours earlier.

Witnesses said Jerry was drinking White Russians, stumbling around a pool table, dropping his cue stick several times. He was so drunk he couldn't even play the game. The Swamp's bartender, Dawn Wakely, testified Jerry drank two bottles of Michelob Light and then downed five or six White Russians, a potent mix of Kahlua, milk, and vodka. The Perkins' testified Jerry drank eight or ten White Russians, plus the beer.

If he really died early Saturday morning as the prosecution contended, Jerry's blood alcohol should have measured .165 to

.195, or higher. Unlike cocaine, alcohol did not metabolize after death. When a person who's been drinking dies, their blood alcohol level remains relatively constant. If Dr. Newhouse's tests were correct, and if the prosecutor's witnesses' testimony was accurate, Jerry couldn't have had a .02 blood alcohol level until noon the next day, Sunday, December 7. And at that time, Terry Moore was just leaving church.

If the jury was able to follow the science of what happened to the human body after a bout of heavy drinking, then this was one of the most powerful points in Terry's favor yet produced at trial.

To bolster the sense of doubt he'd worked so meticulously to instill in the jury, Hackett called one last witness. Detective Fred LaBarge was sworn in. Hackett asked only one question.

"Sergeant, the defendant in this case is Terry Moore, and apart from Debra Parmentier's statement, do you have *any* evidence, specifically and including physical evidence, fingerprints, footprints, anything physical, that relates to Terry Moore and would indicate that Terry Moore is responsible—other than Debra Parmentier's statement?"

"No," LaBarge admitted. "We do not have any physical evidence tying to Terry Moore."

If Hackett had his way, the defense would have rested right then. He'd shown there were inconsistencies about how and when Jerry died; he'd questioned whether Officer Dallas was telling the truth; he'd explained why it would have been impossible to fit a man into Walt's walk-in cooler in early December; and he questioned the police investigation as well as the sanity of the only eyewitness.

But Hackett wasn't the defendant, and the decision of when to rest the case wasn't his, it was Terry's. If Terry knew how to do one thing well, it was talk, and he'd been waiting to do it since the first day of jury selection.

Throughout the trial he'd been taking notes, and more than once was so tense he looked like he was ready to spring from his chair onto the witness stand. He wanted to testify in his own defense, and on the morning of August 19, the 39-year-old father of three got his chance. He took the stand. Hackett asked him to introduce himself to the jury and talk about his relationship with his brother, Laurie.

"Laurie and I really didn't have a relationship, as far as doing things together, other than family functions," Terry said.

"How often did you talk to Laurie?" Hackett asked. "Would it be daily, weekly, monthly, or how did that go?"

"I might walk in (to Walt's) and we would call each other 'bro,'" Terry said. "I would say, 'Hi bro,' and that was about it."

"Did you have occasion to loan money to Laurie?" Hackett asked.

"No."

"Did you know Laurie to use drugs?"

"No, I did not."

"Cocaine?"

"No, I did not."

Terry said he knew who Jerry Tobias was, but only as someone who worked in the oil fields. He didn't socialize with Jerry Tobias, didn't ever work with him, and he had never arranged drug deals with Jerry or anyone else.

"What was your reaction when you heard about his death?"

"I just felt sorry for his wife and kids, you know?" Terry said. "That's about all."

Hackett asked Terry if he believed Jerry's death was a conspiracy. Terry answered that if it was, his participation was logistically impossible. He never met Doug Brinkman until his arraignment. He recognized Don Heistand from Walt's, but he'd never even spoken to him. How could he have conspired to plan a murder when he didn't even know two of the men he supposedly conspired with?

Terry said he did know Mark Canter quite well, but only as a concerned advisor, for lack of a better word. Terry worked for Mark's stepfather on an oil rig, and Mark would sometimes tag along when he was just a kid. Over the years they'd stayed in touch, and when Mark got in trouble for drunk driving and parole violation, Terry tried to help by bailing him out of jail.

"I talked to him about the fact that he was going to have to take a giant step forward in adulthood, and grow up and face facts that . . . he would have to be leaving a lot of that stuff he used to do when he was a teenager behind and grow up."

As Hackett's questions came to a close he asked about Debbie.

"Do you know a Debra Parmentier?"

"I do now."

"Can you explain for us when the first time was that you ever heard her name?"

"Probably in the paperwork that I got after I was arrested. The first time I ever seen Debra Parmentier—in my life—was the day she walked into the courtroom."

Chapter 40　"And here I am."

. . . . Friday, August 19, 1988

"Terry, do you have a response to the charge that has been levied against you in this case, specifically First-Degree Murder?"

"Yes, I do. I am kind of upset with it all, because I am innocent of all charges, and I feel that if I had a chance to speak . . . I have never been questioned. They never asked me any questions, whatsoever. I just was charged and arrested and here I am."

Terry explained that he had an alibi for most of the weekend surrounding Jerry's death. If the police and the prosecutor had interviewed him before they arrested him, they would have known that. But no one did.

Terry's girlfriend, Lynn Kaczor, had been transferred from Gaylord to Lansing, and was staying at the Red Roof Inn while she was getting settled. She and Terry talked on the phone Friday, Dec. 5, 1986, from 9:30 to 9:49 PM and again at 11:06 PM for two minutes. After midnight, they spoke again at 12:50 AM and at 1:20 AM for five minutes. These calls were on her hotel bill, all made from Room 134 to Terry's home.

On Saturday, Dec. 6, 1986, Terry went to the lumberyard at 7 AM and was with one of his employees from 8 or 9 AM to the end of the workday. On Saturday evening, Lynn Kaczor left Lansing and drove to Gaylord, arriving at Terry's house between 8 and 9 PM and spent the night. On Sunday morning the couple went to church together and afterward met with a potential customer of Terry's.

Terry's appointment book was entered into evidence, and it showed that he worked all day both Friday and Saturday. Friday he was busy checking on his crew doing a job in Gaylord and making phone calls to employees and customers. Saturday he was at work, insulating a post office.

On cross-examination, Hayes turned up the sarcasm, and called Terry's girlfriend a liar. He accused Terry of knowing the phone calls between he and Debbie were being taped by the police. He even told the jury that he believed Terry had sacrificed his brother, Laurie, for his own self-interest.

"Let me ask you this: Why was (Laurie's trial) such hell? What was going through your mind? Was it because, Mr. Moore, if you came forward to help your brother you would be nailing yourself? Isn't that true?"

If Hayes was trying to get Terry to lose his temper, the effort failed. Terry could be impatient, loud, opinionated, and full of bluster, but he was not dumb.

"No, Mr. Hayes," Terry answered calmly, "that is not true."

Chapter 41 Expert Maneuvering

. . . . August 22, 1988

While defendants automatically have the right to testify, expert witnesses have to earn it. Their expertise has to be proven "material," meaning relevant, in order for them to testify in court. As the trial worn on, Hackett grew even more certain that Debbie was mentally ill, but Terry had opted not to wait for an in-person examination so he was counting on the testimony of psychiatrist Emanuel Tanay, who'd reviewed Debbie's records, to convince the jury of it. First he needed Judge Porter's permission to call him as an expert witness.

Dr. Tanay had impressive credentials. He was board certified by the American Board of Psychiatry and Neurology and by the American Board of Forensic Psychiatry. He was a professor of psychiatry at Wayne State University, a past president of the American Academy of Psychiatry and the Law, and had been a physician for more than thirty years. He'd testified in the trials of serial killer Ted Bundy and nightclub owner Jack Ruby, the convicted killer of Lee Harvey Oswald. Dr. Tanay was known in legal circles for helping put guilty people behind bars but Hackett hoped he'd be just as good at keeping an innocent man free.

Judge Porter excused the jury and held an impromptu hearing on whether Tanay would be allowed to testify. The judge would quiz Tanay on what he planned to testify to, hear arguments for and against from Hackett and Hayes, and then make his decision.

Dr. Tanay explained that he had reviewed Debbie's psychological records from Fairbanks Memorial Hospital in Fairbanks, Alaska; Alpena General Hospital, in Alpena, Michigan; Chelsea Community Hospital in Chelsea, Michigan; Muskegon General Hospital in Muskegon, Michigan; Otsego Memorial Hospital in Gaylord, Michigan; Hackley Hospital in Muskegon, Michigan; and Burns Clinic in Petoskey, Michigan. He had also reviewed reports from psychologist Timothy Strauss of Joy Valley Christian Medical Center in Petoskey and psychologist Walter Grabowski of Bronson Medical Center in Kalamazoo. At the time of the hearing, a written report of his findings had already been submitted to the judge.

"Miss Parmentier has had a life-long history of mental disturbances, starting earlier in her adolescence," Dr. Tanay said in his report. "There's a whole gamut of psychiatric, diagnostic labels that have been applied to Miss Parmentier. These range from personality disorder, sociopathic personality, anti-social personality, manic-depressive psychosis, a judgment disorder, depressive illness, post-traumatic stress disorder . . . there might have been others.

"There are many references to all kinds of injuries that affected the brain, and there are physicians stating that they diagnosed her as suffering from organic brain damage. There was suspicion that there might be an aneurism. Then there is also long-standing involvement with a variety of drugs."

The most relevant diagnosis for the purposes of trial was the one for sociopathic personality, Tanay said, because it was a disorder that remained constant throughout a person's life, which meant Debbie was definitely suffering from it in December of 1986 and continued to suffer from it. Sociopaths are known to lie, even when they seem to achieve no benefit from it.

"Such persons have a tendency—in fact it is a striking symptom of the illness—to be untruthful, to be manipulative, to respond to immediate stimuli, to fabricate something simply on a moment's notice," Dr. Tanay said.

Sociopaths will never admit they didn't tell the truth, even about something as important as a murder, because they don't have a normal conscience and sometimes even believe their own lies.

"There are some who are so engaged in denial of their symptoms that they might not really have a full conscious awareness that they are lying," Dr. Tanay told Judge Porter. "People who have a sociopathic personality structure engage in all kinds of behavior that they provide good explanations for. They do all kinds of terrible things, and they will give you good reasons why it is perfectly normal and acceptable. They may engage in such massive denial that they aren't even aware they're telling a lie."

With the jury waiting in the jury room, Hackett argued Dr. Tanay's testimony was material to the trial because Debbie's truthfulness, or lack thereof, was at the center of the prosecution's case.

"These matters are so crucial to the defense that it appears virtually impossible to offer our case without being able to explain to the jury the background of Debra Parmentier."

If there were only a single medical report or a single psychiatric commitment to examine, Hackett said, the validity of Dr. Tanay's opinion might be questionable. But for fourteen years, from April 1974 to June 1988, Debbie had 42 separate interactions with eleven medical institutions and had received treatment from several dozen mental health workers, lasting anywhere from one hour for a counseling session to a six-week commitment in a psychiatric hospital.

She'd seen psychiatrists, psychologists, social workers, counselors, emergency room doctors, and family physicians, Hackett said, who'd treated her for anxiety, suicidal thoughts, feelings of having two personalities, hearing voices, panic attacks, memory loss, drug use, promiscuity, depression, abnormal brain structure, headaches, and a nervous breakdown.

The report from Hackley Hospital in Muskegon summed Debbie up this way: "She has a long-standing history of erratic behavior, manic depressive in nature. There is some character damage in her behavior. She lies a lot, manipulates her environment, and uses very poor judgment. In dealing with this patient we should keep in mind her manipulation, poor judgment, lack of insight into her problems, and tendency to lie."

These were just the treatments the defense was able to uncover, Hackett said. There were probably others no one knew about.

"Judge," Dr. Tanay said, "if a patient had various mental illnesses, in addition to prescription drugs, periodic drug overdose, making false police reports, false reports of assault, unstable childhood, including running away, staying at a foster home, and drug abuse, periods of delusion and fantasy, and association with criminal activity, there is a strong likelihood that the patient is not an objective, interested witness."

Hackett was not asking to have Debbie disqualified as a witness. He was only asking Dr. Tanay be allowed to testify about her mental health.

When it was Prosecutor Hayes' turn to address the judge, he argued that Debbie's background was inadmissible, and at one point even laughed at Dr. Tanay as he was testifying. This unnerved the doctor, but didn't surprise Hackett.

"Mr. Hayes has been doing things like that throughout the trial," Hackett told Dr. Tanay, who was still on the stand. "Go ahead."

"It is distracting to me, that something I said needs to be laughed at," Dr. Tanay said, looking at Judge Porter for some kind of ruling. "I don't mean it to be comical."

Hayes, still snickering, said, "I will try to control it."

"Please do," said Judge Porter, in a rare public rebuke of the prosecutor.

Hayes' argument against Tanay was simple. The doctor had not made an in-person examination of Debbie, so Judge Porter should deem all of her prior treatments, counseling, drug abuse, and hospitalizations irrelevant and immaterial.

Stacked on the defense table like a paper snowdrift was the pile of medical records Hayes argued were irrelevant. This stack was so tall that if Dr. Tanay had been sitting behind it, his entire upper body would have been obscured. From the stand, Dr. Tanay gestured toward the stack.

"I certainly would welcome examining Ms. Parmentier," he told Judge Porter, "but I do think that the data I have is more than adequate for me, or for *any* psychiatrist, to reach a reliable diagnostic opinion."

The hearing dragged on and took longer than anyone expected. The jury was confused, the attorneys were irritated, and Terry Moore looked increasingly anxious. Everyone felt the effects but Judge Porter. On the contrary, Porter was the exact opposite of Judge Livo. The more tedious and repetitive the trial became, the more he seemed to dig in. According to an attorney well acquainted with his abilities, Judge Porter was "the intellectual superior of most of his judicial peers and of the lawyers who practiced before his bench. He intensely disliked having either his power or his rulings challenged." Instead of cutting the hearing short, Porter asked Dr. Tanay a few of questions of his own.

"Her personality disorder—let me ask you this: is the personality disorder under that circumstance sufficiently severe, by itself, to question her functional capacity . . . make her functionally problematic?"

"That would be my view," Dr. Tanay said. "There are a number of factors, as I said, the neurological problems."

"That is just one of them?" Judge Porter asked.

"There are episodes of depression, which complicate it, and there is substance abuse that even further complicates it. There is the cumulative effect of the lifelong usage of a variety of drugs, and on top of it, you add organic brain impairment, and you have a pretty complex picture."

Dr. Tanay explained that being able to review her entire psychological history was actually a better gauge of her mental health than a single in-person exam.

"Everyone that has examined her saw only part of the elephant. I, even though I didn't see her as a person, I do sort of have a longitudinal view, and these type of people have a cross section, and she appears fairly normal, but if you look at it longitudinally, she looks much sicker than these records here show. To say she is strictly a personality disorder, you may be really saying an understatement."

Judge Porter said he'd heard enough. He closed the hearing and said he'd need some time to think about the issues raised before he made his decision. He was tired, and he was hungry. It had been a long morning, and the doctor had given him a lot to think about.

"I want to go through this very carefully," Porter said. "It is a complex and an interesting issue, to say the least. Also, it is lunchtime."

With some time to ponder and some food in his stomach, Judge Porter called everyone back to court after the lunch break. Dr. Tanay could testify in front of the jury, but what he could testify to would be strictly limited. Porter would allow the doctor to say what he observed in the hospital and counseling reports, but only those that affected Debbie's ability to "observe, remember, recollect, and recount." Dr. Tanay would not be allowed to mention any diagnosis—not those made by other doctors and counselors, and not one he made himself.

On the surface, Porter's ruling favored the defense. In substance, it would do very little to help Terry's case. Dr. Tanay could not reference Debbie's propensity to lie or her prescription for lithium. He couldn't tell the jury she'd been diagnosed with sociopathic personality disorder and manic depression and had experienced several psychotic breaks. Judge Porter admitted as much when he made his ruling.

"It may be that when the chaff is taken out, there will be no wheat," Judge Porter said.

The bailiff called the jury back in, and Hackett called Dr. Tanay to the stand. He hoped the psychiatrist could provide the jury something to help them understand Debbie.

"My opinion is that because of her emotional difficulties, because of her certain psychiatric conditions and diseases that she has been suffering from, some of them throughout her life, some intermittent, there is a strong likelihood that her ability to perceive, and to interpret, and remember certain events, may have been impaired or affected."

If the jury wanted to look into Debbie's mind any further than that, they would have to use their imaginations. Hackett could only hope they would do just that because Dr. Tanay was his last witness. Late in the afternoon of August 31, 1988, the defense of Terry Moore rested.

As he left court, Hackett had a sobering thought. After all the medical reports, testimony, and fanciful stories, the sum of Debbie was this: she wasn't the least bit credible, but she was still somehow *believable*. A strange dichotomy that Hackett could not remember ever observing in anyone before.

Chapter 42   Closing Arguments

. . . . August 31, 1988

For a man so accomplished at holding his emotions in check, a visible sense of relief was still apparent on the face of Judge Porter. He was not a young man and the stress of the trial had exhausted him. Finally it was almost over and after Hackett rested the defense's case, Porter turned to the jury and explained what was to come. Hayes and Hackett would give their closing arguments and then the jury would begin deliberating.

"We anticipate having final arguments presented to you on Thursday or Friday, as well as the instructions, and have the case go to you this week. Very good. Have a nice day."

Judge Porter often spoke directly to the jury, to greet them in the morning, to give them instructions on points of law during testimony, and to say goodbye to them at the end of the day. He did not expect them to respond, just to listen. But when he finished explaining when they'd probably be deliberating, a juror raised her hand. It was juror number eight, a woman named Betty Swarthout. She'd done the calculations and didn't like the result. Labor Day was a week away.

"Does this mean we will be tied up on a holiday weekend?" she asked. "Is that a possibility?"

Judge Porter tried to hide his irritation but failed.

"There are many things in this world that are possibilities," he said, his answer curt. "I don't have any control over them."

But Juror Swarthout wasn't satisfied.

"I have people coming from downstate for the weekend," she complained.

Michigan did not have the death penalty but Terry Moore was still on trial for his life. A First-Degree Murder conviction carried with it a mandatory sentence of life in prison. Terry's future was about to be decided by twelve citizens, and it seemed to Judge Porter that one of them was more worried about inconveniencing her visiting guests than deliberating a fair verdict. The judge was barely able to contain his disdain.

"Small problem," he said, and exited the courtroom.

By tradition, the prosecutor in a criminal case makes his or her closing argument first. That's because the prosecution has a burden the defense does not—the burden of proof. The prosecution has to *prove* the defendant is guilty of the crime. The defense, in theory at least, doesn't have to prove anything.

Chewing on an ink pen, Hayes began his closing argument at 9 AM the next day, September 1. The role of the prosecutor's closing argument was to sum up the case against the defendant and to give his theory of how and why the crime happened. It was similar to an opening statement, with the new opportunity to respond to witness testimony, physical evidence, exhibits, and the defense's case. In order to get a conviction against Terry for First-Degree Murder and Conspiracy, Hayes needed to convince the jury that he beat Tobias to death and that he planned it with others beforehand.

"Was the killing deliberate?" Hayes asked the jury. "Well, ladies and gentlemen, let's think about that. If someone was assaulted, with weapons used, and with their fists, knocked them unconscious, threw them in the back of the pickup and left them outside in the freezing weather, early in the morning, that's all kinds of intent. There are all kinds of premeditation, deliberation. There is no question. No question there. There is no question there was intent to kill."

Next, Hayes gave the jurors a primer on how to evaluate testimony. Some witnesses had said things that didn't match what other witnesses said. An extreme example was Debbie and Terry.

Debbie said that Terry bought and sold drugs, had planned the murder, and that she had witnessed him carry it out. Terry said he barely knew Jerry Tobias, had never bought, sold, or used drugs, and had never even met Debbie. Two very different stories—how should the jury decide what to believe?

"Do you look at any interest they may have for testifying in the manner in which they did?" Hayes asked the jury. "Do they have any bias? Do they have any prejudice? Do they have a relationship to the parties? Was this a case where someone used to go out with someone, and this is a way for them to get back at them, accusing them of a crime? That's what you look at."

Hayes went on to list what Debbie said about Terry. That Jerry owed him money for drugs. That he promised to punish Jerry for not paying the debt. That Debbie saw him strike some of the blows. Hayes didn't dwell on the physical evidence against Terry because there wasn't any. Instead, he focused on his eyewitness.

"Let's talk about Debra Parmentier for a moment, ladies and gentlemen. When I told you about motive, interest, bias, prejudice for a witness testifying, that is how you judge their testimony. Debra Parmentier has not been promised a thing for her testimony, not one thing.

"How did she look on the witness stand? For two days, *two days*, she stood here and looked right at you, and told you what she saw. You heard her testimony over two days. You heard what she said she saw, and you know what the physical evidence is. No one, *no one* could make it up. No one could."

When the investigation was in its infancy, if Hayes had been willing to speak with Leonard Parmentier, he might have thought differently. He might have gotten to know Debbie the way the defense had, and he might have learned what she was capable of and what inspired her to lie. According to Leonard, Debbie had a pathological craving for attention.

Next, Hayes took aim at Dr. Tanay. Not only was his opinion meaningless, the prosecutor said, scoffing dramatically, it was designed to fool the jury.

"What really offends me, and I think it should offend you too, is to have misleading testimony brought forward. You desire to know the facts. You desire not to be mislead, and nevertheless Dr. Tanay got on that witness stand and said to you, 'Well, she's been hospitalized all these times.' They parade Dr. Tanay in here, as an expert opinion, to tell you what you should do or not do. That is really arrogant, really arrogant, and two thousand dollars a day buys a hell of a lot of testimony."

Hayes' message to the jury was that Dr. Tanay was nothing more than a mouthpiece, a man who would say whatever he was paid to say, making his opinion useless. Didn't Debbie look each of them in the eye and tell them what she saw? Tell them she was afraid for her life? To hear Hayes tell it, Debbie was simply a harmless victim, a woman to be admired for having the mettle to come forward. She was a graduate of the school of hard knocks, yet someone who still did the right thing. That was the Debbie that Hayes presented to the jury—not the sociopathic, lying, attention-seeking drug dealer.

"Ladies and gentlemen of the jury, Terry Moore is innocent of the charges that have been brought by this Court and the Prosecutor's Office. Terry didn't have anything to do with any of this. Terry is innocent. We are not looking for a compromise. I am here to tell you that we are asking you to return a verdict of not guilty."

Hackett began his closing argument the same way he did his opening statement. By asserting Terry's innocence. Not innocent by technicality, or by excuse, or by extenuating circumstance, but innocent because he wasn't even there.

"It's easy to verify the truth," Hackett assured the jury. "It's a little tough when you make it up. This is what you get down to when you start thinking about proof beyond a reasonable doubt, instead of some fantasy, instead of some whim. The prosecutor's case is Debra Parmentier, all by herself."

Terry was just an average working guy, about to turn forty, preoccupied with getting ahead, Hackett said. He went to church, he raised his children, he ran his business; he was not someone who spent his time with drug dealers and crazy women. Gaylord was a small town, and Terry only knew Jerry Tobias in passing. He didn't conduct drug deals with him; he didn't conduct drug deals with anyone.

The essence of Hackett's closing argument was that the jury had no choice but to find Terry innocent because the state hadn't proven their case. The prosecution had nothing that put Terry at the supposed murder scene but Debbie's word. And her word wasn't worth the breath she took to tell her tale.

"Was this a woman who was really disappointed with her life, with Leonard Parmentier, and looking to escape from the responsibilities of being a mother of two, and escaping from Leonard? Was she off in a fantasy of helicopters, gun runnings, and Alaska? And cannons, and tracer rounds, and drugs, and money?"

If Debbie really had participated in all of this illegal activity, where, Hackett wondered aloud, was the money? He reminded the jury of one of the few things Leonard was allowed to testify to: "I never saw any money," Leonard had said. The Parmentiers were very poor. When Debbie left Leonard, she couldn't even afford to rent a tiny apartment and so she moved in with friends. After that she found all sorts of men willing to take care of her, and pay all her bills, culminating in the Michigan State Police. If Debbie really was involved in large-scale drug and gun operations, where was the money?

Next, Hackett focused on the victim, and the mysteries that still surrounded his death.

"I am going to talk, just a minute, about Jerry Tobias. Where was he? We don't really know. Where did he get his money? Think about that. How much did he really have to drink? How much cocaine did he inject? When did he die? Where did he die? All of those are unanswered questions."

Hackett didn't see how any jury could vote for a conviction with so much crucial information still unknown.

"An abiding conviction to a moral certainty? Boy, you got to hesitate. Take a look at the Prosecutor's case and tell me what, before you look at Debra Parmentier, what it is about the Prosecutor's case that mentions Terry Moore? Two hundred exhibits, photographs, diagrams, and all kinds of things, and find *one* that ties in to Terry Moore. Find *one* that relates to him."

Last, Hackett talked about his client. Terry was a single father of three children, his youngest daughter just at the edge of adulthood. He was a businessman focused on financial success. He was a workaholic who knew everything there was to know about the insulation business, and often shared more of that knowledge with people than they wanted to know. Terry talked non-stop about insulation—not a topic of conversation most people wanted to spend more than even a few moments on.

That's just how Terry was, Hackett said, and one of the reasons he knew his client was innocent. Not once had Debbie mentioned Terry's insulation business, even though she said the two of them were supposedly in Mark Canter's car together for hours.

"Do you believe you can sit next to that man for three hours and not know anything about him? Do you believe that you could sit next to him for three hours and *not* have him sell you insulation?" Hackett asked the jury.

In summing up, he characterized the trial as a tragedy, a sad and unfair interruption of an innocent man's life.

"He has been falsely accused. He has offered to you his answer to this bizarre affair. He has waited five months to prove to you that he is innocent. This ordeal has been a nightmare for Terry Moore. You must find Terry Moore not guilty. He didn't do it. He didn't have anything to do with killing Jerry Tobias. If Jerry Tobias was, in fact, killed. He didn't do anything wrong. Thank you."

Chapter 43   Jury Deliberations

. . . . September 1, 1988, 4 PM

Before they began their deliberations, Judge Porter gave the jury his instructions. These included the rules they were required to follow when reaching a verdict and a reminder about the seriousness of their task.

"You are the sole judges of the facts in this case, and must determine which witnesses you will believe, and what weight you will give to their testimony," he said. "In doing so, you may take into account the witness' ability and opportunity to observe, his or her memory, his or her manner while testifying, his or her age, and the interest, bias, or prejudice he or she may have, and the reasonableness of his or her testimony, when considered in light of all of the evidence in the case."

Judge Porter also gave the jury strict instructions about how to communicate with each other and with the Court. The jury would not be sequestered the way that Laurie's jury had, so rules of conduct would be strictly enforced. They could talk about the case in the jury room only. When they were on lunch breaks, dinner breaks, in the courthouse hallway, or when they were recessed for the day, they were to cease all talk about the case immediately. If they had a question about something, they could only communicate it to Judge Porter—not with either of the attorneys, not with the bailiff, and not with any of the witnesses.

All communications with the judge would be in writing. If they needed something, or if they had a question, they were to have the jury foreman write it down and give the note to the bailiff; the bailiff would give it to Judge Porter, and he would provide what they needed and/or answer their questions.

"A verdict in a criminal case must be unanimous. In the jury room you will discuss the case among yourselves, but ultimately each of you will have to make up your own mind. Any verdict must represent the individual, considered, judgment of each juror. I am going to ask you now to retire to the jury room to begin to deliberate and decide your verdict. We will await you."

By now, the trial was big news in Gaylord. Readers of the *Gaylord Herald Times* waited for any bit of news the paper published. While the public waited for a verdict, they could read editor Victoria Naegele's op-ed in the September 1 issue. No one in the news media had spent more time covering Jerry Tobias' death, and the resulting trials, than she had. As the second jury settled in to deliberate, Naegele was particularly struck by the differing styles of the attorneys.

"Superficially, both are conservatively dressed lawyers, dark-haired men sporting facial hair. But here the similarities end," Naegele observed. Mike Hackett was 6' 6", Norm Hayes was 5' 9"; Hackett was married with five kids, Hayes was single with no children. "While Hayes relies on scorn and incredulity, Hackett inflects disgust and tedium as tools in cross examination. When Hayes raises an objection, he does so strenuously. The more softly an objection is stated by Hackett, the more significant it is likely to be. While the bearded and slightly graying Hayes turns to his prosecuting team and smiles knowingly at witnesses' responses,

Hackett, who sports a small moustache, huddles closely with his associates and Moore to discuss testimony given."

Hackett drove a BMW; Hayes a Pontiac.

It was 5:47 PM when the waiting began. The investigation had been long; Laurie's trial had been long; this trial had been long too—a full seven weeks—and all indications were that the jury deliberations would go long as well. At 8:05 PM, the first communication was received from the jury. A note brought in to the judge's chambers from the bailiff read, "Are we able to get any witness testimony or not?"

It was far too soon for the court reporter to have the hundreds of thousands of symbols she entered into her stenotype machine transposed into readable text. Judge Porter wrote back that if the jury wanted to re-visit witness testimony as part of their deliberations, they could ask for specific parts to be read to them aloud by the court reporter.

At 8:15 PM another note. "We need a determination—we need a definition of first and Second-Degree Murder. We are not all sure."

Judge Porter brought the jury back into the courtroom and spent a good half hour explaining the difference between the two charges. In essence, First-Degree Murder meant the defendant had planned the crime. That the killing was deliberate. Second-Degree Murder required the defendant to know that his actions could cause death, but no pre-planning was involved.

A betting person would say that this was a good sign for the prosecution. Asking for the definition of the two offenses could mean that they had already decided Terry was guilty of something—they just needed to decide what. At any rate, there would be no verdict that night. The jury had been in the courthouse for twelve hours. They were tired and wanted to go home.

"You can call it a night," the judge said. "Again, please remember to not discuss this matter. Your family and friends may want to know where you are, and what they can expect. You can't even try to give them hints or tell them anything. So, please be very careful this evening, and I will see you at nine o'clock tomorrow morning. Have a pleasant evening."

At 9:34 PM the court recessed.

The next morning the jury returned as scheduled, the bailiff escorted them into the jury room, and they began deliberating again. An hour in, they sent a note to the judge asking for all the physical evidence to be brought into the jury room. The photographs, the chicken skewer, the city map, the diagram of Walt's, Jerry's clothing—the jury wanted all of it. Judge Porter directed the bailiff to load the evidence onto a cart and wheel it into the jury room.

Two hours passed and another note. The jury wanted to hear what Debbie said happened inside the butcher shop, and they wanted to hear what the *Gaylord Herald Times* reporter said had been published in the newspaper. Then, minutes later, and even before the judge could respond to their request, another note.

"We want to hear all of Debra Parmentier's testimony, direct and cross. We also want a pencil sharpener."

If the previous communications had been a boon to the prosecution, this note bolstered the defense. There was nothing Hackett wanted more than to have the jury go through all of Debbie's testimony with a fine-toothed comb—or, even better, a sharpened pencil.

Judge Porter arranged for court reporter Sandra Davids to do the reading. Debbie's testimony was voluminous and reading all of it, out loud, to the jury would take seven full hours. After five of them they recessed for the day. It was 9:05 PM. Two more hours of Debbie's tale would be waiting for the jury when they returned in the morning.

"Have a nice evening," Judge Porter said. "We trust that you will get a lot of rest. Good night, all. Good night."

Just as one juror had suspected, the deliberations were continued into the holiday weekend. On Saturday morning, they were back in the jury room. If juror Betty Swarthout was still put out by this though, she didn't say anything about it in front of Judge Porter. She and the rest of the jury listened to the court reporter read back the rest of Debbie's testimony. Then in the afternoon, another note.

"Is it possible to get a list of the witnesses that testified or a copy of all witnesses that both attorneys named off, at the start of this case?"

Judge Porter provided the list to the bailiff and he delivered it to the jury room. At 7 PM, the jury foreman sent another note saying they were done for the night.

Still no verdict.

The Judge made a small day-of-rest concession and allowed the jury to begin deliberating an hour later, at 10 AM instead of 9 AM, on Sunday. This gave the church-goers a chance to attend early services and the others an extra hour of sleep.

"You should begin to discuss, again, the facts and evidence in the case," Judge Porter advised them, "with a view to deliberating, in a manner of deciding upon a verdict. Please."

The day passed uneventfully, without any communication from the jury. They recessed at 6:15 PM.

No verdict.

Labor Day, and while most workers were enjoying a day off, the jury returned to the courthouse and began deliberations at 9:30, a half hour later than usual in deference to the holiday. With a break for lunch, the jury listened to the court reporter read back the testimony of Lynn Kaczor, and some of the testimony of Terry

Moore, and then they listened to the police's taped telephone conversations between Debbie and Terry. Late in the afternoon, they were ready to listen to the remaining testimony of Terry, but were allowed to recess early, at 5:15 PM. The court reporter was fatigued, her voice was cracking under the strain of so many hours of reading aloud, and she could do it no longer.

No verdict.

Tuesday morning the court reporter again read the rest of Terry's testimony out loud. After a lunch break, the jury returned to the jury room. No more testimony was read aloud and they began deliberating in earnest. At 4 PM, another note.

"We have come to a standstill. We don't all agree on a verdict. What do we do now? We have taken three votes, and no change."

Judge Porter called both attorneys into the courtroom and shared the jury's latest communication. State courts are prepared for such circumstances and have extensive jury instructions on file for judges to use in just such a circumstance. It was agreed that Judge Porter would bring the jury into the courtroom and share instruction 3:1:18 with them. Up until now, Porter had been playing "good cop." Now he was being forced to dip into his "bad cop" persona.

"I am going to ask you to please return to the jury room and resume your deliberations, in the hope that after further discussions you will be able to reach a verdict," he told the jury once they were seated in the jury box. "Please keep in mind the following considerations: A verdict in a criminal case must be unanimous. In order to return a verdict, it is necessary that each of you agree upon that verdict. In the jury room you will discuss the case among yourselves, but ultimately each of you will have to make up your mind.

"In the course of your deliberations, do not hesitate to re-examine your own views and change your opinion, if you are convinced that it is wrong. However, none of you should surrender your honest conviction solely because of the opinion of your fellow jurors, or for the mere purpose of returning a verdict. Thank you. Please."

The jury went back into the jury room and continued deliberating, but then recessed at 5:30 PM.

No verdict.

Wednesday was another uneventful day in the jury room, at least from the outside looking in. The jury's deliberations began first thing in the morning and went until the noon lunch break, then they were all back in the jury room from 1:30 PM to 5:30 PM. Still no verdict.

The jury, the attorneys, the court reporter, and the bailiff weren't the only ones weary of the case. Judge Porter appeared to be tiring of it as well. His parting words to the jury were getting shorter, and they no longer contained any well wishes.

"We are in recess until nine o'clock tomorrow morning. Don't discuss the matter with anyone or let anyone approach you. We will see you at nine o'clock."

The beleaguered voice of the court reporter was called into service once again on Thursday. Beginning as soon as the jury was seated, she read back the testimony of a Tobias family relative. They deliberated until 10:30 AM and then sent another note to the judge. The jury wanted the testimony of *eleven additional witnesses* to be read back to them aloud. Included in the list were Jackie Tobias, bar customer Barbara Perkins, Leonard Parmentier, and Howard Moore. This would take several days, if not an entire week or possibly longer. Yet the jury again finished early, recessing for the day at 4:15 PM.

No verdict.

Sandra Davids began reading back Jan Duczkowski's testimony on Friday, followed by that of Melvin Green. After dinner, they heard Leonard Parmentier's testimony. Late into the evening, they asked if they could recess for the weekend and Judge Porter consulted with the attorneys before he made a decision.

Norm Hayes agreed to let the jury have the weekend off, but Michael Hackett did not. Hackett wanted the jury to deliberate until they reached a verdict. If that took them the entire weekend or beyond, so be it. Hackett said he had been watching the jury leave early, take long lunch and dinner breaks, but until now hadn't complained. But he was at his breaking point. A weekend recess wasn't fair to Terry.

"It has become ridiculous, the laid-back fashion in which they've approached the case. They basically have been working a nine to five shift since we started. Your honor, my client is incarcerated, and we feel that his rights continue to be infringed upon, and he has to simply sit back and wait for the people to take their weekends and so on. So I am requesting that the Court have them come in and deliberate over the weekend."

Hackett's pleas went unheeded, and Judge Porter gave the jury the weekend off.

"The jury has been deliberating for nine days straight. Mrs. Davids, the court reporter, is hoarse and has a sore throat and difficulty speaking. So, it is my view that we should, in fact, allow the jury to recess, and the court to recess, for the weekend."

Over the long break, the jury would have access to the local media, to their friends and their family, to social situations where the case would surely be discussed, Hackett said. How would Judge Porter ensure that the jury was protected from outside influences? Judge Porter promised that he would strongly caution the jurors about this very thing.

"I want to re-emphasize with even greater intensity than I have in the past. Do not read any local newspapers. Do not watch any local television news programs. Do not listen to any local radio programs. Otherwise, have a nice weekend."

It was 4:20 PM, Friday afternoon, September 9. The jury had been deliberating for more than sixty hours over nine days.

No verdict.

Chapter 44   Debbie Has a Plan

. . . . September 10, 1988

While Terry's jury enjoyed the beginning of a weekend off, another group of citizens was just getting busy. Debbie, her friend Mark Kerry, her boyfriend Curt Beerens, and her neighbor at Sand Hill Manor, Mike Gilbert, had become, if not friends, then certainly the oddest arrangement of allies. Each man longed for Debbie, and she rewarded their attention with her own, while avoiding an exclusive relationship with any one of them. Instead, she gave them assignments, parts to play in her exciting murder drama.

While Terry's jury was temporarily recessed, Debbie and the three men met in Debbie's apartment to flesh out a plan. If it looked like her life was being threatened, Debbie told the men, she'd have a lot more credibility with the jury. The State Police would take her fears more seriously and the jury would have to believe her testimony.

"I don't want to do another Gleason shooting," Mark Kerry said.

Beerens was still working with Kerry as an EMT—the two men had called a fragile truce—but his side business was firearms sales. He told the group that if they were planning another shooting he might be able to provide the rifle, but he wouldn't pull the trigger.

He had his federal firearms license to think about; plus, he was trained to help people, not shoot at them, even if it was faked.

Debbie waved away the men's objections and said she needed to make it look like someone was trying to kill her, so the plan was to have someone shoot into her apartment. Terry Moore's jury was already deliberating, she explained, but the hadn't reached a verdict. Whatever they decided, it had to happen soon. Saturday night, if possible.

That left Beerens out because he was scheduled to work that night. Mark Kerry said he'd help, but he wouldn't be the shooter. That left Debbie's neighbor at Sand Hill Manor, Mike Gilbert. Gilbert said if Debbie really thought that by firing a shot into her apartment she'd get better treatment from the police, he'd do it on one condition. Gilbert was married and had children. He and his family lived in the apartment directly behind Debbie's, so he'd have to make sure he could get his wife to take their kids and go stay at a neighbor's.

The four agreed on the plan, Debbie drew a diagram of the apartment complex, the parking lot, the road, and the surrounding area. Then she wrote down specific instructions for each participant and ordered the men to follow them exactly.

Curt Beerens' task was to park his car in the Sand Hill Manor parking lot, leave the keys in the ignition and a rifle in the backseat, and then walk to his EMT job.

Debbie would make it look like she left her apartment in a rush and would then walk a quarter mile down the road and wait.

Mike Gilbert would get the rifle from Beerens' car and set up in the woods across the road from Sand Hill Manor. He'd find a tree, brace himself against it, aim at the metal frame around Debbie's sliding glass door, and fire. If he hit it, the bullet would fragment and be unidentifiable. As soon as Gilbert took the shot, he was to run back to Beerens' car, pick up Debbie, drop her off at Beerens' cabin, and then return to his own apartment. When the police arrived, he'd act like a mystified neighbor, awakened by the shooting. He'd say he'd found Debbie walking along interstate M-55, incoherent and in shock, so he drove her to Curt Beerens' cabin.

Everyone agreed that the plan could work and Beerens and Gilbert went outside to the parking lot and Beerens popped the trunk of his car. Inside were two rifles to choose from, a 30/30 and a .308. Gilbert looked them over, thought for a second, and chose the .308. It was a more accurate weapon, and he needed accuracy.

Witnesses told police they remembered hearing a single rifle shot just after three in the morning on Sunday, September 11. But for someone who'd just reported a shooting, Renee Wallace seemed remarkably calm. That was the opinion of State Police Trooper David Mertz, anyway. He and his partner were called to the second floor of the Sand Hill Manor Apartments to investigate the shooting. Wallace led them to a neighbor's house and police found a shattered sliding glass door, a bullet hole clean through the doorframe, and two larger holes in an interior wall.

It was the middle of the night, but the commotion woke people up and when police arrived, the lights were on in several apartments and dozens of residents were milling around in the parking lot. One of them was Mike Gilbert.

Trooper Mertz sought out Renee Wallace, since she'd made the 911 call, and she asked if they could talk privately, somewhere that her neighbors couldn't overhear. Mertz, his partner, and Wallace stepped over the shattered glass in the doorway and went inside apartment #10.

"You know who lives here?" Wallace asked them. "Debbie Nicholson. She's that witness to the murder in Gaylord? The one who testified? I know that's a fake name, though. The State Police got her put up here for safekeeping."

Wallace gestured to several large boxes stacked in a corner. She explained they were Debbie's belongings and were packed up because the police were preparing to move her somewhere else. When Wallace heard the gunshot she went to check on Debbie, but she was nowhere to be found.

Trooper Mertz thanked Wallace and then interviewed other neighbors, including Mike Gilbert. Mertz inspected the damage in Debbie's wall and put a pencil in the bullet hole in the drywall.

"Why don't you just put the pencil in the hole in the door frame, too, and that will give you the direction the bullet came from?" Gilbert suggested.

Mertz ignored him and looked around the apartment. He found a pack of cigarettes and a lighter on the kitchen counter, next to a cup of coffee that was still warm. Music played from a radio. A woman's purse was laying open, which Mertz thought was weird. Even in a panic, wouldn't a woman grab her purse? He looked inside and found a tiny spiral-bound address book. The trooper flipped through it, thinking he might find a family member he could call to ask about Debbie, or at least notify she was missing.

But it was not like any address book most women carried. There wasn't a single Parmentier listed. Instead, hand printed in black ink, were twenty-three names and most were familiar to him. Five were deputies with the Otsego County Sheriff's Department, seven were Michigan State Police Troopers, four were federal agents with the Bureau of Alcohol, Tobacco, and Firearms, one was an attorney, and three were witnesses in the Jerry Tobias murder trials.

Among the names Mertz recognized were Detective Fred LaBarge at work and at home, Troopers Goeman, Ambs, Jenkins, and Commander Bob Moylan. Don and Becky Nelson were listed, as were ATF agents Valerie Goddard and George Stohl.

Mertz was also suspicious of Renee Wallace. In his report he noted her demeanor was not natural for someone whose neighbor had just been shot at and was missing.

"Wallace was extremely calm during this whole incident and showed absolutely no surprise or shock that someone may have just tried to shoot Nicholson," Mertz wrote. "She stated that she felt that Nicholson may have gotten a phone call warning her that something like this was about to happen."

One of the officers listed in the little black address book was Detective Sergeant Doug Wilt. Within the northern Michigan police community, it was widely known that he was in charge of Debbie Parmentier's housing arrangements while she was in protective custody, so Mertz gave him a call. As recorded in Mertz report, Wilt's reaction was just as odd as Renee Wallace's:

> "D/SGT. Wilt was contacted and apprised of the situation and felt that the witness was more than likely safe, and that she would be contacting either him or someone else familiar with the situation shortly. He advised to leave the projectile(s) in the wall and do what could be done in so far as an on-scene investigation. He stated that the victim would have to fill in the blank spaces when she called in."

Mertz also noted: "Debra Nicholson is the name used by the victim, however her actual name is Debra Dawn Parmentier, W/F, 5-1-55. She has not been located to be interviewed as of this writing. Status: Open."

While Mertz was making notes for his report, "Debra Nicholson" was already safe inside Curt Beerens' cabin with Mark Kerry. When Beerens returned, he found them there together. When he left for work the next morning, Debbie was still sleeping, but Mark Kerry was gone. Beerens left early. He had something important to do before reporting in at Northern Emergency Services—call Lieutenant Hardy and tell him about the shooting.

At daybreak, Detective Wilt got an emergency assignment from Lieutenant Hardy. He was to drive out to Beerens' cabin, pick up Debbie, make sure she was okay, and then find out what she knew about the apartment shooting.

Wilt did as instructed and found Debbie alone in the cabin, unharmed. He drove her back to her apartment, helped her load the boxes of her things into his car, and then took her to the Gaylord State Police post. Wilt suspected that the shooting was a set-up, but regardless, she couldn't remain at Sand Hill Manor. She was a protected witness and her cover was blown.

Wilt called Hardy with his update, and the two men discussed options for housing their increasingly unpredictable witness. Wilt said he knew of a hotel across the street from the State Police post in Houghton Lake, and Hardy told him to stash Debbie there temporarily. It was still the weekend but on Monday they'd talk with Hayes and LaBarge and figure out a more permanent location.

Detective Wilt made an addendum to Mertz's report on the shooting. "He (Hardy) was advised that the undersigned (Wilt) was skeptical of several areas of the investigation to date."

Chapter 45   Jury Deliberations Continue

. . . . Monday, September 12, 1988, 8:45 AM

Word of the Sand Hill Manor apartment shooting wasn't reported by any newspapers, radio, or television stations. Michael Hackett, Judge Porter, and the jury in the Terry Moore trial had no idea that the prosecution's star witness had been shot at over the weekend. And if they didn't know about the shooting itself, they couldn't know police believed the shooting had been staged by the witness herself.

Prosecutor Hayes knew about it, because Lieutenant Hardy called him and told him, but he didn't share the information. Debbie Parmentier had been accused of being crazy, and of lying, and yet with great skill Hayes managed to get the case to the jury without her coming completely unhinged. His silence surely meant he wasn't about to jeopardize the case now.

On Monday morning, Judge Porter arrived at the courthouse having every reason to feel optimistic. The jury was returning from their weekend off and would surely focus on their task with renewed energy and a fresh perspective. Perhaps a verdict would come that very day. The judge's hopes must have faded quickly when he checked his phone messages, because when he arrived in the courtroom, his mood was not good.

"The record should reflect that we received a call from an attorney, Jim Sullivan, indicating he had been inappropriately approached by a juror." Judge Porter announced, practically growling. The jury had not been brought in yet, and Porter explained to Hayes and Hackett that Jim Sullivan was boating over the weekend and stopped at the Charlevoix marina. A woman he did not know approached him and asked if he could explain the charge of Second-Degree Murder to her.

Sullivan asked her why she wanted to know, and she told him she was serving on Terry Moore's jury and there had been some question about the two different charges. When Sullivan cautioned her against talking to him or anyone else about the case, she brushed him off.

"It doesn't make any difference anyway," she said. "Because I've already made up my mind."

From Sullivan's description, Judge Porter believed the juror to be Betty Swarthout. The same juror concerned about deliberating over a holiday weekend and inconveniencing her guests. Porter called Hayes, Hackett, and Swarthout into his chambers. Swarthout denied any wrongdoing and said she didn't even know anyone named Jim Sullivan. Hackett was furious—this was exactly the kind of thing he'd worried about when Judge Porter authorized the long weekend off and Porter said he'd get to the bottom of it.

Jury deliberations continued throughout the afternoon while fifty miles south at Sand Hill Manor, a representative from the State Police Crime Lab was at work in Apartment 10. While Lieutenant Hardy and Detective Wilt looked on, the crime tech examined a bullet hole in the apartment's living room wall, reached in with a pair of giant tweezers, and retrieved a large caliber bullet and a bullet fragment.

Since the paperwork on the shooting made no mention of the Jerry Tobias case, the police report of it was given a new incident number. Which meant it would not be included in the Jerry Tobias case file, and the police and the prosecutor would not be obliged to pass it on to any of the defense attorneys.

Just after 5 PM, Monday evening, jury deliberations recessed for the day.

No verdict.

On Tuesday, Judge Porter started an investigation of his own. He was not satisfied with Juror Swarthout's answers the day before, and wasn't ready to let the issue go. He asked Attorney Sullivan to come to the courthouse, sit in the back row of the gallery with the other spectators, and point out the juror he'd spoken to at the marina. Porter called the jury in and Sullivan identified juror number eight, Betty Swarthout. The judge recessed the trial, called her back to his chambers, and again asked her if she spoke to Sullivan.

"I may have asked that question," she snapped at Judge Porter. "What's the difference?"

Judge Porter lectured her about the court's rules, but allowed her to remain on the jury. After a short recess, the jury resumed listening to the court reporter read back more witness testimony. They heard the testimony of Pat Mueller, Don and Becky Nelson, and Howard Moore.

At 6:30 PM, the jury sent Judge Porter another note: "Can we hear the definition of conspiracy?"

Judge Porter brought them all back into the courtroom and explained it in detail. Conspiracy, he said, was when someone knowingly agreed to work in conjunction with someone else to commit a crime.

"The crime of Conspiracy to Commit First Degree Premeditated Murder requires proof of specific intent. This means that the Prosecution must prove not only that the Defendant did certain acts, but that he did the acts with intent to bring about a particular result. There must be a meeting of the minds, an agreement between the parties, in order for there to be a conspiracy."

His explanation must have broken something loose in the impasse stymieing the jurors, because at 7:25 PM on Tuesday, the jury sent their final note to Judge Porter: "We have a verdict."

Chapter 46   Another Verdict

. . . . September 13, 1988

"The jury has indicated they have a verdict," Judge Porter told those assembled in the courtroom. "Please make yourself comfortable. After they return a verdict, the first thing we will do is take the jury out. The onlookers, and everybody in the courtroom should remain quiet, please, during the proceedings, until the Court has recessed. I don't want any verbal demonstrations or any physical demonstrations. After I talk to the jury for a moment, we will be taking them out, to see them to their cars. I think that is all we have to cover. We are ready for the jury."

The jury filed into the courtroom and took their places together in the jury box for the last time.

"Have you agreed upon a verdict as to both counts," Judge Porter asked the foreman, Jerry Miller.

"Yes, sir."

"Are the verdicts unanimous as to both counts? That is, are they agreed upon by each and every juror, as to both counts?

"Yes, sir."

The jury foreman stood and everyone packed in the courtroom seemed to inhale a deep breath together. Terry Moore's mother, Esther Moore, was there and so was Norm Hayes' mother. Several witnesses had returned to hear the verdict, as well as many police officers from city, county, and state jurisdictions. The media was there, print, radio, and television, including Hayes' new girlfriend, a television news reporter for a Traverse City NBC affiliate, TV 7 & 4.

In the pause, everyone held their collective breath.

"We the jury find the defendant, Terry Moore, guilty of Second-Degree Murder, as to count one. We, the jury find the defendant, Terry Moore, as not guilty of Conspiracy, as to count two."

Like Robb before him, Hackett asked for the jury to be polled. Judge Porter called their numbers, and each juror agreed that guilty was indeed their verdict.

"On behalf of all the parties, the court officers, the defendant, the entire society and community, I want to thank you very much for what has been an excruciating experience for you, emotionally, intellectually, and physically," Judge Porter said. "And I would go to great lengths to compliment you for the effort and intensity you put in to this trial. If you would recess to the jury room, please. Will the officers please take Mr. Moore into custody?"

"Your honor, I have a motion," Prosecutor Hayes said.

"Certainly."

"I would move at this time that bond be cancelled."

"Thank you, sir. The motion is granted. The Court stands adjourned."

Chapter 47   Esther Moore

· · · · · · · · · · September 29, 1988

To the Editor:

The purpose of this letter is to express my heartfelt gratitude to all of the gracious and courageous people who have supported me and my family through the most trying of times.

To the many who have given their sympathy and asked what they could do to assist us in our quest for true justice, I answer, please pray for the wisdom of "the powers that be" to right this grievous wrong.

As a mother who has lost my sons to a horrendous mistake . . .you who obviously believe the system is infallible, who trust one does not get arrested and charged with a crime unless there is reason, just cause, and evidence, I can only say to you, I sincerely wish that were in fact true. If it were . . . my sons would not be where they are today.

"The most disturbing question to all concerned, how could a jury reach the decision they did? It is my belief the law abiding, honest citizens of the jury were of the same mind as most of us. They want to believe in the system; they are bound by patriotism, by faith in the integrity of our law enforcers, to think one does not get arrested and charged with a crime unless there is reason, cause, and evidence.

Unfortunately that belief, that faith, clouded the true facts of this case. As for the burning question asked by us all, why would someone just make up such gross untruths? The only answer I can offer is the reason her own husband gave—she believed that in trade for her testimony she would receive a new identity, a new life, and leave all her troubles behind.

I am appealing to one and all who might have any doubt, to those of you who think there is perhaps some merit in what I am saying, to see unbiased outside scrutiny of this matter. To ask another authority to look more closely at the possibility that just maybe the true story of what actually happened to Mr. Tobias some 22 months ago is yet to be discovered.

We the family and loyal friends of Terry and Laurie remain frustrated and bewildered that this devastating crime has been falsely blamed on them; but we stand strong in the truth and knowledge of my sons' innocence, and will continue to struggle for justice to prevail."

Esther C. Moore and Family

Readers of the *Gaylord Herald Times* who were looking for evening entertainment could turn to page nine and find an ironic advertisement. The feature film showing that very weekend at the Gaylord Cinema was this: *Who Framed Roger Rabbit?*

Chapter 48   *People v. Douglas Brinkman*

. . . . September 14, 1988

It was a pretty crappy day for Doug Brinkman. First, he pled guilty to resisting arrest, obstructing a police officer, and being a habitual offender. Second, he was supposed to appear in front of

Judge Porter, but that judge was exhausted from the Terry Moore trial; then he was supposed to appear in front of Judge Davis, but that judge was busy with the Don Heistand and Mark Canter pre-trial activities. Brinkman was eventually taken from the Otsego County Jail in Gaylord and transferred to Grayling, where a third judge was called into service to hear his plea and pronounce his sentence.

Judge Richard Liedel heard Brinkman's plea to an unrelated resisting and obstructing charge and was apprised of Brinkman's past convictions—one for larceny from a building and one for receiving and concealing stolen property—and gave him the maximum sentence allowed. Four years in prison.

To round out Brinkman's rotten day, immediately after his sentence was pronounced, he was charged with Accessory After the Fact in the murder of Jerry Tobias and was transferred from the county jail to Southern Michigan Prison. Brinkman was no stranger to the county jail but he'd never been in prison before, let alone in the state's most feared maximum security prison, a place most people just referred to as "Jackson."

Days later, the intake report from the prison social worker didn't provide him with any good news.

"Mr. Brinkman appears to be a very poor candidate for community supervision. Further, he does not appear amenable to substance abuse treatment and therefore the time and resources needed to put him into a program does not seem worthwhile. Mr. Brinkman does not appear capable of curbing his impulsive and abusive behavior. As such, it is recommended that the sentence for this offense be aimed at removing him from the community for the longest time possible."

The longest time possible was pretty long—life, if he was found guilty on the Accessory charge, and if the prosecutor could make the case that he was a habitual offender.

Chapter 49   Roger Becker's Mistake

. . . . September, 1988

Roger Becker had made some really bad choices in his life, but dodging the FBI wasn't going to be one of them. Becker was Debbie's former boyfriend, the man whose handwriting matched Dean Robb's death threat letter and who had fled to Colorado, just before anyone found that out. But even the Rocky Mountains weren't far enough away from Gaylord, Debbie, and the Jerry Tobias case to give him cover. Now that Terry Moore's trial was over, Mark Canter's trial was about to begin and MacNeil wanted Becker to testify. The police had known for almost three months that it was Becker's handwriting on the Dean Robb death threat letter but had done nothing about it. MacNeil decided to track him down himself by issuing a subpoena compelling him to return to Gaylord.

By the time Becker was served, he opened the subpoena, looked at the date, and realized he was supposed to testify in Michigan the very next day—either that or face a bench warrant for failing to appear. With the threat of arrest hanging over his head, Roger Becker walked into the Glenwood Springs, Colorado office of the FBI and agreed to answer whatever questions the law had for him.

The agent on duty, Frank Phelps, contacted the police in Gaylord, and then began the interview. He started with general questions, and then focused on the letter to Dean Robb.

Yes, Becker said, he had dated Debbie during the summer of 1987. Yes, Debbie did have a diary, he had seen it with his own eyes. Yes, he did go to Florida with her, but no, they never hid the diary in any safe deposit box. There was no bank, no safe deposit box, and no key. Debbie made that up. She never told him about any murder, just that she was scared of an attorney named Dean Robb.

The death threat was Debbie's idea, Becker said. She asked him to write it, told him exactly what to say, where to mail it, and he followed her instructions. There was something about Debbie that just made him want to help and protect her.

Becker seemed mystified by his own behavior and told the agent he was sorry he'd done it. He didn't even know Dean Robb and never meant the attorney any harm. He cared so much for Debbie, might have even been in love with her, and was just doing what she asked. Their relationship ended soon after he wrote the letter when the State Police put her in protective custody.

"My handwriting will match the letter," Becker admitted, and agreed to give the FBI a handwriting sample and be fingerprinted. The agent sent the prints back to Michigan. On file at the State Police crime lab were the three latent prints from the Dean Robb death threat letter. All three matched the ones the FBI sent from Colorado.

Chapter 50   Missing Documents

. . . . September 23, 1988

Ten days passed since the guilty verdict in the Terry Moore case when Prosecutor Hayes received a note from a Gaylord divorce attorney. Michael Cooper was representing Debbie in her divorce from Leonard and had been meeting with her off and on for almost two years. One of those meetings was held Friday, Dec. 5th, and it began at 3 PM and lasted until 4:30 PM. This was the same time Debbie testified she'd been driving around Gaylord with Mark Canter and Terry Moore, selling drugs.

In his note to the prosecutor, Cooper said he was absolutely certain he'd been conferring with Debbie in person during that hour and a half. He even sent along a copy of his appointment calendar to prove it and sent a copy of the correspondence to Ray MacNeil. Cooper's note, and the fact it came from the divorce attorney himself, not from the prosecutor's office, was one more indication to MacNeil that he wasn't getting copies of everything the police and Hayes had amassed on the case. The court's discovery rule mandated that whatever either the prosecution or the defense learned about Jerry Tobias' death be provided to the opposing side. In virtually every criminal trial, this was a given, yet MacNeil believed he was being kept in the dark. When his complaints to Prosecutor Hayes went unanswered, he brought the argument to Judge Davis. On Sept. 26, 1988, Judge Davis issued a court order.

"It is hereby ordered that the Otsego County Prosecuting Attorney and/or the Michigan State Police, as the investigating agency in this matter, shall advise the Defendant of any and all information relative to this matter which is in their possession or which they become aware of before or during the trial."

Like Judge Porter, Judge Davis could be an intimidating force in the courtroom, but according to one attorney familiar with both men, Davis was "cut from another cloth." Davis was "a formidable force in his own right." Sometimes sparkling in wit and good humor, he was on other occasions highly aggressive, occasionally abusive, and frequently emotional. In a phrase, he was "all that his muscular frame, strong handshake, ruddy complexion, and red hair implied."

The court order did generate copies of additional police reports for Mark Canter's defense. But MacNeil couldn't ask for what he didn't know existed. The police report on the Sand Hill Manor shooting was dated September 10, 1988. Subsequent reports from the State Police crime lab on the slug and the bullet fragment were dated September 11, and 12, 1988. These remained filed separately from the Tobias case, and neither MacNeil, nor the defense attorneys for the other men awaiting trial, received them.

Other materials were also missing from discovery the defense received, even after the court order. For example, MacNeil, Felton, and Deamud were given a police report stating that a local man, Ned Brandenberg, had been interviewed, but they weren't given the tape of the interview. Debbie said right before the murder—when she was riding around with Terry, Mark, Doug, and "John"—they'd stopped and sold drugs to Brandenberg. On the taped interview, Ned disputed that.

"Brinkman's a friend of mine," Brandenberg told police. "I was heavily shocked when they picked him up for this because he never told me nothing about it, you know, and we were good friends, me and Doug were."

A State Police detective replied, "You're guaranteeing me that you never had contact with Debbie Parmentier on that night and Mark Canter?"

"Hey," Brandenberg said, "I would like to help you guys as much as the next guy, seriously I didn't see them, you know, like I told them other guys. Do you want me to make something up?"

Chapter 51   Moving Debbie Again

. . . . October 6, 1988

In the weeks following the Sand Hill Manor shooting, police moved Debbie to a hotel near the police post in Houghton Lake and then to a condo at Schuss Mountain, an area ski resort. Keeping her at a resort wasn't cheap, but at least until snow season it was off-season rates and less expensive than a hotel room. Still, Hardy knew it wasn't a long-term arrangement.

Debbie lived at Schuss Mountain alone, but after what happened at Sand Hill Manor, Hardy increased her supervision. Several State Police officers were assigned to take turns checking on her including Wilt, Goeman, and a new man, Paul Dunkelberg.

The routine was straightforward. Whichever officer was on Debbie detail would drive out to the ski resort, knock on Debbie's door, go inside, and spend an hour or so just talking with her. If Debbie wanted attention, and that would keep her out of trouble, Hardy's monitoring plan would see to that. On a day that Detective Goeman was assigned to check on her, he opened the drawer of her nightstand looking for a phone book. What he found instead was a .38 special, two boxes of ammunitions, and a red pill. Goeman had worked narcotics, and the pill looked like a prescription painkiller, Oxycodone.

"What are you doing with all this?" he asked Debbie.

"Ah, in case you forgot," Debbie said sarcastically, "my life is in danger."

The gun was for protection, she told Goeman, and had been given to her by a local drug dealer who obviously cared more about her than the police did. If Goeman wanted to do some actual detecting, Debbie said, this drug dealer had an out-of-state connection interested in expanding into Michigan.

Detective Goeman was skeptical. To him, it just sounded like another one of Debbie's outlandish stories, and he accused her of making it all up. But Debbie held firm. She told Goeman she had specific details about the dealer's operation, including names and places. The dealer's name was Rich Chilson and the out-of-state man was Ken Smith. Debbie was their go-between, and the men were planning a big drug drop. Smith would fly to Michigan on a military plane, cruise directly over Gaylord, and drop the drugs at a remote spot. Debbie was supposed to pick them up and deliver them to Chilson, who would sell them locally. The gun Goeman found in her nightstand was for protection during the exchange.

"It's what the dealers call a 'throw-down' gun," Debbie said, meaning untraceable and easily disposed of. Debbie was so connected to the criminal underworld, she bragged to Goeman, she could get any kind of gun she wanted. Automatics, sub-machine guns, anything, and they were all untraceable.

Goeman said he wasn't convinced, but he confiscated the gun, the ammunition, and the pill, and told Debbie he'd talk to his superiors about her story. Later that day, Goeman logged a .38 Special, Sport Arms, Miami, 3" blue steel revolver, a box of fifty .38 Special cartridges, a box of ten exploder .38 Special cartridges, and one red capsule into evidence. Then he called Hardy.

While the police scrambled to keep tabs on Debbie, MacNeil petitioned the court to require her to undergo a psychological exam. Judge Davis agreed. He was not about to have the shenanigans in his court that dominated Judge Porter's. Debbie Parmentier was either competent to testify or she wasn't, and the University of Michigan's Center for Forensic Psychiatry was chosen by Davis to figure out which it was.

The Center was established by the University of Michigan in 1974 and had developed into one of the premier training sites in the country for people studying the interface of mental health and the law. Dr. Robert Mogy, a certified forensic examiner and one of the Center's directors, was assigned to evaluate Debbie.

"The question at issue is whether or not Ms. Parmentier is legally competent to provide testimony as a witness," the court order read. "It is specifically requested that the report address itself to the question of Ms. Parmentier's 'ability to perceive, recall, and recollect events allegedly transpiring on or about December 5 and 6, 1986.'"

On October 7, Detective Goeman picked Debbie up at the ski resort, drove her three hours south to the Center, and waited while she underwent eight hours of tests.

"Ms. Parmentier appeared for examination at the Forensic Center on October 7, 1988, at approximately 9:00 AM," Dr. Mogy wrote in his report. "She received psychological testing from approximately 9:00 AM until 2:00 PM when she was seen by the present examiner in an interview for a three hour and fifteen minute period, finally ending at 5:15 PM. Ms. Parmentier presented as a well-groomed and kempt, slender, long-haired, Caucasian female who appeared for the examination dressed in jeans, a sweater and blouse, and tennis shoes."

Dr. Mogy determined at the time of the interview, that Debbie wasn't psychotic, suicidal, or homicidal. She wasn't hearing voices, wasn't delusional or hallucinating, and didn't remember ever having a hallucination, except for that one time when she dropped acid and people's faces changed and the trees came alive. She was oriented for the correct time and place, knew who she was, who the doctor was, and why she was there.

Despite her somewhat normal-seeming exterior, Dr. Mogy said Debbie had significant mental problems. The results of the tests and the exam found she suffered from "continued impulsive trends," "exaggerations and outright falsifications," "consistent elements of personality dysfunction," "consistent anti-social conduct," "extensive street drug abuse," "considerable stress, anxiety, and depression," "organic brain trauma superimposed on a pre-existing learning disability," "long-standing organic brain dysfunction," "a rather untrusting nature," "a tendency to engage in manipulation, deception, and anti-social conduct," and, finally, he also diagnosed her with a severe "character dysfunction."

Like Dr. Tanay before him, Dr. Mogy reviewed Debbie's hospital commitment reports and her mental health history. But he also had access to her testimony in the Terry Moore trial, and the false accusations of spousal abuse and rape she'd filed with various police departments against Leonard Parmentier.

"Some of the perplexing and bizarre pattern of rape reports may be more comprehensible as simply Ms. Parmentier's method to escape from a difficult situation," Dr. Mogy wrote to the court. "It seems clear that Ms. Parmentier has taken the tact [sic] that she is justified in saying what she needs to say to get what she wants, whether this is deceptive or not."

Nevertheless, Dr. Mogy determined that none of these mental health problems or character deficiencies disqualified her from being a court witness. In his medical opinion, Debbie would likely lie, but she was still competent to testify.

The costs for Otsego County were mounting. Beyond the emotional toll, the Michigan State Police man hours, Debbie's upkeep, and the tangent investigations into drugs, guns, and shootings that so far had led nowhere, the case was taking a big bite out of Otsego County's budget. The pre-trial exams, arraignments, evidentiary hearings, and trials were bankrupting the city of Gaylord and Otsego County, according to the *Gaylord Herald Times*.

So far the public had spent $27,201.60 on Terry Moore's trial, and the bills were still coming in. It had cost more than $19,000 to prosecute Laurie Moore, even though he hired his own attorney. Mark Canter, Doug Brinkman, and Don Heistand all had court-appointed attorneys and their trials loomed, promising to cost the taxpayers thousands more.

"Now the county is facing the cost of prosecuting the remaining three defendants in the Tobias case, who, unlike the Moore brothers have been granted court-appointed attorneys," the Chairman of the County Commissioners told the *Gaylord Herald Times*. "The county must pay all court-related expenses for Canter, Donald Heistand, and Brinkman, including expert witness fees, independent evaluators and investigators, and attorney fees.

"The pressure on the county coffers is so great that if Mark Canter's murder trial goes as scheduled next week, the county may be forced to choose between delaying payment of the bills until next year, asking for more millage, borrowing money, or cutting hours of operation for county offices."

Following her exam, police moved Debbie again. Lieutenant Hardy was looking into her story about accessing illegal guns and an impending airplane drug drop. If her information proved reliable, the police might want to use her in an undercover operation. If that happened, Debbie needed to be back in Gaylord where the State Police could keep a close eye on her. Keeping her in town would also make it more convenient for Prosecutor Hayes, who was going to need her to testify in the Mark Canter trial. The State Police booked a room for her at a local hotel, the Best Western.

Lieutenant Hardy had a dilemma. He didn't trust Debbie and was frustrated by her unpredictability. Yet he wasn't convinced she'd lied about everything. Perhaps she did witness something at Walt's Butcher Shop and had ties to criminal activity. If so, Hardy believed he had a responsibility to investigate her stories and make sure she was available to testify. If more attention was all she wanted, Hardy decided to give it to her, and once a week he visited Debbie himself.

The slim and pretty former drug addict with a sixth grade education and the State Police lieutenant in charge of detectives and major crimes in 23 counties developed a weekly ritual. Lieutenant Hardy would call Debbie and arrange a time to meet. She would leave her room at the Best Western and wait for him in the lobby. He'd arrive and together they'd go into one of the hotel's empty conference rooms and talk. When their conversation was over, Hardy would leave and Debbie would go back to her room.

The Gaylord Best Western wasn't a luxury hotel, but it was still a busy place. Located right off I-75, the interstate connecting Detroit to Michigan's Upper Peninsula and Canada, the hotel was a popular layover spot for all sorts of travelers. On any given day,

vacationers, traveling salespeople, truckers, and government workers all checked in for a one-night stay, almost always on their way
to somewhere else.

One of these random travelers was ATF Agent George Stoll.
Stoll was based in Grand Rapids, but on Oct. 9, 1988, he was
headed north to Sault Ste. Marie, to consult with his Canadian
counterparts. The trip from his Grand Rapids office to Sault Ste.
Marie, Canada, was a six-hour drive. It was late on a Sunday night,
and Stoll was tired. His plan was to stop partway in Gaylord, get
a good night's sleep, and cover the last hundred or so miles to the
U.S.-Canadian border on Monday morning.

Stoll pulled off the expressway and into the parking lot of the
Gaylord Best Western. He checked in at the front desk, asked the
clerk for the government rate, showed his ATF identification, and
went to his room. Moments later, the phone in his room rang, and
Stoll was surprised to hear the voice of Lieutenant John Hardy on
the other end of the line. The two men were acquainted with each
other; Hardy had recently called Stoll and related Debbie's gun
and drug stories. But Stoll was still surprised to hear his voice. He
hadn't told anyone he'd be in Gaylord because until a few minutes
ago, he didn't know he'd be there himself. So how, Stoll wondered,
did Hardy know where he was?

Hardy told the agent it was just a coincidence. Hardy was housing a protected witness at the hotel, and she'd been in the lobby
and overheard Stoll ask for a government rate and then saw his
ATF ID. She called Hardy in a panic, saying a government agent
was at the Best Western and was after her.

Hardy told Stoll he'd been able to calm Debbie down, but the
two men needed to meet immediately. The witness was the same
one who had the "throw-down" gun, and might have information about illegal guns, including machine guns, Hardy explained.
He also told the agent Debbie's story about Ken Smith and Rich
Chilson.

Stoll said he'd be more than happy to run a check on the confiscated gun and on Smith and Chilson. If Hardy wanted to launch an undercover investigation and have his witness try to buy an illegal machine gun, Stoll would help him set it up. The ATF was always interested in working with local or State Police to get illegal guns off the streets and put criminal gun traders in prison.

Chapter 52 Debbie Gets a Gun

. . . . October 13, 1988, 7:45 AM

Lieutenant Hardy arranged for a tap on Debbie's phone and it rang, just as she said it would, and right on time. A man's voice on the other end of the line said, "The package is not here."

For more than a year and a half, Debbie had been telling anyone who would listen—Blair Robb, the Michigan State Police, the prosecutor's office, and now the ATF— that she had information about illegal gun sales. Finally, someone was taking her seriously. Lieutenant Hardy and Agent Stoll set up an undercover sting, where Debbie would buy a machine gun, an "Uzi," from a black market gun dealer. That was "the package" the mysterious caller was referring to. Hardy and Stoll would stake out the buy and arrest the seller.

Despite these plans, Hardy remained skeptical of Debbie's stories. They were just so outlandish. Buying an illegal automatic weapon was one thing. Blowing up an island with stolen dynamite and rocket launchers, driving crates of stolen military handguns into Canada, flying to Nevada and California in military planes loaded with artillery, and hiring military chopper pilots for drug and gun runs were something else altogether. But as crazy as Debbie's stories sounded, each one seemed to have some small verifiable fact attached, making him feel obliged to investigate them. Including this latest attempt to buy a machine gun.

While the State Police and the ATF listened, a man on the other end of Debbie's phone said he'd call her back next Thursday, Oct. 20, at 3:30 PM. He'd have "the package" for her then.

While the ATF waited, Agent Stoll assigned a colleague to interview Debbie in detail. Detective Goeman picked her up from the Gaylord Best Western on Monday, Oct. 17, and drove her to the Traverse City Post, where agent Valerie Goddard interviewed her a second time.

Debbie was an ATF agent's dream; she wasted no time on small talk, but launched right in to her story. Rogue military men in Nevada, California, and Texas were buying stolen military weapons and selling them to criminals in Mexico and Canada. From a tape of the interview:

Goddard: How are you aware of that, that Texas and Mexico were involved, did they say that or is it something you . . . .

Debbie: They wanted me to go with them down on a three day run, and with me being involved in what I am, I did talk to Doug Wilt about it, and I talked to Fred (LaBarge) about it and they said, no it's not a good idea, so I backed away from them.

Debbie told Goddard she'd witnessed small arms and automatic weapons smuggled into Mexico and Canada. Any large-scale gun thefts in the U.S. were tied to military thefts, and the weapons were then delivered to foreign drug dealers.

At the close of the interview, Goddard told the State Police that she thought Debbie's information was solid, and that from her leads, the ATF could begin a large-scale investigations. She complimented Debbie for coming forward.

Goddard: You've given us enough information to keep us busy for five years.

Chapter 53 *People v. Mark Canter*

. . . . October 18, 1988

In contrast to the lengthy jury selection process in the Moore trials that lasted weeks, the jury for *People v. Mark Canter* was seated in just one day. Late in the afternoon just before court recessed for the day, Judge Davis addressed the jurors.

"As members of the jury you alone must decide this case. You are the sole and exclusive judges of the facts and you alone determine the weight, the effect, and the value of the evidence, as well as the credibility of the witnesses. You must begin this trial with a presumption of innocence foremost in your minds."

Ray MacNeil wondered whether that last instruction was an utter impossibility. Though Mark's trial was being held in Grayling on the case's third change of venue, thirty miles wasn't near enough distance to create the presumption of innocence. The case was headline news throughout the state and all around the Midwest. If anyone on the jury hadn't heard that two men, brothers, had been tried and convicted for the crime, it could only be because they were hermits. Unfortunately for Mark, those people didn't usually get called for jury duty.

Nothing could be presumed in this case, MacNeil knew. Nothing. Not his client's innocence, not that an insane woman shouldn't be allowed to testify, and not even that the prosecutor's office would help him subpoena his defense witnesses.

Serving trial witness subpoenas was normally simple legal housekeeping, but nothing was simple or normal in the Tobias case. A few days before Mark's trial was set to begin, MacNeil called Norm Hayes and asked the prosecutor's office to serve subpoenas to his defense witnesses because he was having trouble hiring a process server. Hayes' answer was an emphatic "No." He complained about the request to Judge Davis.

"Mr. MacNeil has been afforded not only an investigator but also a legal assistant," Hayes griped. "I don't know what the investigator is doing, quite frankly, that the taxpayers are paying for his services, but beyond that, to get (witness subpoenas) dumped in my office at 4:30 on a Friday I felt was unfair."

MacNeil explained his problem to the judge. He'd tried to hire three different men for the task, but all refused it.

The first man turned down the job because his wife worked as a secretary for the Gaylord Police Department, and he was concerned that helping the defense would cause hassles for his wife at work. The second man MacNeil approached was a retired police officer who often did process serving work for local attorneys. He told MacNeil he wanted nothing to do with the Tobias case. So MacNeil tried to hire an out-of-town process server, but that didn't work out either. The man did come to Gaylord, and tried to carry out the task, but was followed by the police, pulled over and questioned several times, and grilled by officers regarding his purpose in Gaylord. It unsettled the man, so he quit and left town.

"You mention the Tobias murder case, and everybody runs for cover," MacNeil told Judge Davis.

Subpoenaing witnesses was important, but it was also routine, and it irked MacNeil that a detail usually so mundane had taken up his, and the court's, time. It was probably indicative of a much bigger problem, and MacNeil was worried. If the investigation was so polarizing he couldn't even get his witnesses subpoenaed without a major ordeal, what were the chances that his client was going to get a fair trial? Probably not good.

Judge Davis ordered the prosecutor's office to assist MacNeil and serve his witnesses with their subpoenas, and the trial opened as scheduled. While motions were being heard, MacNeil plunged into the same morass that sucked in Michael Hackett—the exact level of crazy that affected Debbie Parmentier. He knew Judge

Davis mandated her exam, and that she'd been deemed competent to testify, but he still wanted her psychological records to be admitted as evidence.

"I will permit the reference (to the extensive psychological records) but limit it to that," Judge Davis ruled. "Counsel may not go into any specific instances of treatment at this juncture, nor into any reference to the records underlying the treatment, or that would suggest a diagnosis."

Next, MacNeil made a motion to admit her police record, and her reports of gun-running, drug dealing, conspiracy theories, and black magic. Each would allow a jury to more fully judge her truthfulness as a witness, MacNeil argued.

"Now, on this second can of worms that just got opened up," Judge Davis said, "apparently you wish to make some statement to the jury, referencing statements that this witness had made in the past that would appear to be, on their face, bizarre, is that it?"

That was indeed it, MacNeil said. Ever since he interviewed Leonard Parmentier, MacNeil had spent months investigating Debbie. He'd interviewed people who knew her and had read everything he could find about her in the police record and in the newspaper reports on Terry Moore's trial. He knew that Debbie was on record making outlandish claims including that she and Mark Canter ran guns and drugs for the Iran Contras; that she'd infiltrated a U.S. military armory; and even that she could move objects with her mind. MacNeil's contention was such statements would show the jury she was not a credible witness, and were therefore vital to the defense.

Judge Davis was a careful man. He was well aware of how costly the two previous trials had been. At times, they'd even verged on ridiculous—something that harmed the court's reputation for dignity and fairness. But witness credibility was important both to the defense and to the prosecution, Davis believed, and needed to be respected.

"You're proffering some rather inflammatory material, and the fear is, on the prosecutor's behalf, that once heard it's so prejudicial that it's going to skew the jury . . . That's the fear see, and that's the problem."

MacNeil was being stand-up, and playing by the rules in asking for permission to enter Debbie's strangest statements into evidence. He could have just used them for shock value in the middle of the trial and taken his licks from the judge if they turned out to be inadmissible. Instead, he'd done the ethical thing and asked ahead of time for permission. Judge Davis' reaction had to make him wonder if he should have just snuck them in without warning.

"If we can't do that, our whole theory of the defense is gone," MacNeil argued. "Do you believe Debbie Parmentier? That's the ultimate issue. And Judge, you can write that on the board."

Davis ruled the defense would be allowed some latitude when it came to questioning Debbie on her crazier statements, and that some of them could be presented to the jury. However, MacNeil could not use any of them in his opening statement. That would be too prejudicial.

Motions completed, the rest of the day was taken up with both of the attorneys' opening statements. Hayes made his first; it was the third time he'd given one, and he was getting better at it each time. With Mark Canter as the defendant, Hayes was more succinct, more on point, and more specific.

"The evidence will show that this was payment for a debt," Hayes promised the jury. "That Jerry Tobias' life was the payment for a debt. That while Jerry Tobias was, in fact, struggling for his life that it became, quite frankly, a free-for-all. And that Mark Canter took part in it."

Twice before Hayes faced defense attorneys who questioned Debbie's character. Hayes knew MacNeil would too, and so he used part of his opening statement to try to diffuse that.

"Let me tell you—Debra Parmentier is not the greatest person in the world. All right. She's not. But when you're dealing with a case of this nature, the people involved are not nice. All right? We all understand that, and we all know that."

Hayes told the jury right up front that Debbie wasn't perfect, but explained that was exactly why the jury should believe her. Perfect people didn't get involved in drug murders. Murder was a dirty, nasty business. The police and the courts had no choice but to get a little dirty themselves in order to solve capital crimes, punish the guilty, and keep society safe. The prosecution's eyewitness might not be the greatest person in the world, but she could help send a killer to prison.

When MacNeil's turn came, he focused on Debbie, too.

"My name is Ray MacNeil. I represent Mark Canter. Mark Canter is sitting here charged with Murder and Conspiracy to Commit Murder. Mark Canter did not commit murder. Mark Canter did not know Jerry Tobias. Mark Canter has *never* known Jerry Tobias, nor *seen* Jerry Tobias any time in his life. Mark Canter has never been in the rear of Walt's Butcher Shop. Mark Canter knows *absolutely nothing* about the conditions that caused the death of Jerry Tobias.

"The only question that you have to resolve is: Is Debbie Parmentier telling the truth? If she's telling the truth, then Mark Canter has to pay the price. If she's not telling the truth, this is a cruel, cruel hoax on an innocent man who had nothing to do with the death of Jerry Tobias."

MacNeil verbalized the same shocked refrain as Dean Robb and Michael Hackett had before him. There was no physical evidence linking Mark to Jerry's death, to the butcher shop, or to Jerry's truck. No fingerprints, no hair, no nothing. Not only didn't Mark murder Jerry, Ray said, no one murdered Jerry. He died of a cocaine overdose. Every word the jury would hear from Debbie that said any different was a lie.

"What it comes down to again, I'll reemphasize. Do you believe Debbie Parmentier? I have no personal animosity toward Debbie Parmentier or toward anybody in this case, and I say to you in a legal sense—and in a legal sense only—Debra Parmentier is nuts."

MacNeil abided by Judge Davis' ruling and did not quote any of Debbie's outlandish claims in his opening statement, but he did promise the jury they would be hearing what he called her "whoops testimony."

For example, MacNeil said, first Debbie told police she didn't know anyone named Jerry Tobias, but then she told them they dealt drugs together. Whoops. In her account of what happened at Walt's Butcher Shop the night Jerry died, she said she looked out the back window and saw a police car drive by. Except that Walt's doesn't have a back window. Very big whoops.

The repetition of the word *whoops* became almost comical for a while, but as he finished, MacNeil explained what he believed was the awful truth of the case: "I don't know what happened to Jerry Tobias, and when this case is over, you're not going to know, either."

Chapter 54   Prosecution, the Third Time Around

. . . . October 20, 1988

After opening statements, Hayes called his witnesses, entered evidence into the record, and began the prosecution of Mark Canter.

Employees of Acme Tool described Jerry's truck, and Jackie Tobias again testified about his clothing: the bloodstained shirt, the jeans with the ripped belt loops, the cowboy boots with the scrape on the heel.

On cross-examination, Jackie Tobias admitted to MacNeil that Jerry acted strangely in the months before his death. For example, he drank every day, which was unusual. "The drinking was new to me," she said. "Jerry would (usually) have . . . two beers a week. The last year to six months, he was drinking heavy . . . he was drinking more than normal. . . he was just not himself."

The core of the prosecution's case began, just as it had previously, when Hayes called Dr. Newhouse. The pathologist had already testified in the Laurie Moore and the Terry Moore trials. She had experience performing autopsies on frozen bodies, having completed between ten and fifteen. Dean Robb and Michael Hackett had taken her at her word, but MacNeil dug a little deeper and found that her figures turned out to be literally true, but irrelevant. Newhouse had performed several autopsies on frozen bodies, but she'd done them all *after* she performed the autopsy on Jerry Tobias.

In his re-direct, MacNeil asked her how many autopsies she'd performed on frozen bodies *before* she was assigned to the Tobias case.

"Probably one other," she said. MacNeil said he'd found no record of it in his research on her career.

"Do you remember, by any chance, the name of that one?" he asked.

"No," she said, "I don't."

Newhouse explained that her finding that Jerry died of blunt force trauma was supported by the structure of the brain tissue slides she'd collected and examined under the microscope. But MacNeil had done his own research on frozen bodies and had learned that brain tissue traumatized by a blow to the head and brain tissue frozen looked strikingly similar, even under a microscope.

MacNeil explained that to the jury and then asked Newhouse if, in the single frozen body case she said she'd completed prior to working on Jerry Tobias, she collected and examined any brain slides.

"No," Newhouse admitted. "I did not."

The autopsy she performed on Jerry Tobias was the first time in Newhouse's career she'd ever taken frozen brain matter slides, examined them under a microscope, and used the findings to determine cause of death. MacNeil knew the doctor had far less experience in the delicate work than she previously testified to. He had read all of her transcripts and knew that in Laurie Moore's trial, Newhouse said she'd completed such a procedure two or three hundred times, when the actual number was once, maybe. This could have been an important point for the defense, but since Judge Davis ruled that neither attorney could make mention of prior convictions in the Tobias case, the jury never learned about it.

"Can you perform an autopsy on a frozen body?" Hayes asked, when it was his turn again to question the pathologist.

"You can, but it's certainly much more difficult and you want to have the most optimal circumstance for performing the autopsy so your examination can be complete. In the case of Mr. Tobias . . . the body was completely frozen. It was frozen solid."

On its surface, this admission would appear to favor the defense. The pathologist was testifying that it was difficult to do an autopsy on a frozen body. Something the defense in all three trials had been trying, with limited success, to point out. But Hayes was too skilled to ask the question without a good reason. And, he had one—to justify showing autopsy photos to the jury. They were gruesome and shocking—just what the prosecution needed to horrify the jury and make them want to punish whoever was responsible.

"I do not like to have to admit photographs of that nature any more than anyone else," Hayes said. "However, when defense counsel stands up before the jury, and in his opening statement challenges the credibility and believability of this witness . . . unfortunately for the defense, those photographs depict exactly what you get with blunt force trauma."

MacNeil objected but Hayes' strategy worked. Judge Davis allowed the photographs into evidence after warning the jury about their graphic nature. He handed them to the jury foreman almost reverently and directed them to be passed from juror to juror.

And with that, the day's testimony was over. The jury was left to ponder the disturbing images overnight, knowing that they depicted only the external injuries. The next day, Dr. Newhouse would be back on the stand, detailing the internal ones.

Later that same night, while the jury was assigned to contemplate what they'd heard and seen in the courtroom, Debbie Parmentier and Curt Beerens got into the back seat of a State Police cruiser and directed Agent Stoll and Detective Goeman to a remote house trailer off M-66 near Falmouth Road in Missaukee County. Goeman parked the car, all four got out, and Debbie led the men into a barn behind the trailer. Along a back wall was a woodpile. She rummaged around in the logs for a moment and then pulled out an automatic weapon and handed it to Agent Stoll. It was a 9mm Uzi short barrel that had been converted from a semi-automatic gun into a fully automatic one, making possession or sale of it against the law.

Debbie told the agent she bought it from one of her gun-running contacts for $1,500. If they wanted her to, she could get more.

Chapter 55   Dr. Newhouse Stumbles

. . . . Friday, October 21, 1988

If the jury was disturbed by the autopsy photographs they were forced to view the day before, Friday's testimony was even more stomach-churning. Back on the stand, Dr. Newhouse detailed her autopsy procedures, including removing the scalp, and taking the brain out of the skull. The "very small areas of bright red-purple" she found were proof positive, she said, of brain hemorrhages.

"And is this a significant finding?" Hayes asked.

"The pons, medulla, mid-brain area contain the vital areas for life," Dr. Newhouse answered. "They contain areas that control respiration and cardiac function, and if those areas are damaged, even small areas of hemorrhage and small areas of trauma can cause interruption and cessation of the vital functions."

Trauma like what was depicted in the photographs, she said, would be fatal. MacNeil stood up to cross-examine Newhouse and purposefully rammed his shin into the witness box. It made a soft thump.

"So when a person hits something and that results in a bruise— what we call a bruise—you call trauma and a hemorrhage?"

Newhouse admitted MacNeil's vocabulary was accurate. When used as a medical term, *trauma* had various levels of severity. A slight bruise is trauma and a hard knock to the head is also trauma. MacNeil wanted the jury to know that just because Jerry Tobias suffered from "trauma," according to the pathologist, it didn't necessarily mean it was lethal. All it meant was that he sustained injuries that were not severe enough to break the skin.

Like Dean Robb and Mick Hackett, MacNeil also believed that Jerry Tobias died of exposure caused by unconsciousness and a cocaine overdose. That was difficult to prove, and certainly didn't present the gruesome black, blue, and purple images that trauma, even non-life-threatening trauma, did. Death by cocaine overdose actually presented only a few symptoms that would show up in an autopsy. One of those was "pulmonary edema," or fluid in the lungs.

"Did Jerry Tobias have pulmonary edema?" MacNeil asked.

"Yes, he did," Newhouse said.

That Tobias used cocaine to excess was no longer in dispute. That he shot it in his arms as many as eight times within twenty-four hours of his death was also no longer in dispute. And yet, because of errors Dr. Newhouse made in ordering lab tests following her autopsy, no one knew exactly how much cocaine was in Jerry Tobias' system when he died, and probably never would.

"We don't know what the level of cocaine was in (his) blood back in December of 1986, do we?" MacNeil asked Newhouse.

"I would say at the—" she began, but MacNeil cut her off.

"No," he said. "Do we *know*?"

"It was—it will very closely approximate the amount that we have in '88."

"I don't care if it approximates," MacNeil said. "Do we *know* what it was back in December of 1986?"

"I would say we know the range."

"No. You've talked about exactness here in these other things. Do we know *exactly* what the level of cocaine was back in 1986 in the blood of Mr. Tobias?"

"We know approximately."

"We don't know exactly, do we?"

"No."

The amount of alcohol in Tobias' blood was also up for debate. The amount listed in the police report was close to zero. And yet, witnesses said in the hours before his death he'd had at least two beers and as many as ten White Russian cocktails. Even a heavy drinker would show the effects of that kind of volume and Tobias apparently did. One witness said he'd actually been so drunk that he stumbled and couldn't hold onto a pool cue.

"Do you have an opinion. . . what the blood alcohol level of a person who would exhibit those kinds of symptoms would be?" MacNeil asked Newhouse.

"Probably between .20 and .30," she said.

The range of human behavior when under the influence of alcohol has been well documented by science, with .03 being slight euphoria and .40 being death by alcohol poisoning. The police report said Jerry's blood alcohol level was .00 at the time of death, and Newhouse found it to be .02. But under MacNeil's questioning, she admitted someone who drank what Jerry did shortly before his death should have registered at least ten times that level.

It didn't make sense, and while MacNeil didn't have the answers, he wanted the jury to know that Newhouse and the prosecution didn't have them either. There were other inconsistencies, too. When Jerry was found in his truck, he was fully clothed but his jeans were unbuttoned and his zipper was undone. What he'd been wearing was well detailed in the police report, in the news media, in two previous trials, and in this trial. Much had been made of his torn shirt, his ripped belt loops, and especially his scuffed cowboy boots.

The prosecution contended that the scuffs on his boots were evidence that he'd been dragged. Debbie testified that Jerry had been in his stocking feet inside Walt's Butcher Shop and was in the process of changing from a pair of winter boots into the cowboy boots when the men beat him up. But Jerry was found with his cowboy boots *on*, MacNeil reminded the jury, so that meant the killers put them back on him before they tossed him into his truck.

This sounded logical until MacNeil asked the jury to consider how difficult it would be to put fitted cowboy boots onto the feet of an unconscious man. It was impossible.

"Like trying to put a ten-inch balloon into a five-inch paper bag," MacNeil said. "You can't do it."

Newhouse was still on the stand during MacNeil's discussion of the cowboy boots. To everyone in the courtroom it was obvious she didn't want to confirm his line of reasoning, but in the end, she was forced to.

"In removing the boots, do you recall. . . that the boots were very, very difficult to get off?" MacNeil asked her.

"Yes," she said, curtly.

"You had to have some of the police officers help you get the boots off, didn't you?" MacNeil pressed.

"It was hard to get the boots off," Newhouse agreed. "There's no question."

"And it took at least three of you tugging on those boots to get them off, right?"

"I needed help, yes. I didn't do it by myself and there were three of us who held legs and pulled boots and it was hard."

MacNeil walked away from the witness stand toward the jury box. How, he asked himself, thinking out loud, could anyone get a pair of cowboy boots onto the feet of an unconscious man when they fit him so tightly they could only be removed by a doctor and two police officers pulling with all their might?

It seemed to MacNeil a man who's just been beaten up is not going to help the men who did the beating put his boots on. If Jerry were completely unconscious, the task would be even harder. An unconscious man isn't going to point his toes and push his feet inside even if he had a mind to, it was medically impossible.

As Newhouse stepped down, the image she described of three people pulling the boots off a dead man was a disturbing one. How they got on his feet in the first place, if the prosecutor's theory of the crime was accurate, was just one more question that wasn't going to be answered.

Not in Canter's trial and maybe not ever.

Chapter 56   An Earful

· · · · · · · · · · Friday October 21, 1988

While the image of a dead man's cowboy boots dominated the courtroom, guns were on the mind of Lieutenant Hardy. Debbie's fantastical stories were stacking up, so Hardy decided it was time to go through them, one by one. On Friday, October 21, 1988, the lieutenant called a meeting. Hardy and ATF Agent George Stoll would meet with Hardy's spy, Curt Beerens, and share information.

Beerens hadn't been Debbie's boyfriend since she'd turned her affections toward his partner, Mark Kerry, and his loyalty was shifting away from her and toward the police. Beerens still considered Debbie a friend, but even that relationship was rocky and he was finally willing to tell the police everything he knew about her.

The three men met at the State Police crime lab and Beerens unburdened himself. Her story that the handgun Detective Goeman found in her nightstand was a throw-down gun given to her by a drug dealer was a lie. Beerens said he bought that gun legally, using his federal firearms license. He just loaned it to Debbie because she kept telling him how afraid she was. He believed her when she said she needed it for personal protection.

But Debbie gave them names, Lieutenant Hardy and Agent Stoll said. Did she make those people up, too?

No, Beerens said, the men were real people, they just weren't drug dealers. Ken Smith did live in North Carolina, but he was an old friend of Beerens', not a criminal looking to sell drugs in Michigan. Debbie didn't know him; she had just eavesdropped on a phone call between Beerens and Smith. Rick Chilson wasn't a drug dealer either; he was Beerens' cousin. And there wasn't any large-scale narcotics deal connected to the handgun or the men. There wasn't going to be an airplane drug drop, and her purchase of the Uzi was a scam.

Hardy reminded Beerens that the penalty for trafficking in cocaine in the quantities Debbie described was a mandatory life sentence. Was he certain that Debbie was willing to send the men to prison for life for something they had absolutely no involvement in? Beerens said he was. Whether or not Smith's and Chilson's well-being occurred to Debbie, Beerens couldn't say. Being persecuted seemed to be the price to pay for having your name associated with her.

Agent Stoll wasn't convinced. Debbie knew a lot about guns, he said, and had much more detailed information than the average person would ever know. If she wasn't involved with buying and selling illegal weapons, how did she know so much about it?

Easy, Beerens said. Debbie liked to read. She went to the library and checked out stacks of books about guns and crime. Plus, while the police had her tucked away as a protected witness, she got bored. Someone brought Debbie the newspaper and to pass the time, she read it every day as well as all his back issues of *Shotgun News*. The Iran Contra affair, news of which broke just a month before Jerry Tobias died, was a particular favorite of hers. She followed the case closely and if police checked, Beerens was sure her gun-running stories would mirror what the news media reported about Iran Contra.

As if this wasn't enough, Beerens shared even more damning insight about the woman police had been protecting for almost eight months. He told Hardy and Stoll that the shootings were also a set up. One of Debbie's many boyfriends, Mark Kerry, shot into Cindy Gleasen's house back in July. Another, Mike Gilbert, fired the shot into her Sand Hill Manor apartment.

Hardy, Wilt, and others in the State Police had been skeptical of Debbie's account of both shootings, but were still surprised Beerens knew so much about them. Hardy asked him if he was involved, and Beerens said he was. He explained that Debbie asked him to do them, but he refused. After they happened, she'd occasionally taunt him with the fact that she'd found other men to do her bidding.

There was also one other thing the police should probably know, Beerens said. He spent a lot of time with Debbie, and when she wasn't reading *Shotgun News*, she was reading trial transcripts and newspaper clippings about the Tobias case. Beerens would even often quiz her on the details.

Agent Stoll asked Beerens about the Uzi she'd pulled from the woodpile. He'd seen that with his own eyes and even had the actual gun. How could it not be real?

The gun was real, Beerens said, but the man on Debbie's phone talking about a "package" was actually Beerens' brother. His brother, Debbie, and Beerens worked all the details of the purchase out ahead of time. Debbie couldn't buy the weapon from her drug running contacts because she didn't *have* any drug running contacts.

Then how could she get her hands on an illegal weapon?

Just like when Agent Stoll checked into the Best Western, the deal was the result of a simple coincidence, Beerens explained. Someone he worked with, another EMT, saw him reading *Shotgun News*, pointed to a photograph of an Uzi, and bragged that he could get one. Beerens told Debbie, and she lied about it to the police. Debbie and Beerens bought the gun in the advertisement, stashed it in the woodpile ahead of time, then took Goeman and Stoll there to find it.

In light of this new information, Hardy asked Beerens if he thought Debbie really did see Jerry Tobias murdered. Beerens said he could no longer believe anything Debbie said. But, he did know one thing—she hated Mark Canter and Doug Brinkman. Brinkman was one of Debbie's many ex-boyfriends, and after they broke up, Brinkman and Mark Canter teased her relentlessly. They laughed at her and accused her of being a lesbian and because of that, Debbie swore a vendetta against both of them.

"I don't care if they're guilty or not," she promised. "I'll hang 'em."

Mondays were scheduled as down days in Mark Canter's trial. Judge Davis set aside the day to deal with motions and court activity in the other cases he was presiding over. The jury didn't have to report in, Mark stayed in his cell at the Otsego County Jail, and back in their offices, MacNeil and Hayes separately worked on trial strategy and witness preparation.

That did not mean the investigation went dormant on Mondays. After Beeren's revelations, Hardy called a meeting on Monday, Oct. 24. Prosecutor Hayes, Fred LaBarge, Carl Goeman, John Jenkins, and other detectives were invited. Hardy wanted to share with them what he'd learned from Beerens, and he opened the meeting by saying he had concerns about Debbie's credibility. This was not just some nagging worry in the back of his mind, but strong doubt backed up by a series of bizarre happenings.

Since the moment she came forward as an eyewitness, police knew Debbie was a fringe character of questionable motives. Still, most of the officers who dealt with her thought she had seen *something*. But Hardy said he was no longer certain of that. He told the group what he'd learned from Curt Beerens. That Debbie had accused innocent people of serious crimes, including illegal drug sales and gun dealing. She'd filed false police reports, faked her own kidnapping, may have staged one or more shootings, and possessed illegal weapons. None of this was conjecture; Hardy could document it.

The detectives and Hayes likely already knew bits and pieces of what Hardy told them. They had all heard talk that Debbie embellished her role in the Tobias case, and that some of her stories were too crazy for anyone to believe. But the meeting was the first time all of her known falsifications were detailed. Hardy told the group Debbie accused two innocent men, Ken Smith and Rich Chilson, of gun running and drug dealing. That she bought an illegal Uzi submachine gun, staged discovery of for the police's benefit, and then lied about how she got it. That she was responsible for planning the Gleason and Sand Hill Manor shootings. In light of all this, Hardy said he had serious concerns and reservations about the Mark Canter prosecution.

"If you drop the Canter case," he told Hayes, "it wouldn't bother me, because I don't know if it's worth it with a witness like this. It's your call, and I'll support whatever you decide, but I just want you to know I have concerns and reservations."

After further discussion, it was agreed the Canter prosecution would go forward, as would the cases against Doug Brinkman and Don Heistand. But before the meeting was over, another idea was raised. In the months and years to come, there would be disagreement over who raised it, but all agreed with the idea in theory. If there were another eyewitness to Jerry Tobias' death, someone to corroborate Debbie's story, it would strengthen the state's case. If there were two eye witnesses, the convictions of Mark, Doug, and Don could practically be assured.

After the meeting, Hardy and Goeman returned together to the Traverse City Post. What was discussed in the hour-long drive was never documented. But at 9:49 PM, a LEIN search went out from the Traverse City post, initiated by Goeman. The search was for Sherry Lynn Payton, last known whereabouts Gaylord, and the computer responded to with a hit. Sherry Lynn Payton was wanted for larceny.

Chapter 57   Mark Canter

. . . . October 26, 1988

An unbiased observer would probably look at Mark Canter and simply see a handsome, mustached, lanky but broad-shouldered man in his mid-twenties whose blonde-streaked hair could use a trim. A cursory look would reveal him to be scruffy, perhaps even a bit hapless, but also blue-eyed and happy-go-lucky. Canter was often grinning, and usually looked relaxed and happy, as if he didn't have one worry in any fiber of his body. Drop the walls of a courtroom around him, seat him in a defendant's chair, and have him face his accuser as she detailed his misdeeds from the witness stand, and another impression appeared.

Mark Canter, Debbie testified, was actually a drug-dealing, drug-using, gun-running killer. It was already a full week into Mark's trial when Hayes called Debbie as a witness. Word of her impending appearance made the rounds, and again the courtroom was full.

"I notice that we have an increased audience this morning," Judge Davis remarked. "I assume because there's some importance attached to the testimony of the next witness. I wish to make it very clear to everyone that the decorum of the courtroom will be maintained at all times, under all circumstances, and I will not tolerate disruptions of any kind."

Sometimes, Judge Davis knew, a large audience brought out the worst in attorneys. Any line of questioning, whether by the prosecution or the defense, that might be controversial enough to lead to a mistrial was to be argued privately, he said, and only after he removed the jury and cleared the courtroom.

"Anything less than that will cause considerable consternation on my part. All right. Let's have the jury in."

Debbie was sworn in, and Prosecutor Hayes quickly established that she was a Michigan State Police–protected witness and all of her living arrangements were being paid for. This didn't help the prosecution any, but if Hayes raised it himself, before the defense could, it might take out a little of its sting.

On Friday, Dec. 5, 1986, Debbie said Mark picked her up at the Big Boy restaurant in Gaylord at 1 PM and then the pair drove around town "killing time" and "making connections," for future drug transactions while "letting people know when we were going to get more cocaine in." According to Debbie, Mark Canter had a full pound of the drug to sell.

She said the pair then drove around Gaylord for nine to ten hours before picking up Terry Moore sometime between 9 and

10:30 PM. Then Mark, Debbie, and Terry drove around Gaylord some more, eventually meeting Laurie Moore, someone Debbie didn't know named "John," and Jerry Tobias at Walt's Butcher Shop between 11 PM and midnight. An argument broke out almost immediately, and the men beat Tobias unconscious with their fists. Laurie hit him in the back of the head with an "object with two metal cylinder things on it." Then they dragged him into the walk-in freezer.

After a brief discussion about alibis, Debbie said Doug Brinkman arrived and helped drag Tobias out of the freezer, carry him through the back door of Walt's, and dump him into the bed of his pickup truck.

Hayes asked Debbie what Mark Canter and Terry Moore talked about in the car prior to their arrival at Walt's.

"Terry Moore said that Jerry Tobias had owed him $3,000 and Laurie Moore, $4,000, for cocaine," Debbie said. "And that this time he's not going to beat it. Terry Moore said that he was going to be in for a surprise, and his words were, 'I'll kill that little fucker.' That's exactly what he said.

"Mark Canter made the comment, 'Why don't we just get a gun and blow his brains out? It would be a lot easier.' Terry Moore said, 'No. I want to see him suffer first.'"

Prosecutor Hayes confined his questions to the hours surrounding Tobias' death, but when MacNeil had the opportunity to cross-examine her, he began at the beginning.

"Debbie, I'd like to ask you a few questions first just about your background. Where were you born?"

"I was registered in Muskegon County, but I was born in transit between—in a car between the Arizona Indian Reservation in Oklahoma, into Michigan. I was registered just like if I was born in Muskegon County."

MacNeil shook his head but remembered Davis' warning and said nothing. Even Debbie's actual birth had an unusual story attached to it, he marveled to himself. Publicly, he casually asked Debbie more questions about herself and her life. Debbie explained that she had a black belt in karate, but only had a sixth grade education because she ran away from home when she was eleven or twelve. When she was a teenager she lived on the streets in various cities all round the country, from Indianapolis to Washington, DC. She ate scraps, begged for handouts, and slept in parks and abandoned railroad cars. She sold drugs and was a drug addict by the time she was fourteen, trying anything and everything, including "THC, PCP, LSD, yellow sunshine, purple haze, orange mesc, chocolate mesc."

When MacNeil asked about her current circumstances, Debbie said she was still married, but had been going through a divorce since November of 1986. She had two children, both sons, one of whom was seven and one of whom was twelve.

"You haven't seen your children for over a year, have you?" MacNeil asked her.

"No, I haven't," she said.

"And you've been in police custody since March of 1988, is that it?"

"Yes, it is."

"You've been able to move about freely, as you wished, have you not?"

"To a degree, yes."

"But you never did go see your children. Correct?"

"No, I have not."

The cross-examination was initially going well for the defense. MacNeil established that Debbie was a drug dealer and drug user, a woman who would lie to get what she wanted, and who created fantasies surrounding her life and her circumstances. He wanted to show the jury she was a severely flawed person who prioritized creating fantasies of illegal gun and drug activity over mothering her own children, and some in the courtroom would later say they could feel the jury swaying toward the defense.

But just as MacNeil was hitting his stride, his line of questioning was shut down. He asked Debbie about her drug use, and she willingly told him that the last time she remembered using recreational drugs was when she was fourteen or fifteen. It was a bad acid trip, it frightened her, and she'd sworn off drugs after that.

During that "trip," she said that "tree bark would be more—it would stand out from the tree a little bit more. You could see more into the leaves. You could see the blood running in your veins. Pumping."

But MacNeil argued that her medical records detailed her drug use up to, and even in the months after, Jerry Tobias died. If the medical records were accurate, and Debbie's version was a lie, it would contradict her ability to recall the events surrounding Tobias' death. The jury would never know which version to believe because Judge Davis halted MacNeil's line of questioning.

"Inquiry into that area, under these circumstances, would not be probative of her ability to tell the truth, or to properly attack credibility as to what she was able to see and hear during the events in question in this matter," Davis said.

"Judge," argued MacNeil, "with due respect to the Court's ruling . . . The evidence on the record certainly suggests a long history of drug abuse, and because she now says that she stopped using these drugs at fifteen, the court must (have) accepted that as truth, and thereby bases its ruling. That is not true, and the matters concerning the drug abuse and the use of drugs over the years, continues right up through 1987."

But the drugs MacNeil was referring to, Davis said, were prescription drugs, not street drugs. Debbie's prescriptions were legally prescribed by doctors, and if she had abused them, it must have been by mistake. MacNeil was not able to continue, and no mention was made of the fact that the State Police were regularly paying for very same prescriptions MacNeil was trying to say impeached her ability to tell the truth. No mention was made of the red pill Detective Goeman found with the gun in her drawer because that report hadn't been provided to the defense.

MacNeil couldn't use her drug use to impeach her credibility, so he returned to her character, her illegal activities, and her association with Mark Canter.

Debbie told various stories of where she'd met Mark Canter. Once she said it was at a ski resort in October (impossible since the resort wasn't opened for the season yet), and another time she said she met Mark at a house party in November or December of 1986 when Doug Brinkman, her boyfriend of the moment, had introduced the two them.

"Now, during all these periods of time that you went out with Doug Brinkman, you were married. Correct?" MacNeil asked her.

"Yes, I was."

"When you would go out on these occasions, did you often stay away overnight?"

"Yes, I did."

"Were you dating anyone else in December of 1986?"

"I went out with Steve Wise one time," she said. "Well, a few times."

When she and Doug Brinkman went out on "dates," they didn't go to a motel or to Doug's house, Debbie said, they usually just slept together in his car.

"And how old would you have been at that time?"

"Thirty-one."

"Ok, and at 31 you would often spend the night in the car with Doug Brinkman?"

"Yeah," Debbie answered, her tone growing belligerent. "Why?"

"Well I—it doesn't seem unusual to me, but I thought maybe it might to you."

"No," Debbie said, just as confident as ever. "It didn't."

Next, MacNeil questioned her about her gun-related activities. She said she and Mark had helped smuggle "invisible" weapons to paramilitary groups in Detroit.

"And are these 'invisible' in the sense that when you walked up to them you couldn't see them?" MacNeil asked her, causing snickers in the gallery and barely keeping a straight face himself.

"No," Debbie answered matter-of-factly. "They're invisible in the sense that there's no way to trace them."

The "invisible" weapons were M-16s, sulfur grenades, AK-47s, dynamite, blasting caps, shoulder-mounted rocket launchers, silencers, and infra-red rifle scopes. The list bothered Hayes, and he objected.

"I really don't see what the relevance is to this line of questioning," he said to Judge Davis.

"Your Honor," MacNeil explained, "the evidence will show that Mark Canter was not charged or arrested with this crime until 1988. And it shows a scheme or plan on behalf of this witness through 1987, to attempt to implicate him in various activities involving the running of guns and smuggling of guns to try to get him arrested. That is our position, and this would tend to show that scheme or plan, which eventually led to her accusation that somehow Mark Canter was involved in the death of Jerry Tobias."

Davis allowed MacNeil to continue, and Debbie's story became more and more outlandish. Now would have been a perfect time to introduce into evidence Debbie's statement to Curt Beerens that she was going to "hang" Mark Canter whether he was guilty or not. But since neither the police nor the prosecutor provided that information to the defense, MacNeil had no way of knowing she'd ever said it.

Many of her bizarre and unbelievable statements were on record with police though, had been provided to the defense, and MacNeil mined them for information. For example, Debbie said she and Mark went to the U.S. Army's Camp Grayling, to the weapons warehouse there, and loaded crates of guns and bullets into an army truck and drove it to Detroit. Other times, they hired helicopter pilots and used "choppers" to transport stolen weapons to Miami and someplace in California. Often, she said, Mark Canter's father was the pilot on these illegal missions.

Another time, Debbie said she and Mark were part of a convoy of six or seven Army trucks hijacking military weapons out of an armory in Toledo, Ohio. There was a private landing strip at a Gaylord area resort, Lakes of the North, and she said drug dealers used it to fly weapons and drugs in and out of northern Michigan. These weapons couldn't be sold without testing them first, so Debbie, Mark, and Doug often did the testing themselves. Once, she said, they even used military dynamite to blow up an entire island in Lake Louise, an inland lake northeast of Gaylord.

"Did any of the residents who have cottages on Lake Louise— did any of them complain about the island being blown up, to your knowledge," MacNeil asked, suppressing a laugh.

"I have no way of knowing that," Debbie snapped.

Before he lost all rapport with her, MacNeil moved on to a topic she did know something about. Her diary.

"It's my understanding that you kept a diary of all these events. Is that correct?"

"Yes, I did."

"And presumably, if we had that diary here today, we could document everything that you have told us. Correct?"

Debbie said that she'd recorded license plate numbers, plane numbers, boat numbers, telephone numbers, directions to drug and gun meeting places, and people's names. She couldn't possibly remember everything, so every night she would write these details down in her diary. If her life was ever threatened, the diary could function like an insurance policy. If she was harmed or killed, it was to be delivered to police.

"But we don't have that diary today, do we?" MacNeil asked.

"No. We don't."

In January of 1988, Debbie said she went to Florida with Roger Becker, who was her boyfriend at the time, and stashed the diary in a safe deposit box at a bank. She couldn't remember the name of the bank, the town where the bank was located, or even when she was there. Roger Becker would know all these details, she said, and he even had a key to the safe deposit box.

"What would be the purpose in putting a diary in a safe deposit box in a bank if you don't know where the bank is?" MacNeil asked.

"I didn't think I would ever run into that problem because Roger had a key and I could always have contact with Roger," she said.

"Did that change?" MacNeil asked.

"Yes it did," Debbie admitted. "When I went into protective custody, he disappeared."

Weeks prior, Roger Becker told a very different story to the FBI. According to him, there was no safe deposit box, no key, and no bank. He didn't disappear, he said, Debbie dumped him. That information would have been valuable to Mark's defense too, except yet again MacNeil didn't know it. The Colorado office of the FBI made a report of their interview with Becker and sent it to the Michigan State Police, but no one gave a copy of it to MacNeil.

Chapter 58   Sherry Lynn Payton

. . . . Thursday, October 27, 1988

The next morning, Debbie was scheduled to testify for a second day. Police had moved her again, out of Gaylord and into a hotel in Traverse City, a location more convenient for Hardy's regular visits. The trial was scheduled to re-convene at

9 AM, the courthouse in Grayling was a 45-minute drive, and it was often LaBarge's job to get Debbie there on time.

He picked her up early and somewhere on the drive between Traverse City and Grayling, the two had a conversation that would sharply alter the trajectory of Mark's trial and the entire Tobias investigation. The exact words spoken, and by whom, would only be known by Debbie and LaBarge, but the topic was made public as soon as LaBarge took the stand. There was a new eyewitness to the Tobias killing, and her name was Sherry Lynn Payton.

In the days, months, and even years to come, people would speculate about who uttered her name first. Did Detective LaBarge ask Debbie if Sherry Payton had been at Walt's the night Jerry Tobias was killed? Or did Debbie tell the detective there had been another woman at the butcher shop that night? The witness and the detective were the only two people in the car, and their conversation wasn't taped. LaBarge did make a report of it a day later:

"En route to Court, undersigned had conversation with Parmentier about one Sherry Payton. Parmentier then advised undersigned that Sherry Payton was in Walt's Market with Jerry Tobias the night Jerry Tobias was murdered. Everything else was the same as what she testified to in the past. The same people involved in Tobias' death and it occurred in the same manner. As of this time, extensive efforts are being made to locate Sherry Payton."

LaBarge and Debbie arrived at the courthouse just before 9 AM, and the detective walked straight up to the prosecutor's table, took Hayes aside, and shared the news. When the judge announced that court was in session, Hayes put LaBarge on the stand and the detective said, under oath, that the idea that Sherry Payton witnessed the Tobias murder came to him in a dream the night before.

To MacNeil and Canter, that idea seemed ludicrous. Sherry Payton was a friend of Jerry's, but in December of 1986, when the murder investigation was in its infancy, officers interviewed her and learned she had a solid alibi. She worked at an area ski lodge, and her time card showed she'd been punched in from 6:42 PM on

Friday, Dec. 5, to 1:36 AM on Saturday, Dec. 6, and from Saturday evening at 6:51 PM until 11:43 PM. The drive from the ski lodge to Walt's was at least a half hour.

MacNeil had practically memorized the 1,000-plus-page police report, so he already knew that. But before he could cross-examine LaBarge, Judge Davis suspended the trial and gave police one week to find Sherry Payton. If they could not, the trial would resume without her.

That afternoon, a felony warrant was issued for Sherry Lynn Payton with a charge of "larceny over $100" and Fred LaBarge the complaining witness.

Ray MacNeil felt blindsided. Prosecutors and defense attorneys are required to submit a witness list to the court before a criminal trial, and Sherry Payton's name was nowhere on the prosecutor's list. That meant MacNeil had no time to prepare a cross-examination, no time to ask Mark about her, and no time to devise a defense strategy rebutting not one but two eyewitnesses.

After Judge Davis suspended the trial there was nothing for MacNeil to do but go back to his office and re-group. His plan was to spend the rest of the day researching Sherry Payton, but within the hour he received a surprise phone call from the prosecutor. Hayes said he had a plea offer. If Mark would plead guilty to a lesser charge, corroborate Debbie's story, and testify against Doug Brinkman and Don Heistand, Hayes would let him walk. Mark could be out of jail by dinnertime.

MacNeil listened to the offer, told the prosecutor he'd go to the jail to confer with his client, and get back to him that day. At the jail, MacNeil delivered the news to Mark.

"It's a real chance at freedom," he said. "If you know *anything* about this, then I think you should give it serious consideration."

MacNeil explained that if Mark took his chances with the jury and was found guilty, he'd probably face life in prison.

"I'll tell it to you straight, Mark," MacNeil said again. "If you know anything about this, *anything* at all, and you're turning down an offer of immunity, you're nuts."

MacNeil reminded Mark that he was only 24 and had his whole life ahead of him. He'd made plenty of mistakes, but he'd been in jail for a year and a half, and that should have given him plenty of time to think. Over and over again, Mark had told MacNeil how anxious he was to get out of jail and start making some positive changes, starting by quitting the booze and the drugs. The deal was a good one, MacNeil said, and if Mark took it, he could get started on his new life that very evening.

At first MacNeil was surprised by the plea offer, but on the drive to the jail he thought he'd figured out Hayes' motive for making it. MacNeil was a former prosecutor, so he put himself in Hayes' position. Even with the possibility of a new eyewitness, the prosecution of Mark Canter was not going well. With each trial Debbie's behavior grew increasingly bizarre. She wasn't a credible witness, Sherry Payton hadn't been found, and no one knew what she would say if police did find her. Looked at in this light, the prosecutor's offer wasn't so surprising.

What did shock MacNeil was Mark's reaction. He turned it down.

"It's tempting," Mark said, shaking his head. "I'm not going to say it isn't."

He asked MacNeil about the other guys. Doug Brinkman was one of his best friends, he barely knew Laurie Moore, and had never even met Don Heistand until they were assigned adjacent cells and arraigned in court together. He told his attorney he couldn't lie and say he committed a murder with them. The longer he talked, the more upset he became.

"I don't know anything about it, so I can't lie and say I do!" Mark told MacNeil. "I thought you'd know that!"

MacNeil put his hands on Mark's shoulders, the two men just sat there like that for a moment, then MacNeil asked him if he was sure. If he took the deal, he'd be out of jail that night. But Mark said he was certain. He wasn't going to take any deal.

"I can't go on the stand and lie," he told MacNeil, as tears began trickling down his cheeks. "I just can't do it."

"Well, I can't stand by you if you do," MacNeil said. "So just tell the truth. It'll pay off in the end; it always does."

MacNeil left the jail, returned to his office, and called Hayes. Regardless of what happened in their search for Sherry Payton, he said, his client would not be taking a plea.

"Extensive efforts" did not fully describe what the police were doing to find Sherry Payton. Two eyewitnesses were always better than one, and the prosecutor's plea offer to Mark showed how badly they needed Payton to confirm Debbie's story. Beyond LaBarge's silly-sounding contention that her name had come to him in a dream, MacNeil believed there was something else not quite right about the detective's insistence she was involved.

According to LEIN records, the Michigan State Police started looking for Payton three days before her name was discussed by LaBarge and Debbie in that car ride. Equally curious, it was initiated by a State Police detective who had nothing to do with the Tobias investigation assigned to find her.

"Why would they be searching for Payton three days before LaBarge supposedly came to the conclusion she was there in a dream?" MacNeil would ask later. "Give me a break. Anyone can put two and two together and see what happened."

His contention was the prosecution needed another witness because if Debbie unraveled any further and continued with her stories of grenade launchers, blasting caps, assassination conspiracies, and stolen guns, the jury wasn't going to believe her. And since Debbie's story was the only evidence against Mark, he'd be found not guilty.

A lot was riding on the prosecution getting a conviction. The fate of the first two trials, now working their way through the appeals process, but also the viability of the two yet to come— Don's and Doug's. There were also the reputations of the prosecutor and the police to consider, as well as the cost. The county was going broke prosecuting the five men, and the idea they might actually be innocent, making the trials a waste of time, money, and law enforcement resources, was unthinkable.

Whether or not she witnessed Jerry Tobias' death, Sherry Payton was no stranger to police. The LEIN search on her showed arrests for several misdemeanors and a failure to appear for a court date. In January of 1987, Payton stole a checkbook from a woman whose house she had been hired to clean. She forged several of the checks, the woman reported it to police, and a bench warrant was issued for Sherry's arrest. Instead of turning herself in, she moved to Florida with her boyfriend.

But by the fall of 1988, Payton missed her friends and family and was tired of avoiding Michigan for fear of arrest. Payton's mother, Earldine Payton, missed her daughter and was tired of explaining to friends and family where she was and why. In one of the Tobias case's many strange coincidences, the same week that Detective LaBarge said he "dreamed" she was a witness, Earldine Payton hired an attorney to help Sherry make restitution. Earldine had no idea her daughter's whereabouts were of interest to the

Tobias case detectives, and police had no idea Sherry Payton was making plans to return to Michigan.

The first hint Payton herself had that anything was amiss was when an ex-roommate called to let her know some lawmen from Michigan were in Florida looking for her. The men, whoever they were, had been looking for her at her old address. With her mother's help, Payton made plans to return to Michigan so when she learned of the men's visit, she called the attorney her mother hired to find out what was going on.

"I just heard there was bounty hunters looking for me," Sherry said to attorney Karen Jackson.

"Sherry, they don't do that for bad checks," Jackson explained. "I'm your attorney now, and if they were looking for you, I would know. Let me find out what's going on."

While Jackson made some phone calls, Payton boarded a Greyhound bus bound for Michigan. Her ticket took her as far as Lansing, where she spent the night with a relative, planning to make the final three-hour trip to Gaylord by car the next day. When she arrived in Lansing, she called Karen Jackson for an update. She wanted to find out what arrangements had been made for her to make restitution on the stolen checks.

"Sherry," Jackson said, "are you sitting down?"

"No," Sherry answered, sounding confused. "Why?"

"I found out why they were looking for you," Jackson explained. "Do you know who a 'Debra Parmentier' is?"

Sherry thought about it for a minute, but told her attorney she didn't recognize the name.

"Then we have a problem," Jackson said.

Jackson explained Debbie Parmentier was the prosecution's star witness in the Tobias trials. She helped put Terry Moore in prison, was testifying against Mark Canter, and said Sherry was an eyewitness to the murder, too.

"They've suspended the trial for a week, looking for you," Jackson said.

The story was so strange Sherry didn't know how to respond, and she asked Jackson to explain it again. The attorney repeated it, but the scenario still made no sense to Payton.

"That girl is absolutely out of her mind!" Payton said. "I wasn't there!"

Payton asked Jackson for more details about Debbie Parmentier. Who was she? What did she look like? Jackson had few answers but said Sherry should just continue with her plan to come back to Gaylord and they'd talk in person when she arrived.

While Sherry made her way north, Jackson realized she had a problem of her own. When Dean Robb recused himself from representing Laurie Moore in his appeal, Jackson stepped in. Now that Sherry Payton had been dragged into the Tobias case, Jackson wasn't going to be able to represent her. Since she'd already represented Laurie, it would be a conflict of interest.

Before Sherry even arrived in Gaylord, Jackson made a phone call to Judge Davis, explained her situation, and asked for advice. Davis said Payton would be subpoenaed to testify in Mark Canter's trial and that Jackson should advise her to get another attorney and turn herself in to police. They discussed the situation at length, and by the end of the phone call, Jackson promised to advise Payton to turn herself in but asked the judge to appoint someone competent to be her new attorney. The judge agreed, but Jackson still had a bad feeling about it when she hung up the phone.

"I was very concerned about the pressures that might come to bear on Sherry Payton. I was very concerned that she be protected and insulated from any conduct by others that could influence her testimony."

Chapter 59   Sherry Turns Herself In

. . . . Wednesday, November 9, 1988

When she arrived in Gaylord, Payton headed straight to the Gaylord Motor Inn where her mother had reserved a room. Earldine, Payton's aunt, and Cyrinda, Sherry Payton's sister, were all there to greet her. The women hugged hello and Sherry thanked her mother. It was Earldine who bought her bus ticket and who gave her the money to repay the stolen checks.

"I'm tired of having this hanging over my head," Sherry told her family. "I'm ready to face up to it and put it behind me."

The women said they'd heard a rumor that Sherry was going to be a witness at the Mark Canter trial, and they asked Sherry to explain what was going on.

"It's crazy," Sherry told her family. "I don't know anything about that. And I don't understand why anyone would say I was there, because I wasn't." Sherry said she'd never even met anyone named Debbie Parmentier.

Karen Jackson arrived at the motel, greeted the Payton women, and immediately broke the bad news. Sherry was going to have to be represented by someone else now that she was involved with the Tobias case.

"But I don't have anything to do with that!" Payton insisted.

Jackson explained that her denial didn't matter, at least not as far as the court was concerned. Rightly or wrongly, Payton was now part of the Jerry Tobias murder case, so Jackson could no longer help her—not with the stolen checks, and not with her denials of witnessing Jerry's murder. All Jackson could do was arrange for her to have a new attorney and drive her to his office.

"You are a more reliable witness than that Debbie Parmentier," Jackson told her. "You just go in, and you tell the truth, and everything will be okay. I'll make a note to the judge that you turned yourself in, and that you knew nothing about any of this."

Jackson and Payton walked out of the motel room, got in Jackson's car, and Jackson drove across town to attorney Terry Bloomquist's office. Once there, Jackson escorted Payton inside, introduced her to Bloomquist, closed his office door, and walked away. An hour later, Payton turned herself in at the Michigan State Police Post in Grayling.

A few blocks away at the Crawford County Courthouse, as soon as word was out that Sherry had been located, Mark's trial resumed almost immediately. Prosecutor Hayes put Debbie back on the stand, and she testified about her conversation with Detective LaBarge.

Sherry Payton had also been inside Walt's the night Tobias died, Debbie said. Payton was in the butcher shop when the attack began, but ran outside screaming soon afterward and didn't see Jerry beaten unconscious or put into his pick-up truck.

The introduction of a new eyewitness right in the middle of a murder trial was the stuff of television courtroom dramas or Hollywood movies, but it rarely happened in real life. To combat the shock value gained by the prosecution, MacNeil planned his own surprise he hoped would assist the defense. When it was his turn to cross-examine Debbie, he began by asking her a few questions about her friendship with Payton. Debbie said she didn't know Payton very well, but that their paths crossed occasionally and Payton had definitely been in the butcher shop with her the night Jerry died.

MacNeil listened, nodded, and then pointed to a woman sitting in the gallery and asked her to stand. When she did, MacNeil turned back to Debbie and asked if she could identify the woman.

"It looks like Sherry," Debbie said.

"Is this the lady who was at Walt's Butcher Shop the night of December fifth?" MacNeil asked.

Debbie fidgeted in her seat but didn't answer. She, sighed, blinked, and looked quickly back and forth between Prosecutor Hayes and the young woman MacNeil singled out. Several minutes went by, but Debbie said nothing. Finally, MacNeil asked her again. Was the women who was standing up in the courtroom Sherry Payton?

"Yes," Debbie said.

Judge Davis asked the mystery woman to come to the front of the courtroom and be sworn in. "Please tell us your name," he said.

"Mary Dunkin," she replied.

Mary Dunkin was slim and tiny, with fine features, shoulder-length blonde hair, and blue eyes. Sherry Payton was 5'10" with long dark hair, brown eyes, and a muscular, rugged bearing. The two women looked absolutely nothing alike.

"How could anyone make such an obvious mistake?" MacNeil asked.

"I answered fast," Debbie snapped, "and under pressure."

Chapter 60   A Whipped Dog

. . . . November 10, 1988

While Debbie was on the stand identifying the wrong woman as Sherry Payton, the real Sherry Payton was at the Grayling City Police Station being arrested and fingerprinted. When that was completed, she was led into an interview room where three State Police officers were waiting. Ken Burr, John Jenkins, and Anthony Gomez were sitting around a table, motioning for Sherry and her attorney to sit down and join them. Jenkins and Burr had been assigned to the Tobias case from the beginning, but

Trooper Gomez was new. He was assigned to narcotics investigations, and although he lived in Gaylord, he worked out of the East Lansing post.

Gomez hadn't had anything to do with the Tobias investigation, but was assigned the task of leading the initial interview with Payton. If Gomez thought this was odd, he didn't mention it. He just followed orders, and began questioning the new witness who, he'd say later, "looked like a whipped dog."

An observation that wasn't all that surprising. In two days Sherry travelled more than 1,000 miles by bus, learned lawmen were looking for her back in Florida, apologized to her mother, lost one attorney and gained another, learned she was named as a witness in a murder case she said she knew nothing about, and turned herself into police. On top of all that, Payton had just learned she was pregnant. She was tired, scared, broke, and confused.

"How long have you known Jerry Tobias?" Trooper Gomez asked her.

Payton said she didn't know Jerry very well, just knew he'd had an affair with her friend, Marie Ross, before he died. Once, when Marie was working, Payton and Tobias hung out together. They went to a couple local bars and had some drinks.

"Do you remember the night he was murdered?" Gomez asked.

"No," Payton said. " I didn't know until that following Monday. I didn't hear anything about it."

"Do you know Debra Parmentier?

"By name I don't know her," Payton said, "but by face . . . ."

"How do you know her?" Gomez interrupted.

"I *don't* know her," Payton repeated. "I'm saying that maybe if I saw her face I might recognize her."

"Have you had a chance to follow any of these trials?" Gomez asked.

"No. I read the newspaper last night because Karen Jackson called me and said, 'Do you know that they are looking for you for this case?' I said, 'No, I don't know,' and she told me that this Debra girl said that I was there."

"Is there any truth to what she is telling?" Gomez asked.

"Absolutely not," Payton said. "It's and out-and-out lie."

"Ok," Gomez repeated, "you were not there?"

"Absolutely not," Payton said again. "I don't understand why this girl would even, how she would even get my name, or why she would even say that. I have no idea. She doesn't know what the hell she's talking about."

While Trooper Gomez continued the interview and Burr listened in, Detective Jenkins excused himself and went out into the hallway. Sherry Payton's parents, Raymond and Earldine Payton, had arrived and were just outside the door wondering what was going on with their daughter. They asked Jenkins to explain.

"She says she wasn't there, but we got proof that she *was* there," Jenkins said.

"If she said she wasn't there, then maybe she wasn't," Raymond Payton said.

"No, we got proof she was," Jenkins assured them.

Raymond had bought his daughter a pack of cigarettes, and he went into the interview room to give them to her.

"Dad!" Sherry said, "I wasn't there!"

"Tell them that," Raymond Payton said. Sherry was shaking and crying, and he tried to comfort her, but the police asked him to leave.

"No!" she sobbed as he left the room. "They'll put me away for twenty years."

Back out in the hallway Raymond Payton expressed his concern to Jenkins.

"She's in no shape to testify," he said, getting angry. "And maybe she really wasn't there."

Jenkins said that wasn't possible. He repeated that the police knew she was at the butcher shop the night Jerry Tobias was murdered, and they knew she witnessed the crime. The police were holding her as a material witness, and she would be ordered to testify in the Mark Canter trial. As soon as they were finished interviewing her, Sherry would be moved to the Emmet County Jail in Petoskey, an hour north, and she'd be held there until she testified.

After Raymond and Earldine Payton left, the police arranged for Sherry to take a lie detector test. She insisted she was not at the butcher shop the night Jerry died, did not witness the crime, and did not know anything about his death. She failed the test.

Chapter 61   Another Go at Payton

. . . . Friday, November 11, 1988

The next day Gomez was summoned back to the police station to have another go at Payton and someone in the State Police arranged for him to speak with her alone this time. Burr and Jenkins wouldn't be in the room and neither would Payton's attorney.

Terry Bloomquist was with Sherry when she turned herself in, was with her in the interview room the day before, and observed her lie detector test. Payton did not waive her right to have her attorney with her, but no one told Bloomquist the police were going to interview his client again. And Payton didn't know enough about the law to know she could have asked for him to be there to advise her when they did. The first interview with her was tape-recorded. The second one wasn't, at least not initially, so there were two versions of what went on in the interview room.

According to Payton, she and Trooper Gomez talked alone in the same room where she'd been interviewed the day before. Gomez told her she could be sentenced to serve fifteen years in prison on the stolen check charge. If that happened, her baby would be born in prison and the state would take it away from her. Her child would be raised in foster care or adopted out, and she'd never get to see him or her grow up. On the other hand, if Payton admitted she was at the butcher shop the night Jerry Tobias died, and if she confirmed Debbie's account of the crime, all charges against her would be dropped.

Again Sherry insisted she wasn't there, she didn't know how Jerry died, and she didn't know anyone named Debbie Parmentier.

"Why are you doing this to yourself?" Sherry would later remember Gomez asking her. The police knew Mark Canter and the others were guilty, he told her; they just needed Payton's testimony to back up their case. Otherwise, she was going to prison.

Spending the previous night in jail compounded Sherry's feelings of panic and confusion. She wasn't only afraid, she was also exhausted.

"I'll tell you what you want to hear," she eventually said, resigned, "but just so you know, I told you the truth the first time and you won't believe me. So, what the hell do you want me to say?"

In Payton's version of what happened inside the police interview room, Gomez slid a yellow legal pad across the table with the details of Debbie's account of the crime already written down. Then warned if she reported what transpired, Gomez would deny it. It would be his word against hers, he said, and who did she think people would be more likely to believe, a confessed check forger or a State Police officer?

In both versions Payton picked up the pencil and wrote. When she was finished, Gomez opened the door to the interview room and called in Detective LaBarge. A tape recorder was turned on and the two men interviewed Payton a third time.

From the tape:

"You're at the Butcher Shop," Gomez said. "Now, what happened?"

"Ah," Payton mumbled, "walked in and—"

"Were there other people there when you arrived?" Gomez asked.

"Mark Canter and Laurie Moore, Terry Moore, Debra, and Wendy."

When Sherry said "Wendy," the name stood out like firecracker. Police had already interviewed hundreds of people and no one had once mentioned anyone named Wendy witnessing the murder. Not Debbie, not the police, not the prosecutor, no one. It seems logical that the police would want to follow up on this new revelation immediately, but Detective LaBarge did not.

"Had you ever met Debra before?" LaBarge asked Sherry instead.

"No."

"Can you describe her to me?" LaBarge asked.

"If I had a picture maybe I could," Payton said. "You know, if you could show me a picture."

"Who's Wendy?" Gomez finally asked.

"Wendy Brock," Payton said.

She explained Wendy Brock was Mark Canter's former girlfriend, and then said, "Everybody was just standing around. I wasn't even there a half hour, ah, Mark and Jerry started arguing, I guess about cocaine and money. I didn't really pay too much attention."

"Do you recall any portion of the conversation?" Gomez asked.

"No," Sherry said. "I just remember something about cocaine."

"Can you describe the argument?" Gomez asked.

"It wasn't, it was just like, you know, I don't know, mild yelling I guess, and ah . . . ."

"Do you recall any of that conversation at all, the argument?" Gomez asked Payton a third time.

"Not really," she said. "No."

There were other things that Sherry Payton didn't remember, either. On the tape, her answers sounded more consistent with someone who wasn't there than someone who was. For example, she said maybe the men were drinking that night, or maybe not. Maybe they were smoking pot, but then again, maybe they weren't doing that, either. Payton didn't remember what anyone was wearing, didn't remember what Debbie looked like, didn't know anyone named Don Heistand, couldn't say when Doug Brinkman arrived, or recall a single thing anyone said.

By the time LaBarge joined them in the interview room, Sherry had already been interviewed by Gomez, without her attorney, for more than two hours. The taped portion of the interview lasted 22 minutes. When they were finished, police gave Payton another polygraph test. This time, she said she was in the butcher shop with Debbie and did see Jerry beaten. She passed.

The results of Payton's second test were added to the results of similar tests on others the police already had, and taken together provided a curious look into an increasingly strange investigation. In March of 1988, Debbie Parmentier told police she witnessed the Tobias murder. They gave her a polygraph test and she passed. A month later, both Doug Brinkman and Mark Canter told police they had nothing to do with the murder. They were both polygraphed and failed.

From the police's standpoint, the tests were conclusive—the witnesses who named the killers passed and the men they accused failed. In Michigan, polygraph test results were not admissible in court, but they could be used to bolster the police's theory of how and why the crime happened. Polygraph machines are not infallible, however. No one can be forced by the police or courts to take one, and in many other states the results are inadmissible in court either. In Michigan, even the fact someone has taken or not taken a polygraph isn't admissible in court. In the right hands, a polygraph machine can be a powerful tool; in the wrong ones, it can be disastrous.

A 2002 review by the National Academies of Science found that polygraph tests could be rigged by the examiners, questions could be skewed to produce the desired outcome, and that even objective tests often did not reveal when someone was lying.

Regardless of whether Payton's test was objective or rigged, LaBarge was so pleased with her results, he and two other officers took her out for a steak dinner afterward. Payton remembered watching the police eat their big meals with gusto, but she had no appetite at all. On the contrary, she felt nauseous and only picked at her food.

When they were finished, the police took Payton back to jail.

Chapter 62   "It's all a lie."

. . . . Sunday, November 13, 1988

Back in Gaylord, Earldine and Raymond Payton were growing increasingly worried about their daughter. They knew she was in jail, and in trouble, but they hadn't heard from her in two days and wondered what was going on. On Sunday morning, the Paytons made the hour-long trip to the Emmet County Jail. They hoped their visit would answer some questions, but when they arrived a deputy told them Sherry couldn't have any visitors, so they turned around and went back home.

There was a good chance they passed Ray MacNeil somewhere on their way. He wanted to see Sherry Payton too, and made the same trip from Gaylord to Petoskey. The trial of his client had been halted to find her, and MacNeil could hardly mount a proper defense without knowing what she was going to say on the stand so he made the trip on Sunday morning, too, and was also turned away. Later that afternoon, a friend of Payton's went to the jail, but she was put off, too. The message to the Paytons, the friend, and Mark Canter's attorney was the same: No visitors for Sherry.

The friend, a woman named Leah Eddington, wrote Sherry a letter, and addressed it to her in care of the Emmet County Jail:

> Hi! This is me, Leah. Remember your friend? I don't know what's going on with all of this bullshit. When I heard that you were a witness to this murder, I was in shock. I haven't been able to eat or sleep since I heard the news. The only conclusion I can come up with is that it's all a lie.
>
> I remember the time you, Marie, and I had your mom drop us off at Fireside. I called Terry (Moore) to meet us for a cocktail! Remember? You kept telling me to introduce Terry to you. And to fix you up with him.
>
> Sherry, if you didn't know the guy, how could you have witnessed him murder Jerry? Or how could you of wanted to go out with him after you knew what he had done?
>
> I keep asking myself over and over again these questions and the only thing I can come up with is you _didn't_ witness this bullshit. I know you Sherry, you're one of my best friends, and I know you would never be able to live with yourself if you had and kept quiet about it.
>
> I know you're scared right now. But _please_ don't let the cops and Hayes trick you into saying something that could put 4 innocent men away for the rest of their lives.

> I wish you would talk to Mr. MacNeil. He's not going to let anything happen to you. He and Mark only want the truth. That's what we all want.
>
> Sincerely your friend. Leah

The letter was postmarked Tuesday, Nov. 15. It did arrive at the jail, but no one ever gave it to Sherry Payton.

Chapter 63   MacNeil and Payton

. . . . Monday, November 14, 1988

MacNeil couldn't help but think the prosecution's new witness was bogus, but he wasn't going to be able to do much about it if he couldn't even interview her before she testified. Her appearance was awfully convenient. Just as the prosecution's case against Mark Canter looked like it was falling apart and Debbie's testimony became increasingly outlandish, Payton miraculously appeared. The fact that he was barred from interviewing her was more than just bogus; it was illegal, and there was only one reason he knew the police would keep him away: Sherry Payton was lying.

But MacNeil was not like Sherry or her parents. He knew the law and was not so easily put off. The accused always had a right to confront their accuser, and that meant MacNeil had a right to question Sherry Payton before she took the stand against Mark. Since the police were not cooperating, MacNeil called Judge Davis. The judge signed an order mandating MacNeil be allowed to interview Payton, and that all subsequent interviews with her by police be tape-recorded. Prosecutor Hayes could be present when MacNeil spoke to her, Davis said, but the defense attorney would have access to the new witness before she could be called to testify against Mark. The interview was arranged, Hayes was notified, and police again brought Payton to the police station.

"I represent Mark Canter," MacNeil told Payton. "Mark is facing First-Degree Murder, which is mandatory life in prison. I'll tell you as honestly as I can tell anybody, Sherry. I don't care what you say, because if Mark had something to do with killing Jerry Tobias, Mark should pay a price for it. Ok?"

MacNeil paused then, and studied Payton, trying to gauge whether or not she'd heard him. She hadn't once made eye contact with anyone in the room; she just stared down at the table. She didn't nod, didn't look up when he started speaking, and had no reaction to anything that was said. If MacNeil was hoping to engage Payton in a substantive dialogue, he was disappointed. She just sat in the interview room, hung her head, and said nothing.

"You don't seem to give much reaction," MacNeil said. "Are you not going to talk to me or . . . ."

"No," Payton said, barely audible. "I'm listening."

"Mark has maintained to me from day one that he had absolutely nothing to do with Jerry Tobias—he didn't even *know* Jerry Tobias. And I guess . . . do you have . . . I'm just asking, do you have any information that would contradict what Mark has told me? Did you ever know him to be in the presence of Jerry Tobias? Do you know anything about the murder?"

"About the murder itself?" Payton asked.

"Yeah," MacNeil said.

"No," Payton said. "Just that I was there at the butcher shop that night."

"Do you know how Mark got there?" MacNeil asked.

"No," Payton said.

"Did you see any cars around when you got there?" MacNeil asked.

"You see, I didn't, I wasn't even paying attention," Payton said. "We just pulled up there and we went in and I was with him, I don't know, a little while and I went home."

"I don't care what you tell me as long as it's the truth," MacNeil said again. "If it implicates Mark and he's involved, that's fine because I don't care, as long as it's the truth. But if it isn't the truth . . . Mark is looking at life imprisonment for something he didn't do. Do you want my personal opinion, does that count for anything?"

MacNeil was about to tell Payton he thought she was being pressured to testify, but he never got the chance.

"I don't mean to interrupt," Prosecutor Hayes said, "but you know personal opinions, and I don't think Mr. MacNeil will object to my saying this. They just don't count for much. It's what you see, observe, smell, taste, hear, etcetera, etcetera."

Payton then told Hayes and MacNeil she went to the butcher shop with Mark late Friday night or early Saturday morning. The other men were there already. An argument started. She left and walked home. She couldn't remember anymore if Wendy Brock was there or not, couldn't remember what Debbie looked like, didn't remember what anyone wore, what anyone drove, or what anyone said. She didn't remember what route she took from her house to the butcher shop, whether or not the door was locked or unlocked, if Jerry's truck was blue or green, and whether they just walked in or someone let them in. Sherry Payton couldn't remember anything at all, just that she was there.

MacNeil didn't learn one new detail by interviewing Payton, but when the interview was over he was more convinced than ever that something was very wrong with her story.

"Mark's life is on the line here," MacNeil said, packing up his briefcase and preparing to leave. "If you're telling me the truth,

I don't have any trouble with that at all. But if he isn't involved, that's a heck of a consequence to pay . . . and again I would just urge you to tell the truth, *please*, no matter what it might be."

For Sherry Payton, the truth was that if she testified against Mark Canter, and if she made restitution on the stolen checks, her record would be cleared. Not only would all charges against her be dropped, she wouldn't even be sentenced to probation. She'd be a free woman. Free to move back to Florida with her boyfriend, free to raise her baby, free to travel back and forth to Michigan to visit her family whenever she liked. She'd be cleared of everything, instead of looking at fifteen years in prison and having her baby taken away.

Back in court Wednesday morning, MacNeil could object to Judge Davis all he wanted to about Sherry Payton. He could argue that she wasn't on the State's list of witnesses, that she was going to lie, that she changed her story, and that the defense didn't have enough time to prepare a cross-examination. He could and did bring these arguments to the judge's attention, but his objections were all overruled. Sherry Payton would be allowed to testify, Judge Davis said, and without delay.

Prosecutor Hayes immediately put Payton on the stand, and the jury saw that she was indeed a tall and rugged-looking dark-haired woman who did not resemble the petite blonde MacNeil planted in the courtroom days before.

But Payton kept her end of the bargain. She testified she was inside Walt's Butcher Shop, saw Laurie Moore and Mark Canter argue with Jerry Tobias, and said the argument was about cocaine.

"Laurie Moore proceeded to get into the argument," she said. "Mark Canter took a swing at Jerry and hit him in the upper body. I proceeded to leave. Mark asked me where I was going. I said I was going home."

Sherry said she didn't remember many details. Not whether there were any other men—Terry? Don? Doug?—present, not what anyone was wearing or what she herself was wearing, not what vehicles anyone drove to the butcher shop or where they'd parked.

MacNeil seized on Sherry Payton's lack of recall, and the inconsistencies between Debbie's story and hers. Debbie said Sherry Payton ran out of the butcher shop screaming, while Sherry said she just walked out calmly. Debbie said Sherry Payton was drunk and high, while Sherry said she was completely sober. Debbie said two other men, Doug Brinkman and someone named "John" were also in the butcher shop, but Sherry didn't remember either one of them.

"You don't have a very good recollection of the events of December 5 and 6, do you?" MacNeil asked her.

"No," she admitted, "I do not."

While Payton testified, her attorney, Terry Bloomquist, was just going about his day. He was in the courthouse on routine business, peeked into Judge Davis' courtroom out of curiosity, and was shocked to see his client on the stand. Bloomquist had a verbal agreement with Hayes. As Payton's attorney, he was supposed to be notified when she was going to testify so that he could be in the courtroom with her. Bloomquist wanted to be available to provide legal counsel if Payton needed it. But Hayes hadn't notified him, and yet there was Sherry, up on the witness stand.

Bloomquist walked through the door, straight to the front of the courtroom, interrupted the proceedings, explained his arrangement with Hayes to Judge Davis, and asked the judge to call an immediate recess. Davis did, and ordered Hayes, MacNeil, and Bloomquist into his chambers.

"That was not part of our arrangement," Bloomquist told Davis, "to have her testifying without counsel."

Hayes offered no explanation but reiterated that in return for her testimony, he'd drop the four felony charges against her.

Bloomquist was furious, and said he was appalled that it looked like Payton had been willfully deprived of counsel. Davis listened, and then ruled the trial would resume.

Chapter 64   Terry Moore's Prison Sentence

. . . . Wednesday, November 16, 1988

Sherry Payton's testimony didn't only affect Mark Canter; Terry Moore's sentencing had been delayed so Judge Porter could consider what she had to say. Now that she'd confirmed Debbie's account of the murder, nothing was standing between Terry and a long stay in prison.

"It is then the sentence of this court, Mr. Moore, that you be sentenced to the Michigan Department of Corrections for the remainder of your life."

As Porter banged his gavel, weeping could be heard coming from a bench behind the defense. Terry's mother, Esther Moore, sobbed, and then called out her anger and grief.

"That's *justice*?" she wailed.

Terry Moore stood frozen after the verdict was read and showed no reaction. After a pause, he turned toward his mother and his sisters. "They can only have me physically," he told them. "They can't have me mentally. I still know I'm innocent."

Exactly a week later, in another courtroom, in front of another Judge, Norm Hayes rested the prosecution's case against Mark Canter the day before Thanksgiving. Over the long weekend, Esther Moore provided a full turkey dinner to all of the prisoners in the jail, including her son Terry, who wouldn't be transferred out of the county jail and to a more permanent prison until after the holiday.

Chapter 65 Mark Canter's Defense

. . . . Wednesday, November 30, 1988

It was another week until Mark Canter's trial resumed and Mac-Neil began to present the defense. His first order of business was to enter Dr. Tanay's psychiatric report into evidence. This was how the psychiatrist characterized Debbie:

> "Her ability to reproduce events is interfered with by her need to lie. She is driven to tell stories. I don't know if she observed what she said. I just know she is a person who, all her life, has had a habit of making up stories involving other people."

By December, MacNeil was caught in an impossible bind: Reveal his witness list to the prosecution and risk the people on it being intimidated by what he believed was a police and prosecution conspiracy against his client, or not reveal the list and risk being held in contempt of court by Judge Davis. MacNeil reluctantly chose the latter and after six weeks of testimony, the case edged toward mistrial.

"He's been sandbagging the court the whole time!" Hayes protested, when MacNeil tried to call a witness not on his original list. "I've never had a defense attorney do what Mr. MacNeil has done to this court."

MacNeil was just as furious as Hayes. He told Judge Davis that he had tried being up front with the prosecutor about his witness list, only to see his client suffer the results. As soon as his witnesses became public knowledge, MacNeil said, they were interviewed by the police and/or the prosecutor and either changed their story or decided not to testify at all.

"Witnesses have been harassed," MacNeil told Judge Davis. "They are scared to death. They don't want their names released. I'm doing the best I can to represent the defendant. I knew what I had to do and I did it. This has been a dirty, dirty trial all along. If you want to hold me in contempt, then you do it."

MacNeil and Hayes weren't the only ones who were angry; Judge Davis was furious, too. Trial procedure called for each side to submit a list of potential witnesses to the court before jury selection. That way, potential jurors could be asked whether they knew any of the witnesses—sometimes a reason to be excused from duty.

How, Judge Davis asked, was an impartial jury supposed to be selected if the defense didn't reveal its witnesses? MacNeil said he felt he had no choice but to keep his list under wraps. The way the police had strong-armed Sherry Payton was evidence of that, he argued.

"It would be a vast understatement to say I'm displeased," Judge Davis said, his voice filled with anger and frustration.

The trial was allowed to continue, and over the next five days MacNeil called 37 witnesses. The defense's strategy wasn't only to show Mark was innocent of the crime; it was to show Mark didn't even know Jerry Tobias. After all his other witnesses had testified, MacNeil called Mark to the stand to testify in his own defense.

"I've never met Jerry Tobias before in my life," Mark said.

"Were you with Debra Parmentier the night of December 5th and 6th, 1986?" MacNeil asked.

"No sir, Mr. MacNeil, I was not. I've *never* been in the back of Walt's Butcher Shop in my life," Mark said.

"Do you even know what it looks like?" MacNeil asked.

"Well, I've seen pictures of it during the proceedings of this trial," Mark said, "but other than that, no sir."

Chapter 66 Closing Arguments. Again.

. . . . Friday, December 9, 1988

In his closing argument, Hayes apologized to the jury for surrounding them with witnesses who weren't the most upstanding citizens, but explained that was the nature of solving crime.

"Dope murders don't occur in front of bankers and clergymen," he said.

In his closing argument for Mark, MacNeil stated, again and again, that his client had nothing to do with the murder. The only reason he was in the defendant's chair was because of Debbie Parmentier's lies.

"Have you ever thought, 'Thank God she didn't know me'?" MacNeil asked the jury.

Mark was just a victim of "the best manipulator I've ever seen in my life." MacNeil said. "And Sherry Payton would tell you the moon is made of green cheese if you'd dismiss four felonies for her."

The next day, December 10, after deliberating for only five and a half hours, the jury found Mark Canter guilty of Aiding and Abetting and Second-Degree Murder. As the verdict was read, Mark pushed his chair back against the railing separating the defense table from the spectators and threw himself into the arms of his weeping mother. After a few moments, he was led away by the bailiff and MacNeil went to visit him in his cell.

Mark was despondent. MacNeil tried his best to comfort his client, but his words seemed weak and ineffectual. Weighing like a cinderblock on both their minds was the fact that Mark could have walked free if he would have been willing to lie.

The attorney and the convicted man sat together in silence for several minutes when a bailiff arrived with a message for MacNeil.

Judge Davis wanted him back in the jury room. MacNeil said his goodbyes, reluctantly left Mark alone in his cell, and went back upstairs. Waiting for MacNeil in the jury room were Judge Davis, Prosecutor Hayes, and ten of the twelve jurors. A heated discussion was already in progress.

"Why haven't you charged Debbie Parmentier with perjury?" a juror was asking Hayes. "Yeah, and the Nelsons, too?" another wondered.

MacNeil watched as other jurors nodded, one remarking that Don Nelson's testimony in particular was ridiculous and another saying that Debbie was a liar and probably crazy, too.

"Well," Hayes replied, "perjury is a hard thing to prove, and it depends on the state of mind of the person."

MacNeil looked around the room and felt disgusted with the whole lot of them. If they didn't believe the prosecution's witnesses, then why did they convict his client? But it was too late for that. None of their answers would open the door to Mark's cell. He forced himself to listen for a few more minutes, and then turned to leave. Just before he did, one of the jurors, an elderly woman who sat in the back row, answered his question even though he hadn't asked it out loud.

"You know," she said, "without the testimony of Sherry Payton we would never have convicted Mark."

But Mark Canter was convicted; his guilty verdict was added to the ones the prosecutor had won against Laurie and Terry Moore. Only Doug Brinkman and Don Heistand remained and were already behind bars—Heistand because he'd been arrested for open murder and denied bail, and Brinkman because he was serving a two- to four-year sentence on an unrelated misdemeanor charge. Heistand was in the Otsego County Jail, but Brinkman was not so lucky. He was serving his sentence on Twelve Block in Jackson Prison, a curious choice considering it was a facility reserved for prisoners serving life sentences for violent crimes. For Brinkman, Twelve Block lived up to its reputation as being one of the most hated places in Michigan. Less than a week before Mark Canter's conviction, Doug Brinkman was assaulted in prison.

After lunch on December 4, a prisoner dressed all in black approached Doug Brinkman's cell door, used Brinkman's own ID card to open the lock, and once inside, cornered Brinkman and assaulted him.

"I wanted to die," Brinkman would say later, under oath. "I wanted out of there. This guy was able to come and go wherever he wanted. He had obviously been in there for years. Inside, you cannot get away from somebody. There is just no way."

Brinkman stayed in his cell for the rest of the day, and finally at 10 PM asked for a guard. He reported the assault. The guard filed a report, told Brinkman he would see what he could do about protecting him from further attacks, and left his cell.

The next day, Brinkman saw the man who attacked him in a common area of the prison. Brinkman tried to avoid him, but the man approached him and told Brinkman he had better get out of Jackson, go back to where he came from, and do what he was supposed to do, or he'd wind up dead.

For the next week, Brinkman refused to leave his cell. His meals were brought to him on a tray until prison officials moved him to a cell on the first floor of the prison. Brinkman worried that this did not provide any security from the man who'd assaulted him, and that if that guy wanted to, he could do it again.

"It seemed like he knew where I was at, and what I was doing, and who I was and what was going on in my life in Otsego County," Brinkman would later say later, during a deposition for the Michigan Supreme Court. "I figured, either commit suicide or get out."

Chapter 67   Heistand and Brinkman Sentenced

. . . . December, 1988

On December 15, Doug Brinkman became the only one of the Tobias defendants to plead guilty. His charge was Accessory After the Fact to a Felony.

Don Heistand was scheduled to go on trial once Mark Canter's trial concluded. On December 21, 1988, Heistand's attorney, Jack Felton, got a phone call from Prosecutor Hayes alerting him to Brinkman's plea. Not only had Doug pled guilty to Accessory After the Fact, he'd agreed to testify against Heistand. It was Heistand's last chance at a plea, Hayes said. If he would plead guilty to a similar charge, Hayes would dismiss the Second-Degree Murder charge against him. Felton said he'd present the offer to Heistand again, but first he wanted to talk to Brinkman himself.

Brinkman was being held in the Crawford County Jail, so Felton went to see him there. Brinkman confirmed he planned to testify for the prosecution and told Felton that both he and Don Heistand were present when Tobias died.

"If it wasn't Heistand," Brinkman said, "it was his twin."

Felton left the jail feeling confused and defeated. He remained convinced his client had nothing to do with Jerry Tobias' death, yet three men who also proclaimed their innocence were now serving long prison sentences. Felton decided Heistand should consider accepting Hayes' offer.

"I'm prepared to try the case," Felton told him. "But given the unusual and suspicious developments, you should not assume that an innocent man will be automatically exonerated."

Heistand still refused to plead guilty and told Felton he'd go to prison before he'd testify against anyone. Felton asked him if he'd consider pleading no contest if he didn't have to admit guilt or testify against anyone else. If Heistand would agree, Felton would make the counter offer to Hayes. Heistand would still have to go to prison, but he'd get a shorter sentence rather than gambling with life in prison. Heistand again said no, but Felton wouldn't let it alone. He arranged a three-way phone conference between himself, Heistand, and Heistand's wife, Lisa. Once Lisa and Don were on the line together, Felton stepped out of his office with the phone still connected so Don and Lisa could speak privately. The call lasted nearly two hours. When Felton came back on the line, Heistand had a different answer.

"Tell Hayes he won," he told Felton.

The next morning, Felton called Hayes and made the counter offer. Heistand would plead no contest, but he wouldn't testify against anyone. Hayes rejected the counter offer, and said it was a guilty plea or no deal. Felton went back to his client with the news, but Heistand was adamant. He'd face trial and whatever that might bring, rather than plead guilty. Felton mentally prepared himself for trial and called Hayes back a second time to deliver the news. But Hayes changed his mind and agreed to Heistand's terms.

Heistand entered his plea that day and was sentenced to forty to sixty months in prison. Far from feeling vindicated by saving his client from a life sentence, Felton felt defeated.

"I remained deeply bothered by what I viewed as a corrupt prosecution of all the defendants," Felton said later.

But with Heistand's no contest plea, as far as the police, the prosecutor, and the community of Gaylord were concerned, the case was over. Five men had been arrested, three were convicted in jury trials, two took plea deals, and all were in prison.

Laurie Moore's request for a new trial was denied, and his mother, Esther Moore, closed Walt's Butcher Shop. She couldn't keep it going by herself any longer since business had fallen off to almost nothing.

Lieutenant John Hardy and Detective Fred LaBarge retired from the Michigan State Police with lucrative pensions, their retirement earnings computed on their last two years' wages, which were higher than in all their previous years because of the Tobias-related overtime.

Debbie Parmentier's divorce from Leonard was finalized, and she and Curt Beerens were back together. They moved to Cadillac into an apartment paid for by the Michigan State Police.

Betty Swarthout, the juror in the Terry Moore trial who was questioned by Judge Porter for her misconduct, committed suicide.

And a few months after Mark Canter, Doug Brinkman, and Don Heistand were sentenced, a notice appeared in the *Gaylord Herald Times'* District Court report: "Sherry L. Payton, 28, Gaylord, saw charges of larceny over $100 and operating with a suspended or revoked license dismissed in accordance with a plea agreement." Payton had charges pending against her in Kalkaska and Crawford counties, too. By request from Prosecutor Hayes, those charges were also dismissed.

Most people who read the newspaper probably didn't see the notice about Sherry Payton. Or if they did, they read right over it, because it didn't look very important. It was in small print and buried on an inside page next to an advertisement for Rainbow Trophy company. But readers of the *Gaylord Herald Times* probably wouldn't have wanted to see it, even if they knew it was there. The people of Gaylord were just relieved the whole sordid story of Jerry Tobias' death had finally come to an end.

The general attitude toward the case was that a series of nasty and expensive trials were over, the drug-dealing murderers had been shipped off to prison, and at last their little resort town could get back to normal. As one defense attorney put it, people were certain of the men's guilt because it had been "hardened on the anvil of repetition."

"I feel justice has been done," Hayes told a *Herald Times* reporter, "and we can all go on."

PART 3

. . . . The Unraveling

Chapter 68   MacNeil Gets a Phone Call

. . . . Spring, 1989

"**Y**ou know there was something wrong with that trial, don't you?"

The woman on the other end of the line was calling MacNeil collect, at his office, and although she refused to say where she was calling from, MacNeil found the voice sickly familiar. It belonged to someone he hoped he'd never hear from again: Sherry Payton.

Whether by design, default, or a combination of the two, Mac-Neil's reputation was that of a guy you could talk to. A guy who understood how life worked. A compassionate, moral person well aware of what was going on in and around Gaylord—the good, the bad, and the illegal.

Even before he was appointed to represent Mark Canter, Mac-Neil was known as an attorney who would offer you a helping hand, a shoulder to cry on, or a metaphorical swift kick, whichever you needed most. This advice was available for the asking, to clients and non-clients alike. People trusted Ray MacNeil, even when they were in trouble and especially when they were in trouble with the law.

So it wasn't all that unusual for MacNeil to get desperate phone calls from desperate people. But he still never expected to hear from Sherry Payton again. Only a few months had passed since Mark had been sentenced to prison for life and if what that juror told MacNeil was true, it was Payton's testimony that put him there. Still, when an operator asked MacNeil if he'd accept Payton's collect call, he didn't hesitate. MacNeil was still Mark's attorney after all, and there was the appeal to think about.

"There was something wrong with that trial, Mr. MacNeil," Payton repeated. "Gomez should be in jail, and I could be charged with perjury if Hayes finds out I'm saying this, but the guilt is killing me. I can't live with it anymore. I just can't live with the lies."

MacNeil and Payton spoke for several minutes. She alluded to problems with her testimony but refused to say exactly what they were. She was calling him from far away, she said, but she wanted to talk to him in person. She wanted to do it so bad she was willing to come back to northern Michigan to do it. Payton said she could be in Gaylord in a few weeks if MacNeil would be willing to meet with her. He said that he was.

"Just promise you won't tell Hayes you talked to me. That I called you. *Promise.*"

Payton didn't have anything to worry about. Although they both lived and worked in Gaylord, since the end of Mark's trial, MacNeil went out of his way to avoid the prosecutor. He certainly wasn't going to share details of Payton's phone call with him.

Chapter 69   Stuart Hubbell Gets a Phone Call

. . . . April, 1989

While the police, the prosecutor, and the city of Gaylord were happy to see the trials come to an end, behind the scenes and away from the headlines the appeal machinery was slowly grinding on. Ray MacNeil was working on Mark's appeal, and Laurie Moore had been assigned an attorney with the State Appeals Office. Doug Brinkman wanted to appeal but was afraid doing so might negate his plea bargain, and since Don Heistand plead no contest, he couldn't appeal. Terry Moore no longer had adequate legal representation.

Financially destitute from paying for his trial lawyer, Terry requested a court-appointed attorney for his appeal. As his trial judge, William Porter was responsible for assigning one, but when he contacted the criminal lawyers on Otsego County's rotation, every one of them declined the assignment.

Drugs were anathema in Gaylord, and cocaine especially had wrecked lives, infiltrated the local high school, taxed police, threatened tourism, and was at the root of innumerable family break-ups. The Tobias case was irreversibly tainted. Any local attorney already involved with the case wished he or she hadn't been and couldn't be called back into service because of a conflict of interest. Local attorneys not involved with the case intended to stay that way, which proved to be a big problem for Judge Porter.

The Moore appeal was working the tiny two-person law office he'd initially assigned it to right out of business. The six other attorneys Porter contacted all turned him down. Porter's only choice was to look further afield for someone to represent Terry. As a last resort, the judge called Stuart "Stu" Hubbell of Traverse City.

Hubbell had served for a dozen years as prosecutor of Grand Traverse County, and in that time his work approached legend. Once, while shopping in downtown Traverse City on his lunch hour, Hubbell encountered a man he'd just sentenced to several years in prison, walking right down Front Street. Hubbell ducked into a store, called police, went back outside, made a citizen's arrest, and then held the man until police arrived. Hubbell's career as a prosecutor was over, so he was out of public life. He had recently opened his own law practice. His entry into the Tobias case started just like MacNeil's—with a phone call from Judge Porter.

"Stu," the Judge said, "I need a favor."

Judge Porter told Hubbell he knew the case was out of Hubbell's judicial district and that the travel back and forth between Traverse City and Gaylord might cause him some hardship, but six other attorneys had already turned down the appointment and the judge was getting desperate. Court-appointed attorneys were only paid $40 an hour—a third (or less) of the hourly rate many earned in private practice. But Porter promised Hubbell his travel fees would be covered and asked him to represent Terry Moore in his appeal.

"I've heard about that case," Hubbell said. "Of course I don't know all the details, but there's something not right about it. I'd need your word that the proceedings will be legitimate."

"You've got it," Judge Porter said.

Stu Hubbell had all the personal characteristics Porter knew would be needed for any Tobias case appeal. He had an extensive law career and his ethics were above reproach. He'd been a lawyer for the army during the Korean War, the prosecutor of Grand Traverse County, and president of the Michigan Prosecutors Association. He'd served as a Magistrate for the state's Western District and had even worked as Special Council for the U.S. Senate Rules Committee when Gerald Ford was Vice President.

After forty years in the legal profession, not much surprised Stu Hubbell. He was pretty sure he'd seen it all. His first task as Terry's attorney was to send his new client a letter of introduction.

Dear Mr. Moore:

"I have been appointed by the trial court to represent you on your appeal. I have ordered a copy of the transcript of the proceedings in your case and pertinent documents and records. After I receive these and review them, I will make arrangements to discuss your case with you.

"I encourage you to raise any questions you have about the status of your case, appellate procedure, applicable law or any other concerns you have. However, I will not know the issues until I have read the transcript and lower court documents, and completed whatever investigation is necessary to support non-record claims. Therefore, except in the most extraordinary cases, I am not able to give advice about the chances of obtaining relief until I have reviewed the entire record.

　　If you have any questions about the above, please feel free to write to me.

Sincerely,

Stuart D. Hubbell

P.S. Please inform us of any moves and changes in address so that your mail will not be delayed. Also, whenever you write to me please put your name, prisoner number and prison facility on your letter. Thank you.

The subsequent correspondence from his newest client would be as instantaneous as Jackson Prison's bureaucracy and the U.S. Postal Service allowed, not to mention voluminous, well-written, sharply reasoned, and several times grating in its tone and arrogance. Yet Hubbell couldn't help but soften every time he saw those incoming envelopes from Terry.

　　His client would never fail to follow Hubbell's specific instructions for identifying himself, and always included all the information Hubbell required. But Terry would also add his own tagline along the top edge of the envelope: "Liberty and Justice for All!!"

Chapter 70　Meet Stu Hubbell

· · · · · · · · · · Spring, 1989

In a lot of ways, Stu Hubbell wasn't like other attorneys. He'd already had his turn at politics. That part of his career was past, so he wasn't particularly concerned about public opinion. What other attorneys had to say about him didn't matter that much, either. The ones he respected liked him, or at least respected him in return, and that's what mattered to him. The attorneys who didn't like him, Hubbell simply had no time for.

When Porter made the assignment, Hubbell was nearing the end of a career he loved. He knew he was not going to get rich being a lawyer, but he'd made a living at it and raised a family. Three of his grown sons, Joe, Paul and Dan Hubbell, followed in their father's footsteps and were attorneys, too. Now, he just wanted to run his practice ethically and profitably and take on a few more interesting cases before he retired.

Hubbell had the characteristics Judge Porter was looking for in an appeal attorney, and the Terry Moore appeal had the characteristics Hubbell was looking for in a case. So while other attorneys ducked the Tobias case, Hubbell did the opposite. He announced his involvement in it.

The day he wrote to Terry, Hubbell also sent letters announcing his appellate assignment to Terry's two previous attorneys, to Judge Porter, Prosecutor Hayes, the district court clerk, several court reporters, the court administrator, the chief clerk for the court of appeals, as well as the attorneys for all of the other defendants. In each of these letters, Hubbell made sure to cc the others, creating a flurry of correspondence impossible to ignore.

Make no mistake, Stu Hubbell was on the case.

Chapter 71　A Ballistics Match

. . . . June, 1989

"The investigation that would not die." That's what the State Police had taken, among themselves, to calling the Jerry Tobias case. Their unorthodox detective work put five men in prison, but rocks kept turning over, seemingly all on their own, and odd things kept crawling out from under them. The latest of these to surface was a .308 Mauser, a German-made bolt-action military rifle.

The weapon was turned into police by a woman named Sue Kerry. She was Mark Kerry's ex-wife, divorcing her husband soon after learning of his brief affair with Debbie Parmentier. After Mark moved out, Sue started cleaning and found the rifle in the rafters of their garage. It was still loaded, and the Kerrys had three young children. Sue thought it was too dangerous to keep it at her house, so she reported it to the State Police.

A road patrol trooper responded, took the rifle and the box of ammunition found with it, and turned them over to Detective Wilt. Wilt ordered a registration check and ballistic test, and got a match. The gun wasn't stolen, but it was legally registered to someone the State Police were well acquainted with: gun dealer, informant, and former State Police spy, Curt Beerens. Even more surprising than its owner was what the gun had been used for. Shells from the crime lab's test firing matched those recovered in the Sand Hill Manor shooting. The shot that was fired through a sliding glass door in a supposed attempt on Debbie's life more than a year ago came from the gun found in Sue Kerry's garage.

Officially, the apartment shooting was still an open investigation, though police suspected it had been staged by Debbie and Mark Kerry. They'd kept their suspicions under wraps; if any of the defense attorneys got hold of the information, they would have tried to use it at trial to impeach Debbie. It was going to be harder to keep it quiet with new evidence that Mark Kerry was involved. The question for police was what to do with that evidence. Their answer was documented in a police report, but given a separate incident number so it didn't have to be included it with the Tobias case files or provided it to the defense.

On March 3, 1989, Detective Wilt filed an addition to the original apartment shooting report, writing, "Complaint can be closed out, exceptional clearance. There was no crime; it was staged, however no prosecution."

On May 2, 1989, an update on the shell and jacket fragment police recovered in Debbie's apartment: "Items destroyed."

And on June 22, 1989, "Final disposition: Closed."

Chapter 72   Sherry Payton Returns

. . . . July, 1989

Payton kept her promise to Ray MacNeil and returned to Gaylord in July. She was ready, she told him, to tell the truth. She was ready to admit she'd lied in court, that she'd never seen any murder, had no idea who, if anyone, killed Jerry Tobias, and that she'd never even met anyone named Debbie Parmentier.

Payton told MacNeil she only said all of those things in court to save her own skin. When Trooper Gomez threatened her with jail time and promised she'd spend fifteen years behind bars if she didn't testify, she caved.

MacNeil taped their conversation and suggested she get an attorney to represent her. He couldn't do it himself because he was already representing Mark, but recanting her testimony wasn't something she should face alone. Payton said she'd think about it, but in the meantime her conscience was clear and she just wanted to get out of Gaylord and go back to Florida.

When Payton left his office, MacNeil sat back in his chair and exhaled. It felt like he'd been holding that breath for years. Finally, he had real evidence of what he'd suspected all along: Mark was innocent. He'd only been convicted because of perjured testimony. MacNeil believed Debbie lied, the Nelsons lied, and Payton lied. They lied to police, they lied to the prosecutor, and they lied on the stand. Payton was no saint, but at least she was willing to admit her lies—not only admit them, but explain them, too. With no resources and a troubled past, she'd been a malleable witness.

Knowing all that was one thing, but using the information to help his client was another. Even with Mark's appeal looming, what could MacNeil really do? He couldn't go to the prosecutor or police—they were the very people Payton said threatened and coached her. He couldn't go to the trial judge—Judge Davis had chastised Ray harshly during the trial for keeping his witnesses under wraps so MacNeil didn't think he'd be amenable to revisiting testimony now that the trial was long over.

But if what Payton said was true, it was evidence of serious wrongdoing. MacNeil decided it needed to be investigated by the state's highest law: the Michigan Attorney General's office. The state's Attorney General at the time was Frank Kelley, a man with a reputation for being immune to intimidation from anyone, even the State Police. The Attorney General just might be Mark's last hope.

Frank Kelley had statewide jurisdiction in any Michigan case he chose to get involved in. The AG's office ran a special division just to investigate criminal wrongdoing by state employees and that was the office MacNeil wanted to communicate with. But he was also realistic. If he made a formal complaint himself, he'd just look like a sour grapes defense attorney who'd lost a case. He needed someone he trusted, and who the Attorney General's office respected, to intercede on his behalf. MacNeil mulled over this quandary for a few days before someone came to mind. Saginaw County Probate Judge, Edmund Troester.

MacNeil worked with Judge Troester back in the 1970s when MacNeil was a Saginaw County prosecutor, years before opening his practice in Gaylord. MacNeil called Judge Troester, explained the situation, and agreed to contact Frank Kelley.

MacNeil's behind-the-scenes work paid off. Kelley and his chief assistant, Robert Ianni, met with Troester and then agreed to speak to MacNeil. MacNeil detailed issues in Mark's case that bothered him, specifically Sherry Payton's testimony, and a plan was made to investigate Payton's story. Kelley said an agent working for him, former Detroit cop Terry Doyle, just happened to be on vacation in Florida. MacNeil would travel south, meet up with Agent Doyle, and together they would interview Payton. The rest of the investigation would depend on what Payton had to say. To encourage her to tell the truth, Kelley said he'd give Doyle a signed letter of immunity from prosecution.

Chapter 73 The Attorney General's Investigation

· · · · · · · · · · January 10, 1990

According to AG Evidence Tape #T 01-10-90-846, recorded at Sherry Payton's house, in Palm Coast, Florida:

Terry Doyle: I guess, Sherry, we might as well start out, and I want to introduce myself, Terry Doyle from the Attorney General's Office and Mr. Ray MacNeil, the attorney for Mark Canter. As you know, I presented you here with a letter from the Attorney General's Office, which is signed, granting you immunity in the matter of the Tobias murder case. I guess we might as well go back and start at door number one. Why don't you just tell us the story from there.

Sherry Payton: I was living in Florida and I had bad checks out and I wanted to make restitution for them. My mom and Karen Jackson set up an appointment for me to come back to see the judge and turn myself in. Before I left, my old roommate—we moved from the place when we lived on the beach—and my old roommate called me and said the cops were here looking for you. So I called Karen Jackson and she said, "Well, nobody's looking for you that I know."

So, I got on a bus and I went to Lansing and my aunt took me to Gaylord. We met Karen Jackson in a motel room and she said, "You know what, they're looking for you for?" And I said, "No." And she said, "Well, for the murder trial." And I said, "*What*!?"

I hired Karen Jackson because I wanted to come back and face my check charges and turn myself in for that and make restitution. Then when I got back to Michigan, she said, "Debbie Parmentier said you were there. That's why they're looking for you."

Terry Doyle: Ok. And you say they fingerprinted you and processed you. Did the police at that time mention anything about this Tobias murder case?

Sherry Payton: No.

Terry Doyle: Once you get to Gaylord, now what happens? Does this come up about this Tobias murder case?

Sherry Payton: Yes. It was when they started interrogating me. They took me to a big room and Hayes was there and all the detectives were there. And that is when I told them that I *wasn't* there. That I didn't know *nothing*.

Terry Doyle: And what did they do once you told them you knew nothing about this murder, and you weren't at the murder scene?

Sherry Payton: Apparently, they didn't believe me.

Sherry said Hayes left the room, police let Sherry speak briefly with her parents, and then they took her to a jail in Petoskey, where she spent the night. The next day State Police officers came back to the jail, picked her up, and drove her back to the Gaylord post where she was escorted into a small office with Trooper Gomez.

Terry Doyle: Sherry, can you tell us what happened with Gomez, please.

Sherry Payton: Gomez said, "They sent me to talk with you. I am sure I can be your best friend if you just tell me the truth, but the first time you lie to me, then I'm not going to do any more for you." And then he said, "We know, we have proof, that you were there." And I said that I wasn't there and he kept saying, "Why are you doing this to yourself?" He says, "If you just said that you were there, all these charges will be dropped against you. The prosecutor said he will make no deals with you if you don't tell us that you were there. You will go to jail for 10 to 15 years and you're pregnant." And he said to me, "How can you have your baby be born in jail? You'll never see your baby again." After I said, "Ok, what the hell do you want me to say?" He had a big piece of yellow paper and he had things written down and he said, "Well, this is the time that this happened and so on."

Sherry said Gomez coached her on what to say happened the night of the murder, from the time she left work to the time she was supposed to have arrived at Walt's Butcher Shop. He told her who was at the butcher shop, what they did, and when, she said. During these explanations, Sherry explained to Agent Doyle, Gomez turned the tape off; when Sherry got the story straight, he turned it back on again.

Sherry Payton: He told me that everything that was said in the office, if I ever said anything, he would deny it. "It's my word against yours." What it comes down to is they just told me if I didn't tell them I was there, I was going to jail. And I was scared to death and I didn't know what to do. They told me that they had all kinds of proof that Mark and they did it, and I said, "Well, if you have all this proof, why do you need my testimony?" They said, "We just need to ensure they get prosecuted." They told me that my testimony wasn't that important.

MacNeil knew the story well, but it was new to Agent Doyle. If what Payton said was true, the police had told a witness in a murder trial to lie. And there was a good chance an innocent man was serving a life sentence because of it. But Payton wasn't finished.

"You knew Debbie Parmentier, right?" Doyle asked her.

"See? I don't even know her!" Payton said. "I think someone told me she had blond hair or something, blondish brown hair is all I know."

When Doyle took the assignment to interrupt his vacation for a few hours to interview Sherry Payton, the Attorney General's office was only planning to investigate one incident of possible perjury in one defendant's trial. But after talking to Payton, Agent Doyle wondered if she was just the beginning.

"The Attorney General's Organized Crime and Public Corruption Unit has been requested by Attorney Raymond MacNeil to look into the conviction of his client, Mark Canter, for the murder of Jerry Tobias," Agent Doyle wrote in his report of the interview. "Subsequent to that request, information was developed that several witnesses had given perjured testimony during that trial, and it was determined that other witnesses should be re-interviewed."

A month later, Agent Doyle visited Don Heistand in Jackson Prison. With MacNeil's help, the Attorney General's office put together a list of people to interview, and Don Heistand was next in line.

Heistand told Doyle his only crime was being hired as a meat cutter at Walt's Butcher Shop during deer season. Without accepting that part-time job, he never would have had any connection to the Tobias case. He knew the Moore brothers because he worked in the butcher shop, but he'd never met Mark Canter or Doug Brinkman until he was arrested for murder, occupied a cell near their cells, and stood next to them at their arraignment. The victim, Jerry Tobias, was another man he didn't know. Heistand worked for only two weeks at Walt's; he really needed the job, but quit after a having a severe allergic reaction to deer hair.

A week after the Heistand interview, Agent Doyle drove north to the Upper Peninsula and interviewed Doug Brinkman at Marquette Prison.

"Brinkman denied any connection with the death of Jerry Tobias," Agent Doyle wrote in his report of the interview. "He stated he agreed to plead guilty after being raped while in Jackson Prison. While awaiting trial in Otsego County jail, Brinkman was informed that if he talked to (Detective) LaBarge, all harassment would stop. The only reasons he accepted the offer were his desire to get out of Jackson Prison and to avoid the life sentence Mark Canter received."

After Brinkman, Doyle drove to the Upper Regional Chippewa Correctional Facility in Kinross and interviewed Terry Moore. By the time Doyle heard Terry's story, it must have begun to sound like a broken record. Terry Moore also told the agent that he had nothing to do with the crime, suggesting Prosecutor Hayes had a vendetta against his brother, Laurie Moore, that extended back to childhood. After Laurie was convicted, Terry said he tried to secure his brother's release by investigating the case on his own. That attracted the ire of Hayes and, Terry believed, his own arrest and subsequent conviction.

———————

When Agent Doyle left Chippewa Prison, Terry Moore felt ecstatic. The next time he had access to the prison payphone, he called Stu Hubbell. Hubbell was out of the office but a secretary took the emotional message. Terry had just been interviewed by Attorney General investigators looking into his case! And they assured him that if his story could be substantiated, he would be freed. This was going to be his ticket out of prison, he was certain of it. Finally, the truth would come out and he would be vindicated!

When Hubbell returned to his office he read the message and cringed. He knew enough about his client by now to know he had a big mouth and an obnoxious personality to go along with it. The AG investigation might be good news, but if Terry Moore couldn't restrain himself, he could do more harm than good.

"Obviously, this is good encouraging news," Hubbell wrote in a letter back to Terry. "As your visit with the Attorney General's investigator today establishes, there is indeed a real investigation underway.

"Now, I want to caution you most severely. I have perceived in reviewing your file, your correspondence and otherwise, that you have an emotional temperament. This is manifested, as I see it, on occasion by inappropriate behavior and comments. You may not like me stating those perceptions, but I suggest you accept them as being objective observations.

"We are at a critical point here. It is extremely important that you maintain absolute control over your personal behavior and demeanor. Do not screw up there in prison. Do not become a behavior problem. Keep your mouth tightly and absolutely closed about all of this.

"You must accept and realize that to undo this conviction we are undertaking an extremely difficult task. The forces of society, convinced they are in the right, are all lined up against us. But I believe we are making progress."

Terry did his best to take Hubbell's advice while the Attorney General's investigation continued. On February 28, 1990, Agent Doyle interviewed Kelly Morey, whose ex-husband, Bill, worked at Walt's. The night Jerry died, Bill and his brother, Todd Morey, were working at the butcher shop, processing deer. They were the workers who locked the shop after Laurie Moore left to go to the Sportsman's Club Dinner. The agents interviewed Kelly Morey at her house in Shelby Township. MacNeil had represented Kelly in her divorce from Bill and tipped Agent Doyle to something Kelly said about her husband.

The night of the murder Bill Morey came home from Walt's about 11 PM. Todd called him an hour later, and Bill told Kelly he was going out to run an errand. Kelly thought it was odd that her husband would be running an errand at midnight, but Bill refused to give her any details. Kelly went to bed, and when she woke up in the morning, Bill was asleep on the couch.

Several days later, Kelly said she looked out her kitchen window and saw her husband burning a pair of boots in their backyard fire pit. She thought it was strange but was unaware the police were examining footprints and looking for a pair of missing boots in connection with the Tobias case.

Chapter 74   An Idea

. . . . March, 1990

Good ideas often seem obvious in retrospect. Might the appeals of Laurie, Mark, and Terry be more effective if their defense attorneys worked together? Standard defense strategy was often contrary to this idea. When a group of defendants were being tried together for the same crime, one guilty person could bring down the lot of them, even if others were innocent. But what if *all* the accused were innocent? Could reverse logic prevail and one man's innocence actually help the others?

On the morning of March 2, 1990, Dean Robb (Laurie Moore's trial attorney), along with Ray MacNeil, Martin Tieber (Laurie's appellate attorney), and Jack Felton (Don Heistand's attorney) all met with Stu Hubbell in Hubbell's Traverse City office.

"The purpose of this meeting, as we discussed, is to map out collective approaches and responsibilities so as best to effectively and expeditiously bring our clients' causes to a just resolve," Hubbell said, setting the tone.

The men gave updates on their individual appeals and compared notes on the police, the prosecution, and on legal strategy. The normal purpose of an appellate lawyer was not to investigate the case, look for new evidence, or interview witnesses, but to identify mistakes made at trial. The attorneys were prepared to do that, but the complexity of the case, the size of the transcripts, and the inaccessibility of the evidence was making their task difficult. Together, maybe they'd make swifter progress.

MacNeil filled the group in on the Attorney General's investigation and promised as soon as he received the interview reports, he'd pass them on to the others. Hubbell discussed his plans to get Terry's case remanded to the trial court and the difficulties he was having gaining access to trial transcripts and missing police reports. Tieber shared his frustration over what he said was Prosecutor Hayes' stonewalling on providing him copies of lab reports.

Tieber said he'd been working on Laurie Moore's appeal since April of 1988—almost two years—and in that time he'd been trying to get the prosecutor to tell him whether any of Tobias' blood or urine samples from the autopsy remained. Tieber said he also wanted copies of the fingerprints and palm prints found at the crime scene. In letter after letter to Hayes, Tieber promised to pay any costs associated with the evidence, but to no avail. Hayes either didn't respond or gave convoluted answers. This silence from the prosecutor's office was so contrary to anything Tieber had ever encountered, he told the men, so he'd resorted to threats.

"In seventeen years of appellate work I have never received this type of treatment from a prosecutor's office," Tieber wrote in a letter to Prosecutor Hayes dated March 2, 1990. "Your failure to respond to my repeated and legitimate requests for information in any fashion is denying my client his due process right to an effective appeal and clearly constitutes an ethical violation. Unless I receive an immediate response, I will be forced to consider referral of this matter to the Attorney Grievance Commission and/or initiation of court action."

Tieber was eventually informed by Assistant Prosecutor Dawn Pyrek that the prosecutor's office had already supplied the information he was requesting to other members of the "defense team." Presumably Hayes meant the men now gathered at this initial meeting. But they didn't consider themselves a team but rather a group of frustrated attorneys called into service by various judges and state agencies.

Hubbell was empathetic to Tieber's difficulties. He'd been assigned to serve as Terry's court-appointed appellate attorney in June 1989 and didn't receive his client's full trial transcript until November, seven months later. Because of the size of the file, the court had given the two court reporters an extension, the first such extension either women had ever requested in their twelve and fifteen years on the job. The entire transcript of the Terry Moore trial and preliminary hearing, when complete, would extend to several thousand pages and four feet of bound volumes.

"I am under the gun with 38 volumes of trial transcripts, 6 volumes of prelim and assorted other motions hearings, testimony out of the presence of the jury, etc., amounting to over 6,000 pages of grist," Hubbell said.

The prosecution had started grumbling about having to fight a "defense team." But there was no official "defense team." Their client's appeals were filed separately and would remain so. But the attorneys did agree to keep each other informed of their respective successes and setbacks, to share newly discovered evidence, and to make a collective request of the Attorney General's office: Officially support their forthcoming motions for appeal for all five defendants, and do it in court.

Chapter 75 Investigation Expanded

. . . . Spring, 1990

The Attorney General's office acknowledged the request regarding the appeals proceedings, but said a decision would have to wait until their investigation was over and it was looking like that day was still a long ways off. After Agent Doyle's interview with Payton, the Attorney General's office dramatically expanded their investigation. No longer were they concerned only with the veracity of Payton's testimony. Now the office was looking into all Tobias case prosecutions.

Between January and May of 1990, Agent Terry Doyle and several other Attorney General staffers, including Theodore Klimaszewski, the head of the department's Organized Crime and Public Corruption Unit, and Robert Ianni, an Assistant Attorney in charge of the office's Criminal Division, interviewed twenty people who were either centrally or peripherally connected with the Tobias investigation and/or prosecution.

Facts emerged of forged diaries, pilfered trial transcripts and police reports, staged shootings, a fabricated AK-47 purchase, and at least two faked kidnappings. The only common denominator in each of these fantastical dramas? Debbie Parmentier. Trying to interview her would prove to be, not surprisingly, far more difficult and bizarre than the agents bargained for. Even for a seasoned agent like Terry Doyle, Debbie proved to be one of the more slippery witnesses he'd ever tried to interview. Considering his experience in law enforcement, that was saying something.

By the time he was an investigator for the Attorney General's office, Doyle had served a tour in Vietnam and retired from the Detroit Police Department. He'd seen plenty of crime, underhandedness, and illegal shenanigans in his career, though nothing that could have prepared him for Debbie.

But in order to interview her, first he had to find her.

By 1990, Debbie had moved out of Gaylord and into a house in Cadillac with Curt Beerens. She soon got antsy and moved again, this time forty miles south to Baldwin, Michigan, first living with Beerens and then with two other men, Dan Beck and Kent Herrick. Herrick was signing up people for adult education classes and Debbie showed up to enroll.

Twice Doyle and another agent went to Debbie's house in Baldwin, and twice they were turned away by Beck. He didn't know where Debbie was, he said, and hadn't seen her in weeks. He did give them one lead, the Baldwin offices of the Michigan Department of Social Services (DSS). Beck said that was where Debbie's mother worked, and perhaps she could help them find her.

The agents visited the DSS office and found a woman working there named Edith Parmentier. She told them that she did have a daughter named Debbie, but her daughter was not the Debbie they were looking for. That Debbie was crazy, the woman told them, and had caused all sorts of problems for her daughter. Agent Doyle sympathized, and said as long as he was there in the social services office, perhaps Edith would be willing to run a record check on Debra Dawn Parmentier. Maybe the computer database knew where she was.

Edith Parmentier ran the check, printed the information from her computer, and passed it to Doyle. What he read made him want to sit down. Not only was Debbie Dawn Parmentier in their system, and not only was her address the same as Dan Beck's, but she'd been receiving social security disability benefits since 1989 for "emotional distress."

Agent Doyle was incredulous. If what more than two dozen witnesses had told him over the past four months was true, Debbie inserted herself into a murder investigation; concocted imaginary scenarios of gunrunning, kidnapping, and conspiracies; put five innocent men in prison; and during it all had been completely supported financially by the police. Her rent, heat, electricity, cable TV, groceries, prescription medication, and even pocket money were all provided for by the Michigan State Police. Now she was receiving disability checks from the federal government for emotional distress.

With that information in hand, Agent Doyle left the social services office and drove straight to the local sheriff's office. He believed the chances were good that Debbie would have run contrary to local law enforcement at least once. Maybe there were warrants out for her arrest or, if he was lucky, she might even already be in jail for something. If not, the sheriff could at least help him find her.

Yet again, nothing in Doyle's experience prepared him for what he learned.

The Lake County Sheriff's Office was indeed familiar with Debbie. But she wasn't in their jail, she was on their payroll. Since June of 1989, Debbie had been working for them as a criminal informant, setting up drug buys. The program was on hold after $18,000 from a law enforcement narcotics fund came up missing and Debbie was nowhere to be found.

After more than five months of work, Agent Doyle had plenty to do just looking into improprieties in the Tobias trials; he wanted no part of what looked like a bungled undercover drug operation.

Debbie was supposed to be his final interview in the AG's investigation. He just wanted to find her, interview her, and submit his report.

Doyle wished the sheriff good luck in finding out what happened to the money and went back to the last known address for Debbie. He knocked on Dan Beck's front door and was surprised to find that Debbie was not only there, but even invited him in. She didn't act at all surprised to see him, and seemed almost casual about being sought by the state's Attorney General's office.

"I know you're working for the defense," Debbie told the agent. "The State Police told me what you're doing and I'm not feeling so good today. I'm not sure I want to be interviewed by you."

Agent Doyle explained that the full power of the Michigan Attorney General's office was behind his investigation, and that if she didn't agree to an interview voluntarily, she could be compelled to give one via subpoena.

"Well," Debbie said, seemingly unruffled by this information, "I want to talk to Norm Hayes first before I say anything to you."

A week later, Doyle got word via the State Police. Debbie wouldn't be consenting to an interview. Not now, and not ever.

Chapter 76   Back to Hayes

. . . . July, 1990

What Ray MacNeil thought was going to be a blessing—the expanded Attorney General's investigation—was about to become a nightmare.

Just like MacNeil expected, the new investigation had uncovered plenty of probable cause that Sherry Payton, Debbie, and others committed perjury in the Mark Canter and Terry Moore trials. Whether or not that perjury affected the verdicts was for a judge to decide, and the Attorney General was now considering supporting the defense's motions for new trials. For MacNeil, that was the good news.

But the investigation also uncovered evidence that Debbie helped stage the shootings into her Sand Hill Manor apartment and into Mike and Cindy Gleason's house. This appeared to investigators to be some disturbed attempt to make it look like she was in grave danger, so that her stories would be believed and the police would continue to keep her in protective custody and pay her bills. The shootings were a crime, and the Attorney General's protocol when uncovering evidence of a crime was to send notice of it to the local prosecutor, who would decide whether to file charges.

When he learned this, MacNeil was furious. The Attorney General planning to send Debbie's case right back to Hayes. If that happened, MacNeil was certain the trip to Florida, the interview with Sherry Payton, the subsequent interviews with other witnesses, and the entire Attorney General's investigation, would be for nothing.

"As far as I'm concerned, Mr. Hayes is in this up to his neck," MacNeil wrote in a four-page letter to Frank Kelley. "The bottom line in this case is that my client, Mark Canter, is totally innocent. He did not even know the victim and had nothing to do with the murder.

"The reason that Debra Parmentier has been able to pull off what she has done is because it has been with the explicit approval and assistance of the Otsego County Prosecutor and the State Police investigating officers in this case. To ask them now to go back and charge Debra Parmentier is simply ludicrous.

"This young lady has committed a felony of perjury in front of a Circuit Court Judge, in front of the local prosecutor, and in front of a Circuit Court Jury, which is punishable by life imprisonment. Yet she walks the streets freely while at least three totally innocent people, and possibly five innocent people, sit in Michigan prisons.

"There is a point where right is right and somebody has to step up and hold people accountable for their actions, and that includes the Otsego County Prosecutor and the State Police Investigators who perpetuated this fraud. I cannot believe that all of the work that has been done on this case by your office could all go for naught by turning it over to the local prosecutor to do something with it. It might as well be buried, if that's what happens."

Chapter 77 Mark Canter Appeals

. . . . September 13, 1990

As futile as it seemed to be, the court clock was ticking and MacNeil still had to file the proper paperwork on time to request the court dismiss the verdict against Mark or give him a new trial. The Attorney General's office might continue to investigate or the agents might be finished and about to release their report. MacNeil didn't have the luxury of waiting around to see which. His client was in prison, and would be there for the rest of his life if MacNeil couldn't get him a new trial. His only option was to use the only new evidence he had, Sherry Payton's recant, to request a new trial for Mark.

On September 13, MacNeil filed two motions. One asked Judge Davis to dismiss the case, and the other requested a new trial. MacNeil tried to be hopeful, but it wasn't easy. His motions would be argued in front of the same man who sent Mark to prison for life. All he could do was try to tip the balance in his favor.

Over the next month MacNeil deluged the court with paperwork. He sought to have the Otsego County Prosecutor disqualified, he sought to get permission for the TV media to film the pretrial hearing, he sought to enter new evidence, and for the court to recognize the letter of immunity given to Sherry Payton by the Attorney General's office. Between mid-September and Halloween, MacNeil hit the court and the prosecutor's office with everything he had—more than thirty motions, briefs in support, and witness affidavits, including his own.

On September 18, the Attorney General's office sent a letter to Hayes, updating him on the status of their investigation:

> As you know, this office has conducted an investigation into serious allegations that certain witnesses in the *People v. Mark Canter* case committed perjury. After a lengthy investigation, we are unable to conclude with reasonable certainty whether or not the allegations are valid. The Department of Attorney General is not planning additional investigative action as to such allegations at this time.

Prosecutor Hayes told the media he felt vindicated.

"It's truly unfortunate that some members of the media allow themselves to be manipulated by petty politics in the reporting of serious cases," Hayes told a reporter for the local CBS affiliate, 9&10 News. "When the news media base stories on mere allegations by attorneys who have a vested interest in politics rather than on facts and evidence presented in court, it's my opinion the media's performed the grossest disservice to its readers and viewers."

A week later, the *Gaylord Herald Times* weighed in with an editorial, under the headline:

POLITICS MUDDY '86 MURDER CASE

> Justice is taking a back seat to political backbiting in the case of Mark Canter. In one corner is the prosecutor and candidate for district judge. In other, the defense attorneys for Canter and one of his co-defendants, and assorted other attorneys supporting the prosecutor's opponent. Outside the courtroom, the gloves were off and the accusations flew fast and furious. While it may be too much to ask for the veil to be lifted from the mysteries that surround the case, little is served by muddying the waters further with politics.

It looked to MacNeil like all his work on behalf of Mark would be in vain. On November 2, Judge Davis denied his motion to disqualify Prosecutor Hayes, refused to dismiss charges against Mark, and denied him a new trial.

"Having tried this case, I am very aware that it is a strong, testimonially large, complex, and often confusing case," Judge Davis said. "I would indicate as well that I am perfectly aware that there was every indication that there was a lot of fabrication in a lot of testimonies from a lot of different people. I dare say that the Court's impression was, with rare exception, that most of the many witnesses who appeared at trial, lied about something."

The judge said he did not believe the lies were severe enough to grant Mark Canter a new trial. He did leave the door open for the defense, if just a crack. Davis agreed to hear what Sherry Payton had to say, if she would be willing to testify on the stand, under oath, in his courtroom. Payton agreed, returned to Gaylord, and when MacNeil put her on the stand, she told Judge Davis exactly the same thing she'd told MacNeil and Agent Doyle many months ago in the safety of her Florida living room.

Her testimony was not scheduled to be given in private in Judge Davis' chambers, but rather in open court. News of her impending appearance spread, and dozens of police officers came to court to hear what she had to say. It could have been out of simple curiosity, but MacNeil believed the officers had a darker purpose. They were there to intimidate Sherry, to keep her from testifying so the police's misdeeds would remain secret.

"I am appalled that all these officers and all these cops have been sitting here for all these days," MacNeil said, facing the spectators. "I'll address myself to them: If there isn't one of you that's got an ounce of decency or common sense to you, that you can come forward because you all know what happened. You all know, every one of you, you know what happened. Pretty funny, isn't it, Mr. Hayes? You all know what happened. And if you can go home and sleep at night, that's fine because, Judge, I was there at the State Police Post the night Sherry Payton was questioned. I heard Mr. Jenkins make reference to her baby. I heard that, myself.

"You take a young lady; take her into custody; she's pregnant; she's totally intimidated. She hasn't eaten for three days. You know what she has to say. You tell her what she has to say. And Mr. Hayes has got the gall to stand up there and say she wasn't threatened. The prosecutor wanted a conviction in this case and they were going to get a conviction no matter what it took. If anybody could listen to what Sherry Payton said yesterday and not believe that she is being truthful, then I'm in the wrong place and in the wrong profession.

"If you want convictions, Judge, I've got some real easy ones for the Prosecutor. Charge Debra Parmentier with perjury. Charge Debra Parmentier with possession of automatic machine guns. Charge Debra Parmentier with shooting through the Gleason residence. Charge Debra Parmentier with shooting through her apartment in Houghton Lake. It would be an open and shut case, if you want convictions.

"Your Honor, during the trial of this case Mr. Canter was offered a deal to walk. He could be a free man today if he'd got on that stand for a hundred and twenty seconds and simply said, 'Yes, Debra Parmentier was telling the right story.' And I have that on my conscience; that he now sits in prison for life, because I told him to tell the truth.

"And if I could go back to October the 27th, I'll tell you, Judge, as an officer of this court, I'd tell Mark, 'Get on that stand and lie. You get yourself out of this mess. Get rid of all these crooked people. Tell them what they want to hear.'

"This case is not going to go away. I don't care how many times it has to come back. It'll come back. Somebody has to step forward and say what's right. Doesn't it matter what the truth is? And what right is?"

Judge Davis listened impassively and then denied MacNeil's request to expand the hearing and allow other witnesses to testify. He refused to admit the Attorney General's report into the record, and he denied remanding Mark's case to the Court of Appeals.

Chapter 78　Hayes Elected

. . . . November 6, 1990

On Election Day, Prosecutor Norm Hayes was elected 87th District Court Judge. An assistant prosecutor, Dennis Murphy, was appointed to serve the remaining two years of his term. Murphy and Hayes knew each other well. They were both assistant prosecutors in Lapeer, an industrial town north of Detroit, and when Hayes moved to Gaylord, Murphy followed.

Dean Robb filed a grievance against Hayes with the State's Attorney Grievance Commission alleging misconduct in the Moore/Canter trials. It was co-signed by Mike Hackett, Stu Hubbell, Ray MacNeil, and Martin Tieber.

"I have been employed with the State Appellate Defender for seventeen years," Tieber wrote in his letter to the Commission, supporting the grievance. "In that time I have raised countless prosecutorial misconduct issues in cases arising out of nearly every county in this state. The matters depicted in our jointly filed grievance clearly constitute the worst case of prosecutorial abuse of process I have ever seen."

Chapter 79   Laurie Moore Appeals

. . . . March, 1991

Laurie Moore was serving the fourth year of his seven- to fifteen-year sentence at Hiawatha Correctional Facility in Michigan's Upper Peninsula. Between July and October of 1989, Martin Tieber had been doing more than just fighting a letter-writing battle with Norm Hayes. He'd also been submitting motions for Laurie's conviction to be reversed, citing thirteen separate arguments. Tieber contended that Judge Livo erred in his instructions to the jury and that Hayes's repeated "histrionics" and animosity toward Laurie, his suppression of critical evidence, and his unwillingness to investigate "other directions" amounted to a "virtual compendium of prosecutorial misconduct."

In order to make certain the appellate court had all the information they needed to make a decision, one of Tieber's motions asked the court for permission to file an oversize brief.

"Even among extraordinary cases this case must be considered exceptional," Tieber explained. Exceptional in complexity, exceptional in legal issues, and exceptional in *size*. Paperwork on the factual summary alone weighed more than fifty pounds.

"This case involves the longest and most complex record ever dealt with by this attorney in over 15 years of appellate work, much of that time handling exceptional and lengthy cases."

The court agreed to allow Tieber to file his oversize brief, and two months later his diligence was rewarded. On March 8, 1991, the Michigan Court of Appeals reversed Laurie's conviction of Voluntary Manslaughter. The three-judge panel never made it past the first issue and ruled that trial Judge Robert C. Livo erred in his instructions to the jury, making Tieber's other twelve other points moot.

Justice, in a way, had finally been served for Laurie Moore. But it was late, and woefully incomplete. The prosecutor had until April 1 to file an appeal of the decision, but Tieber believed that was unlikely. Double jeopardy precluded charging Laurie with First- or Second-Degree Murder or Manslaughter. Laurie was going to be freed on a legal mistake made by the trial judge and not because the appeals court declared him innocent. Because the judges ruled on the legal mistake first, it precluded the appellate court from ruling on Tieber's charges of Prosecutorial Misconduct, Jury Misconduct, and False Arrest.

Laurie was getting out of prison, but he wasn't going to be exonerated; he was getting off on a technicality. An editorial in the *Gaylord Herald Times* headlined, "Did Justice Prevail?" said as much. "To many, the question of guilt or innocence remains."

Still, freedom was freedom, no matter how it arrived. If there was any legal satisfaction for Laurie and the Moore family, it came from the written opinion of Appellate Judge Myron Wahls. He issued what the *Traverse City Record-Eagle* called "a scathing denunciation of police—and of Hayes in particular—charging the newly elected prosecutor of pursuing Moore in a spirit of personal vindictiveness."

In his concurring written opinion Judge Wahls wrote, in part:

> I find it necessary to address certain errors which occurred at trial that were attributable to the prosecuting attorney. In my opinion, the prosecutor's repeated display of personal animosity towards defendant resulted in severe and reprehensible prosecutorial misconduct and denied defendant a fair trial. A careful review of the entire record, including a separate record made outside the presence of the jury, offers an explanation for the prosecutor's misconduct throughout the course of defendant's trial.
>
> Apparently, the seeds of the prosecutor's enmity toward defendant were sown when the prosecutor and defendant knew each other as children. The prosecutor's rancor toward defendant further increased when defendant dated and later married the prosecutor's former girl friend, a prominent Gaylord attorney. It is very clear from the record that the prosecutor's deportment in this case was not the result of overzealous advocacy but rather fervent vindictiveness.

It took two weeks of legal paperwork and a hearing, but on Friday night at 7:30 PM, March 22, Laurie Moore walked out of prison a free man. His joy and relief were tempered by the fact that his brother, Terry, and four other innocent men were still in prison.

"I'm sure it will only be a matter of time for the reversals for the other alleged co-defendants in this travesty," Laurie told the

Gaylord Herald Times, pledging to help on their appeals in whatever way he could. "There's nothing I'm ever going to say that's going to change the negative people. I was convicted in Gaylord before the trial was over."

Laurie said he felt sadness for Jackie Tobias and the Tobias family. "I feel bad for them—that all this has happened. I feel bad this travesty has happened and kept the wound open for her."

Laurie said he didn't know what he was going to do with the rest of his life. His family's store was closed, so he couldn't go back to work there. The only thing he knew for sure was that he would not be staying in Gaylord. The place didn't feel like his home anymore.

Chapter 80   Hubbell's Resolve

. . . . Spring, 1991

Stu Hubbell was emboldened by the success of Laurie's appeal. He'd been Terry Moore's appellate attorney for two years, and though Terry was still in prison, Hubbell knew his case inside and out. The law had put Terry behind bars, and Hubbell thought he might have come up with a way to use the law to get him out. If successful, it would be unprecedented in Michigan. Hubbell planned to ask the court to give him authority to depose anyone he wanted to, interview them under oath, and get to the truth. Hubbell no longer had any confidence in the justice system in Otsego County and believed secret depositions were the only way he'd ever get Terry out of prison.

It was an unheard of idea—defense attorneys weren't grand juries, and they couldn't take the law into their own hands just because they believed their client was innocent.

But *can't* was not a word Hubbell had much use for. He filed a brief in support of the court granting something never before attempted in a Michigan courtroom: an Order of Confidentiality of Discovery Process. His brief read:

> Appellant has been charged with the responsibility of ferreting out the truth in what has become a notorious public scandal in this and allied cases. What is needed is a cathartic, which utterly cleanses the process of this case and allied cases, of all such claims. It may very well be that what Appellant has proposed is actually insufficient to accomplish that essential task. The reaction of the judiciary to date in response to these crucial allegations . . . has been to ignore or bury the allegations . . . there has been a circling of the wagons on an unprecedented scale.

Mark, Don, and Doug were also still in prison, and their attorneys were also feeling optimistic following Martin Tieber's successful appeal for Laurie. Tieber made his research available to Hubbell and MacNeil, saying he hoped Laurie's freedom foretold the future for the others.

"This is the first tremor. Ultimately I think this whole thing is going to crumble like a house of cards."

The Attorney General's investigation, which at one time had seemed dormant, marched on. The agents assigned expanded their work and began to look into possible police misconduct. Frank Kelley's right-hand man instructed the State Police to back off the case while the AG's agents did their work. Lieutenant John Hardy had long retired, but in May of 1991, Kelley's office sent a letter to his replacement, Captain Tim Baker:

"I am requesting that 7ᵗʰ District personnel not directly investigate the Jerry Tobias case without my prior knowledge and approval," Kelley's chief assistant, Robert Ianni, wrote. "The Attorney General is currently investigating aspects of this case, including allegations of State Police misconduct."

Ianni cautioned Baker not to "interfere and obstruct our investigation" and closed by saying that if the State Police had problems with the way the case was being handled, they should contact Attorney General Frank Kelley directly.

That letter must have dropped in the 7th District like an atom bomb. For the past year and half, rumors, conjecture, and half-truths circulated that the Attorney General's office was doing everything from conducting a witch hunt to trying to disbar Hayes, to signing arrest warrants. None of that was true; the AG's office was only following the tangents they'd uncovered to see where they would lead.

Ianni got a quick response to his letter, not from the State Police but from Norm Hayes' replacement, Prosecutor Dennis Murphy. Murphy complained about the AG's tactics and informed Ianni about some newly uncovered evidence supporting the prosecutions. A prison snitch was willing to testify against Terry Moore in exchange for a reduced sentence. Murphy closed his letter to Ianni by expressing frustration with the Attorney General's ongoing investigation.

"Furthermore, as this office has not been apprised of any of the activity of your investigators, we have no way of knowing what, if anything, is being done by your office."

Murphy's complaints were sidelined. The prosecutor's office had been provided with summaries and transcripts of all the Attorney General's interviews. Considering that possible prosecutor misconduct was one of the things the Attorney General was investigating, Ianni obviously wasn't going to make any of those parts of his investigation available to the very office under scrutiny.

Chapter 81   Hubbell Marches Forward

. . . . May, 1991

66 I can't imagine they envisioned what he plans here."
Prosecutor Murphy had identified a worst-case scenario, but he refused to believe it could actually come true. The *they* he referenced was the Michigan State Supreme Court, the *he* was Stuart Hubbell, and the *plans* were indeed barely imaginable for the prosecution.

On April 30, 1991, Hubbell had his first bit of success. The Court of Appeals remanded Terry's case back to the trial court for an evidentiary hearing. Judge Porter—the same judge who presided over Terry's original trial—would be deciding the parameters of the new hearing. Hubbell asked for "broad discovery authority," so he believed the Court's decision gave him the ability to take secret depositions from potential defense witnesses, including police officers, Attorney General's investigators, and even Prosecutor Murphy and Judge Hayes. It was the only way to determine, Hubbell said, whether or not there had been police and prosecutorial corruption and if so, to keep it from happening again.

A deposition is part of a discovery process conducted when the defense and the prosecution are building their case. A witness is questioned by both defense and prosecution attorneys and their statements are recorded by a court reporter. This process is usually allowed in civil, not criminal, trials.

Prosecutor Murphy disagreed with Hubbell's assumption, telling Judge Porter he was certain Hubbell misinterpreted the Court's ruling. Murphy filed a motion asking Judge Porter to deny the powers sought by Hubbell.

Prosecutor Murphy vowed that Laurie's overturned conviction would not be a harbinger of things to come. With Hayes winning the District Court judgeship, Murphy was now in charge of guarding the guilty verdicts against Mark Canter and Terry Moore, and the sentences given Doug Brinkman and Don Heistand in their plea deals. Don, who'd plead no contest to being an Accessory After the Fact to murder, had only a few months before he'd be eligible for parole. Double Jeopardy precluded Prosecutor Murphy from retrying Laurie, but he told the media that the other men the State had already convicted would not be so lucky.

Even though the Michigan Supreme Court together with the Court of Appeals had remanded Terry's case back to the lower court for an evidentiary hearing, Murphy said he refused to believe Terry Moore would actually be given a new trial. The idea was preposterous, and so was the latitude that Hubbell was asking the Court for.

"I don't think it's legally proper in a criminal case to have depositions," Murphy argued in front of Judge Porter. "We have nothing to hide; therefore the case should proceed in open court" and not via secret depositions.

Hubbell explained to Judge Porter that he didn't just want to take depositions. He wanted to sequester witnesses and make them sign orders of confidentiality. He wanted to put them in jail if they refused to testify. He wanted to exclude non-witnesses, including the police, from the proceedings. And he wanted all of their testimony, and even the fact that they gave testimony at all, to stay secret until Terry Moore's evidentiary hearing.

It was bold, it was brash, and it was unprecedented in Michigan's legal history, but it was also necessary Hubbell argued.

"There is strong suspicion that great wrongdoing occurred," Hubbell said. "I'm trying to make sure that when we get done with this, whatever the outcome, everyone believes we got the truth."

Judge Porter listened to the two men argue their points and then decided not to decide. Porter was a careful man and wanted to preclude the theatrics and the legal morass he'd seen develop unchecked in front of Judges Livo and Davis. Instead of ruling on the matter himself, he sent a letter to the Court of Appeals asking for a clarification. Would the Court please let him know if their ruling meant the defense could conduct the unprecedented secret depositions?

It took a month, but Porter did receive an answer: "No."

Not, "No," the defense couldn't do what it was asking to do, but "No," the Court of Appeals would not clarify their opinion, which put Judge Porter in a pickle.

"Whatever decision he makes, the losing party is likely to appeal the case once again," read an editorial in the *Gaylord Herald Times*. "The appellate court ruling is more than just another bizarre twist in the case. It is another delay in a case that has already been dragging through the legal system for years."

Nearly five years had passed, and no one felt the weight of them more than Terry Moore, Mark Canter, and Doug Brinkman. Terry was having difficulty adjusting to prison and asked a guard if he could see the prison psychologist for advice. "Nothing goes right," he told the doctor. "The court is taking my entire life to decide."

But the delays weren't over. Porter denied Hubbell's motion, and the newspaper's editorial prediction came true: Hubbell appealed to the State Supreme Court. But this time the defense would not be content to just sit and wait for a decision from on high. Instead, Stuart Hubbell, Ray MacNeil, Michael Hackett, Dean Robb, Martin Tieber, and Jack Felton joined forces and signed a motion asking Judge Davis, the trial judge in Mark's trial, to impanel a grand jury to investigate Debbie Parmentier's alleged crimes.

Ample evidence connected her to the death-threat letters sent to Robb and Gleason, the shootings into two residences, the lies to police and the court, the defrauding of the Social Security Administration, the possession of illegal weapons, the slandering of innocent people, and even the defaulting on a loan used to buy new furniture.

Why, the attorneys asked the Court, had she not been arrested? The men demanded that Debbie be charged with Conspiracy to Commit Assault with a Dangerous Weapon (the shootings into Cindy Gleason's house and her own Sand Hill Manor apartment, plus the illegal Uzi in the woodpile and the handgun in her bedside table), Conspiracy to Obstruct Justice (filing false police reports), and Perjury (lying on the witness stand in several hearings and trials). Two prosecutors, Hayes and Murphy, had been given ample time to arrest Debbie but had not. At the very least, by impaneling a grand jury, the Court could bypass the prosecutor and issue a warrant for Debbie's arrest.

There might be another, larger role a grand jury could play, too.

"If this court will summon a grand jury . . . and require the attendance before it of the necessary officers and all witnesses . . . and require those witnesses to give testimony under oath, complainants believe that sufficient information will be secured which will enable law enforcement officers, who have no complicity in respect to the offenses, to apprehend the persons guilty."

In other words, perhaps a grand jury could do what the police, the prosecutor, and the courts had so far failed to do: find out what really happened to Jerry Tobias.

While the Michigan State Supreme Court considered the legality of Hubbell's secret depositions, Debbie had other priorities. She wanted to re-invent herself, and have a new life. Step one was to change her name from Debbie Parmentier to Brieanna Farrell. Step two was to get married. Perhaps, she told those closest to her, these combined efforts would protect her from the law.

On September 4, 1991, Brieanna L. Farrell, a.k.a. Debra Dawn Parmentier, a.k.a. Kim Gray, a.k.a. Dawn Harris, a.k.a. Deb Nicholson, married her latest boyfriend, middle school social studies teacher, Kent F. Herrick.

Chapter 82   Hayes Is Cleared; Otsego County Pays

. . . . Wednesday, September 18, 1991

Throughout the legal back and forth over the past year, Norm Hayes stayed out of the public fray. He was a judge now and acted accordingly. Hayes didn't comment on any of the appeals, rehearings, or motions. He'd love to have his say, he told more than one reporter, but the judicial Canon of Ethics precluded him from commenting as long as any defendants were still seeking reversals of their murder convictions. Mark and Terry's appeals were ongoing, and Doug was considering whether to appeal his conviction.

Something happened in September to loosen Hayes' tongue: The state dismissed the professional misconduct grievance against him.

"I am grateful that the Judicial Tenure Commission has exonerated me from any conduct that was falsely alleged and subsequently reported by various newspapers and television stations," he said in a written statement.

Then Hayes fell silent again, declining any further comment.

Dean Robb was happy to speak on the record, and as usual, his comments were off the cuff and uncensored.

"It does not mean he did not engage in misconduct," Robb said. "It only means they couldn't prove it."

Robb told reporters that he was convinced that when Hayes was the prosecutor, he condoned Debbie's perjury, coached Dr. Newhouse, pressured witnesses, and looked the other way when police made obvious errors in logic, judgment, and ethics.

"And," Robb said, "he got away with it."

A week later, on September 24, the national television news program "Inside Edition" featured the Laurie Moore case in its broadcast. Gaylord locals might have been titillated that a case from their little town made the national news, but Otsego County commissioners must have been sick to death of it when they got Ray MacNeil's bill a week later.

MacNeil, appointed by Judge Davis to represent Mark Canter at trial and handle his appeal, submitted the Canter legal bill to the county: $62,162 for the trial and another $27,104 for the appeal, which was still ongoing. Hubbell was also court-appointed, and had yet to submit his bill for Terry Moore's appeal, but it was expected to be somewhere in the five figures. The only reason the county hadn't heard from Hubbell was because he was too busy researching Terry's case to file one.

These amounts seemed like a fortune to Otsego county taxpayers. Often, appeals were handled by the state's Attorney General's office, who would appoint an appellate attorney and then pay the bill. That was true in Laurie's case, but when it came to the remainder of the Tobias defendants, the state declined to do so. The cases were too complex, there was too much to learn to get a new attorney up to speed, and taking them on would unduly strain the AG's small appellate staff.

The legal bills were only going to get larger. On October 29, the State Supreme Court agreed to consider Hubbell's appeal. The court would decide whether or not he could take secret depositions and use what he learned in Terry's evidentiary hearing. But in order to make a decision on Hubbell's request, the three-judge panel said they needed more information.

Hubbell was ordered to file a supplemental brief within 21 days addressing why he was seeking "superintending control." Why were depositions necessary? Why couldn't he just examine witnesses in open court like every other defense attorney?

"I've got to establish to them, to their satisfaction, why they should order it," Hubbell said. "I know if I can take (the witnesses) one at a time, I can get somewhere. We need this discovery to get to the bottom of this. It's a cancer that needs to be opened."

Hubbell said the wrongdoings in Otsego County were so blatant that "they would be apparent to a schoolchild." He filed a 55-page brief alleging the same old, same old: witness perjury, police cover-ups, and coercion by the prosecutor. This was old news to many, but brand new to Michigan's Supreme Court.

If they agreed to allow Hubbell to go forward, what he found could help Terry and Mark, but would have little or no effect on Heistand or Brinkman. Heistand was released on parole October 30 and Brinkman two weeks later.

Chapter 83   Why Hasn't Debbie Been Charged?

. . . . December, 1991

While the six defense attorneys' request for a Grand Jury churned through the court, there was an unexpected boost. On December 5, Judge Alton Davis, the judge who presided over Mark Canter's trial, the judge who sentenced him to life and then refused to grant MacNeil's appeal, wrote a letter to attorney general Frank Kelley. Davis was supposed to be deciding on the motion from the six attorneys whether or not to impanel a Grand Jury. But he couldn't make a decision until he got the facts. Was the Attorney General's investigation still ongoing? And if so, Davis wondered, why hadn't Debbie been charged with any crimes?

"Before the court proceeds to further consideration of petitioners' request, the court respectfully requests that you determine whether there is some articulable reason why your office . . . is unable to effectively and lawfully enforce the laws."

Assistant Attorney General Robert Ianni told Judge Davis there had indeed been criminal activity by Debbie, but said the charges should come from the Otsego County Prosecutor. However, he did admit that his office had received more than 400 letters asking for charges to be brought against her.

Gaylord Herald Times reporter Vicki Naegele had been covering the trials almost since their inception. Earlier in the year she was given an award from the Michigan Press Association for her coverage of the case and in December 1991 ran an analysis on the newspaper's front page: "Claims of innocence by those convicted of a crime are hardly a rarity, but in the Tobias case plaguing questions have given more than the usual amount of credence to these claims."

"If the five men convicted in the Tobias murder case were indeed all guilty, would they keep a code of silence, even after the convictions? Mark Canter was . . . offered a chance to walk away a free man if he told police one thing new about the murder. Canter refused. He said he would not lie on the witness stand. Days later he was convicted of Aiding and Abetting Second-Degree Murder.

"Were the convictions achieved in the Tobias case so important to then Otsego County Prosecutor Norman R. Hayes and police officers that they were willing to put their careers and reputations in jeopardy by skewing evidence and committing other illegal acts?"

Chapter 84   Porter's Power

. . . . February, 1992

"Unprecedented power"—not everyone agreed it was warranted, but everyone agreed that's what Judge Porter now had. After sitting on the request for two months, the state Supreme

Court granted Porter the option of allowing secret depositions to be taken in Terry Moore's retrial hearing.

The decision was a first. Never before had depositions—testimony of a sworn witness not given in open court but rather in another location—been used in a criminal trial in Michigan.

"They did something extraordinary here," Hubbell said. "It's never happened before in the state."

The victory for the defense was only partial, however. Hubbell asked the court to compel Porter to allow him to be able to conduct the depositions himself, out of the presence of a judge or prosecutor. Instead, the Supreme Court gave Porter permission to include depositions in the retrial hearing only if he saw fit, and directed Hubbell to supply Porter a list of witnesses he wished to depose and the reasons their testimony should be kept secret.

Hubbell would be allowed to conduct the depositions, and they would be kept secret, but both Judge Porter and the Otsego County prosecutor could be present, and would also be allowed to ask questions of witnesses.

The Circuit Court's other judge also had his hands full with the Tobias case again. On the day Judge Porter received his answer from the Supreme Court, Judge Davis received his answer from the Attorney General's office.

"It is our policy to refer cases of this nature to the appropriate prosecuting attorney . . . to determine whether a warrant is necessary. Our investigation did not, however, reveal sufficient evidence to support charges of perjury or obstruction of justice (at least as it involved law enforcement officials). Therefore, criminal proceedings were not initiated by our staff. However, although we do not plan to prosecute in this instance, that decision should not be viewed as a determination that the available evidence does not support further investigation or prosecution."

Options were available to Judge Davis, the AG office said. The judge could appoint a special prosecutor to work only on Debbie's alleged crimes, or he could impanel a grand jury for the same purpose.

The AG's office gave Stuart Hubbell the same information.

"The Attorney General has asked me to respond to your request that this office initiate prosecutions relating to two shootings purportedly orchestrated by Ms. Debra Parmentier in 1988. As you know, the incidents in question were part of the investigation by this office into the circumstances surrounding the Tobias homicide case. Although the focus of that investigation was the question of your client's guilt, evidence of the Parmentier shootings was referred to the appropriate prosecutors to consider whether prosecution was warranted.

"Our decision to refer this matter to the appropriate county prosecutors was based on Michigan law, which has always placed primary responsibility in criminal matters in the office of the prosecuting attorney."

Staffing and budget limitations did not allow the Attorney General's office to assume the responsibilities of locally elected prosecutors, he added.

July 13, 1992

Hubbell began taking his depositions. The order of confidentiality from the Supreme Court not only barred witnesses from speaking about the process, but kept Hubbell quiet about it, too. As much as he might have wanted to, he could not tell Ray MacNeil about the depositions or whether he'd uncovered anything helpful to Mark Canter's appeal.

MacNeil was not under the same constraints. He thought he might have something helpful to Hubbell, and was under no legal order not to share it.

Dear Stuart,

We have not talked in a while and I don't know just exactly where you are or what you are doing in any proceedings that may be going on, but I was thinking the other day about a question that you had asked sometime ago concerning Leah Eddington. After Sherry Payton testified in the Mark Canter trial, (Leah) went to Sherry Payton's house along with Emmogene Ross, and I am informed that in the jist of that conversation, Emmogene Ross and Leah Eddington confronted Sherry Payton as to why she had lied on the stand.

The reason for Emmogene Ross being at that conversation was because when Sherry Payton was first put in jail by the police, she contacted Mrs. Ross from the jail and told Mrs. Ross that in fact she had lied and that the police had made her lie by telling her that if she did not say she was there, she would go to jail for fifteen years and would never see her baby.

Leah was there as a friend of Sherry Payton and somebody that Sherry could trust. There is no question that Sherry Payton, at least from what I understand, was aware that she was "between a rock and a hard place" because if she said that she lied on the stand, it would come back to [MacNeil] and it would then become a swearing match as to who was telling the truth again. In spite of that, I am advised by Leah Eddington and Emmogene Ross that Sherry Payton did admit to them that she lied on the stand, and that she did so out of fear for her own personal well-being and safety. She was extremely angry at the police and at the prosecutor for what they had done to her.

Finally, during Mark Canter's trial, somehow Norm Hayes found out that Leah Eddington had gone out to visit Sherry and basically confronted Sherry and kept asking Sherry, "Why are you lying, why are you lying." Sherry Payton, as I understand it, would make no response to those questions, but Hayes approached me one day during the trial and said to me that the was thinking about bringing charges against Leah Eddington for obstruction of justice or attempting to intimidate or influence a witness. I can't remember exactly what it was that Hayes said, but certainly he was getting the message across to me that he didn't want anybody talking to Sherry Payton.

The reason for that is very obvious, in that Sherry knew she had lied and if she were to change her story before the trial was over, that certainly would throw everything up in the air and would probably have resulted in a verdict of acquittal.

In fact, even after Hayes had cut the deal with Payton to dismiss the charges against her in return for her testimony, he would never dismiss those charges until after Canter's sentencing. In other words, he was protecting himself even prior to sentencing so that Sherry Payton could not change her story and come in and tell the truth about how she had been coerced.

I told Sherry that I would pass on this information to you for whatever reason you would have to make use of it and I told her that I would get back with her as soon as I hear from you. I would appreciate it if you would let me know if you have any reason to contact Sherry Payton, if that is possible. If not, then let it be.

Very truly yours,
Ray J. MacNeil

Hubbell had months to go before his deposition process would be finished, so the judge's order barred him from talking with MacNeil about Leah Eddington, Sherry Payton, or anything else having to do with the Tobias case. As the weeks went by, as far as MacNeil knew, Hubbell was indeed "just letting it be."

Hubbell did depose both women, however. Eddington confirmed for Hubbell what MacNeil had written in his letter: "Just from knowing her and just—I mean, that we just knew that she had lied."

When Hubbell asked Eddington what Sherry had lied about, Eddington said she "lied about being at the scene, at the butcher shop."

When Hubbell asked her if she knew why Sherry changed her testimony, Eddington said she did: "She just said that she was scared, and that they had threatened her, and she was scared and didn't want to go to prison."

Chapter 85   Mark Canter Appeals

. . . . October, 1992

With no communication from Hubbell, MacNeil had no choice but to move forward on Mark's appeal. In his motion to the Court of Appeals, MacNeil presented fifteen allegations of trial errors from perjury to recanted testimony. He alleged the prosecution knew Debbie Parmentier had studied trial transcripts and newspaper articles before trial, that she had staged shootings, that the prosecutor had intimidated witnesses.

"The perjury was so rampant that the entire trial process was warped," MacNeil argued. His arguments centered on Debbie's perjury and Sherry's recanted testimony.

In the meantime there was another new prosecutor of Otsego County. Like Norm Hayes before him, Dennis Murphy also became a judge and another assistant prosecutor, Kevin Hesselink, took over as prosecutor. And like his predecessors, Hesselink argued against the court granting Mark Canter a new trial: "The key to this case is not if he got a perfect trial, but a fair trial."

No trials were ever perfect, Hesselink said, but a jury of his peers had convicted Mark and they'd done so fairly. As far as the prosecutor was concerned, that conviction should stand and Mark should stay in prison.

It took more than two months, but the Court of Appeals finally reached a decision on December 21, 1992. Mark's case would be sent back to the trial court. Judges Richard Allen Griffin, Janet T. Neff, and Maura D. Corrigan announced their verdict in the Canter appeal:

> We affirm in part and remand for further proceedings. The absence of a testimonial record precludes us from determining whether defendant's due process rights were violated because of either prosecutorial nondisclosure of information, or intimidation of witnesses. We are satisfied that justice demands that defendant should be afforded an evidentiary hearing on these issues. Accordingly, we remand to the trial court for this purpose.

Initially, the hearing on whether or not Mark should be given a new trial was to be held within eighty days, but MacNeil asked for and received an extension so he could have more time to prepare. The extension gave him until June 21, 1993. He was hoping Hubbell would be finished with his depositions by then and that there would be new information he could use for Mark's cause.

Chapter 86   A Real Defense Team

. . . . May, 1993

Hubbell was exhausted. It took him a full year but he had secretly deposed 110 witnesses. He was finished and told Judge Porter he'd done all he could do. A month before MacNeil had to file Mark's appeal, Porter lifted the confidentiality order. The "defense team" Hayes referenced years ago never really existed. The assorted attorneys met occasionally and compared notes, but there was no real team. But that was about to change.

Back in the spring of 1989, when Hubbell was asked by Judge Porter to take on Terry Moore's appeal, Hubbell had never heard the name Debbie Parmentier and knew very little about the police's investigation into Jerry Tobias' death, or the courtroom antics of the prosecution.

Four years later, thanks to his exhaustive research and extensive interviews with witnesses, Hubbell knew more about the case than anyone. That was a blessing and a curse. His knowledge would be helpful to Terry Moore, but it also meant he knew exactly how much work was still ahead. He couldn't do it all alone.

Hubbell believed that MacNeil would help, and he was right. But he worried that even two experienced attorneys would not be enough legal manpower to undo the wrong that had been done to their clients. Hubbell and MacNeil needed someone with trial experience to help them, and Hubbell believed he knew just the guy.

Bruce Donaldson worked for one of the state's elite law firms, Dykema-Gossett. Founded in 1897, the firm was one of the largest and most financially successful in the Midwest. They'd represented Chrysler, Ford, General Motors, Honda, Nissan, Toyota, and Volvo, along with banks, hospitals, and national retailers. Even at that level of litigation, Bruce Donaldson stood out. He was known among his peers as a brilliant trial lawyer. In case after case, a whole team of Dykema Gossett lawyers would often be assigned to a trial, but it was almost always Donaldson who stood and argued the case in front of judges while the others sat silent at the table.

Hubbell and Donaldson were introduced to each other by their wives, who were childhood friends. Over the years, the men became friends too and at holidays and weekend gatherings often discussed points of law. Hubbell knew one of the perks of working at Dykema Gossett was senior attorneys were allowed to perform a few hours of pro bono work every year on cases they cared about.

Hubbell contacted Donaldson and discussed the Tobias case. He explained that Terry Moore's and Mark Canter's retrial hearings were going to be combined, and he and Ray MacNeil needed help. Donaldson agreed to join the team, and told Hubbell he'd give the case fifty free hours of his time.

"It is a case worthy of advocacy," Donaldson told his bosses.

Chapter 87   Canter's Retrial Hearing Begins

. . . . June 2, 1993

MacNeil made good use of his extra time. He submitted a complete list of witnesses to Judge Davis this time around and seventy names were on it. Prosecutor Hesselink submitted a witness list, too, and all the familiar names were on it: Former Prosecutor Norm Hayes, Retired Lieutenant John Hardy, and Detectives Fred LaBarge, Carl Goeman, and Doug Wilt, plus a few other officers.

Hesselink told reporters that he was convinced the retrial hearing was nothing more than a formality and that Mark's conviction would be reaffirmed.

"I have not seen anything in the meantime that's changed my mind," he said.

First thing Wednesday morning, June 2, MacNeil called Norm Hayes to the stand. It would be the first time in the case that Hubbell's friend Bruce Donaldson questioned one of the Tobias case witnesses. And if anyone in the courtroom thought that this out-of-town lawyer might be intimidated by the idea of questioning a district court judge, they'd have been wrong.

"You knew Parmentier was a liar, didn't you?" Donaldson asked Hayes.

"Sure," Hayes said. "But was she telling the truth about what happened December 5ᵗʰ and 6ᵗʰ, 1986? That's the question."

Were there times when Hayes doubted his star witness, Donaldson asked.

"Sure," Hayes said again. "There wasn't a day that went by I didn't question things she indicated."

As an example, Hayes said Debbie accused Judge Porter of fixing cases, and Hayes said he did not believe that was true. He didn't even investigate it because he was so certain she was lying.

"She was a false story a minute, wasn't she?" Donaldson asked.

"Except when she was testifying, in my opinion, about the things that occurred December 5ᵗʰ and 6ᵗʰ," Hayes said.

On the stand Hayes said he faithfully executed his duties as prosecutor, and all of his efforts were because he believed Debbie witnessed Jerry Tobias being beaten to death. The decision to charge the men with murder had been his to make and he would not second-guess it now, despite all the controversy it caused.

Donaldson asked Hayes if he provided Debbie with newspaper reports and trial transcripts to study in order to bolster her testimony. Hayes said he did not.

"If you're looking for a head to hang," he challenged Donaldson, "here it is."

By the end of the week, the Attorney General's office came through for the defense. Chief Assistant Robert Ianni filed a motion for Judge Davis to give immunity to Cindy Gleason. On their own, the defense team also asked the judge to grant immunity to Doug Brinkman.

While those motions were being hashed out, Don Heistand testified for the defense on Friday, telling the court his conviction was not because he was guilty of anything, but because of Hayes' vindictiveness.

Heistand had pled no contest to an Accessory After the Fact charge. He testified he did so to save his marriage and to save himself from a long prison term. Heistand said he believed Hayes was out to get him after he declined to testify the way the former prosecutor wanted him to in the Laurie Moore trial. According to Heistand, Hayes tried to make it look like Laurie was asking Heistand, a big man, to strong-arm Tobias, which wasn't true.

"After that he was pretty upset at me because I did not point the finger at Laurie," Heistand said. "He had an attitude."

That week an article in the *Gaylord Herald Times* summarized the progress of the rehearing: "Many of the last vestiges of Parmentier's credibility were stripped away by a parade of defense witnesses."

Chapter 88   Debbie Returns

. . . . June 7, 1993

Debbie testified in Mark Canter's retrial hearing on June 10 and 11, but only because she didn't have any choice. She was arrested for perjury in Toole, Utah, where she'd been living with her husband, Kent Herrick, and extradited to Michigan. Donaldson asked her if in her early statements to police she had told them Sherry Payton was present at the murder.

"No, I didn't," Debbie said.

"What occurred, or prompted you, to correct your testimony?" Donaldson asked.

"I was asked a direct question," she said. "The officer asked me and I answered it."

The officer was Detective Fred LaBarge, she said, and his direct question was, "Was Sherry Payton present?"

Next, the defense called Sherry Payton. She shuffled to the witness stand, slumped in the chair, and started to cry soon after Donaldson's questions began.

"I thought if I didn't say I was there, I was going to jail, and would never get out," she sobbed. "Gomez said I could go to jail for fifteen years and my baby would be born in jail, and I would never get out to see it."

After being threatened, Payton said she buckled under police pressure and changed her story.

"I said, 'All right, I was there.' I made things up as I went along. It was all a lie."

Payton said Trooper Gomez told her the police had other witnesses and other evidence against Mark Canter and that her testimony wasn't all that important.

"I found out later it was solely my testimony that put Mark away," Payton said. "That's why I'm here now. To tell the truth."

Following Payton's testimony, Judge Davis made a decision on the immunity for Cindy Gleason and Doug Brinkman, denying both. Gleason decided to testify anyway, but invoked the Fifth Amendment against self-incrimination whenever she was asked a question about her diary. Judge Davis eventually reversed himself, granted Gleason the immunity, at which point she admitted to putting false entries in her diary and lying to police. Both of these actions were at Debbie Parmentier's request.

"She convinced me to write in my diary that she was not home, that I had dropped her off at the Big Boy for lunch on December 5, and she was gone until Monday morning," Gleason said.

"To what extent did she tell you what to write?" Donaldson asked.

"She told me everything to write down," Gleason replied.

Chapter 89   The Banker's Box

. . . . June 22, 1993

The combined retrial hearing for Mark and Terry was winding down. Donaldson, MacNeil, and Hubbell had almost completed their argument for why the men deserved a new trial. The four men were guardedly optimistic, and there were only a few things left to do. The important one was paying a visit to the State Police post to compare the information the defense had with the information the police had. The police report on the case was voluminous, and the defense wanted to make sure they had been given everything uncovered in the investigation.

Judge Davis agreed and ruled that the defense team be allowed to examine the State Police's file on the case stored at the Gaylord State Police post.

MacNeil and Donaldson went together, and when they arrived the police led them into an interview room where all the reports, files, and evidence were stored in file cabinets, cardboard boxes, and also spread out in large stacks on a conference table. While the police looked on, the two attorneys spent considerable time perusing the materials, finding little of importance they hadn't already seen. But when they were getting ready to leave, Donaldson noticed a single cardboard box, separate from the rest of the material, sitting on the floor in the far corner of the room.

"What's that?" he asked the officers.

The officers looked at each other, initially said nothing, but then one of them reluctantly retrieved the box and lifted it up onto the table with the rest of the evidence. Donaldson opened it, and he and MacNeil peered in. It was filled with papers. The attorneys looked at each other and then dug in. Inside the box they found thousands of pages of police reports, lab reports, investigative notes, and other documents dated as far back as the day after Jerry Tobias was found but that had never been provided to any of the defense attorneys.

What first caught MacNeil's attention were the more than one hundred pages of Detective LaBarge's handwritten notes. As the man in charge of the investigation, LaBarge was privy to every aspect of the case, and the defense had repeatedly asked police to include his notes in their discovery. The defense had only a few notes from the detective, and they were convinced there were others. But whenever they asked a judge to compel the police to provide them, LaBarge testified that he already had.

"It's beyond comprehension," said MacNeil, back in court in front of Judge Davis. "These are the very things they've denied under oath even knowing where they are."

Davis ruled that the attorneys could take the box of papers to MacNeil's office and would have ninety minutes to examine them, at which point they would be turned over to the judge. An hour and a half was not enough time to examine all the documents, but MacNeil had a plan to make the best of a frantic situation. Back at his office, MacNeil shared his idea with Hubbell and Donaldson.

"Just pull out random pages and make copies," he said. "That way, the police won't know what we have copies of and what we don't."

The three attorneys dug through the box as fast as they could. Some reports were useless, while others could have been trial gold. Even more shocking to MacNeil than finding Detective LaBarge's notes was finding material related to Debbie that the defense had never seen and didn't know existed. There was her handwritten note stating Jerry was stabbed to death behind Glen's Market. There was a copy of her telephone bill when she was in police protective custody that showed a 48-minute call to then-prosecutor Hayes at 1:11 AM on May 6, 1988, which was the day after Jerry's blood tested positive for cocaine and less than two hours before Debbie's boyfriend, Mark Kerry, fired a shot through Cindy Gleason's window.

"This would have been a cross-examiner's dream," Donaldson told Judge Davis about the new material. "We can say with confidence that there has been a massive withholding of evidence. To the extent the prosecutor was aware of these events constitutes prosecutorial misconduct of titanic proportions."

It would take days for the defense to understand the significance of the find, Donaldson said. Judge Davis had no choice but to grant the defense whatever time they needed to review the contents of the box. Mark Canter and Terry Moore's retrial hearing would be delayed indefinitely.

One of the more gruesome finds in the banker's box was a videotape of Jerry's autopsy. MacNeil sent the tape, along with several tissue slides and photographs, to renowned medical examiner, Werner Spitz. In contrast to former Otsego County pathologist, Patricia Newhouse, Spitz was a board-certified forensic pathologist and had performed more than 60,000 autopsies, hundreds of which had been on frozen bodies. If pathology had a rock star, Spitz was it. He'd consulted on the independent commissions that looked into the assassinations of President John F. Kennedy and Martin Luther King, Jr., and had testified in the Mary

Jo Kopechne civil case against Ted Kennedy, about the incident known as Chappaquiddick.

The defense wanted to know if Tobias' wounds were consistent with a chicken skewer attack, and whether or not Dr. Newhouse performed the autopsy properly.

Spitz was planning to testify for the defense on both these matters when the retrial hearing began again, which was scheduled for July 13, 1993. That date changed when Bruce Donaldson met with Judge Davis in his chambers and told the judge that Doug Brinkman still wanted to testify for the defense, even without immunity.

But during the break in the trial, Davis had done some investigating into the life and character of Doug Brinkman. He'd gone to the jail and retrieved Brinkman's incarceration records and didn't like what he found. Davis believed the records showed that Brinkman was a terrible inmate, combative and disrespectful. Davis told Donaldson he did not want Brinkman in his courtroom.

"He's a fucking liar," Judge Davis said to Donaldson. "That S.O.B has no place on the witness stand."

Donaldson was shocked and told the judge he thought his comments were inappropriate. A judge was supposed to be impartial, Donaldson reminded Davis, and even questioned whether or not the judge could provide a fair trial for the defense. Davis said his comments were only being made privately, in chambers, where he should be free to express himself. Such statements made in the heat of a discussion did not preclude him from being objective on the bench.

"I have no feeling for Brinkman one way or the other. He is simply another witness."

But when Donaldson told Hubbell and MacNeil what Davis said about one of their potential witnesses, they worried about it, too. The defense had come this far, and they did not want to see their efforts sabotaged by a judge prejudiced against one of their witnesses. MacNeil said he worried that Judge Davis "had abandoned his role as an impartial adjudicator and had taken over the role of prosecutor."

Prosecutor Kevin Hesselink wouldn't hear of having another judge take over. The retrial hearings had already been delayed several times and removing Davis would only add another. Just because the Judge called one of the defense's potential witnesses "a fucking liar," Hesselink argued, didn't mean that he couldn't be impartial.

But the defense team felt they had no option but to file a motion to have Judge Davis disqualified. They'd come this far, and they weren't going to give up on a fair trial now. If Davis wouldn't disqualify himself, the men would take their argument to the district court's chief judge, William Porter.

Chapter 90   Equal Justice for Lawyers

. . . . August, 1993

L ying under oath, illegal gun sales, shooting into an apartment building, and perjury were all felonies—and many wondered, why had Debbie still not been charged with anything? Judge Richard Benedict of Traverse City put that question to the test when he issued a bench warrant for the arrest of Debbie Parmentier for obstruction of justice. The felony charge was for directing Roger Becker to write the death threat letter to Dean Robb.

The warrant had certainly been a long time coming. Hayes, Murphy, and Hesselink had refused to issue a warrant for Debbie's arrest for anything. The Attorney General's office referred the matter back to Otsego County, and Otsego County said the letter to Robb was opened in Grand Traverse County, so it was a matter for that county's prosecutor, Dennis LaBelle. LaBelle refused to act, saying the matter "principally affects Otsego County."

Though obstruction of justice caries a maximum penalty of five years in prison and a $10,000 fine, Benedict's warrant turned out to be ineffective. Without agreement by Otsego or Grand Travese counties to extradite Debbie back to Michigan, officials in Utah refused to arrest her. Despite all the other work they had to do, Hubbell, MacNeil, and Donaldson, with the help of Dean Robb, went back to court and asked a Traverse City judge, Phillip Rodgers, if he would appoint a special prosecutor. That special prosecutor's sole purpose would be to extradite Debbie from Utah back to Michigan.

"So many times in history lawyers who fight and stick to their guns, they get in trouble with the police and the prosecutors who should be on their side," Robb said. "That's the case here. We had this feeling from the beginning that there was almost a conspiracy between the State Police—who should be our protectors—as far as handling all of the misdeeds of this lady."

But Judge Rodgers had very little knowledge of the Tobias case and was confused by Robb's assertions.

"Is there some reason to believe that this claim could not be brought in Otsego County?" Rodgers asked.

"We have, I think, 26 counts against Miss Parmentier for criminal acts, and they wouldn't issue a warrant on any of them," Hubbell said.

"So it's beyond venue," the judge said.

"It's not venue at all, your Honor," said Hubbell.

Rodgers appointed Grand Traverse County's assistant prosecutor, James Hunt. On November 23, Grand Traverse County Special Prosecutor James Hunt and Attorney General Frank Kelley jointly authorized a warrant to charge Debbie with extortion. Alone, Hunt didn't have the authority to up the charge from obstruction of justice (punishable by five years in prison) to extortion (punishable by twenty), but Kelley could. The plan was to try to get Debbie to surrender voluntarily and turn herself in to her local sheriff's department in Utah. If not, she'd be found, arrested, and extradited back to Michigan to face the felony charge.

"The regrettable part of all of this, of course, is that these charges have been buried for so long by the prosecuting authorities, starting with Norman Hayes," Robb said.

"My client is serving a life sentence in prison because of the testimony of this woman and this woman alone," Hubbell said. "Prosecutor Hayes not only failed to provide the information as to Parmentier/Herrick's criminal acts and perjury, he buried it so that it could not be discovered."

Hayes consistently declined comment, citing judicial ethics forbidding a judge from commenting on pending cases. Nothing of the sort precluded Hubbell and Robb.

"I can assure you, this step will be followed by another and another until this entire miscarriage of justice is finally and fully disclosed," promised Hubbell.

Robb pledged that no taxpayer expense would be needed—private money would be raised to prosecute Debbie. He established an ad hoc group, the Committee for Equal Justice for Lawyers, with the goal of raising $10,000. The president of the American Bar Association, George Bushnell, Jr., and a dozen past presidents of the Michigan Bar Association, donated money and joined the committee.

Chapter 91 Waiting

. . . . Fall, 1993

"Tf they can arrest me, try me, and convict me in six months, should it take six years to go the other way?"

While the defense did seem to be making progress from a strictly legal standpoint, Mark and Terry were still in prison. Six years for Terry and five for Mark.

"It goes on and on," Terry said. "They're just prolonging the agony."

Two years had passed since the State Supreme Court decided Judge Porter could allow Hubbell to take secret depositions. Those depositions were over and on September 9, Hubbell had asked for the case against Terry to be dismissed or for the court to grant him a new trial. But as of early November, making a decision on that motion wasn't even on the court's docket.

"I'm a prisoner of corruption," Terry Moore said. "They don't want to air their dirty laundry."

Terry called the system that put him in jail a "conviction system," not a justice system. He and Mark were both at the same prison now, the Chippewa Regional Corrections Facility in Kincheloe, a small town in Michigan's upper peninsula. Stu Hubbell said he understood Terry's distress.

"His bitterness and frustration with the system—perhaps even with his counsel—make complete sense when seen from behind the bars which deny him freedom," Hubbell said.

And, there was yet another delay in the retrial hearing. Judge Porter refused to hear the motion to disqualify Judge Davis. He was too close to the case, he said, and too close to Davis personally to be impartial. A court administrator for the state would have to name an impartial judge, that judge would have to get educated about the Tobias case and then make a ruling. Only then would the retrial hearing resume. Judge Charles Corwin of Cadillac was appointed, the waiting continued, and Prosecutor Hesselink said he expected the new judge to rule in the prosecution's favor.

"It's easy to make allegations of misconduct, but difficult to prove them," he said. "I feel very comfortable and confident we'll prevail."

From left: Stuart Hubbell, Ray MacNeil, Bruce Donaldson. (Courtesy Ray MacNeil)

From left, Bruce Donaldson, Stuart Hubbell, Terry Moore, and Mark Canter during Canter and Moore's retrial hearings. (Used by permission of the *Traverse City Record-Eagle*)

Terry Moore is greeted by his family after a day in court. (Used by permission of the *Traverse City Record-Eagle*)

Lieutenant John Hardy is questioned by Stuart Hubbell. (Used by permission of the *Detroit News*)

Don Heistand visited by his family in Jackson State Prison, Jackson. (Courtesy Don and Lisa Heistand)

Ray MacNeil, Bruce Donaldson, and Stuart Hubbell are congratulated by Mark Canter and Terry Moore upon receiving the Michigan Bar Association's Champion of Justice Award. (Courtesy Ray MacNeil)

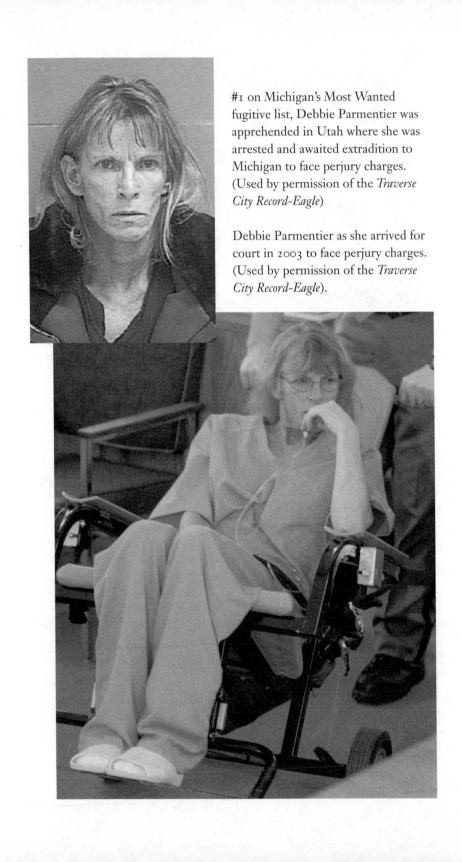

#1 on Michigan's Most Wanted fugitive list, Debbie Parmentier was apprehended in Utah where she was arrested and awaited extradition to Michigan to face perjury charges. (Used by permission of the *Traverse City Record-Eagle*)

Debbie Parmentier as she arrived for court in 2003 to face perjury charges. (Used by permission of the *Traverse City Record-Eagle*).

Chapter 92 Terry Moore's Retrial Hearing

. . . . February 4, 1994

Both Dawn Pyrek, Hayes's assistant prosecutor at the time of Terry's trial, and Detective LaBarge testified and tried to distance themselves from the Tobias investigation's decision-making process. That was all up to Hayes, they said. Pyrek explained she ran the day-to-day business of the prosecutor's office and prosecuted other cases so Hayes could concentrate on the Tobias trials. LaBarge said he just did what he was told.

Hubbell reminded Pyrek that she had declined to issue a warrant for assault against Leonard Parmentier all those years ago because of the "credibility of the complainant." The complainant was Debbie Parmentier. Pyrek admitted the question of Debbie's credibility was "ongoing." She also admitted telling several prosecution witnesses they did not have to talk to the defense.

When asked if he provided the defense with all exculpatory evidence, Detective LaBarge said he did not know what exculpatory evidence was. Evidence important to the defense, Donaldson told him.

"I don't know what would be important to the defense and what wouldn't," LaBarge said. "I'm sure there's some things they didn't get."

"Who decided?" asked Donaldson.

"The prosecutor would generally give me the instructions," LaBarge said.

On Thursday, Feb. 17, 1994, Hayes took the stand and dropped a bomb: Terry Moore had tried to have him killed. Under oath

Hayes said Moore tried to arrange a "hit" on him from his prison cell. Not only that, but the Attorney General's office was biased against him and quashed an investigation into the incident. The former prosecutor accused the Attorney General's office of interfering with the Tobias trials on behalf of the defense, the most blatant example of which was issuing a letter of immunity to Sherry Payton.

Chief Assistant Prosecutor for the Attorney General's office, Robert Ianni, took the stand, and said Hayes' allegations were "absurd" and "bald-faced lies."

"Why Mr. Hayes is saying these things," Ianni said, seeming to be truly mystified, "I don't know."

But Hayes said he believed he'd been persecuted unjustly and that the media coverage of the trials was skewed in the defense's favor. He was even considering filing libel suits against the news department of a CBS affiliate, Channels 9 & 10, plus the *Detroit News* and the *Traverse City Record-Eagle*. Hayes explained he'd asked for retractions from these news outlets but had received none. He accused the *Traverse City Record-Eagle* of comparing him to Saddam Hussein and had spoken to several attorneys about a potential lawsuit.

"One might even have been in your firm," Hayes said to Donaldson, his voice and manner taunting.

"I'm sure we refused," Donaldson answered coldly.

Hayes insisted he had given the defense all the information he had, though his tone communicated just the opposite. A story in the *Gaylord Herald Times* reported that Hayes' responses "dripped sarcasm."

When the hearing recessed for the day, Hubbell drove back to his office and did some checking. Had his local Traverse City newspaper *really* compared the prosecutor to Iraq's brutal dictator?

Hubbell could hardly believe it. He was quite sure he'd read every newspaper article published about the case, especially the ones in his local paper, and couldn't remember any of them mentioning Saddam Hussein.

Hubbell opened a file cabinet and pulled out all of the folders containing clippings of newspaper articles related to the case. They were organized by year, from 1986 to the present, with one legal-sized folder devoted to each year. Most were stuffed to overflowing. In the folder marked "1991" Hubbell found what he was looking for.

On Sunday, March 17, 1991, the *Traverse City Record-Eagle* ran four stories on its front page. A big feature about St. Patrick's Day, with a color photograph right in the center of the page; an international news story across the bottom of the page about Russian President Mikhail Gorbachev's efforts to save the Soviet Union; and two additional stories, one on top of the other, along the right side.

The story in the upper right hand corner had this headline: "Saddam says Iraq to move to democracy" and was accompanied by a small black and white photograph of Saddam Hussein. The story immediately below it had this headline: "Court ruling raises doubts over Gaylord slaying convictions" and was accompanied by a small black and white photograph of Norm Hayes. Both men did have dark hair, dark eyebrows, and dark moustaches, and the photographs were exactly the same size. But nowhere was Norm Hayes compared to Saddam Hussein.

Which got Hubbell thinking. If that tenuous connection was all it took for Hayes to accuse the newspaper of wrongdoing, what was behind the "hit" he accused Terry Moore of arranging from prison? Surely it was going to come up in Terry's retrial hearing, so Hubbell planned to look into it. If past actions were an indication of his future behavior, he would have ferreted out the truth, whatever it was.

But Hubbell was not a young man anymore. He was 66 years old, and the fifteen-hour workdays, the sixty-mile commute, the sleepless nights, and the stress were taking their toll. He refused to admit his health was declining and soldiered on, but it was apparent to others he was suffering. On February 4, Judge Porter called a recess and ordered Hubbell to be driven home. Before he had a chance to look into Hayes' accusation against Terry, he was hospitalized for exhaustion. His doctor released him a few days later, but ordered Hubbell to rest for at least a month before going back to work. Hubbell followed orders and spent the next four weeks recuperating in Florida.

With time to think, he tried to read through the case file objectively, as both a defense attorney and a former prosecutor. He tried to consider the entire case, and not just Terry Moore's appeal. He looked into Jerry Tobias' death, the subsequent police investigation, and the arrests and trials of the other men.

"I began to have grave doubts about the whole case," Hubbell said. "I'm now not even sure Tobias was murdered."

That was the same conclusion Dean Robb, Michael Hackett, and Ray MacNeil had all reached after their own research. Maybe no one knew what really happened to Tobias, Hubbell decided, and maybe no one ever would. The only surety was that Terry Moore's case was going to be delayed. Again.

Chapter 93   Davis Out, and Porter In

. . . . Sunday, February 28, 1993

While Hubbell was getting his strength back and preparing to return to Michigan, Judge Corwin removed Judge Davis from the Canter retrial hearing.

Corwin said Davis presided over Mark's trial "with the highest degree of judicial skill and fairness" but that there was still "an air of prejudice." Not because Davis couldn't be impartial, but because his private in-chambers remarks were reported by the media. Any future decisions by Judge Davis in the Tobias cases would be second-guessed and over-scrutinized by the public. Therefore, Canter would get a new judge.

Hesselink criticized the defense for their tactics, but Donaldson said he didn't regret telling Hubbell and MacNeil about Davis' off-the-cuff remarks about Doug Brinkman. MacNeil said he didn't regret letting the news reporters in on the incident.

"The media was the only vehicle we had to get the truth out in this matter," MacNeil said. "Without the media, we were lost."

Hesselink said he was disappointed in the decision. A new judge would have a lot of reading to do to get up to speed, he argued, and would still be unaware of all the details and the personalities impacting the case. The court files filled eleven large cardboard file boxes. MacNeil said he thought Corwin made the right decision, but agreed a new judge would have a lot of work to do. Perhaps that would mean re-calling witnesses for live testimony, instead of having whoever was appointed simply read transcripts.

"You lose the flavor of the incredibility of a Debra Parmentier and the very believeability of Cynthia Gleason," he said.

"There are certain people you have to watch and listen to," agreed Porter, "there's no question about that."

Which gave Porter an idea. Since it would be difficult to find an impartial judge in the area who hadn't already had some connection to the Tobias case, and equally as difficult for a brand new judge to read the thousands of pages of testimony and view hundreds, even thousands, of exhibits, why not combine the two re-trial hearings into one and preside over it himself?

And that is what he decided to do. He'd hear arguments from the defense attorneys for both Mark Canter and Terry Moore and the rebuttal from the prosecutor. At the conclusion, he would give his opinion to the Court of Appeals regarding whether either man's conviction should stand, be overturned, or if they deserved new trials. When the retrial hearing began again, it was the first joint appearance of any of the Tobias defendants since their preliminary examination in May of 1988.

Robert Ianni was called back to testify. He said he was furious that Hayes would suggest he quashed an investigation. Sworn witnesses are immune from prosecution for slander, but the charge still rankled Ianni.

"If he would say that outside the protection of the courtroom, I'd sue him," Ianni said. "It is not the role of this office, or for that matter any prosecutor, to simply obtain convictions, but rather to ensure the proper administration of justice."

The grant of immunity to Sherry Payton, which Hayes said was meddling, was offered by the Attorney General's office simply to get at the truth, Ianni said. He believed that Hayes was angry at the Attorney General for not blindly supporting him and was just looking for someone to blame now that his cases were unraveling.

Chapter 94   Debbie in the Hot Seat

. . . . March 4, 1994

For the first time, Debbie learned what it felt like to be on the other side of the courtroom. Instead of sitting smug in the witness chair, she stood emotionless at the defendant's table, arraigned for felony extortion. The charge stemmed from information given to police by MacNeil six years ago, when he discovered the handwriting on the Dean Robb death threat letter matched one of Debbie's boyfriends.

Debbie was arraigned in front of Judge James McCormick in Traverse City, posted 10 percent of a $3,000 bond, requested a court-appointed attorney, and immediately went back to Utah. On March 15, 1994, she returned for her preliminary examination, and two of her former boyfriends, Roger Becker and Curt Beerens, testified against her. Becker said he wrote the letter at her direction, and Beerens said she told him she'd dictated it.

She entered a minor twist into a relatively routine arraignment: She signed all of her documents "Brieanna Herrick" although records indicated her legal name was still Debra Herrick and had been since her marriage to Kent in 1991. Debbie was bound over for trial, scheduled for May 2. Dean Robb asked that her $3,000 bail to be increased, so Judge McCormick raised it to $10,000, and Debbie worked with a bail bondsman and posted it.

Incredibly, she would be well compensated by the court for her trouble. She would be paid a witness fee of $100 a day, $1,100 of which would be prepaid. Her medical expenses would be covered, and her transportation back and forth to Utah would also be paid for, as well as the transportation costs of the deputies who accompanied her.

In April, Hayes declared he'd be seeking re-election. Hayes had served as judge of the 87th District Court since being elected in 1990; if his campaign were successful, he'd return to the bench for a six-year term. In his announcement for re-election, he pointed to his eleven years of experience as a full-time prosecutor.

The following month, Ray MacNeil decided to challenge him. In a last-minute filing, MacNeil filled out the paperwork just before the May 10 deadline. The week before Canter and Moore's combined retrial hearings were set to begin, a feature story appeared in the *Gaylord Herald Times*, that summed up the case to date: "In a case that has all the drama of a best seller, all the color of a TV movie, and all the twists and turns of a whodunit, justice, say the attorneys, is the only thing missing."

The three defense attorneys were very much a team now, in spirit, but in an official capacity, too. Since Terry and Mark's retrial hearings had been combined, the men also combined their case files, research, and legal knowledge and began working together in earnest. They even had nicknames for each other: Hubbell was "the Muscle," Donaldson "the Brain," and MacNeil "the Heart." They'd need all three organs to make justice a living thing again for their clients. A retrial hearing doesn't sound like life or death, but in Mark and Terry's case, it was. It would be their last chance to get out of prison.

"If there's anything that gets you mad, it's that you know how the office should work," MacNeil told Hubbell and Donaldson. "If we don't do this, if we're not successful, it could be your kids next. It could be anybody's kids."

"That's the part that really ticks me off," agreed Hubbell. "We're all victims. We're all at risk. Sometimes I wished to God I never heard of this case."

"What we're seeking in a technical, legal sense is the grant of a retrial so a jury can hear all of the evidence and reach a conclusion based on that evidence," said Donaldson.

By granting a retrial, Porter would be saying that the defense's new evidence negated Debbie's testimony. The attorneys believed that would be the same as overturning their convictions. Without Debbie, the prosecution had no case.

"Pragmatically, if Porter grants a new trial, the case is over," Hubbell said.

"Right," agreed MacNeil. "The only way they can maintain the convictions is to fight the retrial."

Chapter 95   Combined Retrial Hearings

. . . . Monday, May 23, 1994

With Hubbell mostly recuperated and Judge Porter assigned to hear the case, the combined retrial hearings were finally underway again. Porter ordered Debbie to produce all her personal documents—letters, notes, diary entries—for an in-court inspection.

Debbie complied, sort of. She produced several letters she said she'd received, and some diary entries, but did not bring her full diary to court. Regardless, as usual she was the star of the show. Debbie was the first witness called by the defense, and the courtroom ability of Donaldson, a.k.a. the Brain, was immediately on display. His style was to ask her a question, often a seemingly innocent one, and then impeach her answer with her own words.

For example, in other trials when asked to recount her childhood, Debbie once testified she'd been imprisoned in a basement by a sex fiend and had to whack him over the head with a wine bottle to get free. In another trial, she said she just walked away when her captor wasn't looking.

"Were those statements true?" Donaldson asked.

"To a degree, yes," Debbie answered.

"Were they the truth, the whole truth, and nothing but the truth?" Donaldson asked again.

On this, Debbie waffled. It was just a story she'd told a friend about something that happened to her when she was young and drifting around the country, so who cared which version was true?

As Donaldson dug deeper, Prosecutor Hesselink seemed to grow increasingly uncomfortable. He objected, insisting the defense's repeated questions were irrelevant.

"There is no purpose served other than to try to beat up the witness," he argued.

Donaldson disagreed.

"The witness is a pathological liar," he argued. "She does not have the capacity, in a serious proceeding, to distinguish between the truth or falsehood. Only by putting her stories on the record can the court see her capacity to weave and interweave facts . . . .to perpetuate this scam on two juries."

Hesselink said such decisions should be saved for a trial, if Judge Porter ruled that there would even be a new trial. The judge considered Hesselink's objection, but overruled him. Debbie's credibility, or lack thereof, was the "central linchpin" of the hearing. There would be rules regarding how she could be questioned, and in the interest of getting at the truth the judge would allow a "broad questioning" of the witness, and Donaldson could continue.

"Why did your friendship with Cindy Gleason fall apart?" Donaldson asked Debbie.

"I didn't like the idea they were bringing in (cocaine) from Chicago and using limousines," Debbie said, accusing her former best friend of being a large-scale drug dealer. For proof, Debbie produced a letter she said was written by Cindy detailing Cindy's entry into the drug world.

Debbie produced other documents as well. There were photocopies of letters supposedly written by Roger Becker and Curt Beerens admitting to serious crimes. These included blackmail, shooting into the Sand Hill Manor apartment, extortion, and threats of violence against her.

One letter read:

> Mark (Kerry) and I had Mike (Gilbert) shoot at Deb and I think it has made an impression. Now that she is scared I can force her to live with me. I will get back at her for the pain she caused.

It was signed Curt (Beerens).

Another letter, supposedly from Roger Becker, read:

> I wish that I didn't lie in court, the attorney said I would go to prison so I told them you made me do it I didn't know what to do. I'm sorry.

Bruce Donaldson, Kevin Hesselink, and Judge Porter each examined the letters and made copies. Even Donaldson had to admit that the handwriting looked genuine but he wanted to be sure. Judge Porter allowed the defense to have the letters examined by a State Police document expert.

Before court recessed for the day, Porter ordered Debbie to return the following morning to face more questions. While the retrial hearing was in session, she was not to leave the courthouse or the presence of her counsel, an indication that Judge Porter had some concern that she might flee. When she returned in the morning she was to bring along her diary and any other papers in her possession. While necessary, the order elicited a groan from both Donaldson and the judge himself.

"I just bring to mind she said she has trailer loads," Porter said to Donaldson.

"The pain is more mine than yours, your honor," Donaldson answered.

Emboldened by Porter's ruling, Donaldson went at Debbie again on Wednesday.

Under his questioning, she admitted to repeatedly lying to friends, family, police, the prosecutor, and to lying on the stand in the Tobias trials. Yet she stood by her testimony of what she'd witnessed at the butcher shop. Because the defense had been unsuccessful getting Debbie declared an incompetent witness, Donaldson continued to pick away at her, bit by bit.

"Is it appropriate to give perjurous testimony if there's a good reason not to tell the whole truth?" Donaldson asked her.

"I don't know," Debbie said. "I answer the questions I'm asked to the best of my ability."

In Terry Moore's trial, Debbie said that it was OK to lie if there was a good reason for it.

As the morning wore on, Donaldson covered Debbie's stories of being a victim of kidnapping—twice—participating in illegal arms sales and drug running, and delved into her active mental health history. Then, Donaldson asked about certain entries in Debbie's diary and the questions took an even weirder turn.

In 1987, Debbie wrote an entry about being privy to a plot to kill President Clinton and Rodney King, whose beating had set off the Los Angeles riot.

"World Congresness (sic) meeting Hungry Horse Montanan (sic) second week in July—members meet every year. KKK will be there. Plans are to leak information about the President and if that fails to assinate (sic) King. Chuck is to move to So Carolina and set up printing press for counterfit (sic) money and meet at headquarters there. Less went to Camp David and to Maryland to take pictures of the CIA and Secret Services men to watch who (sic) many there are and when they change and time the President will be there. Leonard is to go to Arkansas and get information there from headquarters."

Donaldson asked Debbie to read the entry aloud. When she did, he made it obvious he had to fight the impulse to laugh out loud because of how ridiculous it sounded and because Clinton wasn't even president in 1987 (he wasn't elected until 1992). Debbie remained completely serious and showed no reaction to Donaldson. Once he regained his composure, he continued with his questions.

"You're certain they're actual events?" he asked.

"Yes," Debbie said, placid and serious. "I was there."

Donaldson moved to allow Debbie's diary to be accepted into the court record as evidence.

"Your honor," he said, "I believe these entries are either, one, so patently bizarre and beyond the pale of human comprehension that they fall of their own weight. And if they do, the testimony that she records only truthful facts in her diary falls with it."

"Or two, the witness is, or has been, engaged in activity that is the highest criminal act that can be committed in the United States."

Prosecutor Hesselink argued against the admission of Debbie's diary, saying these particular entries had no bearing on the Tobias case. Donaldson was only guessing at their meaning, the prosecutor argued, and guessing was not evidence.

"To allow an evidentiary decision to be based on defense speculation . . . is dead wrong," he said.

Porter allowed the diary in, and when court recessed for the day, he called the U.S. Secret Service. No one was going to threaten the president in his courtroom, even in a diary entry that was probably made up. The Secret Service took the call serious enough to send an agent to Gaylord, and the next time Debbie testified, he was in the courtroom listening. When questioned further about it, along with her knowledge of mafia figures and other crimes, Debbie took the Fifth Amendment against self-incrimination. The agent must have believed President Clinton was safe from Debbie, because he returned to Washington.

Chapter 96   Cut and Paste

. . . . Friday, May 27, 1994

After examining the photocopied letters and the diary entries Debbie brought to court, testing them for fingerprints and putting select portions under a microscope, the State Police's document examiner made some determinations. The letters signed by Curt Beerens and Roger Becker were in their handwriting, but that didn't mean the men had actually written them. They probably hadn't. Instead, someone had cut portions of the men's handwriting out of unknown original documents and glued them onto a blank piece of paper. The forger used correction fluid to repair visible lines and then photocopied the documents several times to get the desired effect. According to the State Police's expert, all of the letters were what he called "cut and pastes." Or, in layman's terms, forgeries.

"I found the same letter formation within this letter that have the same defects, which means these letters had to have a common parent somewhere."

The defects showed evidence of multiple copies using a photocopy machine. Another tip-off was that the letters were just too exact. The human hand is not capable of creating identical letters, he explained.

As for the diary, dating the individual entries was an inexact science, but the examiner concluded they were probably written after Jerry Tobias' death. Under ultra-violet light, it was obvious to the expert that the "lost" pages referring to the murder had similar characteristics to the entries written in 1988, but no similar characteristics to entries written in 1986.

The testimony of the State Police's document expert was obviously quite damning to Debbie's credibility, and Judge Porter asked Prosecutor Hessilink if he would like to cross-examine him about his findings, but the assistant prosecutor declined.

Debbie's boyfriends all testified against her; even Curt Beerens, who'd been loyal to her longer than anyone, turned on her. But the most pitiful story came from Roger Becker. In 1988, Becker said he was in love with Debbie and left his wife and children for her. When Debbie moved in with him, he thought they might get married someday so when he bought a new Chevy pickup truck for $15,000, he put both his and her name on the title. When she went into police custody and their relationship went sour, Becker moved to Colorado and found work as a carpenter. Every month he sent a $317 money order to the Gaylord car dealership that financed the truck.

On October 29, 1993, Becker's truck, full of his carpenter tools, disappeared from his Rifle, Colorado driveway. He filed a police report, but five months went by and he still didn't know what happened to it. Then in March of 1994, Debbie arrived in Traverse City to face an extortion charge, and Ray MacNeil saw Debbie and her husband, Kent Herrick, driving Becker's missing truck to a court appearance. MacNeil called Becker, and Becker called the police. The police found the truck, ran a check on the plates and registration, and then called Becker with the sad news. The truck couldn't be considered stolen because Debbie's name was on the title. Becker sent Debbie paperwork to sign to remove her name, but she never returned it. Not only did she ignore his request, she used parts of his handwritten letter on the cut-and-paste forgeries.

Donaldson questioned Debbie about the truck, the shootings, the forgeries, and whether or not she asked Curt Beerens to drive her to Gaylord over the Fourth of July holiday in 1988 to check whether or not the butcher shop had a back window. She took the fifth on every question. The case was unraveling faster and faster for the prosecution, but Hesselink would not relent.

"At this point, I have not made any determination there was improper police or prosecutorial action," Prosecutor Hesselink said. If he believe that, he told the *Gaylord Herald Times*, it would be his duty to tell the judge, but he didn't.

But when the retrial hearings began more than a year ago, Donaldson, Hubbell, and MacNeil were all of the opinion that if Porter ruled for new trials, the case would collapse. Finally, it looked to the defense like that was a surety.

"I think at this point, enough is enough," MacNeil told the court, just before Porter adjourned the hearings for a week-long break while he heard other cases. MacNeil promised motions would be filed by the defense demanding Debbie be charged with perjury and to grant new trials for Terry and Mark.

Not so fast, said Hesselink.

"That doesn't necessarily mean the case at the time of trial was improper," he said. "The loss of Parmentier's testimony does not necessarily end the men's life sentences. That doesn't necessarily mean the case is over."

Chapter 97　Debbie Goes to Jail

. . . . Tuesday, June 7, 1994

First thing Tuesday morning, Judge Porter ordered the bailiff to take Debbie into custody, and he charged her with eight counts of perjury. She would be housed in the same jail as Terry and Mark while awaiting the results of their combined retrial hearing.

"The court has heard massive and substantive perjury," was all Porter said from the bench, before he signed the warrant for her arrest.

Donaldson argued in favor of the charges. And while Hesselink conceded his experts agreed with the State Police document examiner—the letters Debbie proffered from Beerens and Becker were forged—he asked Porter to appoint a special prosecutor to address her crime. His contention was the forgeries had nothing to do with the Tobias case or the retrial hearings. The defense disagreed.

"Taken separately, these fabrications and forgeries were directly related to the critical issues in these proceedings," Donaldson said, his voice conveying his disgust with Hesselink. "Taken together, had they been accepted as true by this court, and they had the capacity to change the *entire* outcome of this case. It is inappropriate for you, like some Pontius Pilate, to wash your hands of this matter and to defer it over to some special prosecutor."

Donaldson made these comments in haste, before Porter had a chance to rule on the special prosecutor motion from Hesselink, and the judge was not pleased with the Pontius Pilate comment.

"I gently and respectfully take offense that this court would allow perjury," Porter said to Donaldson.

But Donaldson would not back down. "Then send the woman to jail!" he said, and finally Porter obliged. A single count of perjury was punishable by up to life in prison; Debbie was facing eight counts. But as Debbie was led to jail, MacNeil told the court no one should breathe easy because they probably had not seen the last of her.

"She's used this court; she's used Otsego County. Again," MacNeil said. "She's never missed a step and she's a walking, living tornado that leaves nothing but destroyed lives in her past."

With Debbie discredited and jailed, the defense attorneys continued their quest to get Porter to grant Mark and Terry new trials. Witness perjury, recanted testimony, crimes committed by Debbie while she was in police custody, the strong-arming of Sherry Payton—any one of these things, if known by the court, could have produced a different verdict for the two men at their original trials.

"If we had that diary, not only would we have blown Parmentier out of the courtroom, we could have put the truth—verified by Parmentier's diary—into Canter's mouth. Does the system itself feel comfortable with having Mark Canter and Terry Moore in prison based on the testimony of this woman?" asked MacNeil.

Apparently, the system did feel comfortable with it. At least for the time being, because Judge Porter refused to cut the retrial hearing short. It would be argued to its completion, he said, and only then would he make a decision.

His ruling was agony for Mark, Terry, and their attorneys after everything they'd done to get their cases in front of Judge Porter. But it was a victory of sorts for Hesselink. He hadn't won, but he would have more time to fight against either man getting a new trials.

"There has to be a clear establishment that they did not receive a fair trial," Hesselink said, in his support of Porter's ruling. "At this point in the case, that has not been shown to me."

Hesselink said he believed former prosecutor Norm Hayes had an obligation to put Debbie on the stand "warts and all." Plus, despite her lies about everything else, despite her forgeries, crimes, false police reports, and mental problems, Hesselink said he believed Debbie's story of what she witnessed at Walt's was still credible.

"In every murder case, there are always some things that don't go right," he said. "That doesn't mean there was any intention on the behalf of anyone else to 'get someone' or make a mockery of justice. You're never going to have a perfect trial. The only question is, 'Did they have a fair trial?' And unfortunately for them, they did."

The defense put Debbie on the stand again on Thursday, to explain the forgeries, the staged shootings, the faked kidnappings, the convoluted stories of presidential assassination attempts, the gun-running and drug dealing. She'd been in jail for two days, and so Donaldson and the rest of the defense team expected Debbie to be a little defeated, a little less arrogant and sure of herself, a little more submissive and contrite. Donaldson would later say he expected Debbie to "curl into a fetal position on the stand."

Her appearance certainly fit their expectations: Gone was Debbie's styled hair and fashionable clothing; she arrived for court in a jail-issue navy blue jumpsuit. But her demeanor didn't match her outward appearance or Donaldson's expectations. Debbie acted composed and even tough. When the questioning began, she invoked the Fifth Amendment in answer to almost every question. Donaldson was dumbfounded. Debbie had always talked too much; now she wouldn't say anything at all.

"Have you reviewed your diary entries lately," Donaldson asked, taunting her.

"I haven't reviewed anything," Debbie hissed. "I don't *have* anything. I'm in jail."

Chapter 98   Throwing Mud at the Michigan State Police

. . . . Friday, June 10, 1994

The defense team and the defendants weren't the only men who wished Judge Porter would cut the retrial hearing short. Chances were good that so did Police Trooper Thomas Dunneback. With Hesselink refusing to back down, the gloves were off. Judge Porter said he wanted the hearing to be argued to its full conclusion and so that's what the defense was going to do. That meant subpoenaing Dunneback and forcing him to testify about his relationship with Debbie.

In the summer of 1988, Debbie was a protected witness testifying for the prosecution in the Terry Moore trial. Thomas Dunneback was the officer who arranged the apartment for her at Sand Hill Manor. The defense subpoenaed Dunneback and two other State Police officers, but Hesselink argued their testimony would be too prejudicial to allow.

"It does no more than throw mud at the State Police," he said to Judge Porter.

Donaldson disagreed, saying Hesselink opened the door for the subpoenas when he portrayed the police as acting above reproach.

"It is the position of the prosecutor that the law enforcement officers connected with the Michigan State Police conducted themselves in the highest degree of appropriateness and honor; that they are persons of high and unsullied reputations within their law enforcement communities; that this court, in order to find for the defendants, must prove these men breached their duties."

Judge Porter ruled the officers would have to testify.

What the prosecution was trying to keep under wraps was the fact that Trooper Dunneback had a sexual relationship with Debbie while she was in police protective custody. He even introduced her to his family.

"She seemed lonely, and I asked her if I could call her sometime," Dunneback said on the stand. Debbie gave the trooper her phone number, "but she didn't seduce me, if that's what you're asking."

Dunneback worked as an undercover agent for the State Police's drug enforcement criminal investigation unit. He was the officer who kept an apartment at Sand Hill Manor for use in drug investigations. When the State Police needed a place to put Debbie, he suggested the apartment, and he said he met her when he went there to pick up some furniture and check in on her. Under Donaldson's questioning, Dunneback admitted that Debbie told him about drug deals and gun running, but he hadn't filed any police reports about her stories.

"If true, that would have been major criminal activity," said Donaldson.

"Yes," Dunneback said. "I suppose it would. I didn't think it was true."

"So on your bare disbelief you dismissed it?" Donaldson asked.

"Yes," Dunneback said.

"You knew she was an untruthful person, didn't you?" Donaldson pressed.

"At times," Dunneback agreed. "I guess if I thought there was some truth to some portion of that, I would have done something."

Dunneback also said he'd seen Debbie studying documents before and during her testimony in the Terry Moore trial and believed they were court transcripts.

Chapter 99   The Banker's Box. Again.

. . . . Thursday, June 16, 1994

The banker's box of withheld documents came back to haunt the prosecution. After spending a year going through every scrap of paper, every police officer's handwritten note, and every hidden report, the defense learned something so shady that if it surfaced in any other trial, they probably wouldn't have believed it. The investigator Don Heistand's attorney, Jack Felton, hired to corroborate Don's alibi had secretly funneled information to the prosecution.

In May of 1988, when Heistand was in jail awaiting trial, Felton tried to corroborate his alibi. Heistand swore he was innocent and had nothing to do with Tobias' death. He told Felton he didn't know Mark Canter, Doug Brinkman, or Jerry Tobias, and certainly wasn't involved with drugs. Felton believed him, but needed proof Heistand was somewhere else. He hired private investigator Charles Rettstadt and his firm, Research North, to nail down Heistand's alibi.

According to a document found in the banker's box, Rettstadt funneled the information he uncovered to Detective LaBarge,

Lieutenant Hardy, and the prosecutor's office. Assistant Prosecutor Dawn Pyrek's handwritten notes recovered from the box of documents proved it.

"Charlie going to get him to write a stmt & give to Jack." (The defense believed that *Charlie* was Charles Rettstadt, *him* was Don Heistand, *stmt* was statement, and *Jack* was Jack Felton.)

"Charlie says if Terry's convicted, they will all roll over. Charlie believes DP except ID on Don." (The defense believed that *Terry* was Terry Moore, *DP* was Debbie Parmentier, and *Don* was Don Heistand.)

On June 16, the defense called Dawn Pyrek to the stand to explain her notes and confirm the sordid meaning behind them. She said the handwriting was indeed hers, but she had no memory of writing the note. The defense also subpoenaed Charles Rettstadt, who took the stand after Pyrek and denied the allegations.

Heistand was released from prison in October of 1990 after serving out his sentence on a no-contest plea. He had always maintained his innocence and only entered the plea after Terry Moore and Mark Canter were convicted and sentenced to life in prison.

Perhaps equally damning was information the defense uncovered in the banker's box that showed both Hardy's and LaBarge's wives were on Research North's payroll at the time Jack Felton hired the firm and Rettstadt. The defense tried to show that hiring the detectives' wives was actually just a front to employ the detectives themselves, who were barred from moonlighting while they still worked for the Michigan State Police.

While Pyrek and Rettstadt denied the defense's allegations, the blow to the prosecution was a serious one.

"The long-forgotten notes scribbled in the former chief assistant prosecutor's handwriting may be one of the most tangible pieces of evidence yet of misconduct in the Jerry Tobias murder case," reported the *Gaylord Herald Times*.

With Dunneback's revelations of the affair, Debbie's string of 165 Fifth Amendment answers, and the possibility that information was secretly and illegally funneled to the prosecutor, Donaldson again made a motion asking Judge Porter to halt the hearing and immediately grant Terry and Mark new trials. Again the motion was denied.

At the beginning of the retrial hearing, the defense's strategy was to divide their case into three separate arguments, or prongs. Prong One was arguing Debbie was not legally competent to testify, and Prong Two was the newly discovered evidence of her criminal activity. The defense team's plan was to withhold Prong Three—police and prosecutor misconduct—in reserve and only use it if Judge Porter refused to rule in their favor after they presented the first two prongs.

With Prong One and Two complete, it was Hesselink's turn to address what the defense brought to light and argue against either man receiving a new trial. The defense was in a strong position for the first time in almost eight years.

Chapter 100   A Gentleman's Agreement

. . . . Thursday, August 18, 1994

On the afternoon the defense completed presenting Prongs One and Two, but before they rested their case, Ray MacNeil, Stu Hubbell, Mark Canter, and Terry Moore met in the Otsego County Circuit Court's jury room. The attorneys explained their three-pronged strategy to their clients. MacNeil and Hubbell said their inclination was to rest their case and hold Prong Three as a trump card to be used only if Judge Porter declined to grant them a new trial. Their reasoning was it would shorten the retrial hearing and hopefully get the men out of prison sooner. It would also spare the City of Gaylord the embarrassment of having the allegations of misconduct made public.

Mark and Terry listened to their attorneys explain the plan, but both disagreed with it. The men said they'd already been waiting a very long time for justice; they'd be willing to wait a little longer if it meant the allegations of cover-ups and misdeeds would finally come to light.

MacNeil and Hubbell offered the men a compromise. They'd meet with Prosecutor Hesselink and make him an offer: He could go ahead and present the rest of the prosecution's case, but afterward if Judge Porter ruled Canter and Moore deserved a new trial on Prongs One and Two, Hesselink would drop the case. He wouldn't retry the men, he'd drop all charges against them, and they would go free. If Hesselink declined their offer, MacNeil and Hubbell would return to court and immediately present Prong Three.

Mark and Terry conferred and agreed to the compromise. So while a bailiff guarded them in the jury room, the attorneys went to Prosecutor Hesselink's office and made him the offer. Hesselink listened and immediately accepted.

"If you think I'd retry these cases against you assholes, you're crazy," he told them.

MacNeil and Hubbell returned to the jury room and told Mark and Terry they had a gentleman's agreement with the prosecutor. Nothing was signed, but Hesselink had verbally agreed. The next day, he would begin arguing against giving the men new trials and so for now at least, Prong Three would stay under wraps.

The Prosecutor began with a tiny witness list. There were only three names on it: Trooper Tony Gomez, the man assigned to interview Sherry Payton; John Hardy, chief of detectives for the region, and Mark Alsept, a convicted felon who served time with Terry Moore.

Hardy was the prosecution's first witness and he said that while Curt Beerens had come to him with "gut feelings" about Debbie's criminal activities—specifically the Gleason and Sand Hill Manor shootings—Beerens had no real evidence.

Hardy admitted he'd told Prosecutor Hayes he had questions about Debbie's credibility and suggested they back off Mark Canter's prosecution. Hayes made the decision to continue, according to Hardy. When Stuart Hubbell asked Hardy whether he'd checked out Debbie's outlandish accounts of selling stolen guns to Mexican freedom fighters, Hardy said he had not.

"In fact, then, you thought it was unbelievable, didn't you?" Hubbell said.

"I thought part of it was unbelievable," Hardy agreed.

"She was a lie a minute, wasn't she?" Hubbell pressed.

"She was unique," Hardy said.

"If Hardy is telling the truth . . . then a Crime of Conspiracy to Obstruct Justice has been laid bare . . . with Prosecutor Hayes its architect," Bruce Donaldson said to Judge Porter. A Grand Jury must be convened or the case would "leave this stench . . . in the nostrils and minds of the public."

Porter said he'd take the motion under advisement, but was furious with Donaldson for making such a suggestion in open court and in front of the media. It was something better dealt with in chambers, he said. But Donaldson disagreed and would not back off; the public had a right to know what their elected officials were up to, he countered.

"I very much doubt the defense is concerned about Mr. Hayes' position," Hesselink said. "I think it's a ploy to denigrate the testimony of the witnesses in this proceeding. There's no reason to put on a public display like this."

While Judge Porter fumed privately, the hearing wore on publicly, and Prosecutor Hesselink called prison snitch Mark Alsept to the stand. Paroled from prison on six felony counts, Alsept said he and Terry Moore were in Kinross Regional Correctional Facility together. The men became friends, Alsept said, and Terry Moore confessed the murder to him and wanted revenge on Hayes.

"Norm Hayes railroaded him on the case," Alsept testified. "He wanted him hurt. He wanted his arms and legs broke, and his back. He wanted him to suffer for the rest of his life."

According to Alsept, Terry also wanted him to persuade Debbie Parmentier to change her story, or kill her if she refused, and pay off Sherry Payton. Alsept came to the attention of the prosecution when he wrote a letter to Norm Hayes, informing him of Terry's plans. Alsept was serving time for felonious assault, malicious destruction of property, and felony firearms possession, and offered to testify against Terry in exchange for a sentence reduction.

Norm Hayes received Alsept's letter, contacted the State Police, and a plan was made to wire Alsept and set up a prison meeting between Alsept and Terry Moore. Three times the two met, but Terry never mentioned getting revenge on anyone. On the stand Alsept admitted working as a snitch for Kinross' internal investigation unit, but denied working with them when he met Terry Moore.

When Hesselink was finished questioning him, Judge Porter asked the defense if they wanted to cross-examine him. Donaldson said they were waiting to retrieve Alsept's criminal record before proceeding, but reserved the right to cross-examine him later. Porter said he'd allow them to revisit the issue when the hearing continued in a couple weeks. He was calling a break. He needed the time to consider what weight to give to Alsept's testimony and whether to impanel a Grand Jury to look into whether or not John Hardy or Norm Hayes lied under oath.

The defense used the time well. When the hearing resumed, they had two new witnesses. Kinross Deputy Warden Robert Atherton, and a guard, Carl Hanna. The deputy warden testified that because of prison rules Alsept's story could not be true. Alsept could not have visited Terry Moore's cell as many times as he testified to because such visits weren't allowed and would constitute a "major misconduct" citation. While Alsept had fifteen major misconduct citations on his record, none were for unauthorized occupation of a cell. Because of those fifteen citations, Alsept hadn't banked any "good time"—free time to watch TV, go to the prison library, or participate in other recreational opportunities. The warden said the only way for an inmate with such bad behavior to get their good time back would be for them to do something "extraordinary."

The guard backed up Warden Atherto's testimony. "We don't tolerate it," he said, regarding cell visits. Terry was assigned to Kinross months before Alspet was, and it was the guard's opinion that Alsept singled out Terry Moore.

"He associated himself almost immediately with Mr. Moore and that's not a normal action," the guard said, suggesting the friendship was phony and could have been set up by outside interests.

Finally, the prosecution's last witness took the stand. Trooper Gomez denied he ever threatened or intimidated Sherry Payton. He testified he didn't know Judge Davis had ordered police to tape all their interviews with Payton, so it did not seem unusual to him that his first interview with her was not. After Sherry agreed to say she was a witness, Gomez informed Detective LaBarge, at which point LaBarge spoke briefly with Payton and turned on the tape.

"My involvement was very limited," Gomez insisted, but he could not explain why he was brought into the case in the first place.

"Did it seem strange to you that these officers that had been working on this case for almost two years would ask *you* to interview Sherry Payton?" asked Donaldson.

"I've asked myself that question many times since then, and I don't have an answer," Gomez said.

Chapter 101   The Fate of Debbie's Men

. . . . November 9, 1994

On Wednesday, Nov. 9, Debbie was finally bound over to circuit court to be tried for perjury. A condition of her $40,000 bond kept her in Michigan until the trial. In contrast to her usual talkativeness, Debbie stood mute.

But woe to the man who crossed Debbie Parmentier. By the time she was finally in court to face perjury charges, she'd ruined or at least damaged the lives of more than a dozen men. Hers was a "continuing saga of a woman whose life seems to torment those whose paths she has crossed," said the *Gaylord Herald Times*.

Consider the men she'd left in her wake: Mark Canter and Terry Moore were still in prison. Don Heistand couldn't find a job, even after he got out of prison and was on parole. He refused to lie when filling out job applications and few employers looked kindly on convicted felons. Heistand's health was poor. Two years in prison had made his diabetes worse.

Debbie's ex-husband, Leonard Parmentier, was contemplating suing Otsego County because no one in authority had enforced her child support. Leonard was the fulltime caregiver of their two sons, and Debbie was supposed to pay a meager $15 a week. She paid nothing.

Roger Becker just wanted his truck and his carpentry tools back. Trooper Thomas Dunneback had to face the shame of testifying in an open courtroom about his affair with Debbie, and Doug Wilt admitted closing the Sand Hill Manor shooting she was involved in without charging her for anything. Mark Kerry's marriage ended because of his affair with Debbie, and so did his friendship with his EMT partner, Curt Beerens. Beerens' credibility as a firearms dealer was suspect, after providing a handgun to Debbie and a rifle to Mark Kerry for the apartment shooting.

Being associated with Debbie was also expensive. The Social Security Administration wanted to know if she deserved the benefits she'd been receiving for supposedly being disabled by anxiety-related disorders caused by her Tobias trial testimony. The State Police spent $4,146 for her upkeep, but Otsego County got hit the hardest. By the time of the retrial hearings, the rough estimates of the cost of the Tobias case to the county was approximately $2 million.

While Debbie waited for her perjury trial, Mark Canter and Terry Moore's retrial hearings finally came to a close. Judge Porter ordered each side to file "findings of fact." These documents were expected to be voluminous and Porter warned that it would be some time before he could read through them and make his decision.

Chapter 102   MacNeil Gets a Phone Call. Again.

. . . . Thursday, February 23, 1995

It must have seemed like déjà vu to Ray MacNeil. When Sherry Payton wanted to recant her testimony back in the spring of 1989 and admit she lied to police, to the prosecutor, and on the witness stand, she called Ray MacNeil. So at the end of February, a week before she was going to face criminal charges, Debbie wanted to talk to someone, and the someone she chose was Ray MacNeil.

"Brieanna wants to speak with you," Debbie's husband, Kent Herrick, told MacNeil over the phone. "She wants immunity from prosecution."

MacNeil explained that he was an attorney, not a judge. He didn't have the authority to give immunity to anyone. Only the prosecutor, the Attorney General, or a judge could grant immunity. MacNeil said he'd be willing to speak with Debbie, under some very specific conditions: The conversation would be in person, not over the phone, it would happen in his office, another attorney would be present as a witness, and it would be taped.

Debbie agreed, and that same day appeared at Ray MacNeil's office. She said most of her testimony was fabricated at the request of the police and the prosecutor. She said Prosecutor Hayes threatened to charge her with the murder if she didn't alter her story to fit the prosecution's case.

"If I testified the way he wanted me to testify, then he wouldn't charge me with murder, he wouldn't charge me with anything. He told me, 'Either way you look at this, if you pass the lie detector test, you were there. If you flunk the lie detector test, you're lying to us.'"

Debbie said she didn't know Sherry Payton or Don Heistand before the trial, and she only identified Terry Moore in a photo line up because the prosecution showed her a picture of him.

The next day, Debbie disappeared. Her $40,000 bond was revoked, the Attorney General's office labeled her a fugitive, and she was put on the Michigan State Police's Most Wanted list.

"It's interesting to me that she gives this statement just before she flees," Donaldson said. "It's almost as if she wants to put things right before going underground."

Chapter 103   Waiting. Again.

. . . . April, 1995

Six months passed. Debbie was still in the wind and Hesselink hadn't filed his Findings of Fact requested by Judge Porter. The judge said he couldn't make an informed decision on new trials without that document from the prosecutor so Mark and Terry waited in prison.

The defense argued the delay denied the men their right to a speedy trial and filed a motion asking Porter to compel Hesselink to file the document immediately or release their clients from prison. Judge Porter denied it, but Hesselink must have felt the pressure because he filed his Finding of Fact on Tuesday, April 11. Porter promised to put everything on his court docket aside, devote himself to reviewing the materials, and make a ruling soon. Perhaps that's exactly what would have happened, but over the weekend the judge suffered a heart attack. He needed time to recuperate and couldn't return to work until June 1. When his recovery didn't go as swift as hoped, that date was extended, and then the prosecution filed several motions that took up even more of the court's time. So it was January 18, 1996, before Porter finally made his ruling. Mark and Terry were granted new trials.

Porter's written decision ran an unbelievable 600 pages. Much of what he wrote concerned Debbie's ability to con everyone. Her diary was "a web of lies," Porter wrote, but he was particularly impressed with the forgeries of the Curt Beerens and Roger Becker letters.

"The letters would most clearly reflect the ingenuity, creativity and degree of effort Parmentier would utilize to provide false information, statements and testimony in order to enhance her credibility in defendants trials. It perhaps stands out above all other evidentiary items as material for impeachment of Parmentier's credibility."

Porter accused the police of failing their obligation to tell the defense when Debbie started committing crimes and said Prosecutor Hayes should have done a better job of keeping Debbie and Cindy Gleason from collaborating. Porter ruled Mark Canter and Terry Moore deserved new trials, and should the prosecutor actually decide to retry them, Debbie would have no credibility as a witness. What Porter did not know was that the defense team held in reserve that gentleman's agreement with Hesselink. If Porter ruled in their favor, he had agreed not to retry.

The defense was jubilant.

"It's about time," said Laurie Moore. "It's seven years late. I'm as happy as I can be for Terry. She's totally wacko and always has been. Hayes used her nuttiness. She was a tool for the cops."

"It's just a wonderful day," said MacNeil. When he told Mark Canter, his client broke down and wept. "He's been waiting for this for eight years."

"I'm delighted with the decision," said Hubbell. "All the things we said occurred, with one or two exceptions, the judge said we'd proved."

According to the *Gaylord Herald Times*, "It was Hubbell's perseverance, perhaps more than anything, that resulted in the favorable decision for the two men."

Hubbell said it was the "longest and most stressful" case of his career. Donaldson said, "I am delighted not with the thrill of victory in a contest sense, but rather in a much deeper professional manner because I have participated, and the justice system has reached what I consider to be a proper and just result."

Donaldson's rate was $200 an hour, and he originally involved himself in the case on a temporary pro bono basis just to help out Hubbell. When Porter ruled, he'd devoted more than 1,000 hours to it and charged the men nothing. Mark and Terry had been in prison for almost eight years. The ruling soon sparked an effort to clear Don Heistand's name, and his attorney, Jack Felton filed a motion with Porter to set aside Heistand's conviction. MacNeil, Hubbell, and Donaldson filed an affidavit in support. The stress was too much on Heistand though, and weakened by diabetes, he suffered a heart attack on Thursday, Jan. 18. Brinkman wouldn't ever be cleared of the charges against him because he was the only one of the five men who pled guilty.

Porter announced his retirement, but as one of his last acts on the bench, he signed the motion to clear Heistand's record. The judge said Heistand was not at the murder scene, had nothing to do with the murder, and his conviction was a miscarriage of justice.

"It is one of those unfortunate situations where the truth and the legal process were at odds," Porter said.

When the *Gaylord Herald Times* asked Hesselink to comment on Porter's decision, he said it "looks like a big publicity ploy to me."

When Porter announced his decision on the new trials, he suggested that it would be appropriate for the defense to file a motion to set aside the conviction. This would give Hesselink the opportunity to "do the right thing." If not, the issue would be presented to the Attorney General. Hesselink shocked MacNeil and Hubbell by saying that he was considering retrying the men. When Mac-Neil and Hubbell reminded him of their gentleman's agreement, Hesselink said he had no memory of making it. But in 1994, when the retrial hearing was at a crescendo, Hesselink agreed not to prosecute the men at all if Judge Porter granted them new trials. He'd given his word.

With that now meaningless, Donaldson, Hubbell, and Mac-Neil vowed to seek not just an innocent verdict, but a public airing of the last pieces of dirty laundry they'd been holding in reserve. If Hesselink was going to trial, Prong Three would meet him there.

Mark and Terry were released on bond on Thursday, Jan. 18, 1996. Until a decision was made by Hesselink about whether or not to prosecute them again, they'd be under house arrest, electronic tethers attached to their ankles.

Chapter 104   Back to Court

. . . . Thursday, January 25, 1996

The men waited a week for Hesselink's decision.

"I believe in the sanctity of life and I need to vigorously go after those who don't," Hesselink said.

Mark Canter, Terry Moore, MacNeil, Hubbell, and Donaldson all felt betrayed. They'd come so far, uncovered so much, waited so long, and even felt freedom for a brief moment, only to have it languish in limbo. But Donaldson, the Brain of the defense trio, with his confident style and big-city trial experience, was not cowed.

"It's going to get ugly then," he promised.

Hesselink said he didn't care. He would go forward with the prosecutions even if no one could find Debbie or believe her stories once they did find her. Should she turn up, he said might use her again as a prosecution witness. Because of double jeopardy, Mark and Terry could not be tried again for First-Degree Murder. Hesselink's options were Second-Degree Murder or Manslaughter. On the remote chance they were found guilty, their sentences could be less than the time they'd already served. Even supporters of the original prosecutions were skeptical of Hesselink's decision.

"The cost of retrial may punish us all," read an editorial in the *Gaylord Herald Times*. "We understand that there is a man dead and someone should be brought to justice. But the prosecution's main witness . . . has proven to be a pathological liar who can't be relied upon to give a truthful time of day. That this witness lies for no other reason than she is asked a question makes it unlikely it can be proven that Canter and Moore were involved in the murder of Tobias."

Privately, Hubbell and MacNeil were infuriated. The media, Judge Porter, and the people of Gaylord knew nothing about their gentleman's agreement with Hesselink.

Reached at their homes where they were both under house arrest, Terry and Mark said they felt bitter.

"They don't have me physically, but they still have me mentally. It's like a guillotine over my head." Terry Moore said, in a telephone interview with the *Gaylord Herald Times*.

People in Gaylord were not privy to the whole story of the investigation, the cover-ups, and the court maneuvering, and many still believed the men were guilty.

"In a way, that bothers me, but on the other hand, I know the truth," Terry said. "Nobody is going to get one hundred percent of the people on their side all the time. I guess I am just going to have to deal with it."

Mark said he felt dejected, too, but was trying to hope for the best.

"As long as I live, I'll never get over this and what it has done to my family. There will always be permanent scars. I can't begin to express what it feels like to be an innocent man in prison. In all honesty, I am bitter, but I can't let it tie me down. I have to turn it into motivation for something positive."

Mark said he was also aware public opinion was not on his side.

"Sure that bothers me, because there is nothing more I want than people to know I had nothing to do with the death of Jerry Tobias. But as long as I'm proud of the way I'm living my life, and I'm doing the best I can, there's nothing more I can do. Actually, it's more their problem than mine (because) we're closer to the truth now than we've ever been."

After 22 years on the bench, Judge Porter retired February 1, 1996, yet still accepted a re-appointment from Judge Davis to decide on whether or not a speedy trial motion should be heard, and whether or not the defense's Third Prong could go forward. Publicly, Porter told reporters he thought the men were guilty.

Though the defense could not hold Hesselink to his word because there was nothing about their gentleman's agreement in writing, they did file a motion to disqualify Hesselink from prosecuting because of a conflict of interest. He was an advocate for Hayes and the police, they argued, and if the prosecution went forward the defense planned to call him as a witness.

Porter denied the request, and Hesselink refused to disqualify himself. If he wouldn't go, the defense team sought to have Porter removed from the case. He could not have it both ways, they argued. He couldn't publicly state he thought the men were guilty and maintain his impartial status. Human nature didn't work that way, not even for a judge with a sterling reputation.

But Porter refused, and all this legal back and forth took several months, while Mark and Terry waited, confined to their houses and unable to get on with their lives. All they really wanted to do was work. Neither had earned a living in eight years, and the county was charging them $12 a day for their tethers. At $87.50 a week, the costs were mounting, and if they didn't pay the fee they'd go back to jail.

Hubbell asked the court to either let the men work while they waited for trial or suspend the charges against them. When Porter refused, Hubbell paid the fees himself.

On May 1, 1996, a hearing was scheduled on Porter's disqualification. The night before, he withdrew from the case.

"The court has come to the opinion that the interests of judicial economy and a timely processing of the cases is of paramount importance."

Hubbell summed up the defense's reaction: "I find it interesting he's saying he's doing this in the interest of timeliness. I've been on this case for seven years and it took him one and a half years to write his opinion and now timeliness is of the essence."

Hubbell was convinced Porter didn't really care about timeliness; he just didn't want to be cross-examined at the disqualification hearing. Again the court administrator had to go far afield to find an objective judge. Neither Judge Patrick Murphy or Judge Alton Davis could hear the second trials of Mark and Terry because they'd already been involved in the case, Murphy as a prosecutor and Davis as Canter's judge in his first trial. Davis had also made disparaging remarks about Doug Brinkman, they went public, and that disqualified him. Without Porter presiding, Hesselink tried to salvage the prosecutions by offering Mark and Terry a plea deal: plead guilty to a lesser charge on the retrial and be released for time served. The men declined.

The state assigned Judge Joseph P. Swallow from the 26th Circuit Court of Alpena to hear all motions and retrial proceedings beginning June 28, 1996. Under Hesselink's objections, he agreed to give the men work release and signed an order relieving them of the fee for their electronic tethers.

"I don't see any danger to Otsego County," Judge Swallow said. "They were going to be released with time served," he added, referencing Hesselink's plea offer. As the summer wore on, more victories piled up for the defense: Judge Swallow ruled none of Debbie's testimony would be allowed in the second trials and then several prosecution witnesses, including Doug Brinkman and Cindy Gleason, refused to testify. Alsept was in Florida, out on parole, and refused to return to Michigan. Even with all of this, Hesselink still wanted to prosecute, but Judge Swallow advised him to let it go.

"I don't feel that police or prosecution have any reason to hang their heads," Hesselink insisted. "We didn't do anything wrong or improper. Obviously this case was very burdensome, and I spent much more time than I normally would have, but that's part of the job. I have to move on and get ready for the next case."

In a final dig, in September Hesselink filed a personal protection order against Mark Canter and Terry Moore on behalf of Jackie Tobias and her children. The defense moved for it to be rescinded and, in December, it was.

The Brain, the Muscle, and the Heart worked together to prepare the motion to dismiss and submitted it to Judge Swallow. On Wednesday, September 18, 1996, a telephone conference was held between Donaldson, Hubbell, MacNeil, Swallow, and Hesselink.

"There's no evidence the men can be charged with murder," the judge said, encouraging Prosecutor Hesselink to agree to the motion to dismiss. There's no evidence they can be charged with anything."

Hesselink agreed to sign it only after the wording that he had "no objection" to the motion was changed to "no legal objection."

Surrounded by their friends and family, Mark and Terry arrived at the Otsego County Sheriff's office to have their tethers cut off. Several people wept. Terry wore a Statue of Liberty tie for the occasion. "I've worn it to court many times but it never had meaning like today," he said.

Mark Canter was overcome with emotion, but found the words to praise the three attorneys.

"I know, in my lifetime, of no other men who have worked harder in pursuit of justice and liberty."

EPILOGUE

On September 5, 1997, two of the Tobias defendants became the accusers. Mark Canter and Terry Moore sued Otsego County, the State of Michigan, and a dozen people involved in the Tobias case prosecutions, in federal court, for civil rights violations and malicious prosecution. Although this was now a case for the civil and not the criminal courts, the two men were still represented by Ray MacNeil and Stuart Hubbell. Hubbell's health was failing, and so his sons, Dan, Joe, and Paul, assisted.

Mark and Terry were seeking unspecified monetary damages from Otsego County, the Michigan State Police, as well as prosecutors Norm Hayes and Kevin Hesselink, Assistant Prosecutor Dawn (Pyrek) Schumacher, State Police Officers Fred LaBarge, John Hardy, Doug Wilt, Kenneth Burr, and Carl Goeman, Private Detective Charles Rettstadt, Prosecutor's Investigator Jerry Borema, Assistant County Medical Examiner Patricia Newhouse, and Prosecution Witness Debbie Parmentier.

The 134-page complaint alleged the plaintiffs conspired to hide evidence from defense attorneys, coerced witnesses, and forced witnesses to perjure themselves, all in an effort to strengthen the shoddy case against Canter and Moore.

Over the next three years, attorneys for Otsego County, the Michigan State Police and their municipal insurance companies peppered the court with motions in an effort to delay the lawsuit, including making an attempt to get MacNeil and Hubbell disqualified. A U.S. District Court judge ruled the prosecutors (Hayes, Hesselink, Pyrek) named in the suits were protected by "absolute immunity" but that five of the eleven counts could still go forward.

399

"Essentially, we won," Stu Hubbell's son, Dan Hubbell, told the *Gaylord Herald Times*. "I anticipate this won't be the last appeal though. The name of the game for the defendants now is 'Delay.'"

The issues for trial included one count each of malicious prosecution against former State Police Detective Fred LaBarge, John Hardy, and Otsego County; one count of malicious prosecution against Carl Goeman; one count of wrongful imprisonment against Otsego County; one count each of denial of fair and due process against Otsego County, Hardy, LaBarge, Goeman, Burr, and Wilt; and one count each of conspiracy against Hardy, LaBarge, Burr, Wilt, Rettstadt, Borema, and Parmentier.

If and when the case went to trial, the defendants would be easy to locate except, of course, for one. Debbie Parmentier—a.k.a. Brieanna Herrick, Debra Dawn Brown, Brieanna Farrell, Kim Gray, Debbie Walker—hadn't been seen in Michigan since February of 1995, when she'd given a taped statement to MacNeil and Hubbell, recanting much of what she'd testified to. Immediately afterward, she jumped bond rather than face eight counts of perjury and one count of extortion, all felonies. In 2000, the Michigan State Police gave Debbie the #1 spot on their Most Wanted Fugitives list.

A U.S. District Court magistrate, Paul Komives, summed up the whole morass well. Assigned to make a report about the pending lawsuit against Debbie and the others, Komives was in favor of an out-of-court settlement. He said the prosecutorial vindictiveness exhibited in the Tobias case was "fit for a Franz Kafka novel." (Kafka was one of the most influential authors of the twentieth century and among his works is an unfinished novel, *The Trial*. It depicts a man arrested and prosecuted by a remote and inaccessible authority. His crime is never revealed to him or to the reader.)

In February of 2000, Mark Canter and Terry Moore were examined by psychiatrist Dr. Emanuel Tanay in order to determine the extent of the psychological damage they suffered from their false arrest and imprisonment. Canter was 24 years old when he was arrested and said the event was "totally incredible" to him. He didn't even know Laurie Moore, Don Heistand, or Jerry Tobias when he was arrested. Canter's father died two days after his arrest, and he was not allowed to attend the funeral. Although Hayes portrayed Terry Moore as a habitual criminal, the extent of Moore's police record was stealing a watermelon when he was sixteen, using false license plates, and a single speeding ticket. Terry said he was so shocked by his arrest that he originally thought it had to be a joke. In his report to the federal court, Dr. Tanay said the men's symptoms were similar to those suffered by people subjected to political persecution, and diagnosed both men with post-traumatic stress disorder.

Dan Hubbell's prediction of a delay came true, and further federal court maneuvering split the lawsuit into two; one against Otsego County and one against the Michigan State Police. A three-judge panel from the U.S. Sixth Circuit Court of Appeals ruled the police officers should stand trial and further delays by attorneys for Otsego County and the Michigan State Police would no longer be tolerated. They were "thinly veiled attempts to challenge the correctness of the district court's conclusion regarding the sufficiency of the evidence supporting the plaintiff's civil rights claims," the judges said. In the summer of 2001, it looked like the civil lawsuits would finally go forward.

During this time, Don Heistand continued his court battle to clear his name. After seeing Terry Moore and Mark Canter get life sentences, Heistand was advised by his wife, Lisa, and his attorney, Jack Felton, to take the plea deal offered by then prosecutor Norm Hayes. In February of 1989 he pled no contest to an Accessory After the Fact charge and served more than two years in prison. Heistand never admitted guilt, vehemently maintained his innocence, and became known in prison as a true friend to other inmates. He once used his single phone call to call his wife and ask her to buy a pair of shoes and bring them to the jail because a fellow inmate had a scheduled court date, owned no shoes, and Heistand couldn't bear to see him face a judge barefoot. At a 1996 in-chambers conference among MacNeil, Hubbell, Prosecutor Hesselink, and Judge Porter, the judge admitted Heistand's prosecution had been "a miscarriage of justice."

"If Mr. Heistand had not accepted the plea, he very likely would have been convicted and spent more time in prison as a result of Parmentier's perjury before being freed," Porter said. "That does not reduce the tragedy of Mr. Heistand's conviction."

A motion to have Heistand's plea withdrawn was made by Jack Felton following Porter's statement in 1996, but Prosecutor Hesselink left the courtroom before it could be argued. Heistand, who was out of prison and by that time no longer living in Gaylord, made the trip north from his home outside Detroit for the in-chambers conference in the hopes of having his record cleared. He left angry and dejected when that didn't happen and suffered a heart attack on his way back home to southern Michigan from Gaylord. Later, he told reporters that even after gaining his freedom he still felt sad and bitter.

"I feel sorry for the Tobiases. They never got justice. I don't know who killed their son, but I didn't have anything to do with it. I told the truth and I went to prison, but what about all the people who lied in this case? I don't understand it and I don't know how they live with themselves."

The motion to clear Heistand's name languished for years, and Heistand eventually hired a new attorney, Timothy Holloway of Taylor, and the Circuit Court finally ordered Don Heistand's no-contest plea withdrawn in August 2001, five years after it was filed. As if on cue, Hesselink, who was still serving as Otsego County's prosecutor, told the *Gaylord Herald Times* that as far as he was concerned, the ruling didn't exonerate Heistand.

In November 2001, Mark Canter and Terry Moore's case against Otsego County and prosecutor's investigator Jerry Borema was settled out of court for $2.75 million, with no admission of wrongdoing by the county or Borema. In 2002, the case against the Michigan State Police was settled out of court on the eve of trial for $1.25 million, again with no admission of wrongdoing. By the time of the settlements, Otsego County had already spent $2.2 million prosecuting the Tobias defendants.

Despite these settlements, Prosecutor Hesselink was resolute that neither he nor Norm Hayes did anything wrong in their prosecutions of the men. "I believe that those two—based on the evidence I've seen—committed a murder," he told the *Gaylord Herald Times*, referring to Canter and Moore.

And again, the men's attorneys came to their defense. "If you have any evidence," Dan Hubbell said, "then bring it on. What (Hesselink) is really doing is making excuses for costing the taxpayers over $4 million."

The price tag for the Tobias prosecutions was actually quite a bit higher. Otsego County estimates put the cost of the trials at $2.2 million, and the total award in the civil suit settlement was $4 million. While Doug Brinkman's civil suit was dismissed, Don Heistand eventually sued as well and received an out of court settlement of $675,000. So, when it came to prosecutions of the Tobias defendants, the actual cost to "the People" was just shy of $7 million plus the thousands of hours of police time. The cost to the five men was incalculable.

On January 26, 2003, Debbie Parmentier was arrested by FBI agents in Sandy, Utah, a small town south of Salt Lake City, on eight counts of perjury and one count of extortion. The FBI said an anonymous tip led them to a basement apartment where Debbie was living with her husband, Kent Herrick. Debbie chose not to fight extradition, and a Michigan judge ordered her to return to Otsego County and be jailed on a $1 million bond until she faced the perjury and extortion charges in court. A charge of absconding on bond was added to the list.

Suffering from asthma and emphysema, Debbie arrived back in Gaylord on Valentine's Day 2003, thin and diminished, riding in a wheelchair, and hooked up to oxygen tanks.

Even supposedly near death, Debbie rallied and was soon up to her old tricks. There was speculation she'd provided the tip to the FBI herself, hoping to be caught so she could resurface and file her own civil suit. Once in Gaylord, Debbie was assigned a court-appointed attorney who petitioned the judge for a psychological examination. When it looked like her request would be granted, she withdrew it. When all routes of delay were exhausted, Debbie finally faced the charges against her on August 5, 2003, almost seventeen years after she first lied about seeing Jerry Tobias stabbed to death in a grocery store parking lot.

"I am deeply sorry," she said in open court, in a barely audible whisper. Debbie pled no contest to three counts of perjury, taking a plea deal that dismissed all other charges, including the one for extortion. Each count of perjury was punishable by up to fifteen years in prison, but Debbie was sentenced to time served, just 212 days, with the judge explaining his leniency was due to her poor health. Her attorney said she only had months to live.

At the sentencing hearing, one of the people who spoke on her behalf was a surprise: Terry Moore. "The prosecutor created this witness," he said, "made threats and promised her perks for her testimony. No justice is served if she goes to prison. . . . I would recommend instead that charges be brought up against the team." By "team" Moore meant those named in the civil suit.

In 1997, Bruce Donaldson, Stuart Hubbell, and Ray MacNeil were given the Michigan State Bar Association's "Champion of Justice Award" for their extraordinary work on the Tobias case. The award recognizes those who adhere to the highest principles of the legal profession.

"The circumstances surrounding the conviction of their clients came to my attention almost six years ago," wrote Michigan Attorney General Frank Kelley, in a letter of support to the award committee. "As a result of the persuasiveness of Mr. Mac-Neil, I decided to launch an investigation which ultimately convinced me that their clients' convictions were based overwhelmingly on perjured testimony. Unquestionably, without their relentless efforts, and the concomitant financial and physical sacrifice they endured, each of their clients would likely still be in prison."

The trio was also supported by beloved Michigan Governor William Milliken.

"I can't tell you how much I respect you for your courage and perseverance in pursuing justice in this case," Milliken wrote in a personal note to Hubbell. "You are a man of principle and compassion. I admire you for this noble deed."

Detroit News reporter Norm Sinclair, whose five-part series on the case caused a stir when it was published in May of 1991, also weighed in:

"I have never felt compelled to champion the work of subjects of news stories I covered. Until now. The legal saga in which these three lawyers participated was accomplished with much personal sacrifice. MacNeil's practice was nearly financially swamped, Hubbell's health broke down, and Donaldson's three-week pro bono stint turned into three years. In a time when lawyers rank near the bottom of the public's list of villains, these men have been magnificent and honorable practitioners of their profession."

After the Tobias case, all three returned to private practice. Bruce Donaldson died in 1998, Stuart Hubbell died in 2010; and though Ray MacNeil insists he is now retired, he still has a law office in Gaylord, complete with phone line, secretary, clients, and overflowing file cabinets.

In the 2004 Republican primary for Otsego County Prosecutor, Hesselink lost his bid for re-election. He is currently in private practice in Gaylord.

In 2000, when court jurisdictions were re-aligned in northern Michigan, Norm Hayes decided not to seek re-election in the 86th District Court. He ran for probate judge in Antrim County instead and won, was twice re-elected, and continues to serve in that capacity. In 2010, he was diagnosed with colorectal cancer.

On May 22, 2009, six years after her attorney asserted to the court she only had months to live, "Teanna Shiné Herrick" died in Sandy, Utah, of pulmonary degeneration. She was 54. Her obituary read, "Being half Native American, Teanna spent many of her early years on a Native American Reservation. On September 5, 1991, she married Kent Herrick in Hart, MI, and on May 14, 2005, Kent and Teanna were sealed in the Salt Lake Temple. Teanna enjoyed reading, making jewelry, and other Native American crafts. She loved camping, spending time outdoors, and being with her dogs, cats and horses."

POSTSCRIPT

"America has the best justice system in the world," goes the familiar refrain. After spending more than seven years researching a case that sent five innocent men to prison for killing a man I am convinced died of a drug overdose, I still believe that.

But the Tobias case forced me to examine my own feelings about crime, punishment, guilt, and innocence, and I haven't always liked what I learned. No longer do I see a defendant on TV, or read an article in the newspaper about someone being arrested, and automatically assume they're guilty. I'm ashamed to admit I used to do that, which leads me to believe our justice system may indeed be great, but one of its foundations—guilty until proven innocent—is a fairy tale. Our "system" is really just a random assemblage of human beings, people like you and me, each with their opinions, biases, character flaws, strengths, and, of course, ambitions. No matter how smart, well trained, or experienced they are, judges, prosecutors, attorneys, police, private detectives, jurors, and witnesses are still just people, and people make mistakes.

According to a recent article in the *Journal of the International Association of the Chiefs of Police*, faulty investigative thinking is a top reason for an innocent person to be convicted of a crime. An article titled "Failures in Criminal Investigation" listed these primary reasons detectives and prosecutors make mistakes: relying on intuition over reasoning, working from a cognitive bias, taking mental shortcuts, tunnel vision, organizational inertia, and clinging to anchoring assumptions. "It seems most unlikely that, with all the checks and balances of the criminal justice system, someone today could be convicted of a crime he or she did not commit," writes criminologist D. Kim Rossmo. "The unfortunate reality,

407

however, is that it does happen. Like cascading failures in airplane crashes, an investigative failure often has more than one contributing factor." The sad truth for the Tobias defendants is that not just one, but *all* of these failures occurred, over and over again, in order for jurors to reach their unjust verdicts.

My opinion is that almost immediately after Jerry's body was found, Fred LaBarge and Norm Hayes made an assumption about Laurie Moore—that he was guilty of the killing—and they looked for evidence to support that assumption. In law enforcement, that kind of faulty thinking is sometimes called "anchoring." I think the police and the prosecutor really did believe Laurie killed Jerry and were willing to do anything to prove it. But in their zeal they forgot, or maybe just ignored, one important detail. Assumptions aren't truth. Evidence is supposed to be gathered and then the guilty person identified, in that order. Good police work isn't anchored by a personal vendetta and then all effort confined to just a small circle of inquiry for the evidence to support it.

That's how I believe the whole case lost its bearings; by human beings anchoring themselves to a faulty assumption and then looking for evidence only within its boundaries. Anything outside that circle was deemed irrelevant, and I found example after example of that in the Tobias case. Laurie was the first and only suspect; Jerry had fresh needle marks on his arms but his death was ruled a homicide before the toxicology test results were known; the lack of evidence found in the butcher shop was discounted; the package of meat wasn't fingerprinted; the palm prints on Jerry's truck's tailgate were never identified; Laurie had an alibi; someone called Laurie on the phone and threatened him (almost certainly this was Debbie) but no one took the threats seriously. Certainly most devastating of all, Debbie Parmentier's original story was discounted as the ravings of a kook, but then when it changed to fit the assumption, her story became the prosecution's single most important piece of evidence. And with Debbie as a witness, the police's rope swung in a relentless circle catching Terry Moore, Mark Canter, Doug Brinkman, and Don Heistand in its drag.

At some point the prosecutor and the police had to have realized their original assumption was wrong—John Hardy said as much when he finally questioned the Canter prosecution—but by then I can only surmise the resulting fallout seemed too disastrous to do anything about it. I say "surmise" because no one I contacted from the law enforcement side would consent to an interview. However, if the prosecutions had ceased, the reputations of Norm Hayes and the State Police would surely have been damaged, perhaps irreversibly; Otsego County would have been vulnerable to a liability lawsuit, and the whole justice "system" in northern Michigan may have seemed suspect. Even the respected Judge Porter tried to maintain control over the case *after* he retired from the bench. It is this chilling cascade effect that remains particularly troubling to me.

When Norm Hayes was elected judge, his replacement, Dennis Murphy, could have dropped the prosecutions against Mark Canter and Terry Moore but he did not. When Murphy left office and was replaced by Kevin Hesselink, Hesselink could have dropped the prosecutions, but instead he soldiered on with an unfathomable zeal. Even after Debbie's testimony was ruled inadmissible; even after double jeopardy deemed that if Canter and Moore were convicted of anything they'd be released for time served; and even after breaking his gentleman's agreement with the defense, I can think of no other motive behind Hesselink's decision than damage control. For those who might doubt that a county prosecutor would place liability and public embarrassment over the innocence of two men, consider this: Prosecutor Hesselink offered to release the defendants with time served if they would hold the County harmless from civil liability. They declined. And, as soon as the case was finally out from under the control of the Otsego County police, prosecutors, and judges, it was dismissed.

Every possible element of human hubris, ego, stupidness, mis-
placed loyalty, laziness, craziness, and just plain wickedness put the
Tobias defendants behind bars. The one small bit of redemption in
this tragedy is that none were a match for three stubborn lawyers
who knew a wrong when they saw one. With all its failings, that's
what makes our justice system great. That three smart, hardworking men with right on their side can still trump manipulation, ego,
and power. May it always be so.

CAST OF CHARACTERS

JANET ALLEN—Gaylord attorney and Laurie Moore's wife.

MARK ALSEPT—Convicted felon who accused Terry Moore of threatening Norm Hayes' life.

ROGER BECKER—Debbie Parmentier's boss at Beaver Creek Resort and her on again, off again boyfriend.

TERRY BLOOMQUIST—Sherry Payton's second attorney.

JERRY BOREMA—Investigator for the Otsego County Prosecutor's office.

DOUG BRINKMAN—One of Debbie Parmentier's many boyfriends and one of the men she accused of murdering Jerry Tobias inside Walt's Butcher Shop.

WILLIAM BROWN—Judge who replaced Judge Livo and heard Laurie's mistrial and new trial motions.

KEN BURR—Michigan State Police Trooper who discovered Jerry Tobias' body.

MARK CANTER—One of the men Debbie Parmentier accused of murdering Jerry Tobias inside Walt's Butcher Shop.

MICHAEL COOPER—Gaylord attorney who handled Debbie's divorce from Leonard.

MICHELLE CRONAN—Juror Twelve in Laurie Moore's trial and one of the jurors who tried to recant her verdict. The others were Diane MacInnis, Annette Myers, and Sandra Crawford.

DAN DALLAS—Gaylord city patrolman who testified he saw Laurie Moore's van parked outside Walt's the night of the supposed murder.

ALTON DAVIS—Judge in the Mark Canter trial.

DEBRA DEITERING—Friend of Laurie Moore who drove him to Tom Kearbey's cabin the night Jerry Tobias went missing.

JAMES DEAMUD—Doug Brinkman's court-appointed attorney.

TERRY DOYLE—AG's agent who interviewed Sherry Payton in Florida and began the AG investigation into the Tobias case.

FRANK DUFON—Gaylord Police Chief from 1986–1988.

JACK FELTON—Don Heistand's court-appointed attorney.

VALERIE GODDARD—One of the ATF agents who interviewed Debbie about stolen military weapons.

CARL GOEMAN—Michigan State Police detective who worked with Fred LaBarge.

ANTHONY GOMEZ—Michigan State Police trooper who interviewed Sherry Payton.

MICHAEL HACKETT—Terry Moore's defense attorney.

JOHN HARDY—Michigan State Police lieutenant in charge of the 7th District nicknamed "supercop" and who assigned Fred LaBarge to head up the Tobias murder investigation.

NORM HAYES—Otsego County Prosecutor from 1986 to 1990; 87th District Court Judge for Antrim, Kalkaska, and Otsego Counties from 1991 to 2000; Antrim County Probate Judge from 2001 to present (term expiring January 1, 2019).

DON HEISTAND—Brief part-time employee of Walt's Butcher Shop and one of the five men arrested for Jerry Tobias' murder.

STUART HUBBELL—Terry Moore's appellate attorney appointed by Judge Porter. The first attorney in Michigan history to receive superintending control and be allowed to take secret depositions in a criminal proceeding.

ROBERT IANNI—The Assistant Attorney General in charge of the office's Criminal Division.

KAREN JACKSON—Gaylord attorney hired by Laurie to handle his appeal after Dean Robb resigned. She was then hired by Sherry Payton's mother but had to resign from representing her when Payton was drawn into the Tobias investigation.

TOM KEARBEY—Friend of Laurie Moore who owned the cabin where Laurie Moore went the night Jerry Tobias went missing.

THEODORE KLIMASZEWSKI—the head of the Michigan Attorney General's Organized Crime and Public Corruption Unit.

FRED LaBARGE—State Police Detective in charge of the Tobias homicide investigation.

JUDGE LIVO—Presided over Laurie Moore's murder trial.

RAY MacNEIL—Mark Canter's court-appointed attorney.

GARY MAYER—Friend of Jerry Tobias suspected by police of drug dealing. Mayer and Jerry went out drinking together on December 1, 1986, four days before Jerry disappeared. A bartender told police Mayer went to the Fireside bar Friday, Dec. 5 and at 8:30 PM asked if she'd seen Tobias.

ESTHER MOORE—Matriarch of the Moore family and co-owner of Walt's.

HOWARD MOORE—Laurie's youngest brother. He was the one first approached by Debbie Parmentier.

KIM MOORE—Terry Moore's daughter and Laurie Moore's niece. She worked part-time in Walt's Butcher Shop.

LAURIE MOORE—Co-owner of Walt's Butcher Shop and the first man to be arrested for Jerry Tobias' murder.

TODD MOREY—Part-time employee of Walt's who, with his brother Bill, locked up the shop late Friday night, Dec. 5.

BILL MOREY—Part-time employee of Walt's who, with his brother Todd, locked up the shop late Friday night, Dec. 5.

BECKY NELSON—Jackie Tobias' boss at the Yodeler Ski Shoppe and friend to Jerry. She told police she and her husband gave Jerry $200 to buy them some pot but then later admitted the money was for cocaine.

DON NELSON—Becky Nelson's husband. Along with Becky, he gave Jerry $200 for cocaine.

PATRICIA NEWHOUSE—Gaylord pathologist and part-time assistant medical examiner who performed the autopsy on Jerry Tobias. She is the one who determined his death was a homicide.

SHERRY PAYTON—Friend of Jerry Tobias who fled to Florida after writing bad checks and who said she lied on the witness stand and said she was a witness to Jerry's murder after police threatened and bullied her.

GENE PETRUSKA—Janet Allen's law partner.

WILLIAM PORTER—Judge in Terry Moore's trial.

CHARLES RETTSTADT—Investigator hired by Jack Felton to corroborate Don Heistand's alibi.

DEAN ROBB—Laurie Moore's defense attorney.

MARIE ROSS—Jerry Tobias' former girlfriend.

TONY SCHULTZ—Friend of Jerry Tobias suspected by police of drug dealing.

BETTY SWARTHOUT—Juror in the Terry Moore trial who broke the rules and talked about the case during deliberations.

EMANUEL TANAY—psychiatrist who examined Debbie Parmentier's medical records and testified in the Terry Moore and Mark Canter trials.

JACKIE TOBIAS—Wife of Jerry Tobias and mother to his two sons.

JERRY TOBIAS—Oilfield worker, husband and father found frozen in his Ford pickup truck on Dec. 8, 1986.

DOUG WILT—One of the Michigan State Police detectives in charge of keeping track of Debbie when she was a protected witness.

SOURCES AND RESOURCES

PART 1: The Crime

.... Police Documents

Michigan Dept. of State Police report, Incident No. 73-1947-86, murder investigation, original incident dated December 12, 1986.

Michigan State Police crime scene photos for Incident No. 73-1947-86.

Gaylord Police Department Narrative Continuation Case Report Form, 86-2570, dated December 9, 1986.

Autopsy report and photographs of Jerry Tobias by Dr. Patricia Newhouse.

Department of State Police Laboratory Report.

.... Court Documents

Motion For Disinterment, filed Dec. 15, 1986, by Prosecutor Norm Hayes, Otsego District Court.

Circuit Court of Otsego, Trial transcript, People v. Laurie Moore, October, November 1987.

Extensive depositions, Michigan Supreme Court, Court of Appeals

.... Interviews

Author's Interview of Esther Moore

Author's Interview of Laurie Moore

Author's Interview of Dean Robb

Attorney General Special Agent Terrence P. Doyle's extensive interviews with witnesses, May-October, 1991.

Gaylord Police Chief Frank Dufon's interview with Eugene Petruska, dated December 19, 1986.

.... Newspaper Articles

The Bay City Times, May 11, 1987, "Decision near in murder case hearing," by Katie Lou MacDonald.

The Detroit News, October 25, 1987, "Drugs, sex and violence spice upstate whodunit," by Thomas BeVier.

The Detroit News, April 2, 1989, " 'Chicken skewer murder' still haunts Gaylord," by Thomas BeVier.

Gaylord Herald Times, October 23, 1986, "Task force goal: drug crackdown."

Gaylord Herald Times, December 11, 1986, "Probe death of man, 31."

Gaylord Herald Times, March 5, 1987, "Man charged with Tobias murder."

Gaylord Herald Times, May 14, 1987, "Tobias murder charge ruling due," by Vickie Naegele.

Gaylord Herald Times, October 22, 1987, "Laurie Moore murder trial could last up to a month," by Jim Rink.

Gaylord Herald Times, October 28, 1987, "Pathologist shows action of spindle," by Jim Rink.

Gaylord Herald Times, November 12, 1987, "Witness: prosecutor's feelings in the way," by Jim Rink.

Gaylord Herald Times, December 10, 1987, "Judge denies motion for mistrial of Moore," by Jim Rink.

Gaylord Herald Times, February 25, 1988, "Moore defense: new judge means new trial needed," by Jim Rink.

Gaylord Herald Times, May 19, 1988, "Accessory charge for Brinkman," by Vicki Naegele.

Gaylord Herald Times, July 21, 1988, "Attorneys prepare at Kalkaska trial for Terry Moore," by Vicki Naegele.

Gaylord Herald Times, August 4, 1988, "Parmentier story dismissed earlier," by Vicki Naegele.

Gaylord Herald Times, September 22, 1988, "Court postpones trial of Brinkman."

Gaylord Herald Times, October 13, 1988, "County faces growing bills to cover murder costs," by Vicki Naegele.

Gaylord Herald Times, November 3, 1988, "Coping theme of Women '89."

.... Books

Preserve, Protect and Defend: An Illustrated History of the Michigan State Police in the Twentieth Century by Phillip Daniel Schertzing (Turner Publishing Co., 2001).

Dead Man Walking: An Eyewitness Account of the Death Penalty in the United States by Helen Prejean (Random House, 1993).

.... Correspondence

Letter from Det./Lt. John Hardy to Prosecutor Norm Hayes, dated May 19, 1987.

Letter from Harold Moore addressed "Dear Sirs," dated February 22, 1988.

Letter from Angela Moore to Circuit Court Judge William A. Porter, dated September 13, 1988.

Letter from Alice Reed to Circuit Court Judge William A. Porter, dated September 13, 1988.

Letter from Letter from Lynn Kaczor to Circuit Court Judge William A. Porter, dated September 15, 1988.

Letter from Evelyn Lo Curto to Circuit Court Judge William A. Porter, dated September 16, 1988.

Letter from Det./Lt. John Hardy to Colonel Michael D. Robinson, Director of the Michigan State Police, dated May 13, 1991.

. . . . Miscellaneous

Northland Sportsman's Club's newsletter

Gaylord, Michigan Chamber of Commerce statistics.

Michigan Department of Natural Resources statistics.

Pre-Sentence Investigation report for Walter Edwin (Terry) Moore III, filed October 14, 1988.

PART 2: The Trials

. . . . Police Documents

Michigan Dept. of State Police report, Incident No. 73-1947-86, murder investigation, original incident dated December 12, 1986.

Michigan Dept. of State Police report, Incident No.073-927-88, Destruction of Property.

Michigan Dept. of State Police report, Incident No. 070-207-88, Carrying a Concealed Weapon.

. . . . Court Documents

People v. Terry Moore, 46th Judicial Circuit Court Otsego County trial transcript.

People v. Mark Canter, 46th Judicial Circuit Court Otsego County trial transcript.

People v. Douglass Brinkman, 46th Judicial Circuit Court Otsego County proceedings.

People v. Donald Heistand, 46th Judicial Circuit Court Otsego County proceedings.

Circuit Court, County of Otsego, *People v. Walter Edwin Moore, III (a/k/a/ Terry Moore)*, Motion for New Trial, Filed by Michael Hackett, October 5, 1988.

Deposition of John Felton, January 5, 1993, State of Michigan, Michigan Supreme Court, before Judge William Porter, Otsego County Courthouse, Gaylord.

. . . . Newspaper Articles

Gaylord Herald Times, May 12, 1988, "3 bound over in Tobias murder," by Vicki Naegele.

Gaylord Herald Times, August 18, 1988, "Defense witnesses testify Parmentier's story varied," by Vicki Naegele.

Gaylord Herald Times, November 10, 1988, "Tobias witness named," by Vicki Naegele.

Gaylord Herald Times, December 8, 1988, "Elusive witness to testify."

Gaylord Herald Times, December 8, 1988, "Canter denies charges," by Vicki Naegele.

Gaylord Herald Times, December 8, 1988, "Attorney tempers flare over witness list," by Vicki Naegele.

Gaylord Herald Times, December 15, 1988, "Jury finds Canter guilty in murder," by Vicki Naegele.

Gaylord Herald Times, December 29, 1988, "No contest plea by murder defendant closes Tobias case," by Vicki Naegele.

. . . . Journal Articles

"Death Caused by Recreational Cocaine Use: An Update" by Roger E. Mittleman, MD, and Charles V. Wetli, MD, *Journal of the American Medical Association (JAMA)*, Oct. 12, 1994, Vol. 252, No. 14.

. . . . Letters

Death threat letter from Debbie Parmentier to Deb Parmentier, postmarked in Gaylord, Michigan, April 25, 1988.

Death threat letter from Debbie Parmentier to Cindy Gleasen, postmarked in Gaylord, Michigan, April 25, 1988.

Letter from Ray MacNeil to Stuart Hubbell, dated December 22, 1991.

Letter from Jack Felton to Robert E. Edick, Deputy Administrator of the State of Michigan attorney Grievance Commission, dated April 23, 1999.

Letter from Bruce Donaldson to *Detroit News* reporter Norm Sinclair, dated March 16, 1998.

Letter from Bruce Donaldson to *Detroit News* reporter Norm Sinclair, dated March 16, 1998.

. . . . Miscellaneous

Child Custody Evaluation and Recommendations, Otsego County Circuit Court, *Leonard Parmentier v. Debra Parmentier*, compiled by the Family & Law Program, Department of Psychiatry, University of Michigan, June 16, 1988. Prepared by Milton Schaefer, M.S.

Ray MacNeil's typed notes regarding his October 11, 1987 interview with Sherry Payton.

Don Heistand's time cards from November 16, 1986, to January 3, 1987.

Debbie Parmentier's "Little black book."

PART 3: The Unraveling

. . . . Police Documents

Michigan Dept. of State Police report, Incident No. 73-1947-86, murder investigation, original incident dated December 12, 1986.

.... Court Documents

People v. Terry Moore trial transcript.

People v. Mark Canter trial transcript.

People v. Douglass Brinkman court proceedings.

People v. Donald Heistand court proceedings.

Michigan Department of Attorney General Interview synopsis conducted in the Jerry Tobias Homicide Complaint, File 1941, dated May 17, 1990.

State of Michigan Court of Appeals Decision for publication of *People v. Mark William Canter*, dated December 21, 1992, 9:55 a.m.

Felony Complaint filed in State of Michigan's 86th District Court against Brieanna Herrick a.k.a. Debra (Parmentier) Herrick by Stuart Hubbell, June 1994.

Michigan Supreme Court, Court of Appeals, Deposition of Kelly Morey, July 21, 1992.

Michigan Supreme Court, Court of Appeals, extensive depositions taken by Stuart Hubbell in the presence of Judge Porter.

46th Judicial Circuit Court, Otsego County, Bond Hearing, Walter Edwin Moore, Mark William Canter, January 18, 1996.

Michigan Supreme Court, Court of Appeals, Deposition George Stoll, June 15, 1993.

Michigan Supreme Court, Court of Appeals, Deposition of Jerry Wayne Borema, November 17, 1992.

Michigan Supreme Court, Court of Appeals, Deposition of Gary Mayer, November 17, 1992.

Circuit Court of Grand Traverse County Order appointing Special Prosecutor in the matter of *People v. Debra (Parmentier) Herrick* dated July 15, 1994.

Plaintive exhibits and extensive depositions from U.S. District Court, Eastern District of Michigan, in the matter of Mark William Canter and Walter Edwin Moore, Plaintiffs v. Otsego County, Norman Hayes, Frederick LaBarge, John Hardy, Hon. Gerald Rosen, Dawn Schumacher, Kevin Hesselink, Douglas A. Wilt, Charles Rettstadt, Reasearch North, Inc., Carl Goeman, Jerry Borema, Patricia A. Newhouse, Kenneth Burr, Brieanna Herrick a.k.a. Debra Parmentier.

Plaintive exhibits and extensive depositions from Donald L. Heistand and Lisa Heistand, Plaintiffs, v. Hon Gerald Rosen, Otsego County, Norman Hayes, Magistrate Paul J. Komives, Fred LaBarge, John Hardy, Kevin Hesselink, Douglas Wilt, Charles Rettstadt, Research North, Inc., Carl Goeman, Jerry Borema, Brieanna Herrick a.k.a. Debra Parmentier.

.... Newspaper Articles

The Bay City Times, September 24, 1991, "Charges dismissed in Gaylord," by Kathy Petersen.

The Detroit News, March 1991, "Who killed Jerry Tobias?" a five part series by Norman Sinclair.

The Detroit News, September 23, 1991, "Defense alleges misconduct in Gaylord case," by Norman Sinclair.

The Detroit News, December 31, 1991, "2 jailed for Tobias murder bitter over rehearing delays," by Norman Sinclair.

The Detroit News, June 6, 1993, "Kelley backs defense bid to reopen murder case," by Norman Sinclair.

The Detroit News, June 18, 1993, "Woman admits lying over whereabouts of Tobias case witness," by Norman Sinclair.

The Detroit News, June 20, 1993, "Defense moves to arrest star witness," by Norman Sinclair.

The Detroit News, July 6, 1993, "Former prosecutor in murder case accused of hiding box of evidence," by Norman Sinclair.

The Detroit News, July 28, 1993, "Tobias witness accused of making death threat," by Norman Sinclair.

The Detroit News, June 12, 1994, "Trooper admits affair with witness," by Norman Sinclair.

The Detroit News, August 28, 1994, "Cop testifies he told prosecutor witness was liar," by Norman Sinclair.

The Detroit News, March 22, 1995, "Gaylord murder witness missing," by Norm Sinclair.

Gaylord Herald Times, August 25, 1988, "Jurors view 'scene of crime,'" by Vicki Naegele.

Gaylord Herald Times, August 25, 1988, "Long parade of defense witnesses ends," by Vicki Naegele.

Gaylord Herald Times, August 25, 1988, "Tobias whereabouts disputed," by Vicki Naegele.

Gaylord Herald Times, August 25, 1988, "Defense gives another version of Debra Parmentier's allegations," by Vicki Naegele.

Gaylord Herald Times, September 8, 1988, "Hackett: Moore innocent due to unverified witness statements," by Vicki Naegele.

Gaylord Herald Times, November 17, 1988, "2nd witness misidentified," by Vicki Naegele.

Gaylord Herald Times, March 14, 1991, "Appellate court reverses conviction," by Vicki Naegele.

Gaylord Herald Times, March 24, 1991, "No appeal of decision; Moore to be freed," by Vicki Naegele.

Gaylord Herald Times, March 28, 1991, "Moore free; still seeking 'justice,'" by Vicki Naegele.

Gaylord Herald Times, December 19, 1991, "Davis asks Attorney General to decide next step in Moore case," by Vicki Naegele.

Gaylord Herald Times, September 26, 1992, "Program rekindles Tobias questions," by Vicki Naegele.

Gaylord Herald Times, June 6, 1993, "Hayes defends Canter charge," by Vicki Naegele.

Gaylord Herald Times, June 10, 1993, "Tobias case draws appeal from Kelley."

Gaylord Herald Times, June 10, 1993, "Canter defense outlines intimidation," by Jim Grisso.

Gaylord Herald Times, June 10, 1993, "Heistand says conviction was payback from Hayes," by Vicki Naegele.

Gaylord Herald Times, June 20, 1993, "Steele testifies she rewrote diary entries," by Dennis Powell.

Gaylord Herald Times, June 17, 1993, "Immunity denied for Canter witness," by Dennis Powell.

Gaylord Herald Times, June 17, 1993, "Defense attacks Parmentier's testimony," by Dennis Powell.

Gaylord Herald Times, June 17, 1993, "Payton denies witnessing Tobias murder," by Dennis Powell.

Gaylord Herald Times, June 24, 1993, "Canter case delayed to review 'lost' files," by Dennis Powell.

Gaylord Herald Times, July 8, 1993, "Expert reviewing Tobias autopsy tape, tissues," by Vicki Naegele.

Gaylord Herald Times, July 15, 1993, "Canter wants new judge," by Dennis Powell.

Gaylord Herald Times, September 16, 1993, "Moore's attorney ready to head back to courtroom," by Vicki Naegele.

Gaylord Herald Times, September 23, 1993, "Tobias witness faces extradition," by Vicki Naegele.

Gaylord Herald Times, November 4, 1993, "Moore says justice slow," by Vicki Naegele.

Gaylord Herald Times, November 18, 1993, "Porter bows out of Canter issue," by Vicki Naegele.

Gaylord Herald Times, November 25, 1993, "Defense attorneys allege Hayes protected Parmentier," by Vicki Naegele.

Gaylord Herald Times, November 25, 1993, "Parmentier faces 20-year felony," by Vicki Naegele.

Gaylord Herald Times, November 25, 1993, "AG charges Parmentier in extortion," by Vicki Naegele.

Gaylord Herald Times, December 23, 1993, "Special judge sets Jan. 25 hearing in Davis disqualification matter."

Gaylord Herald Times, February 17, 1994, "Prosecutor's team says Hayes made decisions," by Vicki Naegele.

Gaylord Herald Times, February 24, 1994, "Hayes says life threatened," by Vicki Naegele.

Gaylord Herald Times, March 3, 1994, "Davis removed from Canter case," by Vicki Naegele.

Gaylord Herald Times, June 9, 1994, "Linchpin witness jailed for perjury," by Vicki Naegele.

Gaylord Herald Times, June 16, 1994, "MSP trooper reveals affair with key witness," by Vicki Naegele.

Gaylord Herald Times, June 16, 1994, "Prosecution fails in attempt to quash trooper subpoena," by Vicki Naegele.

Gaylord Herald Times, September 1, 1994, "Hardy says Hayes knew Parmentier not credible witness," by Dennis Powell.

Gaylord Herald Times, September 1, 1994, "Tobias case defense demands grand jury," by Vicki Naegele.

Gaylord Herald Times, September 1, 1994, "Alsept: Moore confessed to murder," by Vicki Naegele.

Gaylord Herald Times, September 29, 1994, "Trooper denies he threatened key Tobias witness," by Vicki Naegele.

Gaylord Herald Times, October 27, 1994, "Herrick headed to Nov. 4 perjury hearing," by Vicki Naegele.

Gaylord Herald Times, October 27, 1994, "'She crewed up a lot of people's lives:' Heistand," by Vicki Naegele.

Gaylord Herald Times, March 30, 1995, "Parmentier admits lying," by Dennis Powell.

Gaylord Herald Times, April 13, 1995, "Canter, Moore lose latest freedom bid."

Gaylord Herald Times, January 25, 1996, "Retrial to target prosecutor, police," by Dennis Powell.

Gaylord Herald Times, March 14, 1996, "Appeals court orders hearing," by Dennis Powell.

Gaylord Herald Times, March 14, 1996, "Herrick bond forfeiture adjourned," by Dennis Powell.

Gaylord Herald Times, April 25, 1996, "Hearing set to disqualify Porter from Canter-Moore case," by Dennis Powell.

Gaylord Herald Times, May 2, 1996, "Porter drops Canter-Moore case," by Dennis Powell.

Gaylord Herald Times, May 9, 1996, "Alpena judge to hear Tobias case," by Dennis Powell.

Gaylord Herald Times, July 11, 1996, "Hayes alleges Root misconduct," by Michael Hartz.

Gaylord Herald Times, July 25, 1996, "Tobias case to proceed Prosecutor confident," by Dennis Powell.

Gaylord Herald Times, September 19, 1996, "Judge reduces bond Canter, Moore tether-free," by Lee Dryden.

Gaylord Herald Times, October 3, 1996, "Finally . . .Canter, Moore charges dropped," by Lee Dryden.

Gaylord Herald Times, September 19, 1996, full page advertisement, "Tobias Case: Free at Last."

Gaylord Herald Times, April 22, 2000, "Federal judge delays start of Canter/Moore civil rights trial," by Frank Michaels.

Gaylord Herald Times, August 24, 2000, "Parmentier 'most wanted' state fugitive," by Frank Michaels.

Gaylord Herald Times, August 6, 2001, "Heistand case 'miscarriage of justice'" by Frank Michaels.

Gaylord Herald Times, November 7, 2001, "Canter, Moore share $2.75M settlement," by Peter Comings.

Gaylord Herald Times, August 6, 2003, "Tobias murder 'witness' makes 'no contest' plea to 3 perjury charges," by Michael Jones.

Gaylord Herald Times, August 27, 2003, "Herrick freed," by Michael Jones.

The Traverse City Record-Eagle, March 17, 1991, "Court ruling raises doubts over Gaylord slaying convictions," by Mike Norton.

The Traverse City Record-Eagle, November 1, 1991, "Supreme Court may allow statements in Tobias case," by Lori A. Hall.

Traverse City Record-Eagle, January 23, 1994, "Tobias case pricetag: Over $1 million," by Dan Heaton

Traverse City Record-Eagle, February 6, 1994, "Moore's attorney puts prosecution team on trial."

Traverse City Record-Eagle, May 29, 1994, "Letter called a forgery," by Mike Norton.

Traverse City Record-Eagle, June 12, 1994, "Attorneys speak of conspiracy," by Mike Norton.

Traverse City Record-Eagle, August 31, 1994, "Defense renews charges of misconduct," by Karen Norton.

Traverse City Record-Eagle, January 26, 1995, "Retiring judge a legend among state attorneys," by Will Scott.

Traverse City Record-Eagle, March 23, 1995, "Murder witness recants her testimony," by Rich Bachus.

Traverse City Record-Eagle, April 2, 1995, "Search is on for Herrick," by Rich Bachus.

Traverse City Record-Eagle, January 31, 1996, Editorial, "Tobias case facts seem to demand end to prosecution."

Traverse City Record-Eagle, October 5, 1999, "Former convicts hope for restitution," by Dan Sanderson.

Traverse City Record-Eagle, January 28, 2003, "Tobias case fugitive arrested in Utah," by Dan Sanderson.

Traverse City Record-Eagle, February 23, 2003, "Botches follow botches," by Mike Norton.

Traverse City Record-Eagle, February 24, "Case begins to unravel," by Mike Norton.

. . . . Miscellaneous

Diary, Debbie Parmentier

Diary, Cindy Gleason

Extensive trial notes made by Bruce Donaldson. Undated.

Handwritten "Index of Police Reports" compiled by Stuart Hubbell. Undated.

Motion for Oral Argument, request for Superintending Control, filed in the State of Michigan Supreme Court by Stuart Hubbell, August 19, 1991.

People v. Mark Canter Evidentiary Hearing Transcripts, 46th Judicial Circuit Court, Otsego County, June 1993.

Motion for New Trial, Circuit Court Count of Otsego, *People v. Terry Moore*, September, 1993.

Motion for New Trial, Circuit Court County of Otsego, *People v. Mark Canter*, July 1994.

Letter from Stuart Hubbell to Grand Traverse County Prosecuting Attorney Dennis LaBelle, dated July 27, 1994.

Letter from Stuart Hubbell to Grand Traverse County Prosecuting Attorney Dennis LaBelle, dated August 9, 1994.

Letter from Grand Traverse County Prosecuting Attorney Dennis LaBelle to Stuart Hubbell, dated August 11, 1994.

Letter from Stuart Hubbell to Grand Traverse County Prosecuting Attorney Dennis LaBelle, dated August 12, 1994. Marked "Hand Delivered."

Letter from Grand Traverse County Prosecuting Attorney Dennis LaBelle to Stuart Hubbell, dated August 17, 1994.

Letter from Stuart Hubbell to Grand Traverse County Prosecuting Attorney Dennis LaBelle, dated August 17, 1994. Marked "Hand Delivered."

Letter from Stuart Hubbell to Ray MacNeil, dated June 6, 1993.

Letter from Norman Hayes to Kenneth L. McGinnis, Director of Michigan Department of Corrections, dated July 3, 1996; re: Request for Internal Invest.

Letter from Bruce Donaldson to Norman Sinclair, dated March 16, 1998.